隆天知识产权代理有限公司 组织编写
LUNG TIN INTELLECTUAL PROPERTY AGENT LTD.

知识产权律师论丛

（第 1 辑）

主　编　郑泰强

副主编　郭晓东

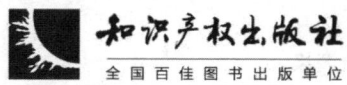
知识产权出版社
全国百佳图书出版单位

图书在版编目（CIP）数据

知识产权律师论丛 . 第 1 辑/郑泰强主编 . —北京：知识产权出版社，2014.9
ISBN 978-7-5130-2976-6

Ⅰ. ①知… Ⅱ. ①郑… Ⅲ. ①知识产权-文集 Ⅳ. ①D913.04-53

中国版本图书馆 CIP 数据核字（2014）第 207161 号

内容提要

本书包含中英双语两部分内容，其中中文部分为"知识产权律师观点"、"知识产权实务探讨"和"知识产权法律研究"三个章节，英文部分为"Insider's Look：Exploring the Intricacies of Chinese IP Law"，是隆天知识产权代理有限公司组织的知识产权律师就近年行业热点和日常知识产权实务所做的一些探讨和评析。本书旨在为知识产权从业者提供一线的律师观点，为企业的知识产权确权与保护实践提供切实可行的建议，并与同行就相关的知识产权法律问题进行交流和探讨。

读者对象：知识产权从业者、企业法务工作者等。

责任编辑：黄清明　　　　　　责任出版：刘译文
装帧设计：黄清明　　　　　　责任校对：谷　洋

知识产权律师论丛（第 1 辑）
Zhishichanquan Lüshi Luncong

主　编　郑泰强

副主编　郭晓东

编　委　向　勇　徐擎红　闫　华

出版发行：	知识产权出版社有限责任公司	网　址：	http：//www.ipph.cn
社　址：	北京市海淀区马甸南村 1 号	邮　编：	100088
责编电话：	010-82000860 转 8117	责编邮箱：	hqm@cnipr.com
发行电话：	010-82000860 转 8101/8102	发行传真：	010-82000893/82005070/82000270
印　刷：	保定市中画美凯印刷有限公司	经　销：	各大网上书店、新华书店及相关专业书店
开　本：	720mm×960mm　1/16	印　张：	21.75
版　次：	2014 年 10 月第 1 版	印　次：	2014 年 10 月第 1 次印刷
字　数：	490 千字	定　价：	78.00 元

ISBN 978-7-5130-2976-6

序

当今世界的主题之一是"Change"，这是一个造梦的年代。站在新的历史起点上，实施知识产权战略，建设知识产权强国，建成创新型国家，这是知识产权事业的"中国梦"。众所周知，中国的知识产权事业仅有30多年的历史，与世界发达国家相比，起步虽晚，但发展迅速。从2011年开始，我国已经成为全世界专利申请量第一大国。从知识产权大国到知识产权强国，虽然还有很长的路要走，但很显然，我国在国际知识产权舞台的地位在不断提高，我们的知识产权事业也步入了稳步发展的上升通道，而这一切，都离不开高素质、高水平的知识产权工作者，这其中就包含着知识产权律师这样一支带动整个知识产权行业前行的群体。

《知识产权律师论丛》一书共收录40余篇文章，作者中的大多数都是奋战在知识产权代理行业一线的律师和代理人，这些文章集理论研究和实务探讨为一体，是对近年知识产权法律、行业热点和日常实务操作所做的一些探讨、评析和总结。所选内容以小见大、指向性强，对于立法修法、同行借鉴、客户引导都颇有意义。

我相信"星星之火可以燎原"。《知识产权律师论丛》一书不仅能为关注知识产权行业的企业、人群提供一线的律师观点和切实可行的建议，同时也能促进与同行就相关的知识产权法律问题进行更深入的交流和探讨，从而对完善中国的知识产权制度，提升知识产权整体水平起到积极作用，令中国的知识产权事业在全球格局下更上一层楼。

田力普
2014 年 8 月于北京

序

　　人类进入工业社会已经二百多年。知识产权是伴随工业文明发生的一种新的财产形态，与之相匹配，已经形成了一套相对健全、完善的全球普遍接受的法律制度。新中国成立 30 年后才逐步建立知识产权制度，对于本就不熟悉法治的国人来说，就属于更新的法律领域。近二十年来，随着市场经济的建设与发展，涌现出的各类知识产权问题层出不穷，令这个领域充满了机遇与挑战，因此也需要更多的知识产权从业者参与到相关的学术探讨和研究中，以探索出更好的知识产权法律制度、司法程序和有效地解决问题的方式、方法。

　　《知识产权律师论丛》，是隆天知识产权代理有限公司（以下简称"隆天公司"）为纪念公司创立二十周年，集结隆天知识产权律师对于近年来知识产权法律、行业热点话题和实务问题的研究、分析和探索所形成的一份智慧成果，确是用心之作。这样一份成果，无疑是献给社会、献给自己的最珍贵的礼物。知识产权工作者的敬业精神都通过文章中这些精辟的观点、独到的分析呈现出来。

　　本书有中英双语两部分内容的文章共 40 余篇，多数文章已被各大专业刊物刊载，另外还有数篇为 2012、2013 年度的人大法学院"隆天知识产权论文奖"获奖论文。其中中文部分包含"知识产权律师观点"、"知识产权实务探讨"和"知识产权法律研究"三个章节，英文部分为"Insider's Look：Exploring the Intricacies of Chinese IP Law"。

　　勤于思考，工于心得，须知厚积薄发，须耐得寂寞。这正是知识产权工作者的写照。

刘春田

2014 年 8 月于北京·人大明德法学楼

目录

知识产权律师观点

如何助力中国计算机软件、网络、通信、商业方法类发明
　孵化出美国专利"金蛋" …………………………………… 张浴月 / 3
浅析宣告专利权无效程序中专利文件的修改　……………… 阚梓瑄 / 12
创造性与非显而易见性：洞察中美两国专利审查实践之不同 ……… 张浴月 / 17
从《专利法》第 33 条和第 26 条第 4 款的差异解读
　"修改超范围"的审判实践　…………………………… 冯志云 / 22
生物领域的审查原则到了需要改变的时候
　——《专利法》第 26 条第 4 款的理论与实践 …………… 吴小瑛 / 29
构造强大的防御体系
　——重视说明书的作用　………………………………… 付永莉 / 34
如何认定对比文件附图的公开内容
　——中国审判实践案例启示 …………………………… 聂慧荃 / 41
论混淆可能性在商标共存判定中的重要意义　…………… 梁晓敏 / 45
浅谈类似商品或服务的认定　………………………………… 吴 滌 / 51
浅谈纺织企业品牌保护　…………………………………… 蔡瑜萍 / 57

知识产权实务探讨

浅谈发明专利的加快授权方法　……………… 魏 彦　金相允 / 65
浅议常用技术手段在创造性审查实践中的认定　………… 聂慧荃 / 71
浅谈外观设计的设计自由度/设计空间　………………… 黄 艳 / 80

浅探外观设计专利的申请程序和维权问题 ……………… 黄　艳 / 85

浅谈相似外观设计与成套产品的外观设计 …………… 董雅会　金相允 / 89

对中国专利实践中的权利要求包含"坏点"的讨论 …………… 吴小瑛 / 94

浅析我国专利侵权判定中的权利要求保护范围的扩张

　　与限制之新进展 ……………………………………… 张永康 / 99

浅析《专利法》中的遗传资源保护制度 ………………… 张永康 / 112

浅析功能性限定权利要求的"以说明书为依据" ………… 张永康 / 125

浅析专利创造性判断中的"事后诸葛亮" ……………… 张永康 / 133

知识产权法律研究

论不可避免披露原则及其对我国商业秘密保护的启示 ………… 程　稆 / 143

我国著作权法上技术措施保护的完善 …………………… 罗明东 / 150

大数据时代的挑战：互联网环境中隐私权的保护

　　——以美欧的隐私政策为例 ………………………… 张家祺 / 162

我国知识产权领域反垄断问题研究 …………………… 赵　雪 / 174

中外专利法比较研究

　　——以中外专利法之修改超出原始公开的范围规定为例 …… 贺　兰 / 183

中日专利法之专有权比较及我国专利制度的发展与完善初探 … 赵　雪 / 192

论部分外观设计的保护 ………………………………… 柴耀田 / 200

中美发明专利创造性比较研究 ……………………… 史兆欢 / 211

Insider's Look: Exploring the Intricacies of Chinese IP Law

Claim Definitions Undergoing Change

　　…………………… Xiaoying Wu & Zongliang（Stephen）Zou / 223

Chinese Practice on Design Freedom Degree / Design Room

　　for Design Patents ………………………………… Yan Huang / 229

Expedited Patent Examination in China：

　　Options and Practical Tips ………… Yan Wei & Xiangyun Jin / 235

Issues and Tips Relating to Software-Related Inventions

　　to Be Patented in China ………………………… Yuyue Zhang / 243

Trademark Coexistence：Issues and Practice in China …… Xiaomin Liang / 249

Amendment to Claims in Invalidation Proceedings ·············· Zixuan Kan / 257

Assessing Inventiveness in China: Whether the Specification

　　Passes a Threshold of Disclosing Enough ······ Xiaoying Wu, Qinghong Xu / 263

Rights of Joint Patent Owners in China ········· Yunling Ren & Yan Hong / 269

Design Patent Prosecution and Enforcement:

　　Latest Issues and Developments ············· Qinghong Xu & Yan Huang / 293

Exceptions to the Unity Principle

　　—Brief Discussion on Similar Designs and Designs

　　　of Products in Set ························· Xiangyun Jin & Yahui Dong / 300

Inventiveness and Non-obviousness: Insights into

　　Prosecution Practice in China and the United States ········ Yuyue Zhang / 307

Chinese Law and Practice on Determining Proximity of

　　the Goods or Services ················· Di (Deland) Wu & Qinghong Xu / 313

Eye on Amendments That Go beyond Original Disclosure ······ Zhiyun Feng / 319

Discussions on "A Defect Point" Included In a Claim

　　under Chinese Patent Practice ································ Xiaoying Wu / 327

Patent Protection: Defenses-Options and Strategies

　　·· Yan Hong & Qinghong Xu / 333

知识产权律师观点

如何助力中国计算机软件、网络、通信、商业方法类发明孵化出美国专利"金蛋"*

张浴月

问题的由来

在新一轮技术革命推动各种产业的智能化、通信互联的革新浪潮中，计算机软件、网络、通信、商业方法领域中的创新越发成为一颗颗引人注意的明珠。中国企业除了在本土进行专利申请外，也在积极寻求美国市场的占领。

然而，由于计算机软件、网络、通信、商业方法领域中的专利法律规定与实践在中国与美国存在较大的差异，企业如果只是沿用其在中国的专利申请策略去美国申请专利，将面临各种法律风险，导致其投入了专利申请费用却不能达到顺利通过美国的专利审查阶段、获取美国专利的目的，或者更甚之，其获得的专利并不能真正成为威慑对手、获得赔偿的利器。

问题的解决

一、可以要求保护的主题有哪些？

1. 专利适格性

美国在其专利法第 101 条中规定了较宽的法定可授权客体范围，其比中国的客体范围宽的一个体现存在于软件以及商业方法类发明的领域。虽然范围宽，但也要在了解中美之间可授权客体范围差异的前提下，选择适当的保护主题和撰写方式，才能孵化出"宽"的专利之"蛋"。

首先，与中国在其《专利法》第 25 条第 2 款中明确排除了科学发现、智力活动的规则/方法的专利适格性相似，美国通过司法判例将抽象思想拒于法定可授权客体的门外。因此，当权利要求指向单纯的商业方法、算法、数据结构、帧格式、协议、软件，即权利要求没有记载计算机、智能终端、网络等机器的应用时，中美两国的专利实践对此的态度都比较明确，即不是可授权客体。如：

---

* 原文刊于中华全国专利代理人协会所编《高质量的专利申请文件》，获 2013 年专利审查与专利代理学术研讨会优秀论文奖。

案例 1（参见 2010 年 Bilski v. Kappos 案）

一种管理由商品供应商以固定价格出售的商品的消费风险成本的方法，包含以下步骤：

（a）在所述商品供应商与所述商品的消费者之间发起了一系列的交易，其中，所述消费者以一个基于历史平均水平的固定费率购买所述商品，所述固定费率与所述消费者的风险状况相对应；

（b）识别与所述消费者有一个相反风险状况的所述商品的市场参与者；

（c）在所述商品供应商与所述市场参与者之间发起一系列以第二个固定费率进行的交易，使得所述一系列市场参与者的交易平衡所述一系列消费者的交易的风险状况。

案例 2

案例 1 被认为太抽象了，美国最高法院在其 Bilski 案中指出与机器联系可以作为专利适格的线索。

若将案例 1 的主题名称进一步改为以下内容，这种写明由计算机等机器执行的方法在中美两国结果不同。

一种管理由商品供应商以固定价格出售的商品的消费风险成本的方法，**该计算机终端被编程以执行该方法。**

在中国，案例 2 可能不被认为属于中国《专利法》第 25 条第 2 款规定的不能获得专利保护的情形，但会采用《专利审查指南 2010》第二部分第九章规定的"三要素测试法"（解决技术问题、采用技术手段且获得技术效果），来判断其是否属于《专利法》第 2 条第 2 款规定的发明专利的可授权客体。由于三要素测试法不考虑商业模式上的创新，而只是检验是否存在技术上的创新，例如扩充了存储空间，或改善了橡胶模压成型工艺，防止了橡胶的硫化欠硫化测试等，或改善了图像质量等（《专利审查指南 2010》第二部分第九章），因此案例 2 在中国可能被《专利法》第 2 条第 2 款挡住。当然，如果除了包括新的商务模式，还包括一种技术创新，就属于中国的可授权客体。

在美国，在审查阶段，案例 2 可能会顺利过美国专利法第 101 条这一关。参见美国专利商标局根据 Bilski 案判决调整的美国专利审查指南（MPEP）2012 版中以下考察因素（节选）：

"既要考虑发生有助于专利适格性影响的因素，又要考虑发生削弱专利适格性影响的因素。发生有助于专利适格性影响的因素满足机器或转换测试标准，或者提供了抽象思想已经被实际应用的证据。"

"该方法是否包括特定机器，或被特定机器执行。"

"在权利要求'对计算机如何辅助该方法、计算机在多大的范围辅助该方法，或计算机对该方法的执行的重要性上保持缄默时'，在一个涵盖了抽象概念的权利要求中增加'计算机辅助'的限制，没有其他限制的话，是不足以使该权利要求适格的。需要清楚写明计算机被编程以执行该方法的步骤。"❶

"机器或装置是否执行了方法步骤很重要。集成使用机器或装置以实现方法的执行将发生朝向适格性的影响，与如果机器或装置只是方法步骤的对象则发生远离适格性的影响相反。❷ 姑且不论网络是否可视为机器，上诉人辩解说其方法权利要求捆绑在机器上的原因是'没有网络，该方法将是可不能的'，不能说服我们很清楚网络不能执行该方法权利要求的欺诈检测方法。"

因此，在美国，如果在撰写商业方法、软件类发明的权利要求时，写入机器执行方法的步骤等特征，一般可以推定具有专利适格性。这是源于，美国的许多法官认为，应将软件与硬件放在一起考虑（如案例2），这样它们可构成一个足以克服要求保护的发明太抽象的意见的新机器，即成为可授权客体。

案例3

然而，商业方法、软件类发明是否应授予专利？如果是，边界在哪儿？这在美国却又起波澜。美国联邦巡回上诉法院（CAFC）近来作出裁决（CLS Bank v. Alice，2013年5月10日）说："抽象思想不能仅仅因为与机器联系了就变成可专利的客体"。具体来说，由法官Lourie领导的5人法官阵营，采取了一种特别洞察入微的观点，以涉案专利中的权利要求的计算机限定特征仅仅是"相对于该抽象思想而言无关紧要的事后解决方案（post-solution）……"为由，认为在计算机上运行程序并不能改变计算机，或减少软件的抽象属性，裁决介质权利要求以及系统权利要求无效。

此案例使得在美国，商业方法、软件类发明的专利适格性更加扑朔迷离。当然，该案可能还会被美国最高法院提审，中国代理人、申请人当拭目以待，根据情况及时调整权利要求的撰写策略。

小结：在美国，除了通过司法判例识别出的例外，基本上都是其第101条可以获得专利保护的客体。这些例外概括而言就是：自然规律、物理现象和抽象思想，或者说是：自然现象，科学原理，只取决于人类智力的系统，无实体的概念，智力过程，无实体的数学算法和公式（参见MPEP 2106）。因此，中国申请人一般而言只要判断其想要保护的不是上面的司法例外，基本上就都可以去美国申请专利，不必像在中国那样只申请有技术创新的发明。例如，如果想要申请一种网络有奖销售发明，或在线玩家终端进行通信的发明，或游戏服务器、数据接入系统的计费发明等只有商务、营销模式创新的

❶ Fed. Cir. 2012：Dealer Track v. Huber，USPQ 2d 1325，1339–1340.

❷ Fed. Cir. 2011：Cybersource v. Retail Decisions，654 F. 3d 1366，99 USPQ 2d 1960.

发明都是可以的。但需按照美国的审查方式、判例等在撰写上进行适当的调整（参见下文）。

2. 权利要求保护主题类别

即使通过初判，确定一个发明创造可以向美国申请专利，还需要注意：需选择适当的、法定的权利要求保护主题类别，获得多个维度的保护形式。

具体地说，除了方法类权利要求中美两国的范畴（可以选择方法、用途等范畴）相似外，在物之权利要求方面，美国除了给予装置、系统等范畴的权利要求形式保护，还比中国多一个介质范畴的保护，例如著名的 Beauregard 形式的计算机可读介质权利要求。并且，撰写时写明权利要求保护的是**非暂态有形**的计算机可读存储介质方可，否则将会覆盖不是法定客体的信号传递的瞬时形式〔CAFC 在 2007 年 In re Nuijten 案（500 F. 3d 1346，84 USPQ 2d 1495）的判决，将机器可读媒介解释为可以包含瞬态信号，以及有形载体的压缩盘〕，而前者被认为属于自然规律。

笔者推荐写入介质权利要求。理由是：在侵权举证时较为容易证明属于美国专利法第 271 条（a）规定的严格责任——直接侵权。且如果侵权者将软件的 master copy 等介质卖到美国之外如中国，装在电脑上的话，美国的介质专利权人还可以主张依据第 271 条（f）要求美国之外的市场如中国市场的销售额作为赔偿基础（CAFC 在 2005 年 Eolas Techs. , Inc. v. Microsoft Corp. 案）。

小结：随着网络技术的迅猛发展，传统的用母盘、光盘分发软件的方式已经发展为通过网络来扩散。若要真正切实给予软件专利保护，是否一定要局限于其载体，中国台湾和欧专局已经说不，它们以形式不能高于实质为由，分别开始允许采用计算机软件产品、数据结构产品的范畴的权利要求来保护软件。作为 IT 技术的领头人美国，未来是否也会给予这种范畴的保护，还是个未知数。但考虑到美国判例对专利审查的实时指导作用，中国申请人也可以在申请之初，就写上这样的软件产品权利要求。

二、易于通过审查的权利要求撰写方式

对于软件类发明申请，需警惕的问题是由中国的一种特殊撰写方式引发的去美国的"水土不服效应"。

《专利审查指南 2010》第二部分第九章给出了一种基于说明书中描述的计算机程序流程或者依据反映了该计算机软件流程的方法权利要求撰写的、由一组软件功能模块限定的产品权利要求。笔者称这种权利要求为中国式"无形"产品权项，即：其所要求保护的产品是一种主要通过说明书中描述的计算机程序实现的抽象的虚拟装置，而不是主要通过硬件实现的实体装置。

中国审查员依据《专利法》第 26 条第 4 款审查这种"无形"式产品权项的保护范围是否符合得到说明书支持以及是否清楚时，会直接根据上述第九章的规定，认为其要求保护的只是软件实现方式，因此能够得到描述了计算机软件流程的说明书的支持且是清楚的。这种审查方式可谓是专用于"无形"式产品权利要求的"特殊"审查方式。

与中国明显不同的是，美国强调产品权利要求保护的产品的有形性，审查焦点在于产品与软件、算法等之间是否存在功能和结构上的关系。笔者称这种旨在保护有形产品权利要求为"有形"式产品权项。这种权利要求也是中国以外大部分国家和地区常用的权利要求形式。

因此，中国申请人若将其中国"无形"式产品权利要求直接翻译成英文去美国的话，很有可能遭遇令其费解的审查意见。例如：

案例 4

一种音乐推荐系统，包括：音乐归属函数获取单元，用于……

用户归属函数获取单元，用于……

粒度相关函数计算单元，用于……

推荐单元，用于……

美国审查员一般根据 MPEP 2106 的两步判断法来判断。第一步是判断是否为专利法第 101 条规定的 4 个法定类别：过程、机器、制品以及物质的合成。第二步判断是否为司法判例识别出来的例外，如信号的传输、无实体的概念、无实体的数学算法和公式。参见下面节选：

"权利要求包括了暗示发明指向产品的术语，例如记载了'机器，包括……'，但是在最宽最合理的解释方式下没有包括赋予具体形状的限定特征，这种权利要求并未被限制到一个实际应用，反之整体上包含了发明赖以作为基础的概念。这是不允许的，因为这种权利要求范围将会延伸到应用该抽象思想的所有方式。"

"权利要求为'根据公式 $F=ma$ 运行的机器'，没有任何有形的结构元素，覆盖了基于该公式的操作原理，而对权利要求的范围没有限制。"

因此，美国审查员轻则将产品权项的某一个功能模块通过援引美国专利法第 112 条第 6 款对应至说明书中某个有形物理实体，重则认为该权利要求覆盖某个算法的所有实际应用的产品，从而挥舞专利法第 101 条的"大棒"拦下该权利要求。

因此，中国申请人在撰写权利要求时，要注意写入产品权利要求的具体结构，再写上结构特征与软件流程各步骤特征之间是否具有功能上和/或结构上的联系。例如：

案例 5（苹果、三星大战中的美国专利 7469381 的权利要求 19）

一种装置，包括：

触摸显示屏;

一个或多个处理器;

存储器, 存储有一个或多个程序, 被配置为由所述一个或多个处理器**执行, 所述程序包括:**

显示电子文档的第一部分**的指令;**

检测触摸屏上或附近对象的移动**的指令;**

响应于对运动的检测, 在第一方向上翻译触摸屏上显示的电子文档**的指令**, 以显示电子文档的第二部分, 其中第二部分不同于第一部分……

三、说明书应当披露的信息

中美差异的一个重要体现在于, 说明书公开何种性质的信息才能构成中国"无形"式产品权利要求的支持。此外, 说明书的信息由于在侵权诉讼中起着解释、支撑权利要求的支柱作用, 更当予以重视, 否则有可能使专利权人用专利武器辅助其商业策略的如意算盘落空, 如下文提到的"2012 年 Noah Systems, Inc. v. Intuit, Inc., 675 F. 3d 1302 案"。

这种差异主要是对中国申请人产生不利影响, 因为中国申请人是使用其在中国的在先申请作为优先权向美国提出申请的。由于中国申请文件的说明书是按照《专利审查指南 2010》撰写的, 虽然可以用来支持中国"无形"式产品类权利要求, 但是经常由于没有描述该产品在现实世界中对应的硬件结构而不能符合美国专利法第 112 条第 2 款的"书面描述"该产品的要求。由于作为优先权的中国申请没有这一部分内容, 导致这种缺陷有可能成为难以克服的硬伤, 从而不能使其产品权利要求获得授权。

美国给予的涉及计算机软件的产品权利要求与中国的产品权利要求的概念是不对等的, 其含义与其他技术领域的产品权利要求基本相同, 即: 该产品需具有作为有形载体的物理实体, 并特别强调该物理实体与该软件之间的功能和/或结构上的关系。因此, 对于产品权利要求, 要求说明书公开该产品的具体构造的各种例子。

因此, 中国申请人在最初向中国提交申请时, 如已经准备进入美国市场, 则需要在说明书中做好铺垫, 即清楚描述软件依托的硬件运行环境和设备。以脉搏血氧测量领域为例, 其发明的新型软件算法在说明书中描述为: "主要是对一定时间内采集到的脉搏波波形进行处理, 特点是对乘法的需求极大, 所涉及的数据处理量为 1k 左右。因此基于 8051 内核的 51 系列单片机不能很好地运行该软件算法, 而使用采用了哈佛总线结构和硬件乘法器、内部设置多个并行操作的功能单元和大量的片内存储器的 DSP 器件, 虽然能提高运算速度, 但成本价格较高。"因此, 从处理能力与成本上都与该软件成为最佳拍档的硬件是"美国微芯科技股份有限公司推出的采用 RISC 和哈佛结构的 PIC 系列单片机"。参见"基于 PIC 单片机的脉搏血氧测量仪的研制"（李文耀，王博亮，戴君伟，《厦门大学学报》第 44 卷第 4 期）。

还需注意的是，产品的具体构造并不能一刀切式地在所有申请中拷入模板型的描述，如"该软件由微处理器来执行。依赖于所需要的配置，可以包括任何类型的一个或多个微处理器，包括但不限于微处理器、微控制器、数字信号处理器或其任意组合"，"该软件存储在存储器，例如，易失性存储器（例如，随机读取存储器）、非易失性存储器（例如，只读存储器、闪存等）或其任意组合"等。而要根据情况，判断是否还需要描述清楚执行该软件的专用处理器及必要的算法。参见"2012 年 Noah Systems，Inc. v. Intuit，Inc.，675 F. 3d 1302 案"，因专利说明书中没有公开能够支持其权利要求的特征"为第一方和/或代理人提供到所述财务会计计算机的档案的访问，从而第一方和/或代理人能够执行一个或更多所选定的行为的装置"对应的特定算法，该专利被无效掉了。

小结：笔者建议，除了继续按照中国的要求，在说明书中写清楚实现软件的功能的各组成模块、关系和流程外，还需要注意软件对硬件的或强或弱的依赖性，以及该软件各个步骤涉及的算法，全方位写明该软件运行所需的软硬件信息。

四、易导致侵权诉讼的权利要求撰写方式

计算机软件、网络、商业方法、通信类的发明经常涉及不同终端、客户端、服务器端各自的操作，以及之间的通信，这些不同端经常由不同的法律主体实施，属于不同的企业或个人，甚至还可能位于不同的国家，即不同的法域。针对这个特点，这里单独讨论与美国侵权诉讼有关的权利要求撰写方式。

规定了直接侵权的美国专利法第 271 条（a）是侵权时法律争议最少的有效工具，其最典型的场景是：一个法律责任主体（如一个人或一个企业）实施专利权利要求的所有特征才算是侵权，并且一般需要专利权利要求的所有特征都在美国境内实施。

虽然也存在多个主体实施所有特征时，其中一个主体也承担直接侵权责任，但这种责任的性质是替代责任，因此认定非常严格。其要求实施了专利方法的所有步骤的多个法律主体之间有代理关系这种意思联络，甚至他们就是一体的，而不是简单的客户关系。而如果无代理关系、策划关系，对于彼此互不相识的多个主体，或者只是一般正常的客户服务商关系，虽然共同实施了专利方法的所有步骤，那么法院一般不会将这些不相干的主体的行为聚

合起来认定为直接侵权。而在计算机、网络、通信领域，这种不相干的主体之间完成权利要求所有特征的场合是很常见的。例如下面的案例就是由客户端的消费者、服务器端的运营商共同实施的多方行为权利要求。

案例 6❶

一种磋商安全通信会议的方法，包括：

发送请求给服务器，

响应该请求，从服务器提供一个包括服务器公钥的服务器证书，

客户端生成唯一的私钥，将该私钥通知给服务器；以及

使用该唯一的私钥和所述服务器公钥获得的加密算法来进行通信。

虽然这个权利要求可能满足所有专利性条件而获得授权，但在将来行使专利权时，却很难甚至不能，导致专利权人空有权利却得不到救济。

由于中国尚未有此类多方行为权利要求专利的侵权判例，因此中国申请人在撰写权利要求时，很容易关注各个端的操作，从各个端的角度进行撰写（如案例 6），从而出现权利要求的所有特征是由多个法律责任主体实施的多用户权利要求（Multi-User Claims）的情况，即分散式或分布式权利要求。这些法律主体有的甚至不在美国，或分散在多个国家。

这种分散式权利要求在美国专利侵权判定实践中也是较为复杂的，导致侵权事实难以认定而对专利权人不利。

例如 2008 年 Muniauction, Inc. v. Thomson Corp. 一案中，上诉法院撤销了地方法院已经给予专利权人对在电子网络上进行原始市政债券拍卖的方法专利 7700 万美元的损害赔偿。理由是，该方法的步骤是由债券发行方市政机构、投标认购人，以及汤姆逊三方实施的，虽然汤姆逊控制了对其被指控的系统的访问，但当其使用其被指控系统进行拍卖时，也没有让其他两方为了其利益而去做，因此不应承担替代责任，并建议将方法权项写成单方接收和提供方法步骤的每个元素的形式。❷

案例 7 演示了服务器端集中式权利要求的写法。这是一种单用户行为权利要求，其从服务器端描述了方法的所有步骤，这些步骤全部是服务器端完成的。

案例 7 ❸

一种磋商安全通信会议的方法，包括：

---

❶ MARK A. LEMLEY, DAVID O'BRIEN, et al. Divided Infringement Claims [J]. Aipla Quarterly Journal, 2005: 255-284.

❷ JANICE M. MUELLER. Patent Law: Chapter 9 patent infringement [M]. 3rd edition.

❸ MARK A. LEMLEY, DAVID O'BRIEN, et al. Divided Infringement Claims [J]. Aipla Quarterly Journal, 2005: 255-284.

接收客户端发送的请求，

响应该请求，从服务器提供一个包括服务器公钥的服务器证书，

接收客户端用所述服务器公钥发送的唯一的私钥；以及

使用该唯一的私钥和所述服务器公钥获得的加密算法来进行通信。

案例7虽可降低没有一个单独的侵权者从而没有直接侵权的风险，但不能避免难以对将服务器放在美国境外导致难以主张直接侵权的风险。此时，可以写一个与之互补的以客户端为中心的权利要求，如案例8：

案例8❶

一种磋商安全通信会议的方法，包括：

发送请求到服务器，

接收来自服务器的包括服务器公钥的服务器证书，

生成唯一的私钥，并用所述服务器公钥，将该私钥通知给服务器；以及

使用该唯一的私钥和所述服务器公钥获得的加密算法来进行通信。

案例8针对的法律主体是分散的消费者。但在美国，由于消费者的行为构成直接侵权，专利权人就有了起诉侵权企业间接侵权的基础，例如指控侵权企业通过指导或许可消费者进行了一个以消费者为中心的集中式方法权利要求的所有步骤，即引诱消费者直接侵权。规定引诱侵权的美国专利法第271条（b）不像第271条（a）那样要求引诱行为发生在美国境内。因此，指控"引诱"可以说是一个强有力的工具，可以用来应对计算机、网络、通信类发明创造的国际化侵权。

结束语

技术上，软件、网络、通信技术、商业方法类发明具有自身的特点，且还在不断演进中。法律上，美国专利法律体系较为复杂。因此，专利代理人应当深谙企业发明的技术特点，更应当对中美两国法律知己知彼，从而给上述领域的发明创造量身定做好在中美两国都能获得最佳保护的法律外衣。不仅要帮助中国企业顺利获得美国专利，更要助其专利在日后的维权阶段屹立不倒，从而提高专利"金蛋"的含金量。

---

❶ MARK A. LEMLEY, DAVID O'BRIEN, et al. Divided Infringement Claims [J]. Aipla Quarterly Journal, 2005：255-284.

浅析宣告专利权无效程序中专利文件的修改

阚梓瑄

近年来，随着专利申请量逐年增加以及专利维权意识的不断提高，宣告专利权无效案件量也大幅上升。专利复审委员会对于专利是否有效有着独立的裁判权❶，无论是否存在与之对应的专利侵权诉讼案件。专利复审委员会的决定必须遵守法律的规定并基于所记载的事实而作出。专利复审委员会遵照执行的无效程序中的审查标准由《专利审查指南 2010》（下文简称《审查指南》）所规定，其初步规定了宣告专利权无效程序中修改专利权利要求书的主要方式，但规定较为笼统，加之尚有一些实践中所遵循的标准，因此本文旨在结合具体案例详细阐明宣告专利权无效程序中权利要求书的修改方式。

《专利法》第 45 条规定，自国务院专利行政部门公告授予专利权之日起，任何单位或者个人认为该专利权的授予不符合《专利法》有关规定的，可以请求专利复审委员会宣告该专利权无效。

《审查指南》规定了宣告专利权无效程序中，发明或者实用新型专利文件的修改仅限于权利要求书，并进一步规定了专利文件的修改原则、修改方式等。

宣告专利权无效程序中修改权利要求书的具体方式一般只限于 3 种方式，即权利要求的删除、权利要求的合并和技术方案的删除。其中，删除方式的修改时机，例如权利要求的删除、技术方案的删除时机可以在专利复审委员会作出审查决定之前；合并方式的修改有较为严格的规定，仅在下列 3 种情形的答复期限内才能以合并方式修改权利要求：

（1）针对无效宣告请求书；

（2）针对请求人增加的无效宣告理由或者补充的证据；

（3）针对专利复审委员会引入的请求人未提及的无效宣告理由或者证据。

《审查指南》仅对宣告专利权无效程序权利要求书的修改作了原则性的笼统的规定，不易理解。下面举例说明《审查指南》规定的在无效宣告程序中允许的三种修改方式。

---

❶ 专利复审委员会独立于专利局。

例1

授权公告文本的权利要求书为：

1. 一种 A，其特征是 B。

2. 如权利要求 1 所述的 A，其特征是 C。

3. 如权利要求 1 或 2 所述的 A，其特征是 D。

4. 如权利要求 1 所述的 A，其特征是 E。

5. 如权利要求 4 所述的 A，其特征是 F 或 G。

（一）以删除权利要求的方式对授权文本的权利要求书进行修改

权利要求的删除是指从权利要求书中去掉某项或者某些项权利要求，被删除的权利要求可以是独立权利要求，也可以是从属权利要求。

例如，删除原从属权利要求 5，则修改后的权利要求书为：

1. 一种 A，其特征是 B。

2. 如权利要求 1 所述的 A，其特征是 C。

3. 如权利要求 1 或 2 所述的 A，其特征是 D。

4. 如权利要求 1 所述的 A，其特征是 E。

通常，在某项从属权利要求不清楚等情况下，可在宣告专利权无效程序中删除该从属权利要求。

又例如，删除独立权利要求 1，则修改后的权利要求书为：

1. 一种 A，其特征是 B+C。

2. 如权利要求 1 所述的 A，其特征是 D。

3. 如权利要求 1 所述的 A，其特征是 E。

4. 如权利要求 3 所述的 A，其特征是 F 或 G。

通常，在某项独立权利要求缺少必要技术特征、不具备新颖性或创造性、不能得到说明书支持等情况下，可以在宣告专利权无效程序中删除该独立权利要求。

（二）以删除技术方案的方式对授权文本的权利要求书进行修改

技术方案的删除是指从同一权利要求中并列的两种以上技术方案中删除一种或者一种以上技术方案。

上述授权公告文本的权利要求书中，仅有权利要求 5 中包括两种并列的技术方案，可以删除技术方案的方式进行修改。

例如，删除权利要求 5 的技术方案 F，则修改后的权利要求书为：

1. 一种 A，其特征是 B。

2. 如权利要求 1 所述的 A，其特征是 C。

3. 如权利要求 1 或 2 所述的 A，其特征是 D。

4. 如权利要求 1 所述的 A，其特征是 E。

5. 如权利要求 4 所述的 A，其特征是 G。

通常，在某项权利要求的并列技术方案中的一个或多个不清楚或不具备创造性等情况下，可在宣告专利权无效程序中删除该技术方案。

（三）以合并权利要求的方式对授权文本的权利要求书进行修改

权利要求的合并是指两项或者两项以上相互无从属关系但在授权公告文本中从属于同一独立权利要求的权利要求的合并。在此情况下，所合并的从属权利要求的技术特征组合在一起形成新的权利要求。该新的权利要求应当包含被合并的从属权利要求中的全部技术特征。

由于《审查指南》规定了"在独立权利要求未作修改的情况下，不允许对其从属权利要求进行合并式修改"，因此以合并方式修改权利要求只能建立在独立权利要求有修改的基础之上。

例如，删除独立权利要求 1（对独立权利要求 1 进行了修改），则对权利要求书可进行如下修改：

（1）原从属权利要求 2 形成新的独立权利要求；

（2）原从属权利要求 3 引用原独立权利要求 1 的部分可形成新的独立权利要求；

（3）原从属权利要求 4 可形成新的独立权利要求；

（4）均从属于原独立权利要求 1 的原从属权利要求 2、3 可合并为一个新的独立权利要求；

（5）均从属于原独立权利要求 1 的原从属权利要求 2、4 可合并为一个新的独立权利要求；

（6）均从属于原独立权利要求 1 的原从属权利要求 3、4 可合并为一个新的独立权利要求；

（7）均从属于原独立权利要求 1 的原从属权利要求 2、3、4 可合并为一个新的独立权利要求；

（8）原从属权利要求 5 形成新的从属权利要求；

（9）原从属权利要求 3 引用原从属权利要求 2 的部分形成原从属权利要求 2（修改后的独立权利要求 1）的从属权利要求，但该从属权利要求的保护范围与上述第（4）项合并从属权利要求 2、3 形成的独立权利要求的保护范围相同，故删除。

修改后的权利要求书为：

1. 一种 A，其特征是 B+C。

2. 一种 A，其特征是 B+D。

3. 一种 A，其特征是 B+E。

4. 一种 A，其特征是 B+C+D。

5. 一种 A，其特征是 B+C+E。

6. 一种 A，其特征是 B+D+E。

7. 一种 A，其特征是 B+C+D+E。

8. 如权利要求 3、5、6 或 7 所述的 A，其特征是 F 或 G。

通常，在某项独立权利要求缺少必要技术特征、不具备新颖性或创造性、不能得到说明书支持等情况下，可在宣告专利权无效程序中删除该独立权利要求，同时对从属于该被删除的独立权利要求作合并式修改。

以上是《审查指南》有明确规定的无效程序中的 3 种修改方式。然而，专利实务中会面临其他更为复杂的情况，例如在删除了独立权利要求及其从属权利要求的情况下，那些从属于该被删除的从属权利要求的各从属权利要求是否可进行合并式修改？下面结合我司的一个无效案例进行说明，为便于阅读及理解，仅给出权利要求书的简化形式。

例 2

授权公告文本的权利要求书为：

1. 一种 A，其特征是 B。

2. 如权利要求 1 所述的 A，其特征是 C。

3. 如权利要求 1 或 2 所述的 A，其特征是 D。

4. 如权利要求 2 所述的 A，其特征是 E。

5. 如权利要求 4 所述的 A，其特征是 F 或 G。

修改后的权利要求书为：

1. 一种 A，其特征是 B+C+D。

2. 一种 A，其特征是 B+C+E。

3. 一种 A，其特征是 B+C+D+E。

4. 如权利要求 2 或 3 所述的 A，其特征是 F 或 G。

上述修改中，删除了独立权利要求 1 及其从属权利要求 2，并对均从属于原从属权利要求 2 的原从属权利要求 3、4 进行了合并式修改，形成新的独立权利要求（见修改后权利要求 3）。虽然《审查指南》中没有明确规定上述修改是否允许，然而专利实务中上述修改方式得到专利复审委员会的确认。根据我们的理解，《审查指南》中有关无效程序中对权利要求合并修改方式的规定，其本意是不创造出授权文本的权利要求书中没有直接或间接给出的技术方案。

由此可见，对于授权专利所允许进行的修改限制确实是非常严格的。不过，最高人民法院对于修改限制则表现出更宽松的态度。在专利复审委员会与江苏先声药业有限公司的行政诉讼案件（案号：执行字 17/2011）中，法院认为专利权人可以以不同于《审查指南》所规定的修改方式来修改其权利要求，并驳回了专利复审委员会关于《专利法》应用方面的严格限制。然而，由于中国并不是一个案例法国家，专利复审委员会关于已授权专利的权利要求的修改依然执行《审查指南》所规定的标准。我们相信，专利复审委员会在未来的无效案审理实践中，会就《专利审查指南2010》中没有明确或者具体规定的修改权利要求的方式，给出更多、更全面、更合理的修改范例或解释。

创造性与非显而易见性：洞察中美两国专利审查实践之不同

张浴月

在各国专利法中，创造性与非显而易见性这两个表述所指的是同一个专利性要求，按照这个要求，确定一个发明是否具有足够的创造力，即是否非显而易见，从而判断是否可以获得专利。虽然创造性与非显而易见性作为基本的法律原则大致相同，但具体的评价却随着不同的国家而变化。中国《专利法》第 22 条第 3 款使用"创造性"措辞，而美国专利法第 103 条使用"非显而易见"措辞。为简化起见，本文在下面的讨论中使用"创造性"。

由于中国与美国是许多专利申请人寻求获得专利保护的国家，本文旨在探求中美两国在专利性最本质的条件"创造性"分析上的异同，❶ 以帮助申请人对于自己的发明在中美两国的审查命运有更好的预测与更适当的应对策略。

一、法律背景的差异及导致的专利申请的审查与审判阶段的差异

美国对于创造性的规定见于美国专利法第 103 条，与中国《专利法》第 22 条第 3 款一样，同样是非常概括的法律条文，仅是措辞不同，美国要求发明需具有"非显而易见性"，中国要求发明需"具有突出的实质性特点和显著的进步"从而具有"创造性"。

在审查发明是否满足创造性要求时，由各自的行政管理机构（即各自的专利局）通过使用具体的行政规则来适用上述概括的法律条文。

不同的是，美国专利商标局（USPTO）适用的审查指南（*Manual of Patent Examining Procedure*，MPEP）不具有法律效力，它需要跟随法院的判例来调整其审查指南中的具体条文，而中国国家知识产权局（SIPO）适用的《专利审查指南》（*Guideline for Patent Examination*，GPE）则属于部门规章，具有法律效力，不随法院的判决而改变。这从例如 USPTO 响应 2007 年最高法院在 KSR Int'l Co. v. Teleflex Inc.（简称 KSR）案中的判决，分别在 2007 年和 2010 年对 MPEP 中的"2141 节，确定显而易见性的审查指南"做的相应的调整和补充可见一斑。

---

❶ 本文针对的是中国发明专利的创造性分析议题，不包括对中国实用新型专利的创造性分析。

之所以有上述不同，是因为两国的法律体系不同，我国是成文法国家，而美国是判例法国家。由此带来的后续不同又有：

（1）在应对审查阶段 OA 中提出的创造性质疑时，在中国，申请人通常需要按照《专利审查指南》规定的审查标准来答复；在美国，申请人则可以援引判例而不一定要按照审查指南的规定来反驳审查意见。

（2）进而如果法院来考虑创造性的争议（例如不服 SIPO 的专利复审委员会的决定而向法院起诉）时，中国的法院将会参照《专利审查指南》的相关规定，美国的法院则遵循先例，若无先例，则会创造先例。

二、创造性的分析路线图的差异

通常，创造性的判断涉及对于客观事实的调查。进行事实调查的主体是在自己的经验和认知水平上进行判断的人，因此不可避免地受到客观局限和其主观因素的干扰。为了尽量去除上述干扰，SIPO 与 USPTO 要求判断者回到过去，穿上法律假设的、在要求保护的发明的申请日（在美国，按照 2009 年改法之前则是发明日）时具有所属技术领域的普通技能的"本领域普通技术人员"的"靴子"或进入他的思想，从这个"假人"的角度来进行客观的判断。

在中国，《专利审查指南》规定了在审查发明"具有突出的实质性特点"时可以采用三步分析法：①识别出最接近的现有技术；②确定发明的区别特征和发明实际解决的技术问题；③判断要求保护的发明对本领域的技术人员来说是否显而易见。《专利审查指南》规定了在审查发明"具有显著的进步"时，是查找要求保护的发明是否能够带来有益的技术效果。

实际上，根据三步分析法，要区分主观要解决的技术问题（原始申请文件记载的）与客观能解决的技术问题。这个客观解决的技术问题是根据最接近的对比文件与要求保护的发明之间的区别技术特征所拟合而成的，因此经常与主观要解决的技术问题并不同。可想而知，当选择不同对比文件作为最接近的对比文件时，这个客观的技术问题也可能会变化。

这种方式带来的后果就是容易将正在被评价创造性的发明当作蓝图使用，而将发明所针对并解决的技术问题当成已知的问题。因而，审查员在将一篇或几篇现有技术文献甚至公知常识进行组合时，可能较少考虑到组合的动机。结果是，如果在发明中的解决其技术问题的改进手段被从与本发明关联度不高的某个现有技术文献中检索出来，则在发明中的某个非改进手段会成为与该现有技术文献相比所具有的区别特征。可想而知，这个"区别特征"很容易被从与本申请关联度较高的对比文件中检索到。因此，这种分析推理的方法导致了更高的创造性标准。

根据上述讨论，中国的分析采用的是"问题-方案分析法"（problem and solution approach）来分析是否显而易见。具体而言就是：调查发明对于客观存在的技术问题提供的解决方案是否显而易见，不同于在美国式体系中调查发明是否显而易见。

在美国，创造性分析路线是一个以复杂的事实判断（factual-determinations）为基础进行的相对而言简单直白的过程，不需要区分主观要解决的技术问题与客观解决的技术问题。在考虑已知的元素是否可以组合时，采用"教导、建议或动机法"（俗称 TSM 测试❶）等方法。按照这种测试方式，只有被引用的几篇对比文件之间关联度较高且能共同指向本发明，即它们与本发明的关联度也较高，才能被考虑"假人"看到它们时能否显而易见地想到本发明。

结果，这种判断方式使得创造性的门槛低于中国。然而，TSM 测试也受到一些诟病。美国最高法院在 KSR 案中称，该测试"以与专利法第 103 条以及本院先例不符的狭窄的、僵化的方式"分析了创造性议题。因此，最高法院在 KSR 案的判决中将创造性门槛略微提高了一些，导致目前在美国专利商标局审查的方式就是：

（1）如果适用 TSM 测试不具有创造性，则作出不具有创造性的决定；

（2）如果适用 TSM 测试不能作出不具有创造性的决定，则还需考虑本领域的普通的技能和公知常识。

三、创造性分析考虑要素的差异

中国与美国通常考虑的事实要素大致相同，类似于美国最高法院 1996 年通过的 Graham v. John Deere Co. 一案中确立的以下 4 个要素（俗称 Graham 要素）：

（1）该领域的普通技能水平（level of ordinary skill）；

（2）现有技术的内容与范围；

（3）要求保护的发明与现有技术的区别；

（4）辅助考虑因素。

关于上述要素（1），在中国，《专利审查指南》对本领域普通技术人员的知识范围（一个知识范围，所属领域的普通技术知识）和能力种类（3 种能力，所属领域的常规实验能力，获知所属领域的所有现有技术的能力，在所解决的技术问题的启发之下获知其他技术领域的相关现有技术、普通技术知识和常规实验手段的能力）作出了定义。美国则需对于上述要素（1）进行

---

❶　参见案例 Winner Int'l Royalty Corp. v. Wang，（Fed. Cir. 2000）。

事实发现，并且需全部或部分考虑以下证据（常以专家证词的形式），来确立该领域的普通技能水平：

（1）发明人的受教育水平；

（2）该领域一般作业人员的受教育水平（例如，高中文凭，本科文凭，研究生文凭如硕士或博士）；

（3）这个技术所遇到的问题类型，以及以前解决这些问题的方案；

（4）该技术发生革新的频度；

（5）该技术的复杂程度（即，发明是鱼饵还是基因克隆方法）。

这种方式使得在美国本领域的普通技能水平会随着例如技术领域、技术问题等而不同。在根据美国专利法第 103 条挑战专利有效性的诉讼中，支持专利有创造性的一方通常会试图建立尽可能低的普通技能水平，使得本发明将能够被尽可能多的人们认为是非显而易见的，反对者通常会寻求提高该水平。

四、美国关于创造性分析的特殊方法

1. 反向教导（teaching away）

美国最高法院在 KSR 案中阐述道："本院依赖这样的推理原则：当现有技术排斥将已知的元素进行组合时，发现将它们进行组合后获得成功的装置更有可能是非显而易见的。"2010 KSR MPEP 也指出 3 种"熟悉的争辩途径仍然是适用的"来克服因缺乏非显而易见性所作出的驳回决定：①反向教导；②缺少合理的成功期待；以及③出乎意料的结果。因此，在 USPTO 的审查过程中，克服显而易见的审查意见的有力的争辩是：要组合的任何参考文件实际上对要求保护的发明给出了反向教导（teach away from the claimed invention），即对比文件中的某些言论与要求保护的发明不一致，不鼓励"假人"做发明人实际上所做的并且已经获得成功的发明，或者将"假人"引导到与发明人所采用的方式不同的改进方向上。

中国在《专利审查指南》中并未明确提出这种判断方式，但实务操作中，对于几篇对比文件的技术方案能否组合时，有时会用这种方法。

2. 其他用于克服显而易见审查意见的证据

美国最高法院在 KSR 案中警示说，根据专利法第 103 条作出的拒绝的分析应当是清晰的。对应地，MPEP 第 2141 节列举了支持显而易见审查意见的几种推理方式：

（1）按照已知的方式组合了现有的元素，产生了可预期的结果；

（2）简单将一种已知元素替换为另一种，并获得了可预期的结果；

（3）使用已知的技术以相同的方式改进了彼此类似的装置（方法或产品）；

（4）将已知的技术用到等待改进的装置（方法或产品）上，产生了可预期的结果；

（5）"显而易见会去尝试"（obvious to try）——以合理的成功期待从有限个、可识别、可预期的解决方案选择出；

（6）在本领域普通技术人员致力的一个领域（one field of endeavor）的已知的工作，如果改变这个工作对于本领域普通技术人员是可预期的，则其可能会受设计驱动或其他市场压力的激发改变这个工作，而将其用在同一个或不同领域；

（7）现有技术存在这样一些教导、建议或动机，其会引导本领域普通技术人员修改现有技术文献或组合现有技术文献的教导，来获得要求保护的发明。

对应地，要反驳这些推理，申请人可以提交反驳性证据，包括："辅助考虑因素"证据。例如：商业上的成功、长期未解决的问题或其他人的失败（在前述 Graham v. John Deere Co. 案中提出的），也可以提交出乎意料的结果的证据。根据美国专利法实施细则 37CFR§1.132 的规定，这些证据可以通过证人证言（affidavit）或声明（declaration）的方式提交。

虽然在中国未明确提出这些推理方式，但类似地，审查意见也有采用本领域普通技术人员通过"合乎逻辑的分析、推理"、"常规选择"或"有限次的实验"可以获得要求保护的发明的方式来反对创造性。并且，在中国，也可以提交额外的实验数据来反驳审查意见。

五、基本相同的发明在中美两国的最终命运小结

由上可知，单从常用的创造性的分析方法上说，中国的创造性门槛要高于美国，因此同样的发明在美国可能获得专利，在中国则未必。但是，由于两国经济、技术发展的不同情况，一项发明在中国获得专利，在美国则未必，例如计算机领域类的发明，由于美国的普通技术水平可能会高于中国，从而导致美国认为该项发明的创造性的高度低。此外，再加上法律上的差异，适合在中美两国申请专利的权利要求的特征与范围可能是不同的，从而进一步加大了创造性分析的差异性。

从《专利法》第33条和第26条第4款的差异解读"修改超范围"的审判实践

冯志云

近年来,中国《专利法》第33条可谓是备受关注的"明星"法条,其在实践中所具有的"中国特色"也致使不少国外律师和代理人难以理解。国外律师和代理人在遇到"修改超范围"审查意见时,其困惑往往会纠结在:我们的修改是完全能得到说明书支持的,为何还会被认为修改超出说明书记载的范围?

因此,此文旨在从第33条"超范围"问题和第26条第4款"支持"问题的差异入手,并结合案例,剖析目前中国审判实践中对第33条的把握尺度,以期能"答疑解惑"。

一、《专利法》第33条及《专利审查指南2010》(以下简称《审查指南》)的规定

申请人可以对其专利申请文件修改,但是,对发明和实用新型专利申请文件的修改不得超出原说明书和权利要求书**记载的范围。❶**

原说明书和权利要求书记载的范围包括原说明书和权利要求书文字记载的内容和根据原说明书和权利要求书文字记载的内容以及说明书附图能直接地、毫无疑义地确定的内容。

二、《专利法》第26条第4款及《审查指南》的规定

权利要求书应当以说明书为依据。

权利要求书中的每一项权利要求所要求保护的技术方案应当是所属技术领域的技术人员能够从说明书充分公开的内容中得到或概括得出的技术方案,并且不得超出说明书**公开的范围**。

如果所属技术领域的技术人员可以合理预测说明书给出的实施方式的所有**等同替代方式或明显变型方式**都具备相同的性能或用途,则应当允许申请

---

❶ 本文仅探讨发明和实用新型专利申请文件的修改,不包含外观设计。

人将权利要求的保护范围概括至覆盖其所有的等同替代或明显变型的方式。对于权利要求概括得是否恰当,审查员应当参照与之相关的现有技术判断。

三、第 33 条和第 26 条第 4 款的异同比较

1. 立法本意

第 33 条和第 26 条第 4 款的立法本意都是"平衡申请人与公众的利益关系",在这一点上二者是存在共性的。不同之处是,第 33 条侧重以"先申请原则"为基准,防止申请人通过修改获得不正当的权益,担当了"黑脸包公"的角色,以白纸黑字来捍卫"先申请原则";第 26 条第 4 款侧重防止申请人通过过度概括获得不正当的权利。

2. 适用时机和对象

第 33 条是针对申请后发生修改的权利要求或说明书,而第 26 条第 4 款是针对申请时的原始权利要求和修改后不超范围的权利要求。一旦权利要求经过修改,则按《审查指南》的规定应先审查修改是否符合第 33 条,然后才能审查第 26 条第 4 款。

3. 依据内容

第 33 条是依据原说明书和权利要求书记载的内容。然而,第 26 条第 4 款是依据原说明书公开的内容,允许在答辩的意见陈述中补充合理预测的等同替代或明显变型方式的内容。

四、解读专利局的审查实践

1. 典型的审查逻辑

公开的范围=文字记载的内容+直接、毫无疑义确定的内容+
　　　　　　合理预测的变型或替代例
记载的范围=文字记载的内容+直接、毫无疑义确定的内容

下面举一个"金属——金、银、铜"的简单例子来说明在目前的审查实践中两范围的差异。如果原始说明书中仅记载了"金、银或铜"来实现导电,未记载文字"金属",那么在审查记载"金属"的原始权利要求时,审查员考虑的公开的范围等于文字记载的"金、银、铜"+本领域技术人员的合理预测的其他金属;然而在审查加入了"金属"的修改后权利要求时,审查员考虑的记载的范围则仅限于文字记载的"金、银、铜",不允许因本领域技术人员根据公知常识推导"金、银、铜"是金属而引入除"金、银、铜"以外的"其他金属"的新内容。

2. 需避免的错误观点

误解 1:修改后的技术方案能得到说明书支持就不超范围。

如前述"金属——金、银、铜"的例子，由于审查支持问题和超范围问题所依据的范围不同，从而导致保护范围相同的权利要求会因第一次是出现在原始申请文本或修改文本中而具有完全不同的命运：授权或驳回。

误解2：权利要求"修改不超范围"就是不扩大原权利要求保护范围，缩小保护范围不会产生"修改超范围"。

权利要求"修改不超范围"的本质含义是未纳入新的技术内容，而不是权利范围大小的问题。因此，曾经也有人研究认为，《专利法》采用的"超范围"一词本身就不准确，容易导致公众误解，应当修改此法条的表达方式。相比而言，美国专利法第132条规定："修改不应在发明的公开中引入新的内容"，其所采用的"不引入新的内容"更易理解、更加科学。对此，我们期待在未来修法时进行完善。

误解3：只要添加至权利要求中的技术特征是原说明书记载的，就不超范围。

修改是否超范围是指修改后的技术方案作为一个整体是否有记载，而不是仅看局部修改或增加的特征本身。例如，即使单个特征本身有文字记载，但与其他特征的组合形成了一个未曾记载过的技术方案，则有可能是"超范围的"。

误解4：在原权利要求保护范围内进行中位概括是不超范围的。

在实践中，概括性的修改内容确实存在较大的超范围风险，但也不是绝对的，要视说明书记载的具体技术方案中不同技术特征之间的关联程度。

例如，原始权利要求1（简称权1）为：一种Y，其包括A、B和C。说明书记载的实施例包括A、B、C、D、E。经过中位概括，修改后的权1为：一种Y，其包括A、B、C和D。如果从说明书看D和E紧密联系（协同关系），则上述修改后的权1倾向于被认为超范围。反之，如果从说明书看D和E不是紧密联系，则上述修改后的权1倾向于被认为不超范围。

五、我司复审成功案例分享

案例1：根据附图修改的内容（中国专利200580008197.2；复审决定书第33336号）

对于涉及依据附图修改的内容是否超范围，目前专利局的审查原则是：本领域技术人员在将所述说明书文字部分和附图结合起来作为一个整体进行理解时，能够直接地、毫无疑义地确定附图所示各部件之间的相对位置、相对大小等定性关系，却不能够仅从附图中直接地、毫无疑义地确定附图所示部件的尺寸参数等定量信息。例如，不允许在申请文件中增加通过测量附图得出的尺寸参数技术特征，以防止对说明书附图所公开内容的过度阅读。实际审查反映的普遍状况是：即使是附图中的定性关系，在实审阶段修改时也常常遭遇 "严格审查员" 的驳回，致使案件答辩难度增加，往往需要进入复审程序。案例 1 就是以附图体现的定性关系内容作为修改依据、实审遭驳回后复审成功的案例。

原说明书记载：

双负压涡轮，具有多个冲击齿板，每个冲击齿板 20 包括安装部 210 和连接安装部的工作部 220。图 1 和图 2 是冲击齿板 20 的正视图和侧视图。

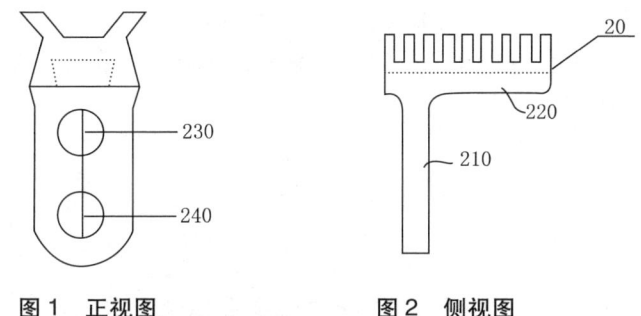

图 1　正视图　　　　　　　　图 2　侧视图

在答辩过程中，为了克服缺乏创造性的缺陷，突出图示中冲击齿板结构能够利用冲击和剪切作用有效地粉碎不易粉碎的物料（例如中药材）的有益技术效果，申请人在独立权利要求中加入了附图才反映的如下技术特征："在该工作部的顶部形成有成对的冲击齿，每对冲击齿的两个冲击齿以齿顶相对远离的方式倾斜，以使每个冲击齿的倾斜方向与所述每对冲击齿的齿根所在的平面之间形成锐角。"

驳回决定的观点：

（1）修改的内容包含了多种情况，例如冲击齿一个向内一个向外延伸，或者两个冲击齿不在同一个横截面内。而图 2 只显示了一种冲击齿的大小、长短、形状等关系。

（2）附图确实是原始公开的一部分，但文字表达的含义比确定的附图的含义广，依据上述文字描述显然可以画出除图 2 以外的其他冲击齿倾斜方式。

复审决定撤销了此驳回决定，认为上述修改不超范围，其观点为：

（1）能由原说明书和图 2 直接、毫无疑义地确定；

（2）不赞同以 "除图 2 方式以外，冲击齿还存在其他倾斜方式" 为由而认定修改超范围。

启发：

不能将附图视为具体下位概念，而将文字视为上位概括。"唯一性" 并不是判断修改是否超范围的标准。

案例2：明显笔误的修正（申请号200710138307.8，复审决定书第45140号）

原说明书记载：

音圈马达定位装置包括：一固定件10、一动件12和一连接件14。动件12可移动地设置于该固定件10上，动件12具有镜头组件120与线圈组件122，固定件10包括第一磁石组件102，第一磁石组件102包括第一磁石1022。线圈组件122导电后产生的电磁场与该磁石组件102散发的磁力线相互作用，以产生一电磁推力致动该动件12。**第一磁石1022固定于镜头组件120，并间隔一可滑动间隙配置于线圈组件122的内部。**

申请人将"第一磁石1022固定于**镜头组件120**"修改为"第一磁石1022固定于**固定件10**"。

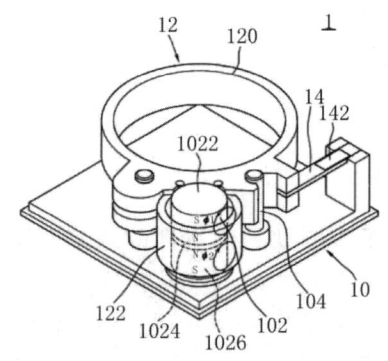

说明书附图

原审查员以上述修改超范围为由作出驳回决定，其理由是：原说明书中对于"第一磁石1022"与"镜头组件120"之间的连接关系的记载自相矛盾，仅能说明第一磁石1022和镜头组件120之间不是"固定关系"，仅能直接、毫无疑义地确定："第一磁石1022"和"固定件10"之间是部分与整体的包含关系。但不能直接、毫无疑义地确定"第一磁石1022"和"固定件10"之间的"固定关系"。

复审委认为：上述原说明书文字记载内容已经清楚表明第一磁石1022属于固定件的一部分，镜头组件120属于动件12的一部分，因此原说明书中的"第一磁石1022固定于镜头组件120"属于明显错误，且可唯一确定"第一磁石1022固定于固定件10"，符合《专利法》第33条的规定。

从案例2反映出，审查员独立审查时往往对于矛盾的技术内容预先设想了多种可能，若无法一一予以排除，则认为修改不是唯一的，无法接受申请人的更正式修改。然而，复审委是更加客观地以本领域技术人员视角作出直接判断，而不是采取排除式的思维判断方式。

六、审查机关和司法机关的实践差异

1. 专利局审查员的 "紧缩" 政策

鉴于专利局有严格质检，审查员会尽可能避免发生因未指出 "超范围" 缺陷而导致重大失误的情形发生，采用 "紧缩" 政策严格执行上述审查逻辑。只要审查员认为修改后的内容可能包含未记载或不能直接地、毫无疑义地确定的内容，就会比较坚守 "修改超范围" 的意见。

2. 专利复审委的 "公平" 政策

相比而言，专利复审委会将兼顾申请文件记载的全部内容和体现的技术贡献，对申请人的修改给予建议，平衡申请人与公众的利益。进而，在某些确实对现有技术作出了贡献而仅因第 33 条被驳回的具体案件上，会表现出相对宽松的 "公平" 政策。上述两案例在一定程度上反映了复审委的审查方式。

3. 人民法院的 "指导性审判"

在审理不服复审决定或无效决定的专利行政诉讼案件过程中，人民法院的审判原则可能不拘泥于《审查指南》，而会从立法本意角度根据具体案情对《专利法》第 33 条产生新的解读。中国虽然不是 "判例法" 国家，但最高法院的判决对未来相关法律法规的修改还是具有深远的 "指导" 意义。

例如，在著名的 "墨盒" 案件（郑某对精工爱普生株式会社的发明专利 ZL00131800.4 以其不符合《专利法》第 33 条为由的专利无效行政诉讼）中，北京一中院维持 "修改超范围" 的复审决定。然而，北京高院将实审答辩中的意见陈述和无效程序中对 "存储装置" 解释为 "半导体存储装置" 也作为判断修改是否超范围的参考，作出了修改不超范围的判决。最高法院虽然也作出了与北京高院相同的 "修改不超范围" 的决定，但更进一步地从立法角度阐述了判断修改超范围的新的指导思想，即：不仅应考虑原说明书及其附图和权利要求书以文字或者图形表达的内容，还应考虑所属领域普通技术人员综合上述内容后显而易见的内容；不能将所属领域普通技术人员可以直接、明确推导出的内容理解为数理逻辑上唯一确定的内容。

又例如，"氨氯地平、厄贝沙坦复方制剂"（ZL03150996.7）专利无效行政纠纷案的再审案［（2011）知行字第 17 号］，专利权人在无效程序中依据说明书中氨氯地平 1mg/kg 与厄贝沙坦 30mg/kg 的组合实施例，将授权权利要求中氨氯地平与厄贝沙坦的比值范围 1：10～50 修改为 1：30。复审委认为原说明书记载的是具体剂量，不是比例关系，而且无法确定是否满足 1：30 比例关系的任何具体剂量均能达到相同的技术效果。最高法院认为，对于本领域普通技术人员来说，1mg/kg 与 30mg/kg 表明的是两种成分的比值，而非一个固定的剂量，因此 1：30 比例关系已经记载于原始说明书中。至于是否符合该比例关系的所有技术方案均能够实现本专利发明目的，是属于权利要求是否能得到说明书支持，即《专利法》第 26 条第 4 款的问题，不宜以该理由认定修改是否超出范围。

4. 专利申请过程的建议

（1）新申请撰写时，在说明书和权利要求中对技术方案要多角度、多层次地进行中位、上位概括。

（2）新申请撰写时，注意将附图中体现的结构改进，尽可能地以文字描述方式记载于说明书中。说明书中的改进点尽可能全面地架构于权利要求书中。

（3）在答辩中针对修改内容陈述修改不超范围的理由时，首先，说明直接的文字记载出处；其次，如修改内容确实无文字记载，需充分阐述本领域技术人员可以直接、毫无疑义确定的理由。如确实需要结合申请日前本领域公知常识才能推导出修改内容，则最好辅以适度举证，这也是为未来可能在行政诉讼中占取有利地位做充分的铺垫准备。

（4）在答辩时，对于必须通过中位概括来争取适当保护范围的案件，尽量采用原说明书中所采用的文字表达来进行中位概括。

（5）对于重要案件，要有攻有守，一方面要勇于和善于借助后续的法律救济程序（复审程序、行政诉讼程序），来捍卫真正的发明创造本应获得的权利。另一方面还可以通过提出分案申请，采用"不超范围"的修改方式，先快速获得一个相对保守的专利权。

结束语

随着来自不同国家或地区申请人、专利代理人、律师的呼吁，第 33 条审查实践的过于紧缩的状态已经受到国知局以及相关司法机关的高度关注。我们翘首期待，随着中国专利制度的与时俱进，《专利法》第 33 条能朝着表达更规范、审判实践更合理的方向发展。

生物领域的审查原则到了需要改变的时候

——《专利法》第 26 条第 4 款的理论与实践[*]

吴小瑛

自从 19 世纪 70 年代兴起现代生物技术以来，生物技术得到了迅猛发展。特别是 2000 年 6 月 26 日宣布人类基因组测序基本完成的消息以来，生物技术已经成为全世界、全社会特别关注的热门话题。生物技术广泛应用于各行业，例如农业领域中的转基因植物、动物，制药领域的生物工程药品和临床领域中涉及的病因探究和疾病的诊断，以及工业领域中可以治污的生物酶。在为人类作出贡献的同时，生物技术领域的研发人员或研发机构对具有实用价值的基因和多肽（或蛋白质）请求专利保护的需求也日益增长。在涉及基因和多肽的专利申请中，如何判断基因或多肽序列的权利要求符合《专利法》第 26 条第 4 款规定的权利要求应得到说明书支持的审查原则和审查标准也是业界关注的焦点。

一、《专利法》第 26 条第 4 款的立法本意

《中华人民共和国专利法》（以下简称《专利法》）第 26 条第 4 款规定："权利要求应当以说明书为依据，清楚、简要地限定要求专利保护的范围。"该条款规定权利要求应当清楚、简要，以说明书为依据。本文只涉及以说明书为依据的规定，也称之为说明书支持的规定。

《专利审查指南 2010》（以下简称《审查指南》）第二部分第二章第 3.2.1 节规定："权利要求书应当以说明书为依据的规定，指权利要求书中的每一项权利要求所要求保护的技术方案应当是本领域技术人员能够从说明书中公开的内容得到或者概括得出的技术方案，并且不得超出说明书公开的范围。""对于用上位概念概括或用并列选择方式概括的权利要求，应当审查这种概括是否得到说明书的支持。如果权利要求的概括包含申请人推测的内容，而其效果又难于预先确定和评价，应当认为这种概括超出了说明书公开的范围。"

可见，《专利法》第 26 条第 4 款中有关权利要求应当得到说明书支持的规

---

[*] 原文刊于中华全国专利代理人协会所编《〈专利法〉第 26 条第 4 款理论与实践》。

定的立法本意，在于保证专利权的保护范围与其对现有技术的贡献相当，即与其说明书充分公开的技术内容相适应，从而平衡申请人与第三人的利益关系。

二、关于说明书支持的审查标准

《审查指南》规定，权利要求所要求保护的技术方案应当是本领域技术人员能够从说明书中公开的内容得到或者概括得出的技术方案。如果所属技术领域的技术人员可以合理预测说明书给出的实施方式的所有等同替代方式或明显变型方式都具备相同的性能或用途，则应当允许申请人将权利要求的保护范围概括至覆盖其所有等同替代或明显变型的方式。对于权利要求概括得是否恰当，审查员应当参照与之相关的现有技术进行判断……对于用上位概念概括或用并列选择方式概括的权利要求，应当审查这种概括是否得到说明书的支持。如果权利要求的概括包含申请人推测的内容，而其效果又难于预先确定和评价，应当认为这种概括超出了说明书公开的范围。❶

判断权利要求是否得到说明书支持的主体是所属领域的技术人员。《审查指南》对所属领域的技术人员给予了定义。所属领域的技术人员，也可称为本领域的技术人员，是指一种假设的"人"，假定他知晓申请日或者优先权日之前发明所属技术领域所有的普通技术知识，能够获知该领域中所有的现有技术，并且具有应用该日期之前常规实验手段的能力，但他不具有创造能力。如果所要解决的技术问题能够促使本领域的技术人员在其他技术领域寻找技术手段，他也应具有从该其他技术领域中获知该申请日或优先权日之前的相关现有技术、普通技术知识和常规实验手段的能力。❷

可以说，《审查指南》的关于说明书支持的规定比较宽泛，缺乏一定的细节描述。公众不能确定所属领域的技术人员在从说明书中概括技术方案时会考虑哪些因素来判断能否得到权利要求的技术方案。例如，对于所属领域的技术人员的水平的确定没有进一步规定，因为界定所属领域的技术人员的水平时不仅需考虑申请日这个时间点，还要考虑在这个时间该领域的发展水平。《审查指南》规定"所属领域的技术人员能够合理预测说明书给出的实施方式的所有等同替代方式或明显变型方式都具备相同的性能或用途"，但并没有解释何谓"合理预测"。

三、生物领域中关于说明书支持的审查实践

显而易见，对于一件专利而言，如果竞争对手很容易地通过对权利要求中的基因或多肽序列进行修饰并同时保持该序列的功能从而规避该权利要求

---

❶ 《专利审查指南 2010》第二部分第二章第 3.2.1 节。
❷ 《专利审查指南 2010》第二部分第四章第 2.4 节。

保护的范围，那么这件专利没有任何商业价值。在申请专利时，申请人必将致力于使序列以上位概念概括的方式主张于权利要求（以下简称上位概括的权利要求）中，以避免竞争对手容易地规避。

上位概括的权利要求的撰写方式有多种，例如，同一性权利要求，即将所要保护的序列定义为与参照序列具有至少百分之多少以上的同一性，这是目前大多数国家或地区普遍采用的一种撰写方式；突变式权利要求，即将所要保护的序列描述为参照序列基础上具有取代、添加或缺失的方式。在《审查指南》"关于化学领域发明专利申请审查的若干规定"这一章中，针对涉及基因和多肽（或蛋白质）的权利要求的撰写方式给予了描述。其中，针对蛋白衍生物或编码其的基因的权利要求，《审查指南》列举的就仅有采用取代、添加或缺失方式这一种撰写方式，其中包含功能特征。❶ 这样的撰写方式是《审查指南》中列举的唯一一种上位概括的权利要求的描述方式。

在专利审查实践中，目前针对生物序列的上位概括的权利要求，无论是何种撰写方式都必定面临权利要求得不到说明书支持的审查意见。实审程序中的审查意见和复审程序中的复审委的观点基本一致。自1993年第二次修改《专利法》以来，❷ 生物序列的上位概括的权利要求一直都很难被认可能得到说明书的支持，审查员接受的基本上都只是实施例中验证了功能的具体序列。

为了获得专利权，申请人只能放弃上位概括的权利要求，因此获得权利的权利要求也只有具体序列。不利的是，竞争对手已经从说明书公开的内容获知了发明技术，通过生物领域的常规制备手段如基因重组工程就能容易地获得本来在上位概括的权利要求中所包含的序列，并通过说明书所描述的检测方法或常规检测方法，获得具有所述功能的类似序列。当这种情况发生时，专利权人理应拿起维权大棒来行使权利。那么，接下来需要考虑的问题是，专利权人还能主张这些原本落在上位概括的权利要求范围内而在审查程序中被删除的序列吗？侵权判定时会受到禁止反悔原则的限制吗？虽然目前还没有类似的诉讼案例，但根据近来的案例，尤其是最高法院作出的（2009）民提字第20号"申请再审人湖北午时药业股份有限公司与被申请人澳诺（中国）制药有限公司、原审被告王军社侵犯发明专利权纠纷案"的判决，❸ 可以预见到这种情况适用禁止反悔原则。也就是说，这种修改很可能使权利人的权利仅限于权利要求中的具体序列，导致等同侵权原则无法适用的严重后果，

---

❶ 《专利审查指南2010》第二部分第十章第9.3.1.1节（4）和（5）、第9.3.1.5节（3）。

❷ 自第二次修改《专利法》以后，化学物质可给予专利保护。

❸ 最高人民法院民事判决书（2009）民提字第20号的判决书，在结论（二）中，其观点是："根据禁止反悔原则，专利申请人或者专利权人在专利侵权或者无效宣告程序中，通过对权利要求、说明书的修改或者意见陈述而放弃的技术方案，在专利侵权纠纷中不能将其纳入专利权的保护范围。"

此时的专利证书也就成了一张废纸。

四、关于说明书支持的审查标准细化可借鉴的案例

最高法院于 2010 年 11 月 10 日作出针对再审人（美国）伊莱利利公司与被申请人国家知识产权局专利复审委员会、哈尔滨誉衡药业有限公司、宁波市天衡制药有限公司、江苏豪森药业股份有限公司发明专利权无效行政纠纷案的再审申请通知书，❶ 该通知书涉及权利要求得到说明书支持的判断标准。复审委在无效决定中以"大量的反复实验或者过度劳动"为理由，认为权利要求 1 得不到说明书的支持，并使之无效。专利权人在上诉中指出，"大量的反复实验或者过度劳动"的认定理由没有在《专利法》和《审查指南》中规定，不是判断权利要求是否得到说明书支持的正确依据。北京市一中院和高院在一审和二审虽坚持无效决定的结论，但纠正了权利要求得到说明书支持的判断标准应为"权利要求书的每一项权利要求所要求保护的技术方案应当是所述技术领域的技术人员能够从说明书充分公开的内容得到或概括得出的技术方案"。北京高院还解释了权利要求允许概括的范围是本领域技术人员能够"合理预测"或者按照"常规实验容易确定"的范围。"合理预测"的范围应当理解为本领域技术人员根据说明书的记载，结合其所具有的普通技术知识，能够预见权利要求所保护的技术方案都能够实现。"常规实验容易确定"的范围应当为本领域技术人员根据说明书公开的实施方案，通过简单的常规实验即可实现权利要求的技术方案。而当超出此种"合理预测"或者"常规实验容易确定"的范围，即需要大量反复实验或者过度劳动才能实现的技术方案时，由于专利权人并未给出明确的、毫无疑义的指引，其效果难以预先合理判断，应当认为该权利要求没有得到说明书的支持。最高法院在此基础上驳回了再审请求。

类似地，在美国，生物序列的上位概括的权利要求同样也需满足类似于得到说明书支持的要求，即美国 35U. S. C. § 112 中规定的 enablement require-ment。❷ 在 *Manual of Patent Examining Procedure*（MPEP）中给出了明确的考虑因素。判断权利要求是否符合 enablement requirement 时，判断的标准是所属领域的技术人员是否不付诸过度实验。判断一个上位概括的权利要求是否符合 enablement requirement 的规定时，须判断所属领域的技术人员是否能够根

---

❶ 中华人民共和国最高人民法院驳回再审申请通知书（2009）知行字第 3 号。

❷ 35U. S. C. § 112 第一段：The specification shall contain a written description of the invention, and of the manner and process of making and using it, in such full, clear, concise, and exact terms as to enable any person skilled in the art to which it pertains, or with which it is most nearly connected, to make and use the same and shall set forth the bet mode contemplated by the inventor of carrying out his invention.

据给予说明书的公开内容并结合现有技术不付诸过度实验下制造和使用权利要求范围内的发明。❶ 在判断是否属于不付诸过度实验时，美国考虑的因素主要有以下几个方面：①所需实验的数量；②说明书提供的指导内容数量；③说明书中的实施例；④发明本身的性质；⑤现有技术状况；⑥所属领域的技术人员的技能；⑦本领域的可预见程度；⑧权利要求的范围。❷ 在 MPEP 2164 章节对 enablement requirement 给予了较为详细的解释并列举了一些各领域中适用的情形。判断不付诸过度实验所考虑的因素，从 In re Wands 一案中可窥一斑。法院认为说明书公开的内容与涉案权利要求相适合，权利要求符合 enabling requirement。理由是，说明书中给出了大量的指引和指导，在提交申请时，本领域技术人员的水平为高水平，且所有实施发明的方法都为熟知的方法。经过考虑了所有因素后，法院得出结论，无须付诸过度实验就可以获得本发明的抗体。

五、主要结论和建议

（1）适度放宽审查尺度，充分保障专利权人的权益。通过上述针对生物序列上位概括的权利要求的支持性问题的审查实践的探讨，希望能使业界由此产生一些思考与讨论，更希望能藉此推动审查原则的发展，使审查原则更充分地体现《专利法》的立法宗旨，使发明人权利得到保护的同时，推进社会科学技术的进步。目前，生物领域中针对说明书支持的审查尺度过于严格，导致专利技术被公众得知后，专利权人只能以具体序列作为垄断权的交换，甚至在侵权诉讼中等同侵权的主张都难以得到支持。发明人的权益不能得到保障，发明人甚至可能会认为，技术秘密更利于保护他们的权益。如果这样，将影响先进技术公诸于世，阻碍科学技术的进步。

（2）细化审查标准，增强条文执行的操作性。北京高院在判定中对《审查指南》中涉及的"合理预测"、"常规实验容易确定"等概括性术语给予了明确定义。美国在判断不过度付诸实验时明确列出了至少需要考虑的 8 个因素。上述关于说明书支持问题的案例给我们启示，审查标准的细化不但有助于审查员和复审委在审查工作中统一操作标准，也能帮助申请人和代理人对审查标准获得更清晰和准确的理解，在撰写权利要求时能够恰当地从说明书中概括权利要求的范围。

---

❶ MPEP 706. 03 (c)，also set forth in In re Wands，858 F. 2d 731，8 USPQ 2nd 1400 (Fed. Cir. 1988).

❷ （1）the quantity of experimentation necessary，（2）the amount of direction or guidance presented，（3）the presence or absence of working examples，（4）the nature of the invention，（5）the state of the prior art，（6）the relative skill of those in the art，（7）the predictability or unpredictability of the art，and（8）the breadth of the claim（s）.

构建强大的防御体系

——重视说明书的作用[*]

付永莉

一、说明书的作用

根据《专利法》第 59 条的规定，发明或者实用新型专利权的保护范围以其权利要求的内容为准，说明书及附图可以用于解释权利要求的内容。

而根据《最高人民法院关于审理侵犯专利权纠纷案件应用法律若干问题的解释》，人民法院应当根据权利要求的记载，结合本领域普通技术人员阅读说明书及附图后对权利要求的理解，确定《专利法》第 59 条第 1 款规定的权利要求的内容，并且人民法院应当结合说明书和附图描述的该功能或者效果的具体实施方式及其等同的实施方式，确定该技术特征的内容。

且在《专利法》第 26 条以及《专利审查指南 2010》的相关部分也明确了说明书的撰写要求：说明书应当对发明或者实用新型作出清楚、完整的说明，以使所属技术领域的技术人员能够实现为准；必要的时候，应当有附图。

因此，无论是在专利的审查阶段，还是在授权后的无效、侵权诉讼阶段，说明书都起到非常重要的作用。具体而言，在审查阶段，对发明内容作出清楚、完整说明的说明书不但可以帮助审查员清楚透彻地理解权利要求书中所概括的技术方案，而且可以针对后续的审查意见作为对权利要求进行灵活缩限的重要依据。同样，在无效、侵权诉讼阶段，虽然权利要求的修改方式受限，甚至是不能再修改权利要求，但此时的说明书所能起到的说明、解释作用往往成为案件成败的关键因素。因此可以说，说明书实质上是专利权在获得授权以及后续的保护中能够起到关键作用的防御体系，而我们代理人所要做的就是要帮助申请人构建该强大的防御体系。

二、案例分析说明

以下通过一些案例的分析说明，从反面阐释说明书撰写上的缺陷所导致

原文刊于中华全国专利代理人协会所编《高质量的专利申请文件》。

后续程序中的一些不必要的麻烦。概括而言，说明书撰写上的缺陷不外乎两种，一是未对权利要求提供充分的支持，二是未对发明内容作出清楚、完整的说明。

1. 未对权利要求提供充分的支持

案例 1

该案例涉及一种制冰机，独立权利要求 1 的方案包括：

托盘，具有构造成制造冰块的制冰空间；冰提升单元，构造成提升位于所述制冰空间中的冰块，使得所述冰块的上部位于所述托盘之上；以及冰分离单元，构造成将所述冰块的上部与所述冰块的其余部分分离。

在专利的审查过程中鉴于审查员所印证的对比文件，申请人考虑对上述独立权利要求 1 的方案进行缩限，补入如下的进一步限定："其中，所述冰提升单元包括：至少一个具有螺纹的可转动的螺杆，所述螺纹构造成接触所述制冰空间中的所述冰块的竖直侧壁，以在所述螺杆旋转时提升所述冰块。"其中关于螺杆的特征，申请人想上位成"至少一个"具有螺纹的可转动的螺杆，而说明书中的实施例部分中记载的是"一个或两个"具有螺纹的可转动的螺杆。这样一来，对于新上位的"至少一个"具有螺纹的可转动的螺杆而言，说明书实施例部分的记载"一个或两个"具有螺纹的可转动的螺杆显然是不能够进行充分支持的，实践中，审查员可能会签发超范围的审查意见。按照通常的理解，"至少一个"应该包括如下的情形："一个"、"两个"、"多个"，至少应该包括"一个"和"多个"的情形。

因此在该案例中，申请人可能会面临需要将进一步上位的"至少一个"具有螺纹的可转动的螺杆按照说明书的记载修改为"一个或两个"具有螺纹的可转动的螺杆。且不说上述案件审查员的审查是否过于严格，对于代理人而言，如果在最初撰写说明书的过程中稍微进行拓展，哪怕只是概略地描述一下具有多个螺杆的方案，后续这些不必要的麻烦都可轻易避免。

案例 2

该案例涉及一种隔水管系统。在答复第一次审查意见通知书后的独立权利要求 1 中，限定有：

一种隔水管系统，包括：阀模块壳体，其形成在防喷装置和钻机平台之间延伸的隔水管柱的纵向部分；阀模块，其可释放地固定和密封到所述阀模块壳体中，所述阀模块选择性地允许流体流经所述隔水管柱和防止流体流经所述隔水管柱，以及其中所述阀模块壳体和所述阀模块中的至少之一包括第一锚固装置，所述第一锚固装置可拆卸地将所述阀模块固定至所述阀模块壳体中，由此允许在所述阀模块壳体保持与所述隔水管柱互联的同时安装和收回所述阀模块。

其中的特征"所述阀模块壳体和所述阀模块中的至少之一包括第一锚固装置"为申请人在答复第一次审查意见通知书时新增的限定。而说明书实施例部分所给出的实施例为：其一，阀模块壳体包括第一锚固装置；其二，阀模块包括第一锚固装置。修改后的权利要求中二次概括的限定"所述阀模块壳体和所述阀模块中的至少之一包括第一锚固装置"显然包括如下的情形："阀模块壳体包括第一锚固装置"、"阀模块包括第一锚固装置"、"阀模块壳体和阀模块均包括第一锚固装置"。因此，实践中，审查员必然会以超范围来签发下次审查意见，虽然申请人通过陈述意见试图坚持上述二次概括的"所述阀模块壳体和所述阀模块中的至少之一包括"，但是经过多个回合的答辩，最终还是按照审查员的要求将上述二次概括修改为"所述阀模块壳体或所述阀模块包括第一锚固装置"。

该案例同样反映了说明书撰写中的缺陷使得说明书没有真正成为申请人退守时的防御体系，申请人想要退守到二次概括的范围时，由于说明书撰写得不完美，遭遇失败，只能退到实施例所具体记载的实施例中。

2. 未对发明内容作出清楚完整的说明

案例 3

本案例是笔者在无效阶段遇到的一个典型案例，其涉及一种离心式散热扇构造。其中涉案专利的独立权利要求 1 中的一个关键特征为"至少一径向入风口 13 设于环墙 12 上"。为便于理解，上述特征直观显示于下图中。

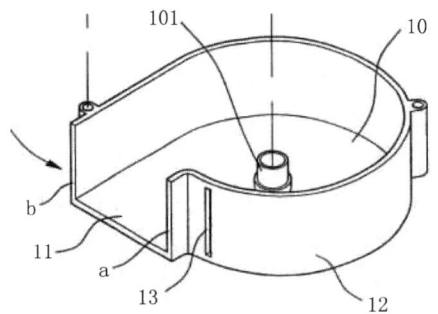

其中的关键性特征径向入风口 13 是设于环墙 12 上的，通过附图可以看出，事实上该径向入风口 13 是设在扇轮壳体的圆形环壁上的。

其中的一篇对比文件附图如下图所示。

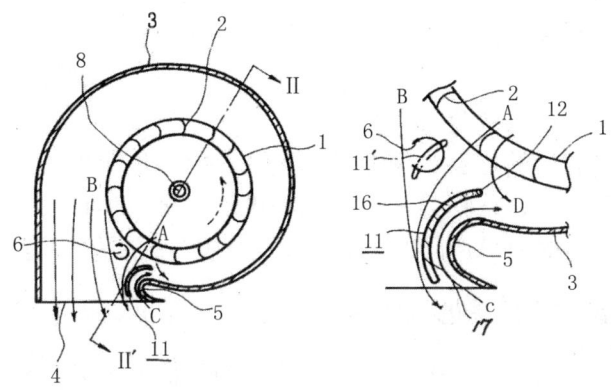

该对比文件中，与上述径向入风口 13 相等同的部件是附图标号 C 所标记的部分，但是通过图示可以看出该对比文件中的辅助入风口实际上是设于风扇扇轮壳体的构成出风口的壁上的。

因此，通过直观对比上述两个图示的方案不难看出，二者的区别在于：涉案专利中的径向入风口其实是设置在圆形部分的环墙上，而对比文件中的径向入风口是设置在构成出风口的扇壳壁上的。因此，此案的关键就在于对"环墙"的理解和限定。也即，所谓的"环墙"究竟是包括所有的壳体壁，包括圆形的墙壁部分以及形成出风口的部分；还是仅仅包括圆形的墙壁部分。遗憾的是，涉案专利的说明书中并未对"环墙"给出任何明确的限定，因此导致在后续的程序中双方当事人开始纠缠"环墙"的确切含义，为此案的答辩带来无尽的麻烦，甚至可能成为此案输掉的关键因素。

此案例带给我们的体会应该是深刻的。事实上，我们在撰写说明书的过程中可能并不能确切地得知哪个特征将是关键性的，应该对哪个特征进行明确具体地限定。笔者认为，可以考虑对整个装置进行全面拆分，然后对各个拆分出的构成部件逐一进行描述，包括每个部件的具体组成、形状、材料，在描述的过程中可以加入变型的、可选的方案的描述。此外，对于申请人的具体产品一定要给出一个全面详细描述的实施例，以此作为最后的防御。

案例 4

该案例也是笔者在无效阶段遇到的，同样涉及一种离心风扇。其中涉案专利的主要发明点在于通过在离心风扇的扇壳上增加辅助径向入风口以实现进风量的增加。而且在该涉案专利的背景技术部分中也介绍有：现有技术中也有在径向出风口的周边设置辅助径向入风口以增加进风量，但是由于气流可能同时通过该辅助径向入风口流入和流出，且可能同时通过该径向出风口流入和流出，因此导致紊乱。

而且，通读涉案专利的说明书都不能够看出，在该专利中是如何避免气流同时通过该辅助径向入风口流入和流出，也即，在该专利的说明书中并没有给出任何的解释和披露，该专利是如何保证其中的辅助径向入风口只可进风不可出风的。因此，对方当事人敏锐地提出了涉案专利说明书公开不充分的问题，给该专利造成致命的打击。

此案例带给我们的体会也是非常深刻的。撰写说明书的一个重要前提是透彻理解说明内容，这往往是从申请人提供的一个具体产品开始的，吃透该具体的一个产品也是对该产品的全部以及部分进行扩展的前提。

三、如何撰写高质量的说明书

上述从反面分析说明的各个案例带给我们的体会和教训应该是非常深刻的，这也是我们在撰写过程中所要尽力避免的。高质量的说明书一定是既可以充分支持权利要求，而且也对发明内容给出了清楚、完整的说明。

笔者抛砖引玉以一般产品类专利的说明书撰写为例说明如何撰写高质量的说明书，以下是笔者认为的撰写说明书的一般流程步骤：

1. 透彻理解技术方案

笔者再次强调透彻理解技术方案的重要性。如果对于申请人提供的产品还没有透彻理解，一定不能开始撰写工作，此时需要查阅资料或者通过与申请人直接沟通来理解发明内容。

在深入理解发明内容的过程中，我们可能还需要对现有的相关技术进行一些检索。通过检索一方面可以更加全面地理解本专利的技术，另一方面也可以了解本专利的主要改进方面，这样可以详细地、有针对性地描述本专利相比于现有技术的改进点，避免出现说明书中对于改进点的公开不充分的问题。

2. 先从总体装配图开始描述

在深入理解了发明内容之后可以着手开始说明书的撰写，而对于产品类的专利申请，建议从总体装配图开始。不论是开始理解技术内容，还是开始着手撰写说明书，都可以考虑先从装配总图开始。对于产品类专利而言，总体装配图给出的信息是最多的，也是对发明内容整体上的一个体现，其包括了构成总体产品的各个组成部件，以及各个组件部件的位置关系、连接关系、动作关系等。因此，在说明书的实施例部分中先结合总体装配图进行上述内容的介绍，可以先对整体产品有一个直观清楚的认识。

实践中我们可能遇到的更多情况是所要申请的专利仅仅是对其中某个或某几个部件的改进，总体装配图可能类同于现有的相关技术。笔者认为，即使在这种情况下，仍然可以结合总体装配图给出产品整体上的描述，以使得审查员或者后续程序中的法官可以首先在整体上理解发明内容，从而可以进一步深入理解发明实质。此外更为重要的是，我们可能无法预期在后续程序中哪个部件将是关键性的，因此，结合整体装配图给出一个概括性的或全局性的说明可能会成为后期退守的保障。

在该部分的描述中还需要考虑总体装配图的各种变型方案和可替换方案，如各个组成部件是否可以省略或更换，各个组成部件的连接关系、位置关系、运动配合关系是否可以进行变更，实现连接关系的各连接部件的数量、形式是否可以变更，或者是否有可替换的连接部件等。

3. 从总体装配图拆分各个组成部分

在对照总体装配图完成描述之后，我们需要拆分该总体装配图，有时可能会需要直接拆分到单个部件的零件图，有时也可能会需要先拆分到几个部件的小组装图，然后再拆分到零件图。在拆分的过程中，我们会再次验证之前对于技术上的理解是否会有偏差。并且在拆分的过程中也可能会获得一些变型实施例。

4. 对照各个组成部分的零件图逐一详细描述

在拆分之后，我们需要对照拆分出的各个附图进行详细说明。对于比较复杂的产品，可能拆分出的附图比较多，那么在撰写过程中，为了增加说明书的可读性，可以考虑按照一定的顺序进行。比如按照关键部分的顺序，或者就是按照从上到下、从外到内的顺序进行描述。由于可能会拆分出包括几个部件的小装配图，那么可以考虑以先整体后单体的顺序进行描述。例如，对于压缩机的总体装配图进行拆分，拆分出壳体单元、动力单元、压缩单元，那么可先按一级顺序进行上述 3 个单元的描述，而在 3 个单元的具体描述中，可按二级顺序逐一描述各个单元的组成部件。例如，在对壳体单元进行整体描述之后，引出组成壳体单元的上壳体和下壳体的描述；在对动力单元进行整体描述之后，引出组成动力单元的电机和传送轴的描述等。

这一点，我们可以从网上查看一下日本的公开专利，即使其所要保护的权项就几个，日本专利的说明书仍然撰写得非常详尽，其通常在开始每个组成单元的描述之前给出一个小标题，这样可以增加可读性和条理性。

在对各个组成部件进行描述的过程中，同样需要考虑各个组成部件的变型方案和可替换方案，如部件的形状、结构、材料、数量等方面的变化。

对于拓展出的各个实施例，如果整体的组装关系发生变化或者部件省略或被其他变型替换等，可以考虑放到第二实施例或第三实施例中以与第一实施例相同的顺序进行描述。当然，为节约篇幅可以考虑省略相同部分的描述。

四、结束语

综上所述，不论在专利的审查过程中，还是在后续的无效、侵权诉讼过程中，说明书都具有非常重要的作用，其真正可以成为申请人在退守时的防御体系。而高质量的说明书既可以对权利要求提供充分支持，同时又可对发明内容作出清楚、完整的说明。我们要提高认识，充分意识到说明书的重要性，努力为申请人撰写出高质量的说明书，对专利申请提供强有力的支持和防御。

如何认定对比文件附图的公开内容

——中国审判实践案例启示

聂慧荃

如何认定对比文件附图的公开内容是专利的新颖性和创造性判断中的一个关键因素。尽管中国《专利法》及其实施细则中并未提及，但是《专利审查指南2010》（以下简称《审查指南》）中具体指出了，现有技术文件的公开内容包括文件中明确记载的内容以及"本领域技术人员能够直接地、毫无疑义地确定的"隐含内容。❶ 中国专利局在审查实践中严格地运用了这一具体标准。

笔者借助最高人民法院（以下简称最高院）所作出的两个无效行政纠纷案例，结合自身的从业经验，对中国审判实践中关于对比文件附图公开内容的认定情况进行剖析，希望能够在中国专利申请保护及专利诉讼方面给大家提供有益的参考。

一、专利审查标准

《审查指南》指出，在新颖性和创造性评价中，现有技术文件（对比文件）公开的内容不仅包括文字明确记载的内容，而且还包括对于所属领域的技术人员来说，隐含的且可直接地、毫无疑义地确定的内容。附图本身作为工程界的语言，对于确定对比文件的公开信息具有重要作用，在认定附图公开内容时，既不能随意扩大附图的公开内容，也不能随意缩小其公开内容。《审查指南》第二部分第三章第 2.3 节规定，审查员在引用附图时必须注意，只有能够从附图中直接地、毫无疑义地确定的技术特征才属于公开的内容，由附图中推测的内容，或者无文字说明、仅仅是从附图中测量得出的尺寸及其关系，不应当作为已公开的内容。

基于《审查指南》的规定，可以理解在对附图公开内容认定的过程中，不仅应考虑附图中图形本身所表达的内容，还应考虑所属领域技术人员综合对比文件记载内容后显而易见的内容，不能对附图所示的内容作机械的理解，将所属领域普通技术人员可以直接、明确推导出的内容理解为数理逻辑上唯一确定的内容。然而，在具体审判实践中，法官对于后者的考虑还是采用了

---

❶ 《专利审查指南2010》第二部分第三章第 2.3 节。

相对审慎的态度。

二、最高人民法院判定

从以下两个实用新型专利权行政纠纷案中，我们可以看出最高院希望审判实践中在"如何认定附图公开的内容"方面所倡导的认定标准。

案例1

在实用新型专利权无效行政纠纷案［（2012）行提字第25号］❶中，最高院指出：对比文件中仅公开产品的结构图形但没有文字描述的，可以结合其结构特点和本领域技术人员的公知常识确定其含义。

该案争议的焦点之一在于：从对比文件1中的主视图来看，直管两端的圆柱形凸起能否被直接地、毫无疑义地确定为"法兰或其他管道连接部件"。对此，一审法院和二审法院持有与专利复审委员会不同的观点，均认为：对比文件1中的主视图只能看到直管以及其两端的圆柱形凸起，不能直接地、毫无疑义地确定该圆柱形凸起为法兰或其他管道连接部件。

涉案专利（CN03274825.6）为"一种带法兰的铸型尼龙管道"，对比文件1为名称为"直管"、授权公告号为CN3205299D的外观设计专利，其主视图中示出了直管和位于直管两端的圆柱形凸起，并且在其简要说明中记载了采用的是"MC尼龙材料一次性铸造成型"。

对此，最高院首先对权利要求所引"法兰"进行了释义，认为："法兰就是结构或机械零件上垂直于零件轴线突出的边缘，可用于管件或设备之间的相互连接。法兰之间的连接可通过螺栓连接、焊接、粘结、卡夹连接等多种方式实现。因此，采用螺栓连接的法兰仅是各种不同法兰连接类型中的一种形式，也存在如下情况，即法兰作为成品时不带有螺栓孔，而是在安装过程中与其连接的另外法兰进行配钻制孔。"

其次，最高院认为："专利权人的相关主张从另一方面证明了本领域技术人员对圆柱形凸起是法兰的普遍认识，对比文件1为一种管道设备，必然和其他管道配合才可以起到分配液体的作用，其两端必然是一个连接部件。虽然对比文件1没有明确说明该圆柱形凸起为法兰，但结合其结构特点和本领域技术人员的公知常识，该圆柱形凸起实际是起到法兰的作用。原审判决关于从对比文件1中的主视图来看，直管两端的圆柱形凸起不能直接地、毫无疑义地确定为法兰或其他管道连接部件的认定存在错误，应予纠正。"

显然，在该案例中，最高院对于对比文件的附图公开内容的认定采用了相对宽松的标准，其明确了对比文件的附图公开的内容不仅包括附图中的图

---

❶ 奚晓明，孔祥俊. 最高人民法院知识产权审判案例指导（第五辑）［M］. 北京：中国法制出版社，2013：250-258.

面所示内容，而且涵盖了本领域技术人员基于结构特征和本领域公知常识所能确定的内容。

案例 2

在实用新型专利权无效行政纠纷案［（2012）行字第 3 号］●中，最高院指出，认定权利要求中的技术特征被对比文件公开，不仅要求该对比文件中包含有相应的技术特征，还要求该相应的技术特征在对比文件中所起的作用和该技术特征在权利要求中所起的作用相同。相应的技术特征在对比文件中所起的作用是指该相应的技术特征在对比文件公开的技术方案中实际所起的作用，而不是该相应的技术特征客观上可具有的作用的全集。

该案争议的焦点在于：证据 1（《国外铁道车辆》2000 年第 1 期"俄罗斯货车用弹性胶泥缓冲器的研究"）是否公开了涉案专利权利要求 1 中的技术特征"沿活塞圆周部位设置有单向限流装置"。对此，专利复审委员会认为"证据 1 的附图隐含公开了权利要求 1 中所限定的单向限流装置"。然而，一审法院和二审法院撤销了第 14603 号无效宣告请求审查决定，均认为：证据 1 的附图 1（a）没有标明单向阀的具体形状和位置，证据 1 文字部分仅仅提到了图 1（a）所示为带单向阀的缓冲器，也没有描述"单向阀的形状和位置"的文字说明，因而该决定与《审查指南》相关规定相悖。

涉案专利（CN01274761.0）为一种快进慢出型弹性阻尼体缓冲器，其中单向限流装置（对应于证据 1 中的"单向阀"）的作用在于调节缓冲器内腔内填充的弹性阻尼体的流量。该单向限流装置被设置为在压缩行程时打开，以使阻尼体的流量增大，从而减小阻尼力；在回复行程时关闭，以使阻尼体的流量减小，从而增加阻尼力，借助于单向限流装置的这种调节作用，达到保护设备和降低噪声的目的。

尽管证据 1 中的文字部分提到了图 1（a）所示为带单向阀的缓冲器，但是证据 1 的附图 1（a）没有公开单向阀的具体形状和设置位置。同时，证据 1 中文字部分还记载了如下内容："图 1（a）所示为带单向阀的方案。2 种缓冲器结构方案的主要区别是活塞杆压缩后返回到初始位置的原理不同。第一种结构方案中（图 1a）为此采用单向阀；第二种结构方案中（图 1b）为此预设高压室。"基于以上内容，最高院认为，在证据 1 公开的技术方案中，图 1（a）中单向阀的作用是使压缩后的活塞杆返回到初始位置，不同于本案专利权利要求 1 中单向限流装置的作用。

由此，最高院认为：涉案专利权利要求 1 中"沿活塞圆周部位设置有单向限流装置"的技术特征，并不能从证据 1 中直接地、毫无疑义地确定；专

● 奚晓明，孔祥俊. 最高人民法院知识产权审判案例指导（第五辑）［M］. 北京：中国法制出版社，2013：32-34.

利复审委员会认定证据 1 隐含公开了沿活塞圆周部位设置有单向限流装置的技术特征，没有事实依据。

与前一个案例不同，最高院在该案例中实际上是结合所限定的技术特征的功能对涉案专利权利要求 1 的保护范围作出了缩限性解释，进而得出"由于相应技术特征的功能不同故对比文件附图没有公开权利要求 1 相应特征"的结论。

三、案例启示及对实践的指导

在案例 1 ［（2012）行提字第 25 号］中，最高院明确提出了"确定对比文件公开的产品结构图形的内容时可结合其结构特点及公知常识"的观点，其将外观设计专利的图示内容和简要说明中的记载内容以及本领域的公知常识相结合来评价涉案专利的创造性。

这对于我们在面对专利文件中没有明确文字记载内容时如何认定附图公开的内容提供了有利的指引，给出了适度引入本领域公知常识来确定附图公开内容的参考案例，有效避免了在审判实践中过于僵化地理解附图公开的内容。在确定对比文件公开的信息时，可以结合本领域的公知常识来考虑其附图所表示的内容，而不能仅仅因为附图所示内容在对比文件中没有相应的文字描述而武断地将其视为非公开内容。基于该案例的指引，当需要证明附图中公开了某些技术特征时，我们可以充分借助于公知常识性证据辅以证明附图中的图形所表达的具体含义，例如图形所体现的部件的结构形状、连接关系、配合关系、相对位置等；可以借助部件的结构特点来证明对于本领域技术人员而言其必然具备的相关功能，还可以借助于公知常识性证据辅以证明本领域技术人员公知的相关部件的基本功能或作用。

在案例 2 ［（2012）知行字第 3 号］中，最高院进一步明确了权利要求的技术特征被对比文件公开的认定标准。最高院强调，认定权利要求中的技术特征被对比文件公开，不仅要求该对比文件中包含有相应的技术特征，还要求该相应的技术特征在对比文件中所起的作用和该技术特征在权利要求中所起的作用相同。由此看出，如果需要认定涉案专利的权利要求中的某一技术特征被对比文件的附图内容公开，那么可能不仅要求对比文件的附图中确实示出了该技术特征，还应当结合对比文件的文字记载内容或本领域的公知常识来证明该技术特征在对比文件中和涉案专利中所起到的作用相同。

在无效案件或侵权诉讼案件中，当需要认定附图所公开的内容时，我们应当不仅仅局限于附图图形所具体显示的内容，还应当有意识地运用本领域的公知常识来辅以证明附图所公开的内容。同时，我们还应当注意附图所在的文件中的相应文字记载内容，明确所涉及的图示的部件在相应技术方案中所起的作用，从而更准确地认定附图所公开的内容。

论混淆可能性在商标共存判定中的重要意义[*]

梁晓敏

商标共存作为商标使用中出现的特殊情形，其与商标侵权的关系十分微妙。一方面，所谓"共存"指的是不同主体所有的相同或近似商标之间的共存；而另一方面，由于商标权是一种排他专用权，如未经商标注册权人的许可，在相同或类似商品/服务上使用与该注册商标相同或近似的商标，即构成对注册商标权的侵害。因此，确立商标共存合法性的基础对维护商标权人的合法权益、防止合理的商标共存被误判为商标侵权显得尤为重要，本文拟就此问题做些探讨。

一、商标共存的概念及特征

商标共存是指不同的市场主体在符合法律规定的情况下，将相同或近似商标使用在相同或近似商品/服务上而不产生混淆的情形。基于这样的概念界定，商标共存具有如下几个特征。

1. 共存商标之间相同或近似

在商标审查阶段，判断商标之间是否构成近似的主要依据是《商标审查及审理指南》，基于音、形、义等多方面进行综合对比。而实践当中，商标之间是否构成近似还取决于商标本身的识别度以及市场相关公众的一般认识。在商标共存的情形下，上述因素都应该纳入商标近似性的判断标准，综合考量。

2. 商标指定使用在相同或类似的商品或服务上

如果商标指定在不同的商品或服务上，就不存在商标之间互相冲突的情形，因此也就没有讨论商标共存的必要了。判断商品或服务是否构成类似，除了依据《类似商品或服务区分表》，还应当联系实际，结合商品或服务的功能用途、销售渠道、消费群体等因素来判定。

3. 商标属于不同的所有人

在商标共存的情况下，共存的商标应该分别属于不同的所有人。如果这些相同或近似的商标都属于同一个人所有，则不属于商标共存。例如，在允

[*] 原文刊于《中华商标》2013年第7期。

许有联合商标的国家，一个商标所有人在相同或类似商品上可以拥有若干个近似商标，这种情况下，商标之间不存在权益冲突，也就不属于商标共存的理论范畴。

4. 商标的共存不会导致混淆

商标是用来区别商品来源的标志，防止混淆是商标保护的基本出发点。❶因此，不产生混淆也是商标共存的前提。

二、混淆可能性是界定商标能否合法共存的核心因素

"混淆可能性"是英文"Likelihood of Confusion"的汉译，指在市场上出现两种相似或相同的商标时，消费者对于两种商品的来源或关系产生的混淆误认可能性。近似商标之间是合法共存还是商标侵权，其最核心的判断标准就是混淆可能性。

实践中很容易将近似与混淆混同起来，认为近似就会导致混淆，这实为一种过于绝对的观点。所谓"近似"，它是指两商标在文字的字形、读音、含义或者图案的构图及颜色或者文字与图形的整体结构相似，是对商标特点的客观描述；所谓"混淆"，则是一般公众对商品或服务来源所产生的混淆，它是对消费者造成的客观后果。因此，近似不等同于混淆，近似也不代表侵权。只有在商标近似且易导致公众混淆的情况下，才有侵权的发生。反之，如果近似但不存在混淆可能性，则应当肯定近似商标在相同或类似商品/服务上共存的合法性。

事实上，很多国际公约和国家的商标法都将混淆可能性规定为判定商标侵权的标准。例如，TRIPS 协议第 16 条第 1 款规定："注册商标的所有人应有专有权来阻止所有第三方未经其同意在交易过程中对与已获商标注册的货物或服务相同或类似的货物或服务使用相同或类似的标记，如果这种使用可能会产生混淆。若对相同货物或服务使用了相同的标记，则应推定为存在混淆的可能。"美国商标法即《兰哈姆法》也明确规定，导致公众混淆是构成商标侵权的要件。《欧共体商标条例》在引言中就强调："混淆可能性构成商标保护的特别条件。"

混淆可能性本身是一个较为抽象而不确定的法律概念，因此，对它的判定也是一个较为复杂的过程。关于如何进行商标混淆可能性的判定，美国1938 年《侵权法重述》第 729 条提出的 4 个要素可作为重要参考：①有关标记与有关商标或商号之间在外表、所用文字的发音、有关图画或设计的字面含义、指示上所存在的相似性程度；②行为人采用有关标记的意图；③在使

---

❶ 吴汉东，等. 知识产权基本问题研究 [M]. 2 版. 北京：中国人民大学出版社，2009.

用和销售方法上，行为人所提供的商品或服务与他人所提供的商品或服务之间的关系；④购买者有可能具有的谨慎程度。❶同时，《侵权法重述》第 729 条的评论指出："一般来说，本条所列举的要素在判定混淆相似性问题中是重要的。但它不是一个排他性的清单，因为还有一些要素在某些特定的案件中是重要的。"❷

借鉴国外的成功经验，笔者认为，我国商标行政机关和司法机关在认定混淆的过程中应当注意如下几点。

（1）判断商标近似与否，应从商标文字部分的音、形、义，图形部分的构图，以及商标整体视觉效果等多方面进行对比，着重于商标的整体印象，而不能将某一个构成要素单独提出来进行比对。此外，比对应该在隔离的方式下进行。

（2）综合考虑各种因素，将商标本身的显著性、知名度、在先使用情况、消费者的认知程度、被告的主观意图等纳入认定混淆可能性的标准之中。一般来说，请求保护的注册商标的显著性越高、知名度越大，混淆的判定就越复杂。

（3）应从相关公众的一般注意力出发。所谓"相关公众"，应该包括商标使用中可能受到影响的所有人，包括但不限于购买者、潜在购买者等。同时，不能完全依据法官自身的主观经验来断定是否有混淆发生，法官必须置身于市场消费者的角度进行判断。

（4）坚持个案审查原则。每个案件的具体情况都有所不同，应当具体问题具体分析，不能简单套用以往的类似判例或类似判例中所形成的观点。

作为 2010 年中国法院知识产权司法保护十大案件之一的"新加坡鳄鱼"和"法国鳄鱼"商标案，就是最高人民法院在审判中结合多方面因素、灵活而全面地对混淆可能性作出认定的典型案例。❸

在该案的判决中，最高人民法院确认了两个"鳄鱼"的合法共存，同时也创设了一条新的裁判原则，即，判定侵犯注册商标专用权意义上的商标近似，除了通常要考虑商标构成要素的近似程度外，还需要根据案件的具体情况，综合考虑被诉侵权人的主观意图、注册商标与诉争标识使用的历史和现状等其他相关因素，在此基础上认定诉争商标是否会产生混淆。这无疑明确了在商标侵权案件中判定混淆的标准，对我国商标司法实践具有重要的指导意义。

---

❶❷ 李明德. 美国知识产权法［M］. 北京：法律出版社，2002.

❸ 参照最高人民法院（2009）民三终字第 3 号判决。

三、混淆理论在我国商标共存实践中的运用和完善

我国对注册商标专用权的保护是行政保护和司法保护并行。商标行政保护的职能机关包括商标局、商标评审委员会和工商局，其中由商标评审委员会（以下简称商评委）负责审理有关商标确权的争议案件，而商标司法保护的职能机关则是人民法院。无论是商评委还是人民法院，现行《商标法》都是它们审理商标争议/侵权案件时的首要依据。同时，针对实践中大量产生的有关"商标是共存还是侵权"的案件，单一适用《商标法》毕竟存在一定局限性，故商评委或法院还会通过一些具体的审查规则或司法解释来作为审判此类案件的参考和指导。

商评委在其 2007 年第 24 次委务会上，就驳回复审案件中申请人提交的"共存协议"问题进行了研究，认为商标权冲突主要是私权纠纷，故对当事人之间的共存协议应该予以考虑，但在决定是否允许共存时还应当综合如下两个因素来衡量共存是否容易造成消费者混淆：①双方商标使用商品的类似程度、双方商标的近似程度及各自的知名度；②双方商标的知名度。下面的案例也能说明商评委在涉及共存协议的案件中对上述标准的把握原则。

A 公司申请注册了"LOWEPRO 及图"商标（见图 1），商标局认为该商标与 B 公司在先注册的"LOWE ALPINE 及图"商标（见图 2）在类似商品上构成近似而驳回了该商标的注册。A 公司向商评委申请驳回复审并提交了 B 公司签署的注册同意书的公证认证件。商评委认为，引证商标的所有人 B 公司已经签署了同意 A 公司商标注册的《同意书》，且两商标的表现形式也有所区别，故认定 A 公司商标与 B 公司商标不存在权利冲突，可以共存。❶

图 1 LOWEPRO 商标

图 2 LOWE ALPINE 商标

从上述案例可以看出，在驳回复审案件中，商评委已经开始有条件地接受当事人双方签订的共存协议，在充分考量上述两方面的因素后，允许两商标按照协议的约定共存。然而，商标是否近似以及商品是否类似，仍是商评委判定商标是否导致混淆、是否能够共存的首要因素。至于双方商标的知名度，本案当事人都没有提及，故商评委着重从商标的近似程度来判定是否会

---

❶ 参照商标评审委员会"商评字 2010 第 36429 号"驳回复审决定书。

产生混淆。由此也可以得出，商标近似性仍是商评委在商标注册过程中认定是否混淆的决定性因素，而该商标市场使用的实际情况和相关消费者对其的认知程度方面，则不是其认定商标是否混淆的必要条件。

人民法院在审理商标确权案件或商标侵权案件的过程中，也融入了混淆理论。《最高人民法院关于审理商标民事纠纷案件适用法律若干问题的解释》第 11 条第 1 款规定："商标法第五十二条第（一）项规定的类似商品，是指在功能、用途、生产部门、销售渠道、消费对象等方面相同，或者相关公众一般认为其存在特定联系、容易造成混淆的商品。"该解释第 9 条第 2 款规定："商标法第五十二条第（一）项规定的商标近似，是指被控侵权的商标与原告的注册商标相比较，其文字的字形、读音、含义或者图形的构图及颜色，或者其各要素组合后的整体结构相似，或者其立体形状、颜色组合近似，易使相关公众对商品的来源产生误认或认为其来源与原告注册商标的商品有特定的联系。"也就是说，"商品类似"和"商标近似"的界定也都以是否导致相关公众的混淆为标准。这一标准在北京高院的《关于审理商标民事纠纷案件若干问题的解答》中得到了具体的展开："足以造成相关公众的混淆、误认是构成商标近似的必要条件。仅商标文字、图案近似，但不足以造成相关公众混淆、误认的，不构成商标近似，在商标近似判断中应当对是否造成相关公众的混淆、误认进行认定。"

德国巴斯夫欧洲公司（以下简称"巴斯夫公司"）1987 年在中国申请注册了"狮马牌"商标（以下简称"引证商标"，见图 3）；湖北祥云（集团）化工股份有限公司（以下简称"祥云公司"）1999 年创立"红狮犸及图"商标（以下简称"争议商标"，见图 4），2005 年注册，2010 年 3 月被认定为"湖北省著名商标"。

图 3　"狮马牌"商标　　　　　　　　　图 4　"红狮犸"商标

巴斯夫公司以祥云公司注册的"红狮犸及图"商标是对其在先申请注册并享有商标专用权的"狮马牌"商标故意模仿、误导公众为由，向商评委提出了注册商标争议申请。其后，商评委以两商标文字部分相近、构成类似商品上的近似为由，裁定撤销祥云公司"红狮犸及图"在化肥、复合肥料、磷肥（肥料）及化学肥料商品上的商标专用权。祥云公司不服，随后向北京市第一中级人民法院（以下简称一中院）提起行政诉讼。北京一中院经审理后认为，对于使用时间较长、已建立较高市场声誉和形成相关公众群体的争议商标，应当准确把握商标法有关保护在先商业标志权益与维护市场秩序相协调的立法精神，充分尊重相关公众已在客观上将相关商业标志区别开来的市场实际，注重维护已经形成和稳定的市场秩序。"狮犸"与"狮马"虽然读音相同，字形近似，但争议商标的图形部分显著性较强，其与引证商标整体视觉效果存在较大差异。商评委未就祥云公司提交的产品宣传手册、销售发票等使用、宣传争议商标的证据予以评述，就此判断相关公众是否能够识别商品来源，属于漏审。据此，一中院判决撤销商评委作出的被诉裁定，并要求商评委在判决生效后针对第 3783811 号"红狮犸及图"商标重新作出争议裁定。❶

上述案件体现了法院在认定商标近似上所采取的混淆标准，同时也反映了行政机关和司法机关在对商标混淆的判定上有着不尽相同的尺度。行政机关在商标注册审查中对是否造成混淆往往简单套用《商标审查及审理标准》的规定，判断商标是否构成近似时，很大程度上仍停留在机械比对两商标各自的音、形、义，并以此作为商标是否会产生混淆的重要依据，而法院更着重于商标的本质，坚持个案原则，除了比对商标本身的构成要素之外，还结合诉争商标在市场使用中的具体情况，只要两商标不构成足以引起市场混淆的近似，即认定商标可以共存。

---

❶ 参照北京一中院（2010）一中知行初字第 2047 号判决。

浅谈类似商品或服务的认定

吴　滁

根据中国❶《商标法》❷ 第 8 条❸可以获知，商标的主要功能在于将自己的商品与他人的商品区分开来，而关于商品或者服务类似及商标近似的判断则是贯穿《商标法》始终的核心，在商标获权及维权的案例中是重要的考虑因素。因此，在判断两个商标是否构成近似时，首先也要判断商品或者服务❹是否构成类似。

在本文中，我们将就中国商标行政机关❺和司法机关❻对于判断类似商品或者服务的依据和最新案例进行探讨。

一、关于判断类似商品或服务的有关规定

1. 商标行政机关对于类似商品或服务的规定

国家工商行政管理总局在 2005 年 12 月发布的《商标审查及审理标准》中规定：

"类似商品，是指在商品的功能、用途、主要原料、生产部门、销售渠道、销售场所、消费对象等方面相同或者近似。

类似服务，是指在服务的目的、内容、方式、对象等方面相同或者近似。

商品与服务类似，是指商品和服务之间存在特定联系，容易使相关公众混淆。"

2. 司法机关对于类似商品或服务的规定

最高人民法院《关于审理商标民事纠纷案件适用法律若干问题的解释》（以下简称《司法解释》）第 11 条规定：

---

❶　本文提到的"中国"，均指中国大陆地区，不包括中国香港、中国澳门和中国台湾地区。

❷　《商标法》指的是 2001 年 10 月 27 日第二次修正的《中华人民共和国商标法》。

❸　第 8 条规定："任何能够将自然人、法人或者其他组织的商品与他人的商品区别开来的可视性标志，包括图形、字母、数字、三维标志和颜色组合，以及上述要素的组合，均可作为商标申请的注册。"

❹　本文提到的"类似商品或服务"包括"类似商品"、"类似服务"、"类似商品和服务"。

❺　本文提到的"商标行政机关"，指的是"国家工商行政管理总局"、"商标局"、"商标评审委员会"。

❻　本文提到的"司法机关"，指的是"法院"。

"类似商品，是指在商品的功能、用途、生产部门、销售渠道、消费对象等方面相同，或者相关公众一般认为其存在特定联系、容易造成混淆的商品。

类似服务，是指在服务的目的、内容、方式、对象等方面相同，或者相关公众一般认为存在特定联系、容易造成混淆的服务。

商品与服务类似，是指商品和服务之间存在特定联系，容易使相关公众混淆。"

从上述规定的内容可以看出，商标行政机关和司法机关在把握判断类似商品或者服务时所考虑的因素基本一致。二者的主要差异在于，商标行政机关规定了考虑因素（比如：功能、用途、生产部门、消费对象等）的近似可以认定为商品类似，但是并没有规定近似的判断标准。而法院的规定未提到考虑因素方面的近似，但是却强调了相关公众构成混淆误认的必要性。但是，虽然从文字内容上看两规定存在差异，但这种差异并没有体现在实务操作中，其仅仅是从不同的角度进行的规范而已。❶

二、《类似商品和服务区分表》在判断类似商品或服务时的作用

我国目前采用的《类似商品和服务区分表》是国家工商行政管理总局以《商标注册用商品和服务用国际分类表》（以下简称尼斯分类）为基础，总结多年的类似商品或服务划分的实践经验制定并公布的，于 2012 年 1 月 1 日正式使用。

1. 商标行政主管机关对于《类似商品和服务区分表》的规定

《商标审查及审理标准》中指明，商标局、商标评审委员会在审理案件时应当参照《类似商品和服务区分表》。在商标驳回复审、异议、异议复审、争议、撤销、撤销复审案件审理中，涉及商品或者服务类似与否的判定问题的，以本标准为原则进行个案判定。

2. 司法机关对于《类似商品和服务区分表》的规定

《司法解释》第 12 条规定，认定商品或者服务是否类似，应当以相关公众对商品或者服务的一般认识综合判断；《商标注册用商品和服务国际分类表》、《类似商品和服务区分表》可以作为判断类似商品或者服务的参考。

从上述规定可以看出，无论是商标行政机关还是司法机关，都认为《类似商品和服务区分表》在判断类似商品或服务时仅起到参考作用，并非确定类似商品或服务的法律依据。

但是，为了维护商标注册秩序的稳定性，在绝大多数行政案件的审理中，商标行政机关还是以适用《类似商品和服务区分表》作为商品或服务类似判

---

❶ 北京市第一中级人民法院知识产权庭. 商标确权行政审判疑难问题研究 [M]. 北京：知识产权出版社，2008：89.

定的原则，以个案突破作为判定的例外。在一些案件中，商标评审委员会认为，在没有充分证据的情况下，不应突破区分表，以保持商标审查及评审标准的一致性。否则，将会破坏商标审查的基本秩序。而北京市第一中级人民法院法官认为，司法审查中基于当事人的主张对商品是否类似进行的判断，正是对《类似商品和服务区分表》的分类是否科学进行的检验，是对商品审查中存在的不当进行的补救，不仅不会破坏商标审查的基本秩序，而且有助于区分表的修订。❶

三、商标确权案例分析：行政机关和司法机关对于类似商品或服务的判断

1. 湖南省长康实业有限责任公司与商标评审委员会、长沙加加食品集团有限公司商标异议复审行政纠纷案❷

被异议商标（申请人：湖南省长康实业有限责任公司）：

类别/群组/商品：29/08/芝麻油

引证商标（申请人：加加食品集团股份有限公司）：

（引证商标一）　　　　（引证商标二）　　　　（引证商标三）

引证商标一的类别/群组/商品：30/15/酱油

引证商标二的类别/群组/商品：30/15，16/酱油，醋，调味品，蚝油等

引证商标三的类别/群组/商品：30/15，16/酱油，醋，调味品，蚝油等

注明：按照《类似商品和服务区分表》，被异议商标指定使用在第29类的商品"芝麻油"与引证商标指定使用在第30类上的"酱油；等"商品并不构成类似商品。

商标评审委员会第34098号裁定认为：被异议商标指定使用的第29类芝麻油商品与3个引证商标核定使用的第30类酱油、醋等商品在生产原料、制

---

❶ 北京市第一中级人民法院知识产权庭. 商标确权行政审判疑难问题研究［M］. 北京：知识产权出版社，2008：94.

❷ 奚晓明. 最高人民法院知识产权审判案例指导（第四辑）［M］. 北京：中国法制出版社，2012：225.

作工艺、销售渠道等方面存在较大区别，不属于类似商品。被异议商标与引证商标一般不易导致消费者混淆误认，未构成近似商标。商标评审委员会裁定被异议商标予以核准注册。

加加食品集团股份有限公司不服第 34098 号裁定，向北京市第一中级人民法院提起诉讼。北京市第一中级人民法院认为：被异议商标指定使用的"芝麻油"与 3 个引证商标核定使用的"酱油"、"醋、调味品、蚝油"等商品对比，其功能均为烹饪调味品，销售渠道、消费群体都无明显区别，应判定为类似商品。况且，商品类似的判断，应当结合商标知名度等因素，在整体上是否容易导致消费者对商品来源混淆误认的角度予以综合考虑。本案中，加加公司提供了大量足以证明引证商标已经取得了一定的知名度的证据。被异议商标与 3 个引证商标中的显著性部分均为汉字"加加"。被异议商标与 3 个引证商标构成了类似商品上的近似商标。2010 年 6 月 18 日，北京市第一中级人民法院作出一审判决，商标评审委员会认定事实错误，应予以撤销。

长康公司不服一审判决，提起上诉。北京市高级人民法院维持原判。长康公司不服二审判决，向最高人民法院申请再审。最高人民法院认为，芝麻油可用作调味，其产品包装类似于酱油、醋等调味品；本案中，相关公众为家庭烹饪用品的消费者，对于此类普通消费者来讲，其普通的认知是芝麻油为调味品的一种。引证商标已经在"酱油"等商品上取得了一定的知名度，普通消费者在看到芝麻油商品上的被异议商标容易产生混淆，以为标注引证商标的酱油等产品均出自同一主体，或者出自特定联系的主体。在此基础上，一审法院、二审法院认定芝麻油与酱油等商品构成类似商品是正确的。2011 年 8 月 31 日，最高人民法院裁定驳回长康公司的再审申请。

2. 杭州啄木鸟鞋业有限公司与商标评审委员会、七好（集团）有限公司商标争议行政纠纷案❶

争议商标（申请人：杭州啄木鸟鞋业有限公司）：

类别／群组／商品：25/01/鞋，靴

引证商标［申请人：七好（集团）有限公司］：

❶ 奚晓明. 最高人民法院知识产权审判案例指导（第四辑）［M］. 北京：中国法制出版社，2012：232.

（引证商标一）　（引证商标二）

引证商标一的类别/群组/商品：25/01/服装

引证商标二的类别/群组/商品：18/01/皮包，旅行袋，公文包等

注明：按照《类似商品和服务区分表》，争议商标指定使用在第25类的商品"鞋，靴"与引证商标指定使用在第25类上的"服装；等"和第18类"皮包"等商品并不构成类似商品。

商标评审委员会第2577号裁定认为：争议商标指定使用的鞋、靴商品与各引证商标指定使用的服装、领带、皮包等所属的范围和领域不同，在《类似商品和服务区分表》中不属于类似商品。争议商标与引证商标未构成使用在同一种或类似商品上的近似商标。商标评审委员会裁定维持争议商标注册。

七好公司不服第2577号裁定，向北京市第一中级人民法院提起行政诉讼。北京市第一中级人民法院认为：争议商标指定使用的鞋、靴商品与引证商标指定使用的服装、领带、皮包等商品不属于类似商品，争议商标与引证商标指定使用在非类似商品上，不会导致消费者对于商品来源的混淆误认。北京市第一中级人民法院作出一审判决，维持第2577号裁定。

七好公司不服一审判决，提起上诉。北京市高级人民法院认为，争议商标与引证商标指定使用的商品虽然不属于同一类似群组，但均为穿戴类商品，在市场上共同使用易使消费者对其商品来源产生混淆、误认。北京市高级人民法院判决撤销一审判决和第2577号裁定。

杭州啄木鸟鞋业有限公司不服二审判决，向最高人民法院申请再审。最高人民法院认为，争议商标指定使用的商品为鞋和靴，引证商标核定使用的为商品类服装等。虽然两者在具体的原料、用途等方面具有一些差别，但是两者消费对象是相同的，而且在目前的商业环境下，一个厂商同时生产服装和鞋类产品，服装和鞋通过同一渠道销售情形较多。争议商标与引证商标中的"鸟图形"虽然略有差别，但两者基本形态相同。根据查明的事实，引证商标通过使用具有较高知名度。在这种情况下，如果两商标在服装和鞋类商品上共存，容易使相关公众认为是同一主体提供的，或者提供者之间存在特定联系。因此，争议商标与引证商标构成类似商品上的近似商标。另外，最高人民法院还认为，在商标异议、争议和诉讼中进行商品类似关系判断时，不能机械、简单地以《类似商品和服务区分表》为依据或标准，应当考虑更多的实际要素，结合个案的情况进行认定。2011年7月12日，最高人民法院驳回杭州啄木鸟鞋业有限公司的再审申请。

四、结 论

从以上两件判例可知，虽然"芝麻油"和"酱油"、"鞋"和"服装、皮包"在《类似商品和服务区分表》中被划为非类似，但法院更注重整体上是否容易导致消费者对商品来源混淆误认的角度（包括商标的知名度、商标的独创性、商标的近似程度、商品关联程度、是否具有恶意等因素，予以综合考虑。最高人民法院认为，对于这些商品，只要是容易使相关公众认为商品或者服务是同一主体提供的，或者其提供者之间存在特定联系，即构成类似商品。

除此之外，需要强调的是，由于在商品类似判断时考虑了个案情况，相关商品是否类似并非是绝对和一成不变的，基于不同的案情可能会得出不同的结论。❶

通过上述案例并结合本公司多年的商标代理经验，我们也发现：在实践中，商标行政机关为了保证执法的统一性和稳定性，一般很难突破《类似商品和服务区分表》。而司法机关由于强调司法对个案的救济性，因此考虑更多的实际要素，并结合个案的情况对于类似商品和服务进行判定。在今后的商标异议、争议等案件中，建议申请人应当尽可能地提供使用证据，因为这些证据有可能成为突破《类似商品和服务区分表》的个案依据。

---

❶ 奚晓明. 最高人民法院知识产权审判案例指导（第四辑）［M］. 北京：中国法制出版社，2012：239-240.

浅谈纺织企业品牌保护

蔡瑜萍

企业的品牌是企业的重要无形资产，保护和维护企业品牌无疑是企业品牌发展的基础。所谓品牌保护，就是对品牌的所有人、合法使用人的品牌实行资格保护措施，以防范来自各方面的侵害和侵权行为。❶ 具体而言，企业的品牌保护中最重要的是对企业商标的保护。在本文中，笔者结合实践中的一些案例来探讨如何做好与纺织集团有关的品牌保护。

一、对企业商标进行注册

我国有独特的商标注册制度，而且在注册商标与未注册商标之间采取鼓励商标注册和强保护注册商标的态度。❷ 因此，对于商标申请注册显然是企业品牌保护的第一环节。经过注册的商标才能享有注册商标专用权，企业才能对商标享有专有使用权和禁止他人在相同或类似商品上使用相同或近似商标的排斥权。企业在商标申请注册阶段，应当注意下列问题。

（一）选择显著性强的商标

企业选择商标要具有较高显著性和独创性，因为商标权的保护范围大小与商标的显著性密切关联。最高人民法院《关于当前经济形势下知识产权审判服务大局若干问题的意见》❸ 指出："认定商标类似和商标近似要考虑请求保护的注册商标的显著程度和市场知名度，对于显著性越强和市场知名度越高的注册商标，给予其范围越宽和强度越大的保护，以激励市场竞争的优胜者，净化市场环境，遏制不正当搭车、模仿行为。"最高人民法院的司法政策强调的便是显著性越强的商标所享有的保护则越高。如本文下面要涉及的案例（无锡宇达纺织有限公司诉国家工商行政管理总局商标评审委员会商标异议行政纠纷案❹）、无锡市世泰盛经贸有限责任公司的"世泰盛"商标就被法院认定为有较强的显著性，并获得了较高的保护。相反，如果企业采用显著性不强的商标作为企业品牌，则很可能和其他企业的品牌相同，而无法突出

❶ 百度百科关于"品牌保护"的定义，摘自 http：//baike. baidu. com/view/280571. htm。
❷ 孔祥俊. 商标法适用的基本问题［M］. 北京：中国法制出版社，2012：44.
❸ 2009 年 4 月 21 日印发，法发［2009］23 号。
❹ （2012）高行终字第 589 号，摘自 http：//hk. lexiscn. com。

本企业的特点，且在商标侵权纠纷案件中，所获得的保护会较弱。如在侵犯"维纳斯"注册商标权纠纷案中，最高人民法院二审判决指出："从商标的显著性考虑，'维纳斯'作为罗马和希腊神话中女神的称谓和著名雕塑的固有含义，弱化了其作为瓷砖商标的显著性。"❶ 由于"维纳斯"作为注册商标在显著性上的先天不足，又没有因为知名度而得以弥补，所以对其采取了弱保护的态度。❷

（二）商标保护范围的选择

根据我国《商标法》的规定，注册商标专用权的范围以核准注册的商标和核定使用的商品为限。企业若想使整个类别都得到保护，必须在该类别的每个类似群组都选择至少一个商品。但是，由于纺织企业的特点决定经营范围不可能无限扩大，所以建议重点选择与主营范围相关的商品以及个别有代表性的商品。例如：以生产西装、衬衫为主的企业在选择商品时，即可以在第25类中重点选择2501群组中的"服装、衬衫、制服"，2502群组中的"婴儿全套衣"，2503群组中的"体操服"，2504群组中的"防水服"，2505群组中的"戏装"，2506群组中的"体操鞋"，2507群组中的"鞋（脚上的穿着物）"，2508群组中的"帽子"，2509群组中"袜"，2510群组中的"手套（服装）"，2511群组中"领带"，2512群组中的"衣服吊带"，2513群组中的"婚纱"。这样，这个企业申请的商标就达到了主要商品和整个类别的商品都能受到全面保护的目的。❸

（三）对企业商标进行跨行业的申请注册

由于经济的高速发展，各个行业都有了密切的联系。对于企业特别是集团公司，其经营范围涉及众多行业。为了保护企业品牌，企业不仅要在本产品所属的行业进行注册，同时还需要考虑在相关联的行业进行商标注册。

在无锡宇达纺织有限公司诉国家工商行政管理总局商标评审委员会商标异议行政纠纷案中，无锡宇达纺织有限公司（以下简称"宇达公司"）于2003年10月14日向商标局申请注册了第3753037号"世泰盛"商标（被异议商标），指定使用在第7类"印刷机器、纺织机；纺织工业用机器；染色机；丝光机；等"商品上，并通过了初步审查而公告。无锡市世泰盛经贸有限责任公司（以下简称世泰盛公司）在法定期限内对被异议商标提出了异议。世泰盛公司在本案中依据了在第25类"服装；成品衣；等"商品上在先注册的第1505195号"世泰盛"商标（引证商标一），第35类"商业信息；广告；

---

❶ 最高人民法院（2004）民三终字第2号民事判决书。

❷ 孔祥俊. 商标法适用的基本问题［M］. 北京：中国法制出版社，2012：49.

❸ 赵家华. 企业的商标策略［J］. 中华商标，2012（3）.

等"服务项目上在先注册的第 773033 号"世泰盛"商标（引证商标二）和在先商号权"世泰盛"。由于宇达公司在第 7 类注册的商品与世泰盛公司在第 25 类和第 35 类注册的商品/服务未构成类似商品或服务，因此，世泰盛公司引用两例引证商标并未获得商标评审委员会或是法院的支持。商标评审委员会和法院都以被异议商标违反了世泰盛公司的在先商号权而认定被异议商标不予核准注册。

上述案件中，世泰盛公司虽然依据具有较高知名度的商号"世泰盛"而使得被异议商标在第 7 类不予核准注册，但是该案件经历了商标局、商标评审委员会、北京市第一中级人民法院和北京市高级人民法院的涉诉过程，世泰盛公司为了本案支付了高额的诉讼成本和时间成本。笔者认为，为了避免他人在相近行业抢注本公司的商标，最好事先就将集团总部和关联公司的商标在多个类别上进行注册。具体而言，纺织集团可以考虑在第 2 类"染料；等"、第 7 类"纺织机；等"、第 22 类"生丝；网织物；等"、第 23 类"毛线；丝纱；等"、第 24 类"纺织品；纺织织物；等"、第 25 类"服装；等"、第 26 类"拉链；服装扣"等商品上，以及第 35 类"商业管理；替他人推销；等"和第 40 类"服装制作；等"服务项目上进行注册。

（四）对企业商标进行防御性申请注册

为了防止他人在不同类别的商品（服务）上使用与其相近似的注册商标，企业可以在确定了自己的主商标后，根据企业的发展战略，在今后有可能涉及的领域（商品或服务）进行防御商标注册，以防患于未然。例如，四川金泰纺织集团有限公司为了保护其" "商标专用权，采用了防御性保护措施，设计了新的" "、" "、" "、" "图形商标、文字图形组合商标、中英文商标，形成了"曲美"系列商标。❶

（五）商标的国外注册

注册商标的保护具有地域性。如果企业将标有本企业商标的商品或服务销售到多个国家，为了保护企业的品牌，就需要在这些国家获得商标专用权。然而，现实中由于企业的品牌国际保护意识不强，往往忽视了企业商标的国

---

❶ 四川金泰纺织集团有限公司保卫"曲美"商标［EB/OL］. http：//www. Haotm. cn/news. htm? id＝3487.

外注册。据国家工商总局最新的不完全统计，国内有 15% 的知名商标在国外被抢注，其中超过 80 个商标在印度尼西亚被抢注，近 100 个商标在日本被抢注，近 200 个商标在澳大利亚被抢注。如"康佳"在美国、"海信"在德国、"科龙"在新加坡等相继遭遇了商标被抢注的命运。每年商标国外抢注案件超过 100 起，其中涉及了服装、纺织品等多个行业。❶ 对于纺织集团而言，商标的国外注册也是开拓国外市场的基础。商标要想在国外获得保护，一般有两种途径，一是通过单一国家或地区申请，即单独在每个国家或地区进行商标注册申请，另一种方式是通过马德里国际注册。相对于单一国家申请，通过马德里国际注册，企业一般只需要提交一份申请，使用一种语言和缴纳一次费用，就可以向加入条约的缔约方提出商标注册申请，手续相对简单，费用相对低廉。

二、合理有效的使用

（一）使用总商标与产品商标的策略

为了树立企业的形象，扩大品牌的声誉，同时在市场营销的过程中避免消费者对新产品和新商标产生的不信任感，企业应考虑在所有产品上使用同一"主商标"，并在不同品种、不同质量的产品上使用不同"子商标"。例如：美国宝洁公司的主商标为 P&G、宝洁，子商标有：飘柔、海飞丝、潘婷、沙宣、伊卡露、玉兰、碧浪、汰渍、舒肤佳、佳洁士等。企业采用这种策略，可以将主商标注册在企业提供的所有产品和服务上，但子商标只需在其所指定保护的单项产品注册即可。❷

（二）使用等级商标策略

所谓等级商标，是指企业在自己生产的同一种类、不同档次的产品上，分别使用不同的商标。纺织型企业的产品相对单一，且容易受到原材料、工人技术、设备等外部因素的干扰而影响产品质量。如果企业在所有产品上使用同一商标，容易损坏企业的声誉。解决这一问题除了严格产品的质量管理之外，还可以对一种质量的产品、确定一种价格、使用一种商标，使消费者一见到某种商标的商品，就能知晓该商品的质量和档次。

三、企业对本集团的品牌进行推广

在企业的品牌获准注册后，企业还需要对品牌进行科学的管理，确保企业品牌价值。既要对本集团和各个关联公司的品牌进行监控、打击侵权行为，

---

❶ 论企业如何进行品牌保护［EB/OL］. 品牌中国网.
❷ 赵家华. 企业的商标策略［J］. 中华商标，2012（3）.

切实维权，又要提升产品服务质量，争创驰名商标，从而保护本集团和各个关联公司的品牌。

在泰丰纺织集团有限公司与山东泰鑫经贸有限公司商标权侵权纠纷一案❶中，原告泰丰纺织集团有限公司（以下简称泰丰集团）在第24类"布；棉织品；床单、被罩"等产品上注册了第3152091号"TAIFENG"商标。原告在经营过程中，大力实施品牌战略，在全国范围内对其商标及产品进行宣传，并先后荣获"山东省著名商标"等多项荣誉称号。2006年11月，原告通过调查发现，被告山东泰鑫经贸有限公司（以下简称泰鑫公司）经销"TAIFENG"牌染布用的化工染料（纺织助剂）。原告在本案中向法院提交了大量的品牌使用证据、该品牌所获得的各种荣誉证明、品牌推广材料、产品质量报告、消费者问卷调查等知名度材料，最终法院认定了原告的"TAIFENG"商标为驰名商标并判决被告停止侵权、赔偿损失。

借鉴泰丰集团能够通过法院认定驰名商标并成功维权的案例，笔者认为可以从以下几个方面进行品牌的推广和保护。

第一，对企业品牌在中国和海外进行商标公告监测，采取有效措施防止他人对企业品牌的抢注。

企业品牌注册后，企业为了有效保护企业品牌，应当主动委托商标代理机构对本企业的品牌在国内和国外进行商标公告监测。商标公告监测主要指的是通过对商标主管机关发布的新申请商标公告进行监测从而发现抢注的情况，通过商标异议程序或者撤销程序来防止他人对企业品牌的抢注。如果没有对企业品牌进行有效的商标监测，一旦错过异议期，企业要想维护自己的品牌利益，需要在时间、精力和费用上付出更多。

第二，对企业品牌进行有效的市场监测，采取有效的措施发现和打击他人的侵权行为。

企业为了维护企业品牌，需要通过市场监测。市场监测主要指的是通过对市场上出现的与企业品牌相同或近似的商标进行监测，一旦发现侵犯企业品牌的行为及时采取法律行动，维护企业利益和保护企业品牌。在上述案例中，原告泰丰集团正是通过对企业品牌进行有效的市场监测和调查，发现被告经销"TAIFENG"牌产品的行为，并通过诉讼程序成功维权。

第三，提高企业产品和服务质量，对品牌进行大量的宣传和推广，并注意收集证据，争创驰名商标。

驰名商标既具有一般商标的区别作用，又有很强的竞争力，知名度高，影响范围广，已经被消费者、经营者所熟知和信赖，具有相关的商业价值。❷

---

❶ （2006）莱中知初字第20号［EB/OL］. http://hk. lexiscn. com.

❷ 中国驰名商标［EB/OL］. http://baike. baidu. com. cn/view/563468. htm.

驰名商标作为企业最重要的无形资产之一，不但代表着企业品牌的商业价值和商誉，并且根据我国相关法律可以得到相对更为全面的保护。企业应当注意在日常的品牌使用时注意收集认定驰名商标所需要的证据材料，如：年销售量、营业收入、净利润、纳税额、市场占有率等主要经济指标的材料；销售合同；广告合同；广告宣传资料和图片；报纸、杂志等宣传材料。因此，企业要从长远出发，切实提高产品或服务质量，提升公众认同感，争创驰名商标，提高品牌保护水平。

一个企业靠什么才能立足于市场？答案无疑是"品牌"。企业如何创立和发展自己的品牌？唯有创新。创新让企业的产品和服务区别于他人，创新让企业的品牌故事得以延续和发展。中国纺织民族品牌"恒源祥"的刘瑞旗董事长曾说过："如果恒源祥有 1 亿元，我坚决不会去买地、买设备，我坚决会将恒源祥的知识产权进行到底。"❶自 20 世纪 80 年代以来，"恒源祥"从绒线单品发展到针织、服饰、家纺、羊绒等多种经营。"恒源祥"1999 年被认定为中国驰名商标，2005 年成功赞助 2008 年北京奥运会，2010 年成为上海世博会特许零售商。纵观"恒源祥"的品牌发展之路，我们得到了这样的启示：只有有了自己独特的品牌，实施了正确的品牌运作之道，企业才能上演不老的传奇。

---

❶ 刘洪 . 恒源祥品牌上演"不老传奇"[J]. 中华商标，2012（8）.

知识产权实务探讨

浅谈发明专利的加快授权方法

魏 彦 金相允

企业为了在市场上占得先机，其技术常常需要尽快获得专利的保护。然而，就如何能够尽快获得专利权而言，随着时代变迁和制度的变动，方式方法不尽相同。众所周知，在中国大陆，实用新型专利和外观设计专利只需初步审查通过就能够在较短时间内获得专利权。因此，在本文中，只浅谈发明专利在中国尽快获得专利权的方法。

一、通常情况下发明专利从提交申请到授权的过程

首先，参照图 1 来说明中国国内的发明专利从申请到授权所需的时间。

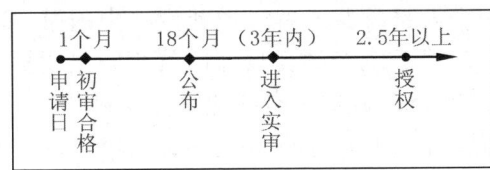

图 1 从申请到授权所需时间

《专利法》❶ 第 34 条规定了 "国务院专利行政部门收到发明专利申请后，经初步审查认为符合本法要求的，自申请日起满十八个月，即行公布。国务院专利行政部门可以根据申请人的请求早日公布其申请"；第 35 条中规定了 "发明专利申请自申请日起三年内，国务院专利行政部门可以根据申请人随时提出的请求，对其申请进行实质审查"。

如图 1 所示，一件发明专利申请从提交申请到授权的过程为：申请→初步审查合格→公布→实质审查→授权。从实务经验看来，通常各阶段所需时间如下：初步审查合格需要从提交申请的申请日起 1 个月时间；如 PCT 国际申请进入中国国家阶段的申请，在自申请日起 18 个月以后初步审查合格的情况下，从该初步审查合格日起 4 个月内进行中文公布；自公布日及实质审查请求日中最晚的日期起 1 个月以内进入实质审查；自实质审查进入日起 3 个月以后才发出第一次审查意见通知书。这样一来，发明专利申请要获得专利

---

❶ 《专利法》指的是自 2009 年 10 月 1 日起施行的经过第三次修改后的《中华人民共和国专利法》。

权，自申请日起一般至少需要 2.5 年以上。

下面，探讨如何加快授权。

参照图 1 可知，发明专利从提交申请到授权的过程主要经历 3 个期间，即：

（1）从申请日到公布日为止的期间；

（2）从公布日到实质审查进入日为止的期间；

（3）进行实质审查的期间。

可见，若能将前两个期间的起始日（申请日、公布日）提前，或将第三个期间的长度缩短，那么就有可能尽快获得专利权。下面，分别探讨提前申请日、提前公布日以及缩短实质审查阶段的方法。

二、提前申请日的方法

提前申请日，主要利用优先权制度。

《专利法》第 29 条规定："申请人自发明或者实用新型在外国第一次提出专利申请之日起十二个月内，……又在中国就相同主题提出专利申请的……可以享有优先权。申请人自发明或者实用新型在中国第一次提出专利申请之日起十二个月内，又向国务院专利行政部门就相同主题提出专利申请的，可以享有优先权。"就在外国首次提出申请的发明专利而言，参照图 2 可知，利用《巴黎公约》制度，能够将向中国专利局提交申请的实际申请日提前到在外国首次提出申请的在先申请日，最多能够提前 1 年。

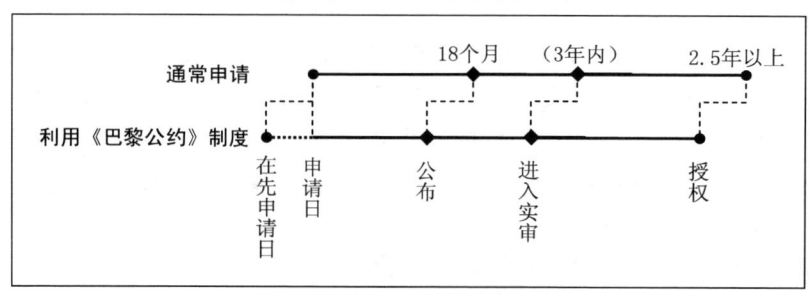

图 2　利用《巴黎公约》制度提前申请日

就在国内首次提出申请的发明专利而言，参照图 3 可知，利用本国优先权制度，同样能够提前实际申请日，最多能够提前 1 年。

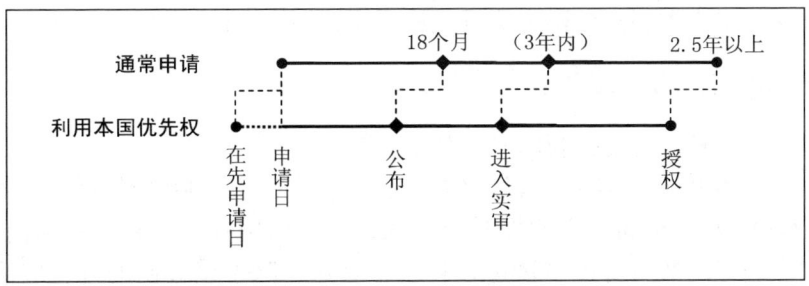

图3　利用本国优先权制度提前申请日

如上所述，无论是利用外国优先权还是本国优先权，从法条的规定上都能够将实际申请日提前到在先申请日。

参照图4，以利用本国优先权的情况为例，如果在发明创造虽还未进入实际研发过程但已有了完整的构想的阶段，先以实用新型专利或发明专利的形式提出专利申请，等到通过具体研发活动来补充完善已提出的发明创造后，再将已提出的该专利申请作为要求优先权的在先申请来申请发明专利，那么，能够大幅度提前发明专利申请的实际申请日。其中，提出在先申请的目的就是为了获得在先申请的申请日及申请号，无须向专利局缴纳任何费用。这样的方法同样也适用于利用外国优先权的情形。

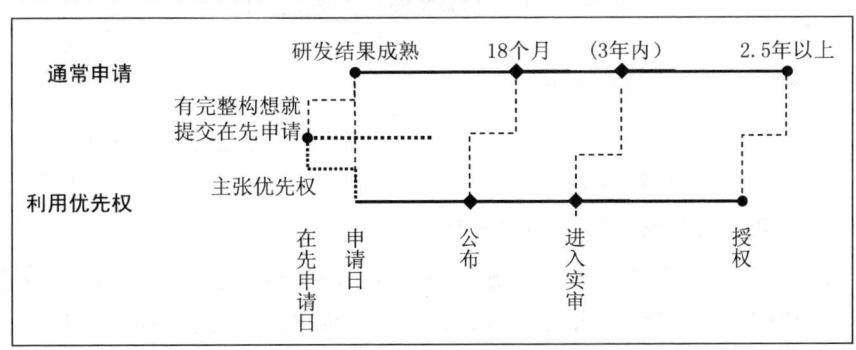

图4　利用优先权提前申请日

诚然，上述在后申请中新增加的在先申请中所不包括的内容，不能享受在先申请的优先权。从法条的规定来看，在后申请中新增加的内容部分，与申请人另行提交一件普通的专利申请没有什么不同。即使如此，以这种方式要求本国优先权对于申请人来说仍可能具有某种价值。❶ 一般情况下，针对一件专利申请的优先权主张是否成立，审查员只审查其是否满足形式上的条件，而很少考虑在先及在后申请之间的实质内容的差异，因此在新申请阶段，这

---

❶ 尹新天 . 中国专利法详解 ［M］. 北京：知识产权出版社，2011：393.

样的优先权主张大多都会得到认可，从而能够加快授权。

三、提前公布日的方法

提前公布日，主要是利用早日公布制度。

根据《专利法》第 34 条的规定以及《专利法实施细则》❶ 第 46 条规定，"申请人请求早日公布其发明专利申请的，应当向国务院专利行政部门声明。国务院专利行政部门对该申请进行初步审查后，除予以驳回的外，应当立即将申请予以公布。"

从实务经验看来，参照图 5，一件发明专利申请若利用上述的早日公布制度，则与通常的发明专利相比，能够将公布日提前 6~8 个月。

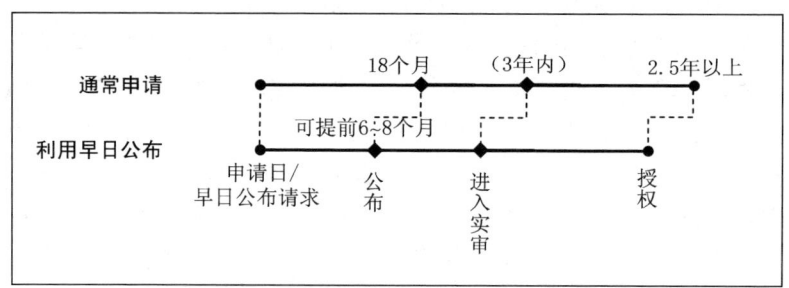

图 5　利用早日公布制度提前公布日

四、缩短实质审查阶段的方法

缩短实质审查阶段的时间，主要是利用专利审查高速公路（以下简称 PPH）制度和优先审查制度。

（一）利用专利审查高速公路制度

PPH 的基本概念是，申请人提交首次申请的专利局（OFF）认为该申请的至少一项或多项权利要求可授权，只要相关后续申请满足一定条件，包括首次申请和后续申请的权利要求充分对应、OFF 工作结果可被后续申请的专利局（OSF）获得等，申请人即可以 OFF 的工作结果为基础，请求 OSF 加快审查后续申请。

图 6❷ 示出了可提出 PPH 请求的 3 种基本情形。

---

❶ 《专利法实施细则》指的是自 2010 年 2 月 1 日起施行的经过第三次修改的《中华人民共和国专利法实施细则》。

❷ 国家知识产权局专利局审查业务管理部. 专利审查高速路（PPH）用户手册［M］. 北京：知识产权出版社，2012：2.

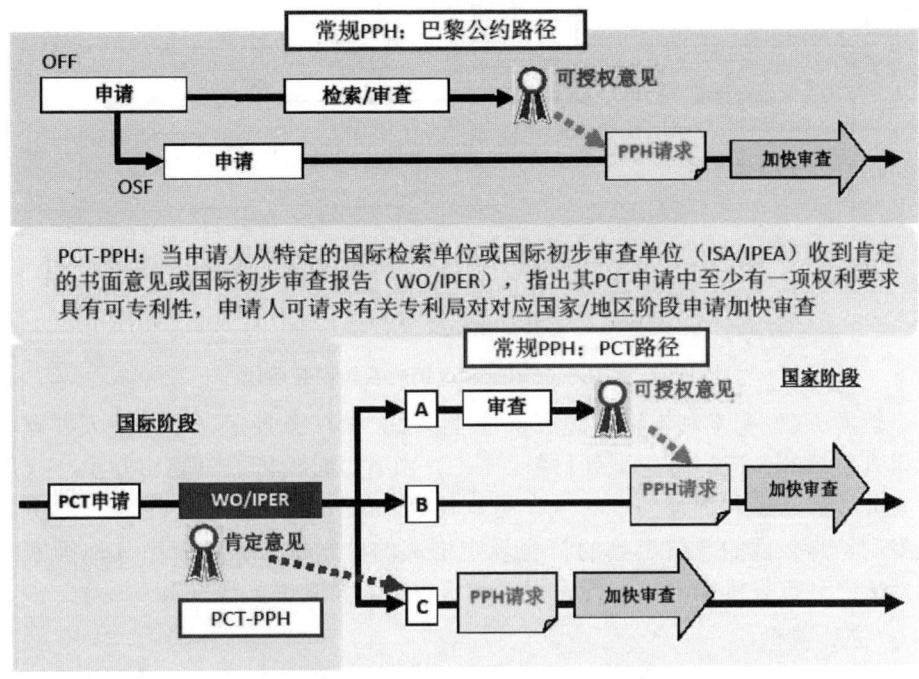

图6 可提出 PHH 请求的 3 种情形

利用专利审查高速公路制度，则如图7所示，能够大幅度提前发出第一次审查意见通知书的时间，通常自 PPH 请求日起 1~1.5 个月（实务经验数据）就发出第一次审查意见通知书，从而能够大幅度缩短实质审查阶段，加快授权。

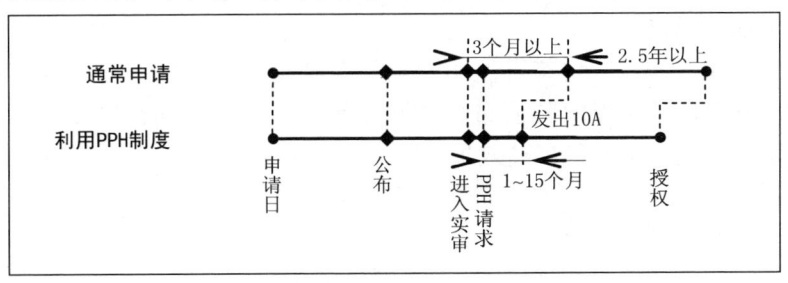

图7 利用 PPH 制度缩短实质审查阶段

（二）利用优先审查制度

利用基于《发明专利申请优先审查管理办法》❶ 的优先审查制度，则如图8所示，自优先审查请求获得同意之日起 30 个工作日内发出第一次审查意见通知书（第9条）并在 1 年内结案（第2条），从而能够大幅度缩短实质审

---

❶ 国家知识产权局第 65 号令，自 2012 年 8 月 1 日起施行。

查阶段。

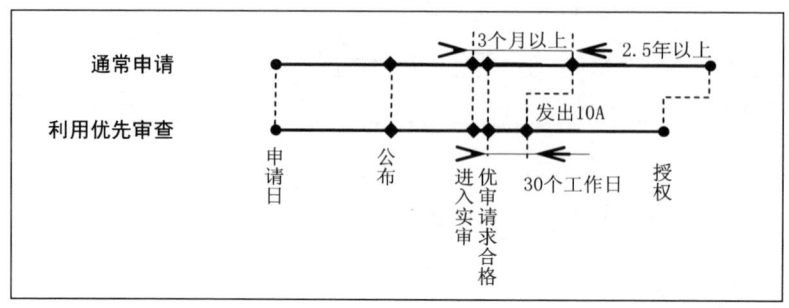

图8　利用优先审查制度缩短实质审查阶段

然而,《发明专利申请优先审查管理办法》第7条规定了"申请人办理优先审查手续的,应当提交下列材料:(一)由省、自治区、直辖市知识产权局审查并签署意见和加盖公章的《发明专利申请优先审查请求书》;(二)由具备专利检索条件的单位出具的符合规定格式的检索报告,或者由其他国家或者地区专利审查机构出具的检索报告和审查结果及其中文译文"。

(三)其他

除上述方法之外,还可以采用大家熟悉的方法来缩短发明专利申请的实质审查阶段。例如:

(1)将审查意见通知书中被指出存在问题而又不急于获得授权的权利要求剥离开来分案申请,从而加快其余权利要求的授权;

(2)灵活利用对权利行使无大碍的缩限修改,来相应地缩短实质审查时间,从而加快授权等。

综上所述,为了尽快获得发明专利的专利权,可以利用上述各种规章制度来提前其申请日、提前其公布日或缩短实质审查的时间,当然也可以适当将各方法进行组合来获得最佳效果。

浅议常用技术手段在创造性审查实践中的认定[*]

聂慧荃

一、引　言

　　专利申请的创造性审查是其能够获得最终授权的关键所在，因而在专利审查实践中保证创造性审查标准的客观化便具有至关重要的意义。在当今世界各国的专利制度中，由于各国主权的限制，尽管各国对创造性的规定在含义上并非完全一致，但是其创造性审查标准实质上都是"非显而易见性"标准。然而，在专利行政和司法实践中，"非显而易见性"的规定在某种程度上将专利的批准推入了自由裁量、主观性色彩较大的境地。

　　为此，在欧洲、美国以及我国的专利实践中，都试图将创造性判断标准客观化，例如将创造性判断的方法（或步骤）客观化、定义本领域普通技术人员等。欧洲专利局审查指南规定，为了客观地、可预期地判断是否具有发明创造性步骤，审查员应该采用所谓"三步法"（又称为"问题-方案法"）；在我国的专利审查实践中，参考欧洲专利局的做法，也常常使用这种"三步法"；根据美国最高法院 1966 年 Graham v. John Deere Co. 一案的判决，美国专利审查指南要求审查员按"Graham 四因素"进行非显而易见性审查，包括：现有技术的范围和内容；现有技术与所审查的权利要求之间的区别；相应领域的普通技术水平；辅助性考虑因素，包括商业上成功、长期渴望解决的需求、他人的失败等。在考虑上述因素后，确定该发明由该领域技术人员看来是否是显而易见的。[❶] 然而，无论采用哪种方法，最核心的仍然在于判断要求保护的发明对于本领域技术人员而言是否显而易见。

　　在对专利申请创造性的审查实践中，审查员最常用的理由便是该区别技术特征为本领域的常用技术手段。本文针对当前审查实践中的这种现状进行了讨论，并结合两个具体案例进行了具体分析，总结了其对审查实践中"常用技术手段"的把握和运用的启示。

---

　　[*]　原文刊于中华全国专利代理人协会所编《〈专利法〉第 22 条创造性理论与实践论文集》。

　　[❶]　U. S. PATENT AND TRADEMARK OFFICE（USPTO）. Manual of Patent Examining Procedure [M]. 8th ed. , 2001.

二、当前审查实践中运用"常用技术手段"所面临的现状

在具体的审查实践中，判断非显而易见性这一环节最容易掺入审查员或法官的主观意见，会不可避免地带有某些主观因素，也是最具争议的一个环节。特别是在当前中国专利审查实践中，我们可以在审查意见通知书中看到，在进行非显而易见性判断时，审查员频繁引用"常用技术手段"为依据来否定发明的创造性，而这也往往会成为申请人与审查员之间争议的焦点。尤其是在面对审查员的这种评述时，申请人普遍会认为审查员的这种认识从客观上缺少具体事实和证据支持。审查员之所以有这种认识源于其对技术方案的宏观把控以及对发明技术效果的深度理解，进而导致创造性审查标准在应用过程中主观性过强，使得发明最终能否获得授权并不取决于发明本身固有的创造性的高度，而纯粹取决于审查员个人的技术理解力及其对发明的认知度。

首先，在现行的《专利法》、《专利法实施细则》或《专利审查指南2010》当中均未涉及"常用技术手段"，而仅仅是简单提及了"所属技术领域的惯用手段"，但并未给出任何与之相关的明确定义或量化概念，也未指明其所涵盖的范围。这也导致申请人和审查员在面对"常用技术手段"这一问题上各持己见，争论不休。

在实践中，常用技术手段被视为属于公知常识的范畴。在《审查指南2001》第二部分第四章的"判断要求保护的发明对本领域的技术人员来说是否显而易见"的示例中，首次以举例的方式对公知常识的概念做了一个简单概括，并且在随后的《审查指南2006》中对该概念进行了修订。据此，我们可以将"公知常识"认定为"本领域中解决发明所要解决问题的惯用手段以及教科书、工具书等披露的解决发明所要解决问题的技术手段"。其中，我们不难看出，所谓的"常用技术手段"实质上等同于公知常识中的"本领域中解决发明所要解决问题的惯用手段"。

其次，对于公知常识的举证问题，《专利审查指南2010》第二部分第八章（实质审查程序）第4.10.2.2节中明确规定"审查员在审查意见通知书中引用的本领域的公知常识应当是确凿的，如果申请人对审查员引用的公知常识提出异议，审查员应当能够说明理由或提供相应的证据予以证明"；另外，《专利审查指南2010》第四部分第八章（无效宣告程序中有关证据问题的规定）中规定："主张某技术手段是本领域公知常识的当事人，对其主张承担举证责任。该当事人未能举证证明或者未能充分说明该技术手段是本领域公知常识，并且对方当事人不予认可的，合议组对该技术手段是本领域公知常识的主张不予支持。当事人可以通过教科书或者技术词典、技术手册等工具书记载的技术内容来证明某项技术手段是本领域的公知常识。"

尽管《专利审查指南 2010》中对于公知常识的举证责任作了如上规定，但在具体的审查与司法实践中，普遍认为常用技术手段属于本领域内公知事实的范畴而不需要提供证据支持。因此，在具体操作中，审查员通常可以将对比文件与所要保护的发明创造的技术方案之间的某些区别技术特征简单认定为常用技术手段便可否定受审方案的创造性，而并不受《专利审查指南 2010》中规定的上述举证责任的限制。虽然这可能有利于简化审查程序，加快审查进程，但也在一定程度上放大了审查员的自由裁量权，使得"常用技术手段"成为审查员在创造性审查实践中最频繁使用的理由之一。

最后，由于客观条件的限制，从事专利审查的审查员并不是严格意义上的本领域技术人员，跨专业审查的现象时有发生，而且部分审查员缺少具体领域的实践与生产经验。在这种情况下，常用技术手段判断的准确性难免会受到很大影响。

由于上述原因，现实中往往导致申请人与审查员眼中的常用技术手段各有不同，无法实现统一的认知标准，从而使得申请人在创造性高度的判断上存在诸多未知因素和不确定性，这将不可避免地会影响其发明创造的积极性。同时，由于当前法律法规对常用技术手段的概念及应用限制无明确规定，这也可能助长审查员在找不到合适证据或懒于寻找证据的情况下，盲目根据自身的技术水平作出"属于常用技术手段"的断言，进而导致以属于常用技术手段为由的权利滥用，无形之中使申请人的利益受到严重影响。

三、实践中应用"常用技术手段"进行创造性判断的几个实例

在对申请文件创造性的审查实践中，即便表面上看来是简单的技术特征，仍然可能赋予整个技术方案突出的实质性特点，并使之具有显著的技术进步。这就要求审查员必须真正站在本领域技术人员的角度，切实从技术方案的整体出发，注重对技术效果的理解，从而实现对所谓"常用技术手段"的客观性评价。以下将结合两个具体案例，对常用技术手段在审查实践中应用时可能存在的问题进行说明。

案例 1

请求保护的发明涉及一种造纸机中的设备，该设备包括：压榨部，其装备有一个或多个压榨压区；以及干燥部，其包括支撑纸幅的递纸部、竖直的冲击式干燥机以及一个或多个烘缸干燥机组，其中，第一烘缸干燥机组的第一干燥机烘缸跟随该竖直的冲击式干燥机。该设备的特征在于其包括直接吹向纸幅的预冲击式干燥机，该预冲击式干燥机紧位于该竖直的冲击式干燥机之前以便在竖直冲击之前预热该纸幅，该预冲击式干燥机的冲击长度为总纸幅冲击长度的 15%~35%。

在审查时，审查员认为请求保护的发明与检索到的对比文件之间的区别在于：“预冲击式干燥机的冲击长度为总纸幅冲击长度的15%～35%”，并认定该区别技术特征属于本领域的常用技术手段，因而该技术方案不具备创造性。

事实上，预冲击式干燥机的冲击长度这一数值范围并不属于本领域技术人员的常规选择，该技术特征并非是单纯的数值范围选择，其隐含决定了预冲击式干燥机和竖直的冲击式干燥机相互之间的位置关系以及两者在该设备中的设置情况。同时，该技术特征保证了预冲击式干燥机与竖直的冲击式干燥机之间的紧凑设置并且使得能量利用最有效。

具体而言，将纸幅从预冲击干燥机传递至竖直的冲击式干燥机时，幅材会因两者之间的距离出现一定程度的变冷。然而，上述技术特征能够最有效地避免在幅材传递过程中的能量浪费，而使得竖直的冲击式干燥机获得具有良好温度的幅材。

另外，预冲击式干燥机与竖直的冲击式干燥机之间的这种紧凑的结构设置，能够更快、更容易地打开造纸设备的冲击罩，这在幅材断裂时非常重要，能够有效避免织物或机器损坏。特别是在竖直的冲击式干燥机中，由于重力部件较小并且断裂的幅材更容易滑落，因而这一点尤为重要。

而在请求保护的发明中，由于预冲击式干燥机的冲击长度采用上述设置，使得预冲击式干燥机与竖直的冲击式干燥机之间的距离远小于现有技术中的情况；也就是说，在利用预冲击式干燥机进行预热之后，纸幅只需行进很短的距离便进入竖直的冲击式干燥机，因此能够获得很好的干燥效果。

由此可见，尽管从表面上看，该区别技术特征似乎是对于冲击式干燥机的冲击长度的一个简单数值范围的选择，但是对于造纸机所属领域的技术人员而言，冲击长度处于该界定范围内的预冲击式干燥机将会使得设备取得显著的技术效果，这显然不是常用技术手段的范畴。再者，本领域技术人员在实践中很难想到以此作为改进点来提高设备的干燥效果，整个技术构思的提出本身已然需要付出创造性劳动。

案例2

请求保护的发明涉及一种包括多个LED芯片单元的发光装置，该发光装置设有透光构件，透光构件与所述LED芯片单元相对应部分处形成多个透镜，用于确定从所述多个LED芯片单元发出的光的取向，并且透光构件除透镜之外的部分由金属制成。

在针对该权利要求的创造性评述中，审查员认为检索到的对比文件1公开了一种LED照明装置，在与各LED芯片714相对应部分处形成多个透镜765，用于对从LED芯片单元发出的光的方向进行调节，透镜765由环764支撑，共同构成透光构件；尽管该对比文件未公开环 764 的材质，但采用金属制成环 764 属于本领域的常用技术手段，因而认为该方案不具备创造性。

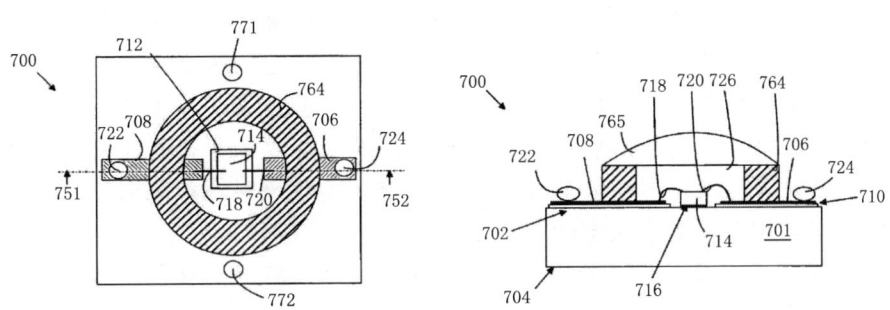

图 1　对比文件 1 参考图

从对比文件 1 的参考图可以看出，该 LED 装置 700 包括透镜 765 和环 764，其中，该环 764 附连在主体 701 的第一表面 702 上，该透镜 765 设置在环 764 上。另外，如图 1 所示，在主体 701 的第一表面 702 上形成有触点 706 和 708，环 764 设置在触点 706 和 708 上。

然而，对于本领域技术人员显而易见的是，如果环 764 具有导电性（例如，当其由金属制成时），触点 706 和 708 将会彼此电连接。因此，在面对该对比文件时，本领域技术人员为避免两触点之间的导通，根本不可能会想到用金属作为构成环 764 的材料。也就是说，从对比文件 1 的技术方案本身出发，其实质上已经排除了使用金属来构成环的可能性。

如此一来，即使本领域技术人员将对比文件 1 与本领域的常用技术手段相结合，也根本不可能得到"所述透光构件除所述透镜之外的部分由金属制成"。

另外，在请求保护的发明中，从其技术方案的整体而言，由于具备以上区别技术特征，该发光装置能够有效控制来自各 LED 芯片单元的光的取向，特别是由于透光构件除透镜之外的部分是由金属制成的，因此与其他完全由合成树脂、玻璃等制成的透光构件相比能够增强导热性能，从而进一步抑制 LED 芯片的结区温度的上升。

在该案例中，我们不难看出审查员忽视了被视为常用技术手段的特征与技术方案在整体上的技术关联。实际上，如果从技术方案的整体上来把控，即便是貌似常用技术手段的特征，也可能是整个技术方案中对发明的创造性作出巨大贡献的特征。可见，在进行常用技术手段认定时，必须对技术有充分的理解且保持审慎的态度。

四、以上案例对"在审查实践中应用常用技术手段"所给出的启示

从以上两个具体案例可以看出，在当前的审查实践中，"常用技术手段"的认定最易受到主观因素的影响，这明显不利于保证创造性审查标准的明确性和客观性。因此，尽可能做到"常用技术手段认定的客观化"是完善创造性审查标准的重中之重，也是我们能够在保护发明创造、激发创造性与避免降低创造性门槛、保证公众合理使用现有技术之间寻求平衡的决定性因素之一。笔者认为，从我国当前的技术发展与审查现状来看，应当着重从以下方面促进"常用技术手段认定的客观化"。

1. 从立法角度而言，应当尽快给出常用技术手段的具体定义或界定其所涵盖的范围

笔者认为，作为创造性的审查标准，应当是内容确定、含义明确，并且在实践中具有可操作性，只有如此才能够保证实施者的客观性和公平性。另外，申请人也能够在申请前基于此对发明创造的可专利性进行一个合理的预估，从而决定其所采用的技术保护策略。因此，细化常用技术手段的具体内容已经势在必行。

例如，笔者认为可以尝试将"常用技术手段"具体界定为：发明创造所属领域的技术人员在从事本领域设计、生产、工艺制造等活动中所普遍熟知及广泛使用的技术手段，所属领域的技术人员基于其所知晓的本领域基础技术水平，无须经过一般性逻辑推理或实验手段便可获得。

2. 始终以是否具备非显而易见性为标准

在进行创造性判断时，审查员应当确保从本领域技术人员的角度出发，从技术方案整体来看该区别技术特征是否属于常用技术手段的范畴；应当重视被视为常用技术手段的区别技术特征与其他特征的技术关联性，在对比文件与所谓常用技术手段的基础上，始终以本领域技术人员能否显而易见地得到要求保护的技术方案为指引。

由于受其自身技术水平、专业领域及工作实践的限制，审查员往往并非严格意义上的本领域技术人员，因而并不完全了解审查所涉及领域的常规设计、生产和制造工艺，也不容易受所涉及领域的固有思维的局限。在这种情况下，审查员就很有可能对发明的创造性高度认识不足。尤其是，审查员是在发明创造完成后才了解发明的技术方案，由于是在先获知了成形的技术构思后进行反推，这往往使其无形中先具备一定的创造力。

因此，笔者认为，在具体审查中，审查员应当充分了解要求保护的发明创造与对比文件之间技术构思的差异性，重视被认为常用技术手段的特征与其他技术特征之间的内在关联性及相互作用关系，关注其所获得技术效果的

区别性，从而力争对创造性评判的客观性，避免对常用技术手段的简单认定。

为使非显而易见性判断客观化，欧洲专利局审查指南提出了"可能-愿意"（would-could）方法：现有技术作为整体是否存在任何教导来使本领域技术人员面对该客观技术问题时，愿意而不只是可能考虑到该教导来修改或调整最接近现有技术，使之实现发明内容。

3. 基于技术背景，区别性对待成熟技术与新兴技术

我国在改革开放30年的时间里，科学技术获得了突飞猛进的发展。在不同的技术领域之间，创造性的难易程度与技术的成熟程度之间有着密不可分的联系。

在新兴技术领域，由于现有技术的公开内容有限，审查员通常可能不容易检索到影响专利性的对比文件，而且产品和方法可改进之处较多，由此发明创造的创造性高度往往容易得到保证，这种情况下对于常用技术手段的认定通常比较明确，不太容易产生争议。

与此相反，对于成熟设计领域而言，由于其已经是成熟设计、规模化生产，这时候的发明创造通常属于改进型发明，相较于开创性发明而言，创造性的高度往往难以判定，这时某些区别技术特征会很容易在审查中被误认为常用技术手段。特别是，在成熟设计领域，本领域技术人员容易受传统固有设计思维的局限，可能会在客观上排除一些设计方案，不可避免地具有某种技术偏见。比如，在规模化生产中，本领域技术人员受部件模块化、集成化的局限兼顾生产成本等因素的综合考虑，在解决某些技术问题时，会避免对某些常规部件进行改动，避免采用非常规设计，从而导致其事实上舍弃了采用某些技术手段的可能性。上述情况在配件生产领域尤其突出。因此，在成熟设计领域，本领域技术人员在技术上的突破程度及所带来的商业价值都有可能被低估。

因此，审查员在对成熟设计领域的发明创造进行创造性审查时，应当格外关注"被认定的常用技术手段"是否确实是本领域技术人员容易想到的，是否背离了本领域技术人员所具备的常规判断能力，是否克服了本领域技术人员的技术偏见，是否能够取得预料不到的技术效果。

4. 在审查实践中适当引入"专业技术人员"来辅助进行常用技术手段的判断

《专利审查指南2010》第四部分第八章（无效宣告程序中有关证据问题的规定）第5.3节"技术内容和问题的咨询、鉴定"中规定："专利复审委员会可以根据需要邀请有关单位或者专家对案件中涉及的技术内容和问题提供咨询性意见，必要时可以委托有关单位进行鉴定，所需的费用根据案件的具体情况由专利复审委员会或者当事人承担。"

另外，在目前的知识产权司法实践中，当专业技术问题成为审理案件的难点时，一些具有专门知识的专业人员逐步进入司法程序，它们凭借所掌握的专业知识对专门技术问题发表意见，以此来帮助法官对涉及专业技术的事实问题作出判断。❶

笔者认为，这对于审查员在进行常用技术手段的判断时同样具有借鉴意义。国家知识产权局可以通过高等院校、研究所、行业协会等机构建立自己的专业人员咨询委员会，利用专业技术人员作为审查员在技术方面的辅助人，借助其更好地掌握行业的发展动态，从而客观地评价申请人所提供理由的合理性，正确认定被争议的技术特征是否属于常用技术手段。必要时，可要求专业技术人员出具相应的专业意见，作为创造性最终裁定的依据。

5. 避免审查过程中对证据把握的不严谨性

由于现阶段法律法规对于何为"常用技术手段"及其所涵盖的技术内容并未提供清晰的概念，因此当申请人已经就被认为常用技术段的特征陈述具体理由后，审查员应当基于申请人的陈述进行针对性的反驳并提供相应的证据支持。作为行政机构的一员，审查员有义务确保证据的客观性和合法性。这对于保护申请人的合法权益，同时维护社会公众的利益都具有重要意义。

KSR 案例是自 20 世纪 70 年代以来，美国最高法院受理的第一件非显而易见性的专利案件。❷ 甚至可以说，KSR 案例为美国最高法院数十年来就专利的显而易见性问题上所作出的最重要的、影响最为深远的判决，对于现行的专利制度也将形成重大的冲击。

2007 年 4 月 30 日，美国最高法院就 KSR International v. Teleflex 一案作出判决：撤销美国联邦巡回上诉法院（CAFC）的判决，认定联邦巡回上诉法院在判断专利权利要求是否显而易见时，采用的"教导-启示-动机"审查标准有悖于最高法院所奉行的"扩展和灵活标准"，并直接裁定 Teleflex 公司的 Engelgau 专利权利要求具有"显而易见性"，因而无效，维持了密歇根州联邦地方法院对该案的简易判决。

美国最高法院的判决写道：创新应当是在现有技术基础上的进步，普通的改进不属于专利法规定的授予排他性权利的主题，如果对于普通的改进授予专利权，不仅不会促进发明创造，还会阻碍进行发明创造。美国最高法院还指出：联邦巡回上诉法院在判断 KSR 案中争议的权利要求的创造性时，对于"教导-启示-动机"标准的运用是狭隘、僵化的，联邦巡回上诉法院在

❶ 北京市高级人民法院知识产权庭. 知识产权诉讼实务研究［M］：北京：知识产权出版社，2008：335.

❷ KSR International Co. v. Teleflex Inc.[EB/OL].http：//www.supremecourtus.gov/opinions/06pdf/04-1350.pdf, 2006-10.

KSR 案对于显而易见的判断，不符合美国专利法第 103 条关于显而易见性的规定，也违反了最高法院有约束力的相关先例。最高法院认为：在判断技术方案的主题是否属于显而易见时，应当以更为宽泛、灵活的方式进行。

对于以上 KSR 案例，笔者认为，该案例的出现并不是偶然的，美国联邦巡回上诉法院所确定的"教导-启示-动机"虽然在客观上防止了审查人员在判定非显而易见性时的主观随意性，但却牺牲了一部分人的创新积极性，一定程度上阻碍了科技的创新。尽管现在的判断标准能够达到一定的平衡，但当这种过低的门槛可能影响到社会的进步的时候，就要打破这种已有的平衡，寻求一种更有利的判断标准从而达到新的平衡。

那么对于常用技术手段的认定而言，也可以借鉴 KSR 案的判决，在审查实践中可以给予专利审查员更多的灵活性，使审查员可以利用其丰富的专业技能，拒绝对于那些仅仅是利用常用技术手段对现有技术进行了显而易见改进的申请授予专利权。然而，审查员也应当担负起对其认定结果的举证义务，保证其审查的客观性与公正性。

五、结　语

随着我国经济技术及对外贸易的发展，知识产权问题已经成为我国与其他国家贸易争端的主要焦点之一。发达国家目前正在积极推行知识产权战略，努力通过各种途径寻求其他国家强化对其知识产权的保护，并以知识产权优势强化其竞争优势。随着专利申请的国际化，大量的国际专利进入我国，造成了大量国际专利技术的垄断从而影响国内企业技术创新的发展。

在这种情况下，如何认定"常用技术手段"对我国当前的知识产权保护战略具有至关重要的意义。总体而言，一方面，我们必须不断地总结经验并借鉴国外做法，为国内立法提供建议，使我国的专利制度向激励企业技术创新的方向更加完善和发展。另一方面，笔者认为，在审查中涉及常用技术手段的认定时，应当遵循"基于国情适度从宽的原则"，应当结合我国科技发展的宏观战略，在推动国民经济发展的重点领域采用适度从宽的认定原则，以形成合理的知识产权保护架构，从长远的角度推进我国科学技术的进步。

浅谈外观设计的设计自由度/设计空间

黄 艳

中国的外观设计专利体系自《专利法》第三次修改后（2009 年 10 月 1 日生效）产生了重大变化，其包括专利性门槛的提升。由于中国外观设计专利无须实质性审查，因此，现有设计［申请日（有优先权的，指优先权日）以前在国内外为公众所知的设计］与授权专利之间的专利性核查主要是在无效程序中进行的，以一般消费者为判断主体，同时基于"整体观察、综合判断"的原则。根据《专利审查指南 2010》的规定，一般消费者是一个假想的人。鉴于很难对一般消费者有一个统一的认定标准，中国近年的专利实践中，在一些案件里使用了"设计空间"的概念，以确定一般消费者的知识水平和认知能力。下面，就结合 OHIM 的一个案例中有关"设计自由度"的分析以及我国最高人民法院针对"设计空间"提出的观点进行讨论，进而提出我们的思考和建议。

一、OHIM 案例

在欧盟共同体外观设计体系中规定：与现有设计相比，外观设计只有具备新颖性和个性特征才能作为共同体外观设计受到保护。特别的，如果既没有相同的现有设计且其不同特征并非仅局限于非重要细节，则该外观设计被视为具备新颖性；并且，如果在考虑设计者开发外观设计时的自由度时，所浏览的外观设计的整体印象明显地不同于浏览现有设计时的整体印象，则该外观设计被视为具有个性特征。设计自由度越受到限制，足以对见多识广的用户产生不同的整体印象的设计之间的差别就可能越小。

近期，笔者阅读了由欧盟内部市场协调局（以下简称 OHIM）作出的第 ICD8611 号无效决定。在该决定中，基于 3 份现有技术，OHIM 宣告维持名称为 "watches（part of -）" 的第 001600560-0001 号注册式共同体外观设计（以下简称"涉案外观设计"）的权利，并结合"设计自由度"详细地进行了分析。

该涉案外观设计的附图见图 1：

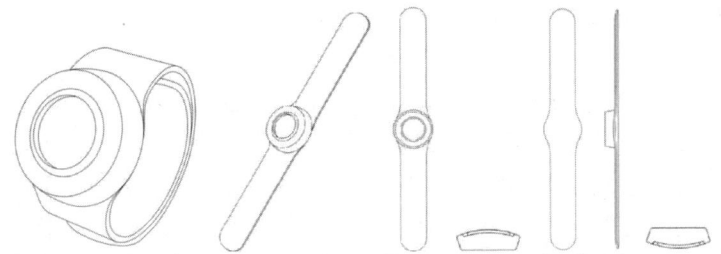

图 1　涉案外观设计的附图

在先设计 1 为法国外观注册 No. 042596-004，其附图如图 2 所示：

图 2　在先设计 1 附图

在先设计 2 为美国外观专利 No. D455,356 S，其附图如图 3 所示：

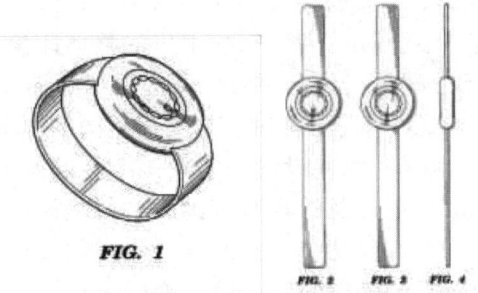

图 3　在先设计 2 附图

在先设计 3 为国际外观设计 No. DM/063479，其附图如图 4 所示：

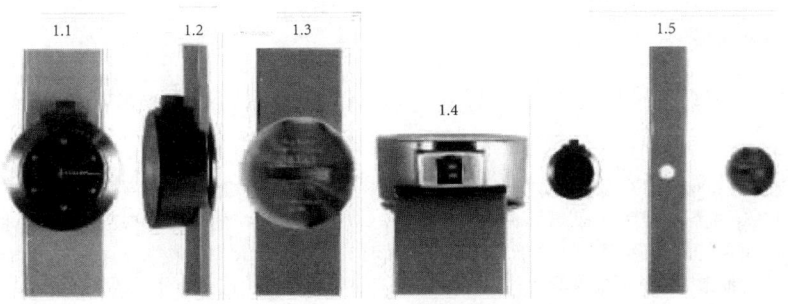

图 4　在先设计 3 附图

针对涉案外观设计以及现有设计披露的内容，OHIM 分别进行了特征对比。

对见多识广的用户产生的整体印象而言，OHIM 认为：见多识广的用户熟知与该涉案外观设计相关的产品的基本特征，并且了解到，这类表的设计者的设计自由度几乎是没有限制的，因为手表的特征（例如表壳或表带）可以具有各种不同的形状、图案和材料。对于设计者的限制仅仅在于手表必须要包括某种类型的表盘以显示时间，并且必须具有将表附接于手腕的装置。然而，手表市场越是琳琅满目，其差异性就越能够对个性特征❶（individual character，独特性）作出贡献。

OHIM 还认为：涉案外观设计与现有设计具有一些共同的基本特征，即圆形的表盘和表壳，这些都是常规特征，因此对见多识广的用户产生的整体印象仅占据很小的份量，而涉案外观设计所具有的巨大的突伸出的表壳以及宽的表框和宽的表带给该手表带来了更为结实、厚重的视觉印象，从而使其明显不同于现有设计的不那么庞大的传统手表的整体印象。

根据 OHIM 的上述认定，可以看到，其在判断整体印象是否与现有设计存在差异的过程中，当考虑设计者的设计自由度时，关注了实现手表的诸如圆形的表盘和表壳等基本功能的设计，并且认为，设计自由度越大，实现基本功能的惯常设计就越不会对见多识广的用户的整体印象产生视觉冲击。之后，OHIM 才根据该涉案外观设计与现有设计进行对比所认定的若干区别特征来判断从整体上涉案外观设计是否能够带来明显不同的视觉印象。

亦即，OHIM 是在考虑了哪些设计是实现该产品的基本功能的设计之后，才基本上确定设计自由度可延及的相对范围。也就是说，对于一项工业设计而言，当至少排除了所有仅起功能、技术效果作用的设计特征之外，其他的设计内容均可以认为属于设计者的设计自由度的范畴，只是一些外观设计的不同特征从整体上仅为"无关紧要的细节"，不能带给见多识广的用户不同的整体印象；而另一些外观设计的不同特征却能够带给见多识广的用户不同的整体印象。

二、中国实践

而中国《专利法》并没有外观设计必须具有个性特征才能被授予专利权

---

❶ 欧盟理事会 2002/6/EC 条例（2001 年 12 月 12 日）关于共同体外观设计（OJ EC No L 3 of 5. 1. 2002, p. 1）第 6 条"个性特征"：1. 在下列情形下，如果见多识广的用户在浏览外观设计时的整体印象明显地不同于其在浏览任何公之于众的外观设计时的整体印象，则该外观设计被视为具有个性特征：（a）对于非注册式共同体外观设计，在要求保护的该外观设计首次为公众所知的日期之前；（b）对于注册式共同体外观设计，提交注册申请的日期之前，如果要求优先权，则在优先权日期之前。2. 在评价个性特征时，应考虑设计者在开发外观设计时的自由程度。

的规定，而是规定授予专利权的外观设计与现有设计或者现有设计特征的组合相比应当具有明显区别。虽然，中国《专利法》没有对"明显区别"给出定义，但是根据最高人民法院（以下简称"最高院"）的司法解释，被诉侵权外观设计应当以一般消费者的观察能力基于外观设计的整体视觉效果进行综合判断。实践中，这一原则亦应用于评价授权外观的专利性。

近年来，在中国外观专利实践中，引入了"设计空间"的概念，与欧盟理事会 2002/6/EC 条例第 6 条中的"在评价个性特征时，应考虑设计者在开发外观设计时的自由程度"的规定相比，存在一定差异，例如根据中国《专利法》的规定，外观设计的相同/相似性的判断主体是一般消费者。❶

即便如此，笔者还是认为，欧共体外观设计保护制度的设计自由度的理念对于中国专利实践还是具有一定的借鉴意义的。

由于"一般消费者"是假想的人，在判断一项外观设计与现有设计是否具有明显区别时，总是要面临到底如何判断在该外观设计的领域内"一般消费者"的知识水平和认知能力，这往往致使人们难以脱离主观因素的影响，而容易导致判断方式以及结论方面的差异。作为原因之一，为了尽可能地进行客观公正的评判，近几年来业内在确定中国外观设计专利性时逐步开始引入"设计空间"的概念。

例如，作为 2010 年最高院知识产权审判案例收录的"摩托车车轮"外观设计专利无效系列案件（ZL 200630110998.7 和 ZL 200730112575.3），从一审到最高院都谈及"设计空间"。在该系列案件中，最高院提出，"设计空间"是指设计者在创作特定产品外观设计时的设计自由度。

最高院指出，设计者在特定产品领域中的设计自由度通常要受到现有设计、技术、法律以及观念等多种因素的制约和影响。特定产品的设计空间的大小与认定该外观设计产品的一般消费者对同类或者相近类产品外观设计的知识水平和认知能力密切关联。对于设计空间较大的产品领域而言，由于设计者的创作自由度较高，该产品领域内的外观设计必然形式多样、风格迥异、异彩纷呈，该外观设计产品的一般消费者就更不容易注意到比较细小的设计差别。相反，在设计空间受到很大限制的领域，由于创作自由度较小，该产品领域内的外观设计必然存在较多的相同或者相似之处，该外观设计产品的一般消费者通常会注意到不同设计之间的较小区别。

---

❶ 根据《专利审查指南 2010》的规定，在判断外观设计相同/相似时，应当基于涉案专利产品的一般消费者的知识水平和认知能力进行评价。作为某种类外观设计产品的一般消费者应当具备下列特点：（1）对涉案专利申请日之前相同种类或者相近种类产品的外观设计及其常用设计手法（常用设计手法包括设计的转用、拼合、替换等类型）具有常识性的了解。（2）对外观设计产品之间在形状、图案以及色彩上的区别具有一定的分辨力，但不会注意到产品的形状、图案以及色彩的微小变化。

从 OHIM 的上述案例以及最高院的上述法律解释不难看出，虽然双方均关注整体视觉效果，但是双方从不同的视角利用设计自由度/设计空间提出了各自对相同或相似性外观设计的判断基础及理解。例如，OHIM 认为产品的市场越丰富密集，设计上的差异性就越可以对个性特征作出贡献，而最高院却认为，创作自由度较高产品领域内的外观设计形式就会越丰富，细节上的差异就不容易被一般消费者所关注。

实际上，最高院已明确：在外观设计专利与在先设计相同或相近似的判断中，可以考虑设计空间或者说设计者的创作自由度，以便准确确定该一般消费者的知识水平和认知能力。在考虑设计空间这一因素时，应该认识到，设计空间的大小是一个相对的概念。同时，对于同一产品的设计空间而言，设计空间的大小也是可以变化的。在专利无效宣告程序中考量外观设计产品的设计空间，需要以专利申请日时的状态为准。

三、结 论

笔者认为，最高院对工业外观设计的"设计空间"进行了详细的阐释和解析，对将来具有一定的指导意义，是对采用整体观察、综合判断进行相似性判断的一种有益的补充。但是，在提及"设计空间"时引入了新的群体"设计者"，其并不同于中国《专利法》意义上的"一般消费者"，二者不可等同和混用。就笔者看来，在中国，当前"设计空间"这一概念的提出应主要用于准确确定"一般消费者"的知识水平和认知能力，因此应从不同的角度来考虑设计空间延伸的范围，而不宜局限于某一视角。

总之，在进行外观设计的相同或相似性判断时，不论是否引入"设计空间"这一概念，对于一项工业品外观设计而言，其"设计空间"都是客观存在的，可以从多个角度来考虑。切不可因引入设计者的"设计空间"而改变"一般消费者"的法律属性。另外，"设计空间"的延及范围应在合理认定仅起功能、技术效果作用的设计特征的前提下予以确定。为此，建议当事人在论及设计空间的大小时进行充分的举证。

浅探外观设计专利的申请程序和维权问题

黄　艳

外观设计专利是一种颇具价值却又经常被忽视的知识产权保护形式，但其能在公司的经营战略上发挥重要的作用。通常，外观设计专利被应用在能够依靠产品的美感提升品牌魅力并且打造客户忠诚度的产业中。苹果（Apple）公司所使用的覆盖了 iPhone 和 iPad 的老辣的进攻型外观设计专利战略就是这样一个实例。

在本文中，我们将就中国外观设计专利的申请程序和维权的最新问题和发展情况进行探讨。

一、关于外观设计专利的申请程序

对于外观设计专利申请而言，中国专利局在进行初步审查之后即授予专利权，而不进行关于现有设计或抵触申请的检索。

1. 简要说明

根据《专利法》❶第 59 条第 2 款的规定，在中国的外观设计专利中需要有简要说明。法律规定"外观设计专利权的保护范围以表示在图片或者照片中的产品的外观设计为准，简要说明可以用于解释图片或者照片所表示的该产品的外观设计"。此外，《专利法实施细则》❷第 28 条还规定，简要说明尤其应当写明外观设计的设计要点。

事实上，《专利审查指南 2010》❸（以下简称《审查指南》）和司法解释❹都已指出，如果将授权的外观设计与现有设计或被诉侵权产品进行对比，应当采用"整体观察、综合判断"的一般原则。然而，目前还不明确法院将如何使用简要说明，尤其是其中描述的设计要点。目前，大多数从业人员以广泛定义要被授权的外观设计的形式来撰写简要说明。

2. 相似外观设计

《专利法》第 31 条第 2 款规定，同一产品两项以上的相似外观设计，或

---

❶　指的是 2009 年 10 月 1 日生效的经第三次修正的中国《专利法》。

❷　指的是 2010 年 2 月 1 日生效的《专利法实施细则》。

❸　指的是 2010 年 2 月 1 日生效的《专利审查指南 2010》。

❹　指的是 2010 年 1 月 1 日生效的《最高人民法院关于审理侵犯专利权纠纷案件应用法律若干问题的解释》。

者用于同一类别并且成套出售或者使用的产品的两项以上外观设计（相似外观设计），可以作为一件申请提出，这是为了解决一件申请的相似外观设计不能被专利保护的问题。

顾名思义，相似外观设计是指"一般情况下，经整体观察，如果其他外观设计和基本外观设计具有相同或者相似的设计特征，并且二者之间的区别点在于局部细微变化、该类产品的惯常设计、设计单元重复排列或者仅色彩要素的变化等情形"的那些外观设计。参见《审查指南》第一部分第三章第9.1.2节。

具体的，《审查指南》还强制性限制一件外观设计专利申请中的相似外观设计不得超过10项。但糟糕的是，如果申请人试图在另一申请中请求保护超出这10项相似外观设计之外的其他实施例，则这两件申请或其中之一可能会因为重复授权❶而被驳回。因此，为了有效获取更大的保护范围，建议对代表设计构思的基本设计的选择，以及对无专利性差异的相似外观设计进行专利申请都要非常慎重。

值得一提的是，一旦以现有设计为基础宣告一件多项外观设计专利权无效，被无效的仅仅是那些无效宣告理由成立的实施例。

3. 参考图

参考图通常用于表明使用外观设计的产品的"用途、使用方法或者使用场所"，参见《审查指南》第一部分第三章第4.2节。

目前的法院判决表明，至少在某些情况下，在确定保护范围时，使用状态参考图被排除于专利保护范围之外，例如"沙发床（普士）"案❷。

在"沙发床（普士）"案中，中级人民法院维持了复审委员会所作出的无效决定（2007年，北京市第一中级人民法院行政诉讼案第97号）。中级人民法院的观点为：使用状态参考图通常用于确定产品类别，不应当作为判断是否与在先设计相同或相近似的依据；当变化状态产品的外观设计作为被比设计时，对其变化状态的比较应以使用状态图为准。

该案上诉后，高级人民法院（下文简称"高院"）维持一审判决。高院认为，《审查指南》中对"使用状态参考图"的上述规定包含了确定该外观设计产品保护范围和显示保护对象的作用，其并不违反《专利法》、《专利法实施细则》的相关规定（2008年，北京高级人民法院行政诉讼案第10号）。

---

❶ 在美国通过使用虚线表示请求保护多个实施例的形式在中国是不被允许的。

❷ 在专利复审委员会作出的一项外观专利"沙发床（普士）"的无效宣告请求审查决定中认定，对于具有变化状态的产品的外观设计权的保护范围的确定，应当以该专利中所有标注有主视图、后视图、左视图、右视图、俯视图和/或仰视图的视图为依据，而没有考虑使用状态参考图，从而作出该外观设计无效的审查决定（第8897号无效宣告请求审查决定）。

因此，考虑到中国的专利实践，申请人应当在外观设计专利中慎重选择和使用"参考图"。

4. 变化状态图

变化状态图被用于一些在销售和使用时呈现不同状态的产品。《审查指南》第四部分第五章第 5.2.5.2 节规定，对比设计的每个视图在与涉案专利进行比较时均可被使用，而对于该涉案专利而言，应当以其使用状态所示的外观设计与对比设计进行比较，其判断结论取决于对产品各种使用状态的外观设计的综合考虑。与使用状态参考图不同，这里的使用状态图作为确定专利性的独立的来源，而两者仅有的区别是前者是被命名为"参考图"提交的。❶ 就此而言，附图名称的选择可能会对中国外观设计专利权的确权和维权产生影响。

推荐的是：采用变化状态图或使用状态图来保护产品的变化状态。

二、关于外观设计专利的无效

外观设计专利权可通过无效程序来挑战其合法性。无效的理由包括缺乏新颖性、创造性，以及与在先权利相冲突，参见《专利法》第 23 条。

1. 一般消费者

就确定外观设计专利相对于现有设计是否具备新颖性或创造性而言，应当基于一般消费者对该外观设计专利产品的知识水平和认知能力进行对比和评价，参见《审查指南》第四部分第五章第 4 节。最近，最高人民法院审理的案件对这种假想的人应该具有什么能力提供了一些解释，即差不多达到一般设计人员的水平。

在本田诉专利复审委员会（2010 年，最高人民法院行政诉讼案第 3 号）和浙江今飞机械集团公司诉浙江万丰摩托有限公司（2010 年，最高人民法院行政诉讼案第 5 号）的案件中，最高人民法院认为，一般消费者除了对外观设计的整体外形轮廓进行观察之外，还能够知晓惯常的设计手段、相关技术和已有设计，以及对外观设计的革新到底是什么，即设计空间（设计自由度）。根据最高人民法院的判例，一般消费者会理解一个特定产品的设计空间（设计自由度），并据此对外观设计的专利性以及专利侵权作出判断。

2. 综合判断

在前述本田一案中，最高人民法院确认"整体观察、综合判断"作为一般原则，并进一步考虑一般消费者所理解的设计空间的认知。法院认为，当

---

❶ 在"沙发床（普士）"一案中，中级人民法院还认为，"使用状态参考图"中可以出现外观设计专利保护范围之外的形状、图案或色彩；而"使用状态图"中禁止出现外观设计专利保护范围之外的形状、图案或色彩。如果两者具有相同的功能，则会在外观设计专利申请初步审查中出现混淆。

某些类型的汽车所采用的外观设计具有或显示出作为一个整体的惯常结构时，这将限制对这种类型汽车的整体视觉效果的影响。反之，局部外观设计特征上的差异，例如前大灯的设计、侧视图和后视图，会对作为一个整体的汽车的设计带来显著的视觉效果，而导致一般消费者能够将该被诉外观设计专利与现有设计区分开。最终，该被诉外观设计专利维持有效。

三、结　论

《专利法》的第三次修正对外观设计专利的授权标准带来了相当大的变化。我们随时准备向我们的客户提供有关这些问题的最新发展和变化，以帮助我们的客户实施其经营战略，并在中国取得成功。

浅谈相似外观设计与成套产品的外观设计

董雅会　金相允

单一性原则被各国专利制度普遍采用。该单一性原则，是指一件专利申请应当限于一项发明创造。但是，单一性原则并不是绝对的。关于外观设计专利申请，《专利法》❶ 第 31 条第 2 款规定："一件外观设计专利申请应当限于一项外观设计。同一产品两项以上的相似外观设计，或者用于同一类别并且成套出售或者使用的产品的两项以上外观设计，可以作为一件申请提出。"本条款规定了外观设计专利申请的单一性原则，同时也规定了两种外观设计专利申请的单一性原则的例外情形：相似外观设计和成套产品的外观设计。

本文将浅谈相似外观设计与成套产品的外观设计的异同及申请策略等。

一、同一产品两项以上的相似外观设计

作为外观设计专利申请的单一性原则的例外情形的相似外观设计，是第三次修改《专利法》时新增加的。修改前的《专利法》所规定的单一性原则的例外情形仅包括成套产品的外观设计，而且修改前的《专利法实施细则》❷第 13 条第 1 款规定，同样的发明创造只能被授予一项专利。

然而，在实践中，设计人在对同一产品的外观提出新的设计方案时，往往会形成一个基本的设计方案和多个与该基本的设计方案相似的设计方案，申请人普遍希望对基本的设计方案和相似的设计方案均获得专利保护。在《专利法》修改前，如果在一件外观设计专利申请中要求保护同一产品的多个相似的外观设计，会因为不符合修改前的《专利法》❸ 第 31 条第 2 款的规定而被驳回；如果分别提出多项外观设计专利申请，会被认为是"同样"的发明创造，而因为不符合修改前的《专利法实施细则》第 13 条第 1 款的规定被驳回。相似外观设计专利申请制度正是为了克服上述令申请人左右为难的情况而增加的。

就同一产品两项以上的相似外观设计提出合案申请时，应当在简要说明中指定其中一项外观设计作为"基本设计"。"相似"的含义为：经整体观察，如果其他外观设计和基本外观设计具有相同或者相似的设计特征，并且

---

❶　《专利法》指的是自 2009 年 10 月 1 日起施行的经过第三次修改的《中华人民共和国专利法》。

❷　修改前的《专利法实施细则》指的是自 2001 年 7 月 1 日起施行的经过第三次修改前的《中华人民共和国专利法实施细则》。

❸　修改前的《专利法》指的是自 2001 年 7 月 1 日起施行的经过第三次修改前的《中华人民共和国专利法》。

二者之间的区别点在于局部细微变化、该类产品的惯常设计、设计单元重复排列或者仅色彩要素的变化等情形，则通常认为二者属于相似的外观设计。[1]

下面列举了几种同一产品两项以上的相似外观设计允许合案申请的情形。

设计1主视图

设计1立体图

设计2主视图

设计2立体图

图 1　相似外观设计（1）

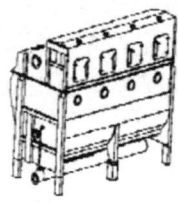

设计1立体图

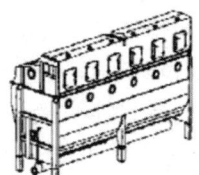

设计2立体图

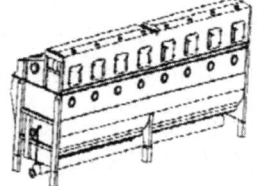

设计3立体图

图 2　相似外观设计（2）

设计1主视图

设计2主视图

设计3主视图

设计4主视图

图 3　相似外观设计（3）

---

❶　摘自中华人民共和国国家知识产权局制定的《专利审查指南 2010》第一部分第三章第 9.1.2 节。

设计1主视图　　　　设计2主视图　　　　设计3主视图

图 4　相似外观设计（4）

还应当注意：就同一产品两项以上的相似外观设计提出合案申请，应当涉及同一产品的外观设计，其产品名称、类型及其用途应当相同；一件外观设计专利申请中的相似外观设计不得超过 10 项。❶

作出"一件外观设计专利申请中的相似外观设计不得超过 10 项"这样的规定的原因在于，在为申请人提供方便的同时，也要注意防止由于合案申请的设计方案数量过多而给专利申请的审查和专利权的保护带来过大的负担。

然而，从 2010 年 2 月 1 日起实施《专利法实施细则》❷ 以来的情况来看，中国知识产权行业对于这一规定的争议较大，普遍认为一件外观设计专利申请中的相似外观设计最多包括 10 项不够满足需求。我们相信，在以后修改《专利法》及《专利法实施细则》时这一条款被修改的可能性很大。

二、用于同一类别并且成套出售或者使用的产品的两项以上外观设计

《专利法实施细则》第 35 条第 2 款规定：《专利法》第 31 条第 2 款所称同一类别并且成套出售或者使用的产品的两项以上外观设计，是指各产品属于分类表中同一大类，习惯上同时出售或者同时使用，而且各产品的外观设计具有相同的设计构思。这里所说的"分类表"指《国际外观设计分类表》。

关于"成套出售或者使用的产品"的含义，是指习惯上同时出售或者同时使用，例如由咖啡杯、咖啡壶、糖罐、牛奶壶等产品组成的多件咖啡器具。

关于"相同的设计构思"，是指各产品的设计风格是统一的，即对各产品的形状、图案或者其结合以及色彩与形状、图案的结合所作出的设计是统一的。

三、相似外观设计和成套产品的外观设计的专利权以及保护

同一产品两项以上的相似外观设计专利申请和成套产品的两项以上外观设计专利申请，一旦授予专利权，一件专利中的各项外观设计是各自独立的，

---

❶ 《专利法实施细则》第 35 条第 1 款所规定的内容。

❷ 《专利法实施细则》指的是自 2010 年 2 月 1 日起施行的经过第三次修改的《中华人民共和国专利法实施细则》。

其中一项被宣告无效，并不必然导致其余各项必然无效。

在宣告相似外观设计专利权无效时，不能以某项相似外观设计与基本外观设计相似为理由宣告其无效。

专利权必须同时转让，就相似外观设计专利权而言，其属于一件专利权，必须要同时转让；基本外观设计不存在的情况下（比如被无效），其他所有的相似外观设计仍必须要同时转让。

四、申请策略

单一性要求是授予专利权的形式条件，而不是授予专利权的实质性条件。对于相似外观设计和成套产品的外观设计的专利申请而言，在授予专利权之前，国家知识产权局可以以不符合如《专利法》第 31 条第 2 款的规定而驳回；而在授予专利权之后，即使认为一项外观设计专利权不符合该条规定，也不能以不具备单一性为理由请求宣告该外观设计专利权无效。

鉴于此，对于申请人来说，在一种产品的外观设计具有相同或者相似的设计特征的情况下，一件外观设计专利申请可以尽可能提出多项相似外观设计（但要满足不得超过 10 项的规定）。即便在初步审查中被审查员指出不相似，也可以通过分案申请来应对。

若针对同一产品作出 10 项以上例如 15 项的相似的外观设计方案，在提出相似外观设计专利申请时，鉴于当前的一件相似外观设计专利申请不得超过 10 项的规定，我们建议申请人将 15 项外观设计分成两件相似外观设计专利申请或者将设计方案缩减为 10 项。通过下面的示意图（图中的数字代表各设计方案，假设相邻的设计方案最相似）来具体描述如下两种方案。方案 1：将 15 项设计方案分为 1~7 和 8~15 的两件相似外观设计专利来提交申请，第一件将设计 4 作为"基本设计"，第二件将设计 12 作为"基本设计"。

方案 2：删除其中相似度高（这里所说的"相似度高"是指设计特征的变化小）的 5 个设计方案，而只保留 10 项。

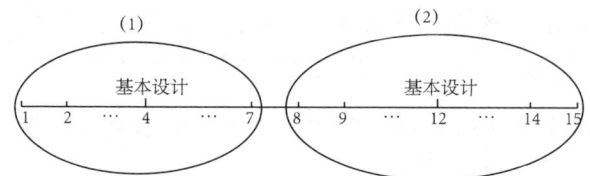

图 5　方案 1：两件相似外观设计专利申请

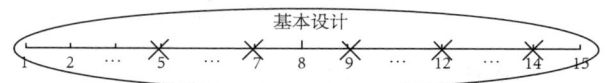

图 6　方案 2：一件相似外观设计专利申请

在采用方案 1 的情况下，由于 15 项设计具有相同或者相似的设计特征，当两件相似外观设计专利申请都被授予专利权后，可能以因第一件专利权（设计 1~7）中的某项外观设计（例如设计 7）与第二件专利权（设计 8~15）中的一项外观设计（例如设计 8）实质相同而属于同样的发明创造为理由，两者中的一项外观设计专利权被宣告无效，即，宣告设计 7 的外观设计专利权或者设计 8 的外观设计专利权无效。但是，即使设计 7 的外观设计专利权被宣告无效，设计 1~6 的外观设计专利权并不必然被宣告无效，所以能够获得最大的保护范围。

需要注意的是，在一件外观设计专利申请中，不能既包含两项以上的相似外观设计，又包含成套产品的两项以上外观设计。如果一件申请中包含了由咖啡杯、咖啡壶、牛奶壶和糖罐组成的成套产品，其中咖啡杯、咖啡壶、牛奶壶和糖罐分别又有 10 项相似外观设计，应当按照相似外观设计进行申请。如果分别提交 10 件由咖啡杯、咖啡壶、牛奶壶和糖罐组成的成套产品的外观设计专利申请，很可能会被认为 10 件成套产品的外观设计属于同样的发明创造而仅能获得一件专利权。

五、结 论

相似外观设计及成套产品的外观设计的合案申请制度，在专利申请、专利权保护等方面均有利于申请人，如果在外观设计专利申请中灵活利用这些制度来确定申请策略，申请人能够在多付出小额费用的情况下获得最大且最稳定的保护范围。

六、附 录

最后，将相似外观设计与成套产品的外观设计之间的区别总结于下面的表 1，供参考。

表 1 相似外观设计与成套产品外观设计的区别

	对产品的要求	判定原则	举 例
相似外观设计	同一产品	具有相同或者相似的设计特征	如图 1~图 4 等
成套产品的外观设计	属于《国际外观设计分类表》中同一大类的产品	习惯上同时出售或者同时使用；具有相同的设计构思	由咖啡杯、咖啡壶、糖罐和牛奶壶组成的咖啡器具

对中国专利实践中的权利要求包含"坏点"的讨论

吴小瑛

对于寻求在中国发展的生命科学企业，中国专利的保护力度和可预见性值得着重关注。是否在中国提交专利申请和如何准备申请文件，知识产权界业内人士也需要针对一些中国特色的审查实践和司法实践给予考虑。本文依据两个最新案例，就权利要求包含不可实施的技术方案，对专利申请的授权和授权后专利的稳定性的影响进行了讨论，并提出我们的观点和建议。

一、何谓"坏点"

"坏点"是指一件申请中，说明书记载的一些无法解决技术问题、实现发明目的的具体技术方案。在概括权利要求范围时，当概括的权利要求的范围包含了这些无法解决技术问题、实现发明目的的具体技术方案时，则该权利要求包含了所谓的"坏点"。

权利要求中包含"坏点"，在专利审查阶段是否会影响专利的授权，专利授权后是否会影响专利权的稳定？本文将以两件最新案例为例对该问题进行探讨。

二、法律依据

权利要求书应当以说明书为依据，清楚、简要地限定要求专利保护的范围（《中华人民共和国专利法》第三次修正，第 26 条第 4 款）。

权利要求书应当以说明书为依据，是指权利要求应当得到说明书的支持（《专利审查指南 2010》第二部分第二章第 3.2.1 节）。

如果权利要求的概括包含申请人推测的内容，而其效果又难以预先确定和评价，则应当认为这种概括超出了说明书公开的范围。如果权利要求的概括使所属技术领域的技术人员有理由怀疑该上位概括或并列所包括的一种或多种下位概念或选择方式不能解决发明或实用新型所要解决的技术问题，并达到相同的技术效果，则应当认为该权利要求没有得到说明书的支持（《专利审查指南 2010》第二部分第二章第 3.2.1 节）。

三、案　例

案例1

此专利是专利号为 93109045.8、发明名称为"立体选择性糖基化方法"、专利权人为伊莱利利公司的发明专利。该专利的权利要求 1 涉及一种 β 异头物富集的二氟核苷的制备方法，权利要求中限定了反应原料及用量、反应步骤、反应温度等。该专利所要解决的技术问题是，提供一种适于得到 β 异头物富集的二氟核苷的制备方法。在说明书公开的 104 个实施例中出现了 11 个得不到 β 异头物富集的二氟核苷的实施例，而这 11 个实施例所涉及的对现有技术作出贡献的反应条件均落入权利要求 1 记载的技术特征的范围内。也就是说，权利要求 1 包含 11 个坏点。本案争议的焦点在于权利要求 1 能否得到说明书的支持。

该专利在 2006 年被提出专利无效宣告请求，专利复审委作出无效宣告审查决定（第 9525 号），宣告该专利权全部无效。该决定认定的主要内容是：权利要求 1 包含的范围包括了过多无法预见 β 异头物富集的二氟核苷产物的情形，所属领域技术人员要通过实验选择能够实现权利要求 1 所要保护的技术方案需要进行大量的反复实验或者过度劳动，因此权利要求 1 不符合《专利法》第 26 条第 4 款的规定。

伊莱利利公司不服该决定提起行政诉讼，认为第 9525 号决定中采用的"大量的反复实验或者过度劳动"的认定理由没有在《专利法》和《审查指南》中规定，不是判断权利要求是否得到说明书支持的正确依据。本专利说明书中虽然有不能得到 β 异头物的实施例，但本领域技术人员会注意到说明书中大量实施例作为一个整体给出的暗示，不会仅仅注意实验中的一个或者某些数据。

北京一中院一审 [（2007）一中行初字第 922 号] 中，一审判决撤销第 9525 号无效决定。一审认为，评价权利要求是否得到说明书支持应当以"权利要求书中的每一项权利要求所要求保护的技术方案应当是所属技术领域的技术人员能够从说明书充分公开的内容得到或概括得出的技术方案，并且不得超出说明书公开的范围"作为标准，复审委在无效审查决定中引入"如果所属技术领域的技术人员根据说明书的教导并考虑本领域普通技术知识，仍然需要进行大量的反复实验或者过度劳动才能确定权利要求概括的除实施例以外的技术方案能否实现"作为标准评判本专利权利要求是否得到说明书支持，其评判的出发点不符合《专利法》第 26 条第 4 款的规定，是不适当的。在评述本专利权利要求是否得到说明书支持时，复审委主要是从无法得到 β 异头物富集物的数据出发进行判断，而没有全面考虑说明书中有关发明目的、技术方案的记载以及大量能够得到 β 异头物富集物的实施例和数据。在判断本专利权利要求是否得到说明书支持时，应将两者结合起来进行综合评判。

专利复审委及无效请求人不服一审判决，向北京高院提起上诉。在北京高院的二审 [（2008）高行终字第 451 号] 中，北京高院判决撤销一审判决、维持第 9525 号决定。北京高院认为，权利要求所要求保护的技术方案应当是所属技术领域的技术人员能够从说明书充分公开的内容中得到或概括得出的技术方案，并且不得超出说明书公开的范围。如果权利要求的概括包含申请人推测的内容，而其效果又难以预先确定和评价，则应当认为这种概括超出了说明书公开的范围。如果权利要求的概括使所属技术领域的技术人员有理由怀疑该上位概括或并列所包括的一种或多种下位概念或选择方式不能解决发明或实用新型所要解决的技术问题，并达到相同的技术效果，则应当认为该权利要求没有得到说明书的支持。在说明书中披露的部分实施例不能达到发明目的或发明效果的情况下，应当认为该权利要求没有得到说明书的支持。

专利权人伊莱利利公司不服北京高院的二审判决，向最高人民法院（以下简称最高院）请求再审，最高院驳回了该再审请求。最高院认为，权利要求所要求保护的技术方案应当是所属技术领域的技术人员能够从说明书充分公开的内容中得到或概括得出的技术方案，并且不得超出说明书公开的范围。如果权利要求的概括使所属技术领域的技术人员有理由怀疑该上位概括或并列概括所包括的一种或多种下位概念或选择方式不能解决发明所要解决的技术问题，并达到相同的技术效果，则应当认为该权利要求没有得到说明书的支持。本专利说明书中有 11 组数据不能制备得到 β 异头物富集的二氟核苷。根据说明书的描述，影响该立体选择性方法的因素较多，权利要求 1 概括的制备方法的各因素的范围是十分宽泛的。本领域技术人员有合理的理由认为，除了 11 个不能实施的情况外，该权利要求 1 的概括还包含众多其他不能解决发明所要解决的技术问题的技术方案，所属技术领域的技术人员不容易从各种反应条件的排列组合中通过常规实验或者合理推测得出能够解决技术问题的技术方案，而是需要大量反复实验或过度劳动才能确定权利要求 1 的范围。因此，权利要求 1 没有得到说明书的支持，不符合《专利法》第 26 条第 4 款的规定。

案例 2

申请号为 200480006411.6 的中国发明专利申请，发明名称为 "α-淀粉酶家族酶的变体"，在实质审查程序中于 2010 年 2 月 12 日被驳回，然后于 2012 年 3 月 16 日被复审委维持驳回。维持驳回的理由是由于说明书包含不能解决技术问题的实施例，导致本领域技术人员无法合理预期权利要求 1 中的酶变异体都可以实现发明目的，由此权利要求 1 得不到说明书的支持。该申请中，权利要求 1 请求保护分离和/或纯化的酶变异体,该酶变异体相对于参照酶而言发生了氨基酸突变 A230V,或者在 A230V 突变的基础上于 230 以外的位点发生取代、插入或缺失一个或几个氨基酸残基。所述酶变异体具有增强的酶外特异性,即提高的总水解活性和/或减弱的内活性。虽然实施例中大部分的酶变异体具有增强的酶外特异性,但实施例 4 中包含了在 Tabium CGTase 的基础上构建的双变异体 A231V/F260E 显示出的相互排斥的结果,该酶变异体的水解活性相对于野生型酶而言不仅没有提高反而降低了。因此,本领域技术人员有理由怀疑在参照酶的基础上将 A230V 突变与 230 以外位点取代、插入或缺失一个或几个氨基酸残基的突变进行组合后,所得到酶变异体的水解活性相对于野生型酶而言可能会提高,也可能会降低,因而根据说明书公开的上述内容本领域技术人员无法合理预期在参照酶的基础上发生 A230V 组合突变后所得到的酶变异体都可以实现发明目的。因此,权利要求 1 不符合《专利法》第 26 条第 4 款的规定。

四、专利局、复审委和法院对"坏点"的态度

从上述两个案例可以看到,在授权程序以及授权后程序中,针对包含"坏点"的权利要求,专利局、复审委和法院都得出该权利要求得不到说明书支持的结论。但是,从上述各结论中,我们可以看到所述权利要求包含了"坏点"并不是得出得不到说明书支持结论的直接原因。决定和判决中的结论是:"权利要求所要求保护的技术方案应当是所属技术领域的技术人员能够从说明书充分公开的内容中得到或概括得出的技术方案,并且不得超出说明书公开的范围。如果权利要求的概括使所属技术领域的技术人员有理由怀疑该上位概括或并列所包括的一种或多种下位概念或选择方式不能解决发明所要解决的技术问题,并达到相同的技术效果,则应当认为该权利要求没有得到说明书的支持。"

五、思考和建议

上述案例可能会给人们带来疑问,如果申请人并未披露这些坏点,或者在权利要求 1 中将所述坏点排除掉,那么案例 2 的权利要求 1 能否被授权,或案例 1 授权后的权利要求是否不会被宣告无效?尽管专利局、复审委和法院的结论中都没有将"坏点"作为导致权利要求得不到说明书支持的直接原因,但我们是否可以这样理解,它的存在为本领域技术人员提供了"有理由怀疑该上位概括或并列所包括的一种或多种下位概念或选择方式不能解决发明所要解决的技术问题,并达到相同的技术效果"的证据,也就是使得这种怀疑是有理由的。

事实上，在专利审查期间，审查员不可能对专利申请人提交的实验结果进行验证。对于审查案件的审查员在不经过实验验证的前提下，如何做到"有理由怀疑"呢？最信服的途径是找证据。当一件专利申请文件中包含了不可解决技术问题的技术方案时，可以说，这就给本领域技术人员提供了"有理由怀疑"的证据。设想上述案件中如果没有记载这些"坏点"，本领域技术人员怎样做到"有理由怀疑"呢？这样看来，不将"坏点"写入说明书中对专利权人是有利的。可是，隐瞒真实数据的做法会违背有些国家对诚实披露实验数据要求的严格规定。因此，重要的是，如何既能诚实地披露数据，又能不损害专利权人的利益，争取适当的权利要求保护范围，并维护专利权的稳定性。

针对案例 1，权利要求存在"坏点"是在专利授权后的无效宣告请求程序中被指出的。对于专利权人，在无效宣告请求审查阶段的修改是十分受限的。此时的修改方式通常为删除技术方案或权利要求，或者是合并权利要求来缩小权利要求的保护范围。如果此时通过删除坏点或包含坏点的范围来修改权利要求 1，则通常是不会被允许的。这就需要在撰写权利要求时具有层次，为日后的修改留有余地。在撰写权利要求书时，不仅要注意权利要求的概括是否合适，更重要的是要体现独立权利要求与从属权利要求之间以及各级从属权利要求之间的层次性，既有包含"坏点"的大范围，又有排除"坏点"的小范围，从而既可能获得尽可能大的保护范围，又能稳定保护核心技术方案。以这样有层次的权利要求应对多个国家或地区的审查要求，即便在审查要求较为严格的中国，也能避免如案例 1 被无效时专利无路可退的被动局面。

浅析我国专利侵权判定中的权利要求保护范围的扩张与限制之新进展[*]

张永康

一、引　言

在专利侵权判定中需要对权利要求中记载的技术方案进行解释，来确定专利权利要求的保护范围的界限。在对该界限进行确定时，为了平衡专利权人与社会公众的利益，我国已发展出了等同原则、禁止反悔原则以及捐献规则等对专利权利要求的保护范围进行扩张与限制的各种原则及规则。

首先，关于等同原则，该原则是上述原则及规则中最早确立的，是在最高人民法院于2001年6月22日发布的《最高人民法院关于审理专利纠纷案件适用法律问题的若干规定》（以下简称《2001年专利纠纷案件规定》）的司法解释中明确确立的。

等同原则的含义是，专利权的保护范围既包括权利要求书中明确记载的技术特征所确定的范围，也包括与该技术特征相等同的特征所确定的范围。等同原则扩张了专利权利要求的保护范围，从而更加有力地保护了专利权人的利益，鼓励了发明创造。

其次，关于禁止反悔原则，该原则正式确立是在最高人民法院于2009年12月28日发布的《关于审理侵犯专利权纠纷案件应用法律若干问题的解释》（以下简称《2009年专利纠纷案件解释》）的司法解释中确立的，但在我国的司法实践中已经早有运用。[●]

禁止反悔原则的含义是，专利申请人、专利权人在专利授权或者无效宣告程序中，对权利要求、说明书进行修改或者进行意见陈述，放弃了某些技术方案，该放弃的技术方案不应在侵权判定时又纳入专利权保护范围。禁止

---

[*] 原文刊于知识产权出版社2011年3月出版的《实施国家知识产权战略　提升专利代理服务能力》一书中。

[●] 虽然在最高人民法院于2001年6月22日发布的《最高人民法院关于审理专利纠纷案件适用法律问题的若干规定》中，没有明确确立禁止反悔原则，但是最高人民法院民三庭在"如何理解最高人民法院关于专利法（2001）法释字第21号司法解释"中，认为"人民法院应当准确适用禁止反悔原则，将等同原则的适用限制在一个合理的范围内"。另外，在很多的早期判决中也采用了禁止反悔原则，例如，"手机自动隐形拨号报失的实现方法"发明专利侵权纠纷案［北京市第一中级人民法院（2005）一中民初字第3254号、北京市高级人民法院（2005）高民终字第1262号］。

反悔原则限制根据等同原则主张侵权的权利要求的等同特征范围，排除了在专利申请的审批过程中通过限制性修改或者限定性的陈述放弃了的等同特征。

再次，关于捐献规则，该规则是在上述《2009 年专利纠纷案件解释》的司法解释中首次确立的。

捐献规则的含义是，仅在说明书或者附图中描述而在权利要求中未记载的技术方案，视为专利人将该技术方案已经捐献给社会，该技术方案不会通过等同原则而再次包含在该专利权利要求的保护范围内。

对上述原则及规则的理解以及运用，对相关当事人来说是至关重要的。但是，由于上述原则及规则的适用往往与案件所涉及的具体技术方案等实际情况直接相关，司法解释中只能作出一些原则性规定，从而导致在对上述原则及规则的理解以及运用上产生诸多困难。

本文中，笔者希望通过对相关法律规定以及人民法院的一些近期案例进行分析，探究上述司法解释字面含义背后的真正内涵，以求能够使读者更加深入地了解并能运用上述原则来保护自己的合法权益。

二、专利权利要求保护范围的扩张与限制

1. 等同原则

目前，世界各国专利法大都规定专利权的保护范围以权利要求的内容为准。从理论上讲，按照该规定，应该严格按照权利要求的字面内容来判断被控侵权物或方法是否落入专利权的保护范围，以保证权利要求的公示性。

然而，由于语言文字的局限性，申请人在撰写权利要求时，难以真实地界定出自己的发明的界限。而且，由于技术的发展，一些器件更新换代，在撰写权利要求时不可能想到技术特征在侵权发生时成为公知常识，如果实施的客体与权利要求相比没有实质上的不同，则不被认定为侵权，则将不能很好地补偿专利权人为社会作出的贡献，造成专利权人与社会公众的利益失衡，影响申请人进行发明创造的热情，进而导致专利制度鼓励发明创造、推动发明创造的应用、提高创新能力、促进科学技术进步和经济社会发展的作用受到影响。

因此，各国普遍建立了等同原则，以对权利要求所表达的保护范围作出一定程度扩张，从而不仅对表现在权利要求的文字上的技术方案进行保护，而且还能够对文字背后真实地体现发明创造的实质的技术方案进行保护。

具体到我国，在《2001 年专利纠纷案件规定》第 17 条中，对于等同原则有如下规定：

"专利法第五十九条第一款❶所称的'发明或者实用新型专利权的保护范围以其权利要求的内容为准，说明书及附图可以用于解释权利要求'，是指专利权的保护范围应当以权利要求书中明确记载的必要技术特征所确定的范围为准，也包括与该必要技术特征相等同的特征所确定的范围。

等同特征是指与所记载的技术特征以基本相同的手段，实现基本相同的功能，达到基本相同的效果，并且本领域的普通技术人员无须经过创造性劳动就能够联想到的特征。"

那么，该如何理解上述条文呢？

下面，笔者从 3 个方面结合相关法律规定以及人民法院的一些案例对上述条文进行分析，以期能够使上述的原则性规定明晰化，便于读者掌握。

（1）上述司法解释中的必要技术特征是指在权利要求中记载的所有的技术特征。

首先，在《2009 年专利纠纷案件解释》第 7 条中，对于判定被诉侵权技术方案是否落入专利权的保护范围，有如下规定：

"人民法院判定被诉侵权技术方案是否落入专利权的保护范围，应当审查权利人主张的权利要求所记载的全部技术特征。

被诉侵权技术方案包含与权利要求记载的全部技术特征相同或者等同的技术特征的，人民法院应当认定其落入专利权的保护范围；被诉侵权技术方案的技术特征与权利要求记载的全部技术特征相比，缺少权利要求记载的一个以上的技术特征，或者有一个以上技术特征不相同也不等同的，人民法院应当认定其没有落入专利权的保护范围。"

根据该 2009 年的司法解释，在侵权判断时，应当审查权利要求中记载的全部技术特征，也即权利要求中记载的全部技术特征均对权利要求的保护范围具有限定作用，由此上述《2001 年专利纠纷案件规定》中的必要技术特征应该改读为全部技术特征。

另外，在 2005 年作出的"混凝土薄壁筒体构件"实用新型专利侵权纠纷案❷判决中，最高人民法院的审理法官也认为：

"凡是专利权人写入独立权利要求的技术特征，都是必要技术特征，都不应当被忽略，而均应纳入技术特征对比之列。"

综上可以明确，专利权的保护范围应当以权利要求书中明确记载的全部技术特征所确定的范围为准，也包括与上述技术特征相等同的特征所确定的

---

❶ 在《最高人民法院关于审理专利纠纷案件适用法律问题的若干规定》第 17 条原文中，记载的是"第五十六条第一款"，但是由于《专利法》进行了修改，该"第五十六条第一款"应该对应于"第五十九条第一款"。

❷ 最高人民法院（2005）民三提字第 1 号。

范围。

（2）等同特征的判断标准是"与所记载的技术特征以基本相同的手段，实现基本相同的功能，达到基本相同的效果，并且本领域的普通技术人员无须经过创造性劳动就能够联想到的特征"，国家标准仅是一种行政管理措施，在国家标准中公布的可替换技术方案，并不能作为是否是等同特征的判断标准。

首先，关于等同特征的判断标准，最高人民法院民三庭在"如何理解最高人民法院关于专利法（2001）法释字第 21 号司法解释"中，进一步解释为：

"等同特征必须同时具备两个条件：

一是与权利要求中的技术特征以基本相同的手段、实现基本相同的功能、达到基本相同的效果。也就是说，等同特征与权利要求书中明确记载的技术特征必须在手段、功能和效果 3 个方面都没有实质性区别，而是简单的替换或者变换。这是认定构成等同的客观标准。

二是本领域的普通技术人员无须经过创造性劳动就能够联想到，或者说对本领域的普通技术人员是显而易见的。这是认定构成等同的主观标准。所谓普通技术人员，是一个抽象的概念，应当以侵权发生期间该专利所属领域的平均知识水平为标准衡量，是指具有该技术领域中的一般知识和能力的技术人员，既不是该领域的技术专家也不是不懂技术的人。在司法实践中，由于普通技术人员是一个假想的群体，因此界定的难度较大。在判断被控侵权产品与原告权利要求中的技术特征是否构成等同时，如果委托有关技术鉴定单位进行比较鉴定或者请相关技术领域专家发表意见，则应当考虑鉴定结论或者专家意见是否是从普通技术人员的角度出发作出的。"

由此，可以看出最高人民法院民三庭将《2001 年专利纠纷案件规定》中的判断等同的标准进一步解释成包括客观标准（三个基本相同）和主观标准（一个容易想到）两个部分，要构成等同特征必须同时满足上述两个部分。

另外，在"一种防治钙质缺损的药物及其制造方法"发明专利侵权纠纷案❶中，最高人民法院认为：

"国家药品监督管理局国药管安（2000）131 号《通知》附件中，虽然公布了可以'用盐酸赖氨酸 10g 代替谷氨酸 10g'，但这只是国家采用的一种行政管理措施，并非专利法意义上的等同替换，不能据此就认为被诉侵权产品的盐酸赖氨酸技术特征与涉案专利权利要求 1 记载的'谷氨酸或谷氨酰胺'技术特征等同。"

---

❶ 最高人民法院（2009）民提字第 20 号。

综上可以明确，等同特征的判断标准，是包括客观标准和主观标准两个部分的"以基本相同的手段，实现基本相同的功能，达到基本相同的效果，并且本领域的普通技术人员无须经过创造性劳动就能够联想到"的标准，而所谓的国家标准仅是一种行政管理措施，在国家标准中公布的可替换技术方案并不能替代上述标准来判断技术特征之间是否等同。

（3）功能性技术特征所覆盖的范围，是通过说明书和附图描述的该功能性特征的具体实施方式及其等同的实施方式来确定。

首先，在《2009年专利纠纷案件解释》第4条中，对于功能性特征限定的范围，有如下规定：

"功能性特征限定的范围，应当结合说明书和附图描述的该功能性特征的具体实施方式及其等同的实施方式，确定该技术特征的内容。"

而且，早在作出上述司法解释之前，在"除臭吸汗鞋垫"实用新型专利侵权纠纷案❶中，北京市高级人民法院的法官也认为，"对于采用功能性限定特征的权利要求，不应当实现该功能的具体方按照其字面含义解释为涵盖了能够实现该功能的所有方式，而是应当受到专利说明书中记载的方式的限制。具体而言，在侵权判断中应当对功能性限定特征解释为仅仅涵盖了说明书中记载的具体实现方式及其等同方式。"

综上可以明确，权利要求中记载的功能性特征所限定的范围，应当结合说明书和附图描述的该功能性特征的具体实施方式及其等同的实施方式来确定，而不能解释为涵盖了能够实现该功能的所有方式。

2. 禁止反悔原则

禁止反悔原则限制根据等同原则主张侵权的权利要求的等同特征范围，排除了在专利申请的审批过程或无效过程中通过限制性修改或者限定性的陈述放弃了的等同特征。

具体到我国，在《2009年专利纠纷案件解释》第6条，对于禁止反悔原则，有如下规定：

"专利申请人、专利权人在专利授权或者无效宣告程序中，通过对权利要求、说明书的修改或者意见陈述而放弃的技术方案，权利人在侵犯专利权纠纷案件中又将其纳入专利权保护范围的，人民法院不予支持。"

那么，该如何理解上述条文呢？

下面，笔者从4个方面结合相关法律规定以及人民法院的一些案例对上述条文进行分析，以期能够将上述原则性规定明晰化，便于读者掌握。

（1）"通过对权利要求、说明书的修改或者意见陈述而放弃的技术方案"

---

❶ 北京市高级人民法院（2006）高民终字第367号。

指的是放弃了技术方案的客观结果，而不论造成该结果的原因。

首先，关于《2009年专利纠纷案件解释》中对于禁止反悔原则的规定，最高人民法院的法官解释❶为：

"该条强调的是，专利申请人、专利权人客观上所作的限制性修改或者意见陈述。该修改或者陈述是权利人主动还是应审查员要求所为，与专利授权条件是否具有法律上的因果关系以及是否被审查员最终采信，均不影响该规则的适用。"

其次，在"一种防治钙质缺损的药物及其制造方法"发明专利侵权纠纷案❷中，最高人民法院的法官认为：

"根据禁止反悔原则，专利申请人或者专利权人在专利授权或者无效宣告程序中，通过对权利要求、说明书的修改或者意见陈述而放弃的技术方案，在专利侵权纠纷中不能将其纳入专利权的保护范围。因此，涉案专利权的保护范围不应包括'葡萄糖酸钙'技术特征的技术方案。"

在上述审理中，法官判断为禁止反悔时，如上述文章中所述，并没有论证该修改或者陈述的原因以及该修改或者陈述与专利授权条件是否具有法律上的因果关系。

综上可以明确，只要是书面声明或者修改对专利权利要求的保护范围作了限制承诺或者部分地放弃了保护，不管该修改或者陈述的原因，以及该修改或者陈述与专利授权条件是否具有法律上的因果关系，均禁止反悔。

（2）在审查或无效阶段中，只要是书面声明或者修改对专利权利要求的技术特征作了限制承诺或者部分地放弃，则限制承诺或者部分地放弃后的该技术特征限定的范围与之前的技术特征限定的范围之间的范围均为放弃的内容，禁止反悔。

上述观点，是笔者在考察了禁止反悔原则的历史演变而得出的。

具体地讲，在2003年，最高人民法院曾发布了《关于审理专利侵权纠纷案件若干问题的规定》（会议讨论稿），在该会议讨论稿第13条中，对于禁止反悔原则，有如下规定：

"专利申请人或者专利权人在专利授权或者维持程序中，为满足专利法及其实施细则关于授予专利权的实质性条件的要求，在专利文件中或者通过书面声明或者记录在案的陈述等，对专利权保护范围所作的具有限制作用的任何修改或者意见陈述，对权利人有约束作用，在专利侵权诉讼中禁止反悔。

人民法院不应将禁止反悔的技术内容认定为权利要求记载的技术特征的

---

❶ 孔祥俊，王永昌，李剑.《最高人民法院关于审理侵犯专利权纠纷案件应用法律若干问题的解释》适用的若干问题 [J]. 电子知识产权，2010（2）：76-80.

❷ 最高人民法院（2009）民提字第20号。

等同特征。但对于在专利授权和/或维持程序中修改过的技术特征，在适用禁止反悔原则之后，权利人仍然有权主张对保留的该技术特征适用等同原则。"

该 2003 年的会议讨论稿虽未正式生效，但是经过最高人民法院正式公布，必然对当时的侵权判定产生很大的影响，将其与上述《2009 年专利纠纷案件解释》中的关于禁止反悔的记载进行比较，可以看出在 2009 年颁布的司法解释中，删除了"但对于在专利授权和/或维持程序中修改过的技术特征，在适用禁止反悔原则之后，权利人仍然有权主张对保留的该技术特征适用等同原则"的规定。由此应该可以明确，对于在专利授权和/或维持程序中修改过的技术特征，在适用禁止反悔原则之后，权利人不能再主张对保留的该技术特征适用等同原则，也即限制承诺或者部分放弃后的该技术特征限定的范围与之前的技术特征限定的范围之间的范围均为放弃的内容，禁止反悔。

究其原因，等同原则所体现的利益平衡是社会公众与专利权人之间的动态平衡，其内涵会随着时代的演变而演变。当今社会技术发展迅速，各个领域的发明创造也日益密集，如果过度适用等同原则，将会严重影响到新技术开发的自由空间，也为社会公众创立了太多的模糊区域。通过如上所述适用禁止反悔原则，除能够对等同原则进行一定的限制之外，还能够减少模糊区域，更大程度地保证权利要求的公示作用，使社会公众能够容易地自行判断能够自由实施的空间。

（3）被控侵权人未主张适用禁止反悔原则时，人民法院可以主动适用禁止反悔原则。

在"汽车地桩锁"发明专利侵权纠纷案❶中，最高人民法院的法官认为："禁止反悔原则是对认定等同侵权的限制。现行法律以及司法解释对人民法院是否可以主动适用禁止反悔原则未作规定，为了维持专利权人与被控侵权人以及社会公众之间的利益平衡，亦不应对人民法院主动适用禁止反悔原则予以限制。因此，在认定是否构成等同侵权时，即使被控侵权人没有主张适用禁止反悔原则，人民法院也可以根据业已查明的事实，通过适用禁止反悔原则对等同范围予以必要的限制，以合理地确定专利权的保护范围。"

由此可以明确，被控侵权人未主张适用禁止反悔原则时，人民法院可以主动适用禁止反悔原则。

（4）禁止反悔的是专利申请人、专利权人在专利授权或者无效宣告程序中，通过对权利要求、说明书的修改或者意见陈述而放弃的技术方案，而非在其他场合下放弃的技术方案。

对于该问题，笔者认为专利文件是一个法律文件，其能够产生法律效力

---

❶ 最高人民法院（2009）民申字第 239 号。

在于其履行了申请的审查甚至无效过程中的审查的法律程序，只有在上述过程中的申请人或专利权人的陈述或修改才是该法律文件的不可或缺的一部分。

而在其他程序中，例如其他的诉讼程序中的陈述则是对该法律文件的解释过程，该过程中的解释具有自认的效力，但该效力应该仅限于该诉讼程序，在其他诉讼程序中并不必然产生自认或禁止反悔的效果。

3. 捐献规则

由于如在第二节所论述的等同原则的适用，导致专利申请人在申请专利时会采取如下的策略。即在专利申请时，权利要求采用比较下位的概念，而在说明书及附图中又对其进行扩张解释，然后，在侵权诉讼中主张说明书所扩张的部分属于等同特征。

由于在专利申请时权利要求采用比较下位的概念容易获得授权，而在侵权诉讼中又能够将其扩张到说明书中所记载的范围，因此通过该策略能够扩大专利权的保护范围。

然而，专利制度的价值不仅要体现对专利权人利益的保护，同时也要维护权利要求的公示作用。因此，为了维护权利要求书的公示性和平衡专利权人与社会公众的利益关系，在很多国家的侵权判定中都确立了捐献规则及其类似的规则。❶

具体到我国，在《2009 年专利纠纷案件解释》第 5 条，对于捐献规则有如下规定：

"对于仅在说明书或者附图中描述而在权利要求中未记载的技术方案，权利人在侵犯专利权纠纷案件中将其纳入专利权保护范围的，人民法院不予支持。"

这一原则是随着《2009 年专利纠纷案件解释》的司法解释的颁布而引入我国的，在实践中尚未有任何的司法案例。在此，笔者提出以下两点，与读者一同讨论学习。

（1）仅在说明书或者附图中描述，而在权利要求中未记载的权利要求的技术方案的技术特征的等同特征构成的技术方案以及在权利要求中未记载的覆盖权利要求的技术方案以外的部分的技术方案是被捐献的技术方案。

首先，最高人民法院的孔祥俊法官等在《电子知识产权》杂志上撰文，对捐献规则解释如下：❷

"该规则是指，对于说明书记载而权利要求未记载的技术方案，视为专利权人将其捐献给社会公众，不得在专利侵权诉讼中主张上述已捐献的内容属

---

❶　例如，美国法院确立了捐献规则及可预见规则，日本确立了意识限定论。

❷　孔祥俊，王永昌，李剑．《最高人民法院关于审理侵犯专利权纠纷案件应用法律若干问题的解释》适用的若干问题 [J]．电子知识产权，2010（2）：76-80．

于等同特征所确定的范围。捐献规则实质上是对等同原则适用的一种限制。之所以如此规定是考虑到以下情形：专利申请人有时为了容易获得授权，权利要求采用比较下位的概念，而说明书及附图又对其扩张解释。专利权人在侵权诉讼中主张说明书所扩张的部分属于等同特征，从而不适当地扩大了专利权的保护范围。实际上，这是一种"两头得利"的行为。专利制度的价值不仅要体现对专利权人利益的保护，同时也要维护权利要求的公示作用。"

由此可以理解，该条司法解释的目的是通过制止上述"两头得利"的行为，以维护权利要求的公示作用。因此，仅在说明书或者附图中描述而在权利要求中未记载的权利要求的技术方案的技术特征的等同特征构成的技术方案，以及仅在说明书或者附图中描述而在权利要求中未记载的覆盖权利要求的技术方案以外的部分的技术方案，均可认定为是上述两头得利的行为，应该要制止。

另外，在孔祥俊法官等在《人民法院》杂志上刊登的撰文❶中，还举出如下案例：

"权利要求明确记载某一个技术特征是"三个螺丝"，而说明书又称，该螺丝也可以是 5 个、8 个、10 个。如果被控侵权产品的相应特征是 8 个螺丝，权利人主张该 8 个螺丝与 3 个螺丝等同，依据司法解释第 5 条的规定，权利的上述主张不能成立，因为，权利要求未记载而说明书或者附图描述的技术方案，不属于等同特征限定的专利权保护范围。"

上述案例作为举例，明确说明了仅在说明书或者附图中描述而在权利要求中未记载的权利要求的技术方案的技术特征的等同特征构成的技术方案，应被认定为是两头得利的行为，应该要制止。

（2）被捐献的技术方案仅包括说明书中明确记载的技术方案，不应该包括与说明书中明确记载的技术方案相等同的技术方案。

关于该点，笔者想说明的是，被捐献的技术方案仅包括说明书中明确记载的技术方案，而不应该包括与说明书中明确记载的技术方案相等同的技术方案。

也即，在上述案例中，说明书中记载该螺丝也可以是 5 个、8 个、10 个，如果被控侵权产品的相应特征是 7 个螺丝，权利人主张该 7 个螺丝与 3 个螺丝等同，此时，不能依据司法解释第 5 条的规定，将上述 7 个螺丝与 5 个、8 个、10 个螺丝相等同而进行捐献，相反应该可以按照上述等同原则判断该 7 个螺丝与 3 个螺丝是否等同。

究其原因是，虽然上述规定是为了控制两头得利的行为，但是，从捐献

---

❶ 孔祥俊，王永昌，李剑.《最高人民法院关于审理侵犯专利权纠纷案件应用法律若干问题的解释》适用的若干问题 [J]. 人民法院，2010（3）：27-33.

的法理来说，更应该考虑当事人的意愿，不能要求其捐献本不想捐献的部分。

三、实务上的指导

1. 专利权人（申请人）的应对策略

（1）通过"三个基本相同、一个容易想到"的上述判断标准来证明被控侵权的技术特征与权利要求中记载的技术特征相等同。

如上述第二节等同原则中所述，等同特征的判断标准是"与所记载的技术特征以基本相同的手段实现基本相同的功能，达到基本相同的效果，并且本领域的普通技术人员无须经过创造性劳动就能够联想到的特征"。

因此，若要想专利权的保护范围能够通过等同原则而扩张到覆盖被控侵权对象，必须按照上述判断标准，积极证明被控侵权对象中的技术特征满足下述两个条件：一是与权利要求中的技术特征以基本相同的手段、实现基本相同的功能、达到基本相同的效果；二是本领域的普通技术人员无须经过创造性劳动就能够联想到，或者说对本领域的普通技术人员是显而易见的。

（2）主张所涉技术特征不是功能性特征。

如上述第二节等同原则中所述，功能性特征所限定的范围，应当结合说明书和附图描述的该功能性特征的具体实施方式及其等同的实施方式来确定，而不能解释为涵盖了能够实现该功能的所有方式，由此将该特征严格限定在了说明书中所记载的具体实施方式及其等同的实施方式上，有时可能会导致保护范围不适当地缩小。

因此，在侵权判定时，某项技术特征是否作为功能性特征来对待，有时变得非常重要。而由于对于文字的表现方式的认识的不同，同一个技术特征有可能既可认定为是功能性限定特征也有可能认定为是结构性特征，此时应极力主张该特征并非是功能性限定，而是一种结构性特征。

（3）在撰写权利要求时，撰写适当保护范围的权利要求。

如上述第二节禁止反悔原则中所述，在审查或无效阶段中，只要是书面声明或者修改对专利权利要求的技术特征作了限制承诺或者部分地放弃，则限制承诺或者部分地放弃后的技术特征与原先的技术特征之间的所有范围均为放弃的内容。明确地说，只要进行了限制性陈述或部分地放弃，则对于该修改后技术特征就不能再适用等同原则。

因此，笔者认为，申请人在撰写权利要求时，撰写策略不应该是撰写保护范围尽可能宽的权利要求，而应该是撰写保护范围适当的权利要求。

为了使读者容易理解上述观点，笔者举出下述案例：

专利申请的权利要求为一种氮化硅陶瓷的生产方法，其烧成时间为2～12小时。审查员检索到一篇申请日前公开的对文件，其公开的烧成时间为10小时。申请人将权利要求改为一种氮化硅陶瓷的生产方法，其烧成时间为 2~8 小时，然后获得了授权。

获得授权后的专利权人发现有人实施的氮化硅陶瓷的生产方法的烧成时间为 8.5 小时。此时，能否适用等同原则来判断实施氮化硅陶瓷的生产方法者侵权呢？

笔者认为，此时已经不能认定实施该氮化硅陶瓷的生产方法为侵权行为。原因在于，申请人将烧成时间限制为 2~8 小时，就已经放弃了 8~12 小时之间的所有"领地"，应该适用禁止反悔原则。此时，即使实施该氮化硅陶瓷的生产方法的烧成时间非常接近于权利要求的烧成时间，也不能再适用等同原则了。

但是，假如在撰写时能够撰写一个合适的范围，而非尽可能大的范围，例如将权利要求撰写为一种氮化硅陶瓷的生产方法，其烧成时间为 2~8 小时，则此时可以主张等同侵权，而不受禁止反悔的制约。

（4）说明书中记载的所有的实施方式都要涵盖在权利要求书中。

如上述第二节捐献规则中所述，仅在说明书或者附图中描述而在权利要求中未记载的权利要求的技术方案的技术特征的等同特征构成的技术方案，以及在权利要求中未记载的覆盖权利要求的技术方案以外的部分的技术方案是被捐献的技术方案。

因此，若想自己的发明成果不会作为捐献的技术方案而被社会公众所自由使用，就应该将说明书中记载的所有的实施方式都涵盖在权利要求书中而不让上述条件成立。

2. 被控侵权人的应对策略

（1）通过"三个基本相同、一个容易想到"的上述判断标准来证明被控侵权的技术特征与权利要求中记载的技术特征不相等同。

如上述第二节等同原则中所述，等同特征的判断标准是"与所记载的技术特征以基本相同的手段实现基本相同的功能，达到基本相同的效果，并且本领域的普通技术人员无须经过创造性劳动就能够联想到的特征"。

因此，若要想专利权的保护范围不能够通过等同原则扩张到覆盖被控侵权对象，必须按照上述判断标准，积极证明被控侵权对象中的技术特征不能满足下述两个条件：一是与权利要求中的技术特征以基本相同的手段实现基本相同的功能、达到基本相同的效果；二是本领域的普通技术人员无须经过创造性劳动就能够联想到，或者说对本领域的普通技术人员是显而易见的。因而，被控侵权对象中的技术特征与权利要求中记载的技术特征不等同。

（2）主张所涉技术特征是功能性特征。

如上述第三节中所述，由于对于文字的表现方式的认识的不同，同一个技术特征有可能既可认定为功能性限定特征也有可能认定为结构性特征，此时应极力主张该特征是功能性限定，从而将该技术特征的范围限定到说明书和附图描述的该特征的具体实施方式及其等同的实施方式上。

（3）查看申请档案，寻找禁止反悔的证据。

如上述第二节禁止反悔原则中所述，在审查或无效阶段中，只要是书面声明或者修改对专利权利要求的技术特征作了限制承诺或者部分地放弃，则限制承诺或者部分地放弃后的技术特征与原先的技术特征之间的所有范围均为"通过对权利要求、说明书的修改或者意见陈述而放弃的技术方案"，明确地说，只要进行了限制性陈述或部分地放弃，则对于该修改后技术特征就不可能再适用等同原则。

尽管在认定是否构成等同侵权时，即使被控侵权人没有主张适用禁止反悔原则，人民法院也可以根据业已查明的事实，通过适用禁止反悔原则对等同范围予以必要的限制，以合理地确定专利权的保护范围。但由于能否适用禁止反悔原则在多数情况下将直接关系到诉讼的胜败，作为被控侵权人应该主动查阅专利权的审查档案，仔细研究，查看其修改及陈述对技术特征的限定，寻找禁止反悔适用的依据，从而尽可能地争取到有利的诉讼结果。

（4）研究被控侵权物（方法）实施的技术是否是属于未在权利要求中记载但却在说明书中有明确记载的技术。

如上述第二节捐献规则中所述，仅在说明书或者附图中描述而在权利要求中未记载的权利要求的技术方案的技术特征的等同特征构成的技术方案，以及在权利要求中未记载的覆盖权利要求的技术方案以外部分的技术方案是被捐献的技术方案。

因此，作为被控侵权人应该仔细阅读说明书及其附图，寻找仅在说明书或者附图中描述而在权利要求中未记载的权利要求的技术方案的技术特征的等同特征构成的技术方案，以及仅在说明书或者附图中描述而在权利要求中未记载的覆盖权利要求的技术方案以外部分的技术方案，来查看自己实施的技术方案是否是专利权人已经捐献的技术方案，如果是，则作为证据证明自己不侵权。

四、结 论

本文详细介绍并分析了在专利侵权判定中，在确定专利权利要求的保护范围的界限时所采用的等同原则、禁止反悔原则以及捐献规则等的对专利权利要求的保护范围进行扩张与限制的各原则及规则。

对上述原则及规则的理解以及运用，对相关当事人来说是至关重要的。但是，由于上述原则及规则的适用往往与案件所涉及的具体技术方案等实际情况直接相关，司法解释中只能作出一些原则性规定，不可能划定统一的标准，从而导致在对上述原则及规则的理解以及运用上产生诸多困难。

因此，笔者希望通过对相关法律规定以及人民法院的一些近期案例进行全面分析，探究上述司法解释字面含义背后的真正内涵，以求能够使读者更加深入地了解并能运用上述原则来保护自己的合法权益。

由于相关案例并不是很充足，而且今后法院的立场也会随着时代的推进而演变，文中的许多观点难免有出自笔者的个人主观推断之处，敬请读者谅解。

鉴于笔者水平和经验有限，不妥之处敬请各位业界前辈、同仁批评指正。

浅析《专利法》中的遗传资源保护制度[*]

张永康

一、引 言

2008 年 12 月 27 日第十一届全国人民代表大会常务委员会第六次会议作出了《关于修改〈中华人民共和国专利法〉的决定》，对《中华人民共和国专利法》（以下简称《专利法》）进行了第三次修订，并于 2009 年 10 月 1 日起施行。随后，2010 年 1 月 9 日国务院作出了《国务院关于修改〈中华人民共和国专利法实施细则〉的决定》，对《中华人民共和国专利法实施细则》（以下简称《专利法实施细则》）进行了第二次修订，并于 2010 年 2 月 1 日起施行。紧接着，国家知识产权局也对《审查指南 2006》进行了修订，修订后的《专利审查指南 2010》（以下简称《审查指南》）也自 2010 年 2 月 1 日起施行。

本次修改中，一个重要的方面，是在中国的专利制度中首次引入了遗传资源保护的内容，其主要体现在《专利法》第 5 条第 2 款以及《专利法》第 26 条第 5 款中。其中：

《专利法》第 5 条第 2 款规定，对违反法律、行政法规的规定获取或者利用遗传资源，并依赖该遗传资源完成的发明创造，不授予专利权。

《专利法》第 26 条第 5 款规定，依赖遗传资源完成的发明创造，申请人应当在专利申请文件中说明该遗传资源的直接来源和原始来源；申请人无法说明原始来源的，应当陈述理由。

笔者希望通过本文对《专利法》中的遗传资源保护制度进行分析探讨，使读者更好地理解并能灵活运用《专利法》中的遗传资源保护制度，或者能够对决策者在修改、执行或司法过程中起到些许作用。

二、遗传资源保护制度相关术语解析

随着遗传资源保护制度导入《专利法》，出现了许多专业术语。下面，先对相关术语进行分析探讨。

---

[*] 原文刊于知识产权出版社 2011 年 3 月出版的《实施国家知识产权战略 提升专利代理服务能力》一书中。本文被评为中华全国专利代理人协会第二届知识产权论坛征文优秀论文。

1. 遗传资源

《专利法实施细则》第 26 条第 1 款中规定，专利法所称遗传资源，是指取自人体、动物、植物或者微生物等含有遗传功能单位并具有实际或者潜在价值的材料。

《审查指南》第二部分第一章第 3.2 节中进一步规定，遗传功能单位是指生物体的基因或者具有遗传功能的 DNA 或者 RNA 片段。遗传功能是指生物体通过繁殖将性状或者特征代代相传或者使整个生物体得以复制的能力。取自人体、动物、植物或者微生物等含有遗传功能单位的材料，是指遗传功能单位的载体，既包括整个生物体，也包括生物体的某些部分，例如器官、组织、血液、体液、细胞、基因组、基因、DNA 或者 RNA 片段等。

2. 依赖遗传资源完成的发明创造

《专利法实施细则》第 26 条第 1 款中规定，专利法所称依赖遗传资源完成的发明创造，是指利用了遗传资源的遗传功能完成的发明创造。

《审查指南》第二部分第一章第 3.2 节中进一步规定，遗传功能是指生物体通过繁殖将性状或者特征代代相传或者使整个生物体得以复制的能力。发明创造利用了遗传资源的遗传功能是指对遗传功能单位进行分离、分析、处理等，以完成发明创造，实现其遗传资源的价值。

无论是《专利法》第 5 条第 2 款还是《专利法》第 26 条第 5 款，均把依赖遗传资源完成的发明创造作为构成要件。因此，对依赖遗传资源完成的发明创造的理解，是理解并把握整个依赖遗传资源保护制度的基础。

因此，笔者根据个人的理解，通过如下案例，对于何者是依赖遗传资源完成的发明创造，何者不是依赖遗传资源完成的发明创造，进行分析探讨。

案例1　一种从野生蘑菇中提取核酸制成的核酸口服液

该野生蘑菇是遗传资源，核酸是遗传功能单位，而且，该发明还对遗传功能单位进行了提取。但是，该核酸口服液仅是普通的保健饮料，该发明创造仅是利用了核酸的化学成分，并没有利用生物体通过繁殖将性状或者特征代代相传或者使整个生物体得以复制的能力，没有实现其作为遗传资源的价值。

从案例 1 我们可以得出，在判断是否是依赖遗传资源完成的发明创造时，判断的核心在于发明创造是否利用了遗传资源的遗传功能，实现其作为遗传资源的价值，而不是在于是否是利用了遗传资源。

案例2　一种通过研究血友病人的基因缺陷而开发出的治疗该缺陷的药物

研究者们通过对血友病人的基因进行分离、分析、处理等，找到了引起致病性的基因片段，然后，找到一种合适的载体，能够将正常基因导入血友病人体内，替换缺陷基因并进行表达，从而开发出了一种治疗血友病人基因缺陷的药物。该药物的开发利用了生物体通过繁殖将性状或者特征代代相传或者使整个生物体得以复制的能力，实现了其作为遗传资源的价值，是依赖遗传资源完成的发明创造。

案例 3

在案例 2 的研究开发过程中，申请人并非直接采取血友病人的基因进行研究，而是通过对科研论文公开的相关基因信息进行研究，从而开发出了一种治疗该缺陷的药物。

研究者们通过阅读相关的科研论文，获知表达致病性的基因片段，然后，找到一种合适的载体，能够将正常基因导入血友病人体内，替换缺陷基因并进行表达，从而开发出了一种治疗血友病人基因缺陷的药物。

该药物的研制，利用了其他研究者对血友病人的基因进行分离、分析、处理等得出的血友病人身上的遗传功能单位上承载的遗传信息，从而完成了发明创造。也即是说，该药物的研制是通过其他个体或组织对遗传资源的利用而间接获知相关遗传信息，从而间接利用了遗传资源。那么，这种情形算不算依赖遗传资源完成的发明创造呢？

关于该问题，张清奎等人曾在《〈专利法实施细则〉修改专题研究报告》❶ 中，从为了让涉及披露遗传资源来源的专利申请数量控制在合理的范围之内的角度出发，认为将"依赖"程度定为直接依赖较为稳妥。

笔者也认为，上述情形不是依赖遗传资源完成的发明创造。笔者作出上述判断的具体理由如下：

第一，在《专利法》中引入遗传资源保护制度的目的是为了维护我国因遗传资源所应获得的正当利益。❷

针对遗传资源的保护，我国作为缔约国之一的国际公约《生物多样性公约》，确立了 3 项核心原则：国家主权原则、知情同意原则和惠益分享原则。我国作为该公约的缔约国，在《专利法》的第三次修改中，明确设立了遗传资源保护制度，以求避免我国珍贵遗传资源遭受剽窃。

既然该制度导入的目的是获得我国因遗传资源所应获得的正当利益，那么，完全可以通过对直接利用者的知情同意而与其设定惠益分享的机制来保证该利益的获得，而无须再延伸至对间接利用了遗传资源的个体或组织进行知情同意。

第二，对于间接利用了遗传资源而完成的发明创造，也要定义为依赖于遗传资源完成的发明创造，有可能造成执法上的困难，甚至执法不能。

因为对于间接利用了遗传资源而完成的发明创造，可能一项遗传资源的

---

❶ 国家知识产权局条法司. 专利法研究 2007 [M]. 北京：知识产权出版社，2008：491-492.

❷ 全国人大常委会法制工作委员会经济法室.《中华人民共和国专利法》释解及实用指南 [M]. 北京：中国民主法制出版社，2009：13-14.

利用会经过很多个体或组织的反复开发或进一步研究，从而造成分不清界限，或者无法确定彼此之间的惠益分享的数额，造成执法上的困难。

第三，给申请人带来过多的负担，而不会对达成本条款的立法目的起到相应的作用。

根据《专利法》第 26 条第 5 款的规定，申请人需要披露遗传资源的直接来源和原始来源，而在间接利用的情形下，申请人可能很难获知自身所依赖的遗传资源的直接来源或原始来源，将难以满足披露遗传资源来源的要求。

3. 发明创造所依赖的遗传资源

根据《专利法》第 5 条第 2 款的规定，当发明创造所依赖的遗传资源是违反法律、行政法规的规定获取或者利用的遗传资源时，不授予专利权，因此，需要判断何者为发明创造所依赖的遗传资源。

另外，根据《专利法》第 26 条第 5 款的规定，依赖遗传资源完成的发明创造，申请人应当在专利申请文件中说明该发明创造所依赖的遗传资源的直接来源和原始来源，因此，也需要判断何者为发明创造所依赖的遗传资源。

因此，笔者通过如下案例，对于何者是发明创造所依赖的遗传资源，何者不是发明创造所依赖的遗传资源，进行分析探讨。

案例 4

在案例 2 的研究开发过程中，采用了与不带血友病致病基因的正常人的基因进行对比的方法

按照对案例 2 的分析，血友病人的基因是发明创造所依赖的遗传资源。但是，该发明创造的完成所依赖的遗传资源，仅是血友病人的基因呢，还是也包括不带血友病致病基因的正常人的基因呢？

为了回答上述问题，笔者曾提出了充分公开发明的客观的判断方法，[1] 也就是说，如果说明书中的该遗传资源存在与否，均不影响本领域技术人员理解及实施本发明，则证明本申请并不是依赖该遗传资源完成的发明创造。

因此，要判断该发明创造所依赖的遗传资源，是否也包括不带血友病致病基因的正常人的基因，需要判断在说明书中省略了与不带血友病致病基因的正常人的基因进行对比的内容之后，本领域技术人员是否仍能实现该发明创造而得到治疗该缺陷的药物。

如果仍能实现，则不带血友病致病基因的正常人的基因不是本发明所依赖的遗传资源，例如，虽然在研究过程中采用了与不带血友病致病基因的正常人的基因进行对比的方法，但主要还是通过对血友病人的基因进行分离、分析、处理等，找到了引起致病性的基因片段，然后，找到一种合适的载体，

---

❶ 张永康. 中国特許法における遺伝資源保護制度の解説 [J]. 知財管理, 2010 (9): 1416-1417.

组入人工合成的正常基因，从而完成了发明的情形。

在不能实现的情形下，由于存在上述的案例 3 中分析的直接利用和间接利用两种情形，则仍需进一步判断该利用是直接利用还是间接利用，若是直接利用则本申请是依赖该遗传资源完成的发明创造，若是间接利用，则本申请不是依赖该遗传资源完成的发明创造。

4. 违反法律、行政法规的规定获取或者利用遗传资源

《审查指南》第二部分第一章第 3.2 节中规定，违反法律、行政法规的规定获取或者利用遗传资源，是指遗传资源的获取或者利用未按照我国有关法律、行政法规的规定事先获得有关行政管理部门的批准或者相关权利人的许可。

但是，在《审查指南》中没有明确地定义"违反法律、行政法规的规定获取或者利用遗传资源"中的"行政法规"应作何理解，即，是狭义的呢，还是广义的呢？也就是说，该"行政法规"包括到哪一层级的"行政法规"呢？

在学理上，凡是行政机关所立的法律规范，均为行政法规。但是根据我国的《立法法》第 56 条第 1 款，❶ 行政法规的立法机关是国务院。也就是说，此处的"行政法规"应作狭义理解，因此，此处的"法律、行政法规"，仅包括全国人大及其常委会所立的法律以及国务院制定的行政法规，而不包括部门规章、地方政府规章等。

下面，进一步深入探讨该术语的含义。

对于"违反法律、行政法规的规定获取或者利用遗传资源"，需要弄清楚的是，怎样的行为算是违反法律、行政法规，怎样的行为不算是违反法律、行政法规。

根据《专利法》第 26 条第 5 款的规定，在《专利法》中，将遗传资源的来源分为直接来源与原始来源两种。根据上述分类，"违反法律、行政法规的规定获取或者利用遗传资源"是仅指遗传资源的直接来源违法还是也包括遗传资源的原始来源违法呢？例如，购买形式合法但销售机构的原始获取形式违法的情形，算不算是"违反法律、行政法规的规定获取或者利用遗传资源"呢？

若是前者，也就是说，仅是直接获取或利用遗传资源的方式违反法律、行政法规的规定并依赖该遗传资源完成的发明创造不授予专利权。这样大家都很容易理解，直接获取或利用遗传资源的方式违法，是申请人自身违法，能够由申请人自身控制，带有主观恶意。若其符合法的构成要件，对其处以不能授予专利权或无效其获得的专利权的惩罚，是理所当然的。

---

❶ 《立法法》第 56 条：依据宪法和法律，国务院制定行政法规。

　　然而，若是后者，也即是说，若是直接获取或利用遗传资源的方式合法但原始来源违法，例如购买形式合法但销售机构获取形式违法的情形，也不能被授予专利权或无效已获得的专利权，很多人就会觉得难以理解，因为，申请人在购买时，很难从销售机构获知自己合法购买的遗传资源在原始获取形式上存在违法行为。从表面上看，这是违反公平原则的，因为，人们只对自己的行为负责，不应该被要求对他人的行为负责。

　　对此，笔者认为，这应该从本法条的立法本意来理解。由于中国的生物遗传资源非常丰富，而保护力度还远远不够，以致被西方发达国家大量掠取而流失，因此，中国的立法专家在《专利法》的第三次修改中，在《生物多样性公约》确立的国家主权原则、知情同意原则和惠益分享原则下，提出了上述合法获取遗传资源的要求。也就是说，立法目的是保护遗传资源的流失，获得应该分享的利益。

　　基于该目的，必然要求不管是直接获取或者利用遗传资源还是原始获取或者利用遗传资源的行为都应该合法。因为，如果只要求直接获取或利用合法，而不追究原始获取或利用是否合法，则导致若不能在原始获取或利用时行使知情同意权，则在后期的直接获取或利用时，再无进行知情同意的机会。此时，作为遗传资源所有人，我国❶将不但无法在前期获得利益分享，而且还可能在后期处于被诉侵权及索要使用费的境地。此时，根本无法有效地保护我国的遗传资源免遭流失。

　　因此，从本质上说，所谓的"违反法律、行政法规的规定获取或者利用遗传资源"，是指针对该遗传资源还未履行过知情同意的手续就进行了获取或利用，而不管该获取或利用是否是原始获取或利用。

　　下面列举出案例5，以使读者更好地理解"违反法律、行政法规的规定获取或者利用遗传资源"。

案例5

　　未办理相关审批手续，向境外输出列入中国畜禽遗传资源保护名录的畜禽遗传资源的情形。❷

　　按照《中华人民共和国畜牧法》和《中华人民共和国畜禽遗传资源进出境和对外合作研究利用审批办法》的规定，向境外输出列入中国畜禽遗传资源保护名录的畜禽遗传资源应当办理相关审批手续，某发明创造的完成依赖于中国向境外出口的列入中国畜禽遗传资源保护名录的某畜禽遗传资源，未办理审批手续的，属于"违反法律、行政法规的规定获取或者利用遗传资源"的情形。

---

　　❶　根据我国《宪法》、《物权法》等法律的相关规定，我国的遗传资源所有人为国家、集体、机构或个人，此处为了记载的方便，仅简单记载为我国。

　　❷　该案例选编自《专利审查指南2010》第122页的内容。

5. 遗传资源的直接来源和原始来源

《审查指南》第二部分第十章第9.5节中规定，直接来源是指获取遗传资源的直接渠道。原始来源，是指遗传资源所属的生物体在原生环境中的采集地。遗传资源所属的生物体为自然生长的生物体的，原生环境是指该生物体的自然生长环境；遗传资源所属的生物体为培植或者驯化的生物体的，原生环境是指该生物体形成其特定性状或者特征的环境。

下面列举出案例6、案例7，以便读者更好地理解何为遗传资源的直接来源和原始来源。

案例6

遗传资源是从保藏机构、种子库（种质库）、基因文库等获得。❶

直接来源是该保藏机构、种子库（种质库）、基因文库等。原始来源，则从保藏机构、种子库（种质库）、基因文库等获得。

案例7　一株采自中国新疆的野生植物，在韩国济州岛进行驯化的情形

如果该野生植物形成其特定性状或者特征的环境是中国新疆，则其原始来源是中国新疆，而非韩国济州岛。

三、法条探讨

前文中已对相关术语进行了解说，下面从整体上分析相关法条。

1. 《专利法》第5条第2款

首先，从法律地位上来说，《专利法实施细则》第53条第一项规定《专利法》第5条第2款是驳回理由；《专利法实施细则》第65条第2款规定《专利法》第5条第2款是无效理由。

其次，从实体内容上来说，该条款规定了不授予专利权的一种情形，对违反法律、行政法规的规定获取或者利用遗传资源，并依赖该遗传资源完成的发明创造，不授予专利权。

符合该情形需满足两个条件：条件一，违反法律、行政法规的规定获取或者利用遗传资源；条件二，发明创造依赖该遗传资源完成。关于上述两个条件的详细含义，笔者已经在上节"4. 违反法律、行政法规的规定获取或者利用遗传资源"、上节"2. 依赖遗传资源完成的发明创造"及上节"3. 发明创造所依赖的遗传资源"中进行了详细地分析探讨，此处不再赘言。

最后，笔者想将该条款的遗传资源保护的规定置于我国的民法体系中进行详细分析，与读者共同对该法律条款的内容进行深入地理解和把握。

《中华人民共和国民法通则》（以下简称《民法通则》）第58条第1款第

---

❶ 该案例选编自《专利审查指南2010》第305页的内容。

（五）项中规定违反法律的民事行为无效，第 2 款规定无效的民事行为从行为开始起就没有法律约束力。因此，如果适用《民法通则》，则"违反法律、行政法规的规定获取或者利用遗传资源"的行为是无效的民事行为，不应发生预期的法律效力，不应产生对遗传资源进行获取或者利用的结果。那么，以该无效的民事行为作为基础，花费各种劳动创造出的知识产权应该归属于谁呢？

对于上述问题，根据民法理论，笔者列出以下两个完全不同的理解。

第一，发明者违反法律、行政法规的规定获取或者利用遗传资源的行为与根据该遗传资源进行发明创造的行为是一个不能分割的整体，属于一个法律关系，该发明创造是物权（遗传资源）上衍生的孳息。既然该无效的民事行为不发生取得或者利用遗传资源的效力，则该发明创造应该归属于所依存的物权（遗传资源）的所有人。即发明创造应该属于遗传资源的所有人，并不应该给予发明人专利权。

第二，发明者违反法律、行政法规的规定获取或者利用遗传资源的行为与根据该遗传资源进行发明创造的行为是独立的两个行为，分别属于两个法律关系。因此，前行为的无效并不会导致后行为的无效。因此，进行发明创造的行为有效，则该发明创造的归属应该由《专利法》来确定。

对于上述两种理解，笔者认为后者更合理。原因如下，按照民法理论❶，孳息是因物或者权益而生的收益，分为天然孳息和法定孳息两种。天然孳息是根据物的自然属性所获得的收益物。法定孳息是依照法律规定产生的收益物。上述发明创造，既不是根据物的自然属性所获得的收益物，也不是依照法律规定产生的收益物。因此，既不是天然孳息也不是法定孳息，不应归类于孳息。不应将实施发明创造的行为与在前的违反法律、行政法规的规定获取或者利用遗传资源的行为归为一个行为而用一个法律关系来解决。

因此，在无效民事行为的基础上，花费各种劳动作出发明创造的行为与在前的违反法律、行政法规的规定获取或者利用遗传资源的行为分属于不同的法律关系，花费各种劳动作出的发明创造的归属应该由《专利法》来确定。

换言之，违反法律、行政法规的规定获取或者利用遗传资源得出的发明创造，在《专利法》修改以前，应该属于对发明创造作出贡献的发明人❷。在《专利法》修改后，发明人已经不能就该发明创造获得专利权。

更明确地说，上述发明创造的归属的结论，是基于《专利法》中对遗传资源的特别规定。在现在的民法体系下，并不是所有的基于无效的民事行为的结果而衍生出来的发明创造，均不授予专利权。仅仅是违反法律、行政法

---

❶ 魏振瀛. 民法［M］. 3 版. 北京：北京大学出版社，高等教育出版社，2007：129.

❷ 根据情况，有时属于发明人所属的单位或者委托该发明人进行发明的单位或个人，为了便于说明，此处仅简单记载发明人。

规的规定获取或者利用遗传资源得出的发明创造，不授予专利权。

2.《专利法》第 26 条第 5 款

首先，从法律地位上来说，《专利法实施细则》第 53 条第（二）项规定，《专利法》第 26 条第 5 款是驳回理由。

其次，从实体内容上来说，该条款为申请人设定了一项义务，即，依赖遗传资源完成的发明创造，申请人应当在专利申请文件中说明该遗传资源的直接来源和原始来源；申请人无法说明原始来源的应当陈述理由。关于依赖遗传资源完成的发明创造以及遗传资源的直接来源和原始来源的详细含义，笔者已经在上述第二节"2. 依赖遗传资源完成的发明创造"及第二节"5. 遗传资源的直接来源和原始来源"中进行了详细地分析探讨，此处不再赘言。

再次，笔者想对申请人履行义务的条件即需要披露来源的遗传资源进行分析。

从《专利法》第 26 条第 5 款的规定的字面上来理解，凡是依赖遗传资源完成的发明创造，申请人均应当在专利申请文件中说明该遗传资源的直接来源和原始来源，没有任何例外。

但是，笔者认为该条款应作狭义理解，❶ 即，仅要求保护的发明创造需要披露所依赖的遗传资源的直接来源和原始来源，而并非申请文件中提及的所有的发明创造均需披露直接来源和原始来源。

上述理解的理由之一，专利制度的本质，国际上比较通行的理论是契约论。❷ 该理论认为专利是以国家的面貌出现的社会同发明人之间签订的一项特殊的契约。这项契约约定，申请人的义务是充分公开技术，权利是获得一定时期的垄断权，社会的义务是保护申请人的垄断权，权利是垄断期后的自由使用权。不言而喻，申请人公开的技术应当与获得垄断权的技术对等，所述以国家的面貌出现的社会，不应当对申请人的要求获得垄断权的技术以外的技术作出任何额外的要求。

由此，不难理解，若要求申请人披露要求获得垄断权的技术以外的技术所依赖的遗传资源的来源，则是要求申请人履行契约范围之外的义务。

上述理解的理由之二，《专利法》第 1 条规定，为了保护专利权人的合法权益，鼓励发明创造，推动发明创造的应用，提高创新能力，促进科学技术进步和经济社会发展，制定本法。该条确立了《专利法》的立法宗旨，是原则性的指导性的规定。也即是说，专利制度的设立是为了保护专利权人的合法权益，鼓励发明创造，推动发明创造的应用，提高创新能力，促进科学技

---

❶ 张永康. 中国特許法における遺伝資源保護制度の解説［J］. 知財管理，2010（9）：1420-1421.

❷ 胡佐超. 专利基础知识［M］. 北京：知识产权出版社，2004：31-32.

术进步和经济社会发展。当申请人面对不寻求专利权保护的发明创造仍被要求进行遗传资源来源披露等时，申请人今后的选择必然是不在专利申请文件中公开不寻求专利权保护的发明创造，从而违背了专利制度的立法宗旨。

具体分析，不妨研究下述案例：

案例 8　一种通过研究血友病人的基因缺陷而开发出的治疗该缺陷的药物

按照对案例 2 的分析，该药物的研制利用了遗传资源的遗传功能，是依赖遗传资源完成的发明创造。根据《专利法》第 26 条第 5 款的规定，申请人应该披露该血友病人的基因的直接来源和原始来源。❶

此外，根据相同的研究思路，申请人还对白化病人的基因进行了研究，并开发出一种治疗白化病的药物，对于该治疗白化病的药物发明，申请人仅仅在上述申请的说明书中进行了记载，而没有在权利要求书中要求保护。对于这种情况，按照上述论述，笔者认为，既然申请人并未在权利要求书中要求对治疗白化病的药物进行保护，自然也不需要披露白化病人的基因的直接来源和原始来源。

最后，笔者想对申请人履行的义务即如何说明该遗传资源的直接来源和原始来源进行分析。

关于遗传资源来源的披露，《审查指南》第二部分第十章第 9.5.2 节规定：

"就依赖遗传资源完成的发明创造申请专利，申请人应当在请求书中予以说明，并且在专利局制定的遗传资源来源披露登记表（以下简称为登记表）中填写有关遗传资源直接来源和原始来源的具体信息。

申请人对直接来源和原始来源的披露应符合登记表的填写要求，清楚、完整地披露相关信息。

如果遗传资源的直接来源为从某个机构获得，例如保藏机构、种子库（种质库）、基因文库等，该机构知晓并能够提供原始来源的，申请人应当提供该遗传资源的原始来源信息。申请人声称无法说明原始来源的，应当陈述理由，必要时提供有关证据。例如指明'该种子库未记载该遗传资源的原始来源'、'该种子库不能提供该遗传资源的原始来源'，并提供该种子库出具的相关书面证明。"

《审查指南》的上述规定中，对《专利法》第 26 条第 5 款中的"申请人无法说明原始来源的，应当陈述理由"进行了进一步的解释性规定，即，"申请人声称无法说明原始来源的，应当陈述理由，必要时提供有关证据，例如

---

❶　根据知识产权局发布的遗传资源来源披露登记表的填表说明，涉及人类遗传资源的，申请人披露其来源信息时，不得公开被采集遗传资源的个人的姓名、身份证号和详细住址。由此，不会引起个人隐私的泄露等的问题。

指明'该种子库未记载该遗传资源的原始来源'、'该种子库不能提供该遗传资源的原始来源',并提供该种子库出具的相关书面证明。"

笔者认为,《审查指南》中的上述规定体现了《专利法》第 26 条第 5 款的立法目的,即,通过在《专利法》中规定专利申请人对遗传资源来源的说明义务,有利于落实知情同意原则,有利于国家掌握本国的遗传资源利用状况,该条款与《专利法》第 5 条第 2 款的规定以及我国的遗传资源保护的专门规定相互配合,有利于加强对我国遗传资源的保护。❶

正如笔者在前文中对违反法律、行政法规的规定获取或者利用遗传资源的情形的分析,为了彻底保护我国涉及遗传资源的正当利益,遏制违反法律、行政法规的规定获取或者利用遗传资源的行为,应既包括直接获取或者利用遗传资源违法的行为,也包括间接获取或者利用遗传资源违法的行为。因此,为了提高该规定的实际操作性,需要精确地掌握发明创造中所依赖的遗传资源的直接来源和原始来源。

因此,笔者认为虽然《审查指南》中的规定是"必要时提供有关证据",但是在实际操作中可能会大量地要求提供有关证据,甚至会演变成一般情况下要提供有关证据,特殊情况下才不需要提供证据的执法状况。

当然,从切实保护我国的遗传资源的角度讲,笔者也认为应该对遗传资源的来源披露进行严格要求,假如可随便地申明自己不知原始来源便可获得专利权,则该条款的辅助查明的作用也就几乎形同虚设。

四、申请人的应对策略

对于上述规定,笔者基于自身的从业经验,试图对申请人或专利权人提出一些有益的建议。

1. 依赖遗传资源进行研究开发

根据《专利法实施细则》第 53 条第(二)项规定,依赖遗传资源完成的发明创造,申请人不能在专利申请文件中说明该遗传资源的直接来源和原始来源,或者无法说明原始来源又无正当理由的,专利申请将被驳回。

因此,申请人在研究开发的过程中应该慎重保存合同、实验记录以及其他相关文件,以防止在未来申请专利时不能披露遗传资源的直接来源和原始来源。

2. 遗传资源的获取或者利用

申请人获取或者利用遗传资源的方式有直接获取或者利用和间接获取或者利用两种。在直接获取或者利用时,申请人可容易地自行判断该获取或者

---

❶ 全国人大常委会法制工作委员会经济法室.《中华人民共和国专利法》释解及实用指南[M]. 北京:中国民主法制出版社,2009:62—64.

利用方式是否合法。但在通过其他机构间接获取或者利用时，申请人则难以判断该遗传资源的原始来源是否合法。此时，假若申请人合法获取或者利用的遗传资源是该其他机构非法获取或者利用的遗传资源，按照上述论述，笔者认为此时仍可能承担不能获得专利权或获得的专利权被无效的后果。因此，申请人在从其他机构间接获取或利用时，应该考虑到后期的风险，签订合法担保协议，若出现获取或利用的遗传资源为该其他机构非法获取或利用的遗传资源时，要求其承担损失。

另外，假如申请人无法从遗传资源权利人处合法获取或利用遗传资源，不妨考虑从公开的科技文献或从其他已获取或利用遗传资源者处，获知相关的遗传信息，进行相关研究开发。

3. 关于遗传资源来源披露的审查意见的答复

在前文中，笔者已经对如何判断哪些遗传资源需要披露提出了自己的一些看法。在此，笔者想对由于未披露遗传资源来源而收到审查意见通知书时的答复策略提出一些自己的看法。笔者认为，由于未披露遗传资源来源而收到审查意见通知书时，可从以下 3 个方面来应对：

第一，如果能够提供，则直接提供遗传资源来源，提交遗传资源来源的披露登记表，具体披露遗传资源的直接来源和原始来源。

第二，具体陈述发明创造并非依赖遗传资源完成的发明创造。根据上述的第二节 "2. 依赖遗传资源完成的发明创造" 中提出的方法进行具体判断，然后具体陈述本发明创造不是依赖遗传资源完成的发明创造，不需要披露遗传资源的直接来源和原始来源。

第三，具体陈述依赖遗传资源完成的发明创造并不是本申请要求保护的发明创造。换言之，具体陈述权利要求中的技术方案的完成不依赖于该遗传资源。

4. 专利权的行使

《专利法实施细则》第 65 条第 2 款规定，《专利法》第 5 条第 2 款是无效理由。

根据该条款的规定，违法获取或者利用遗传资源并依赖该遗传资源完成的发明创造，即使在申请过程中，由于审查瑕疵而获得了专利权，也难以行使权利。因为在行使权利时，作为竞争者，由于涉及巨大的经济利益，必然会进行深入的调查，假如存在违法获取或利用遗传资源的情形也必然会被查出，此时，该专利的权利应被自始无效，专利权人将无法因该专利获得任何经济利益。

因此，专利权人在行使权利前，应该首先自查是否存在违法获取或者利用遗传资源并依赖该遗传资源的情形，判断专利权的稳定性。如果该专利是高度稳定的，则可提起诉讼或许可谈判，若是稳定性很低，则不做任何处理，对竞争者产生威胁反而会更好。

五、结　论

首先，通过对依赖遗传资源完成的发明创造的分析，笔者认为，只有直接利用遗传资源完成的发明创造才是依赖遗传资源完成的发明创造，间接利用遗传资源完成的发明创造不是依赖遗传资源完成的发明创造。

其次，根据《专利法》第 5 条第 2 款的规定，笔者认为，不但直接获取或者利用遗传资源的方式违法的情形不能获得授权，直接获取或者利用遗传资源的方式合法但原始获取或者利用遗传资源的方式违法的情形也不能获得授权。

再次，根据《专利法》第 26 条第 5 款的规定，笔者认为，满足以下两个要件的遗传资源才需要披露来源，若不满足则无须披露来源：第一，发明创造是依赖该遗传资源完成的发明创造，第二，依赖该遗传资源完成的发明创造是要求保护的发明创造。

而且，笔者还认为，为了彻底保护我国涉及遗传资源的正当利益，应该对遗传资源的来源披露进行严格要求，假如可随便地申明自己不知原始来源便可获得专利权，则该条款的辅助查明的作用也就几乎为形同虚设。

综上，本文中笔者举出大量案例对《专利法》中的遗传资源保护制度进行了全面分析探讨，希望能够使读者更好地理解并能灵活运用《专利法》中的遗传资源保护制度，或能够对决策者在修法、执法或司法过程中起到些许作用。本文的分析探讨若能有助于此则幸甚。

浅析功能性限定权利要求的"以说明书为依据"*

张永康

一、引　言

《专利法》第 26 条第 4 款规定"权利要求书应当以说明书为依据，清楚、简要地限定要求专利保护的范围"。

根据《专利审查指南 2010》的规定，权利要求书应当以说明书为依据，是指权利要求应当得到说明书的支持。权利要求书中的每一项权利要求所要求保护的技术方案应当是所属技术领域的技术人员能够从说明书充分公开的内容中得到或概括得出的技术方案。

因此，判断权利要求书是否以说明书为依据，也即是判断权利要求能否得到说明书的支持，也即是判断权利要求书中的每一项权利要求所要求保护的技术方案是否是所属技术领域的技术人员能够从说明书充分公开的内容中得到或概括得出的技术方案，也即是判断在由说明书记载的实施方式扩展到权利要求所包含的所有的实施方式时是否均能解决发明所要解决的技术问题。

功能性特征作为概括方式，仅仅记载了功能而没有结构或步骤的限定，在字面含义上能够获得更大的保护范围，因此，受到了申请人的广泛青睐。但是，由于不是结构或步骤的限定，功能性特征所限定的范围在一定程度上会变得模糊不清，进而为判断权利要求是否以说明书为依据带来了困难。

另外，在现行的法律体系中没有对功能性特征进行定义，而且也没有对采用功能性特征限定的权利要求是否以说明书为依据的判断规则给出清晰的规定。

因此，笔者希望根据自身从事专利代理的实务经验，对功能性限定权利要求是否以说明书为依据的判断规则进行深入探讨，提出一些问题并提供一些解决思路，进而对专利审查指南提出修改建议，以期对完善功能性限定权利要求是否以说明书为依据的判断规则有所裨益。

---

* 原文刊于知识产权出版社 2013 年 1 月出版的《专利法第 26 条第 4 款理论与实践》一书中。

二、我国的法律规定和适用现状

1. 功能性特征的含义

笔者在从事专利代理的实务工作中，曾经收到过将参数特征作为功能性特征而认为权利要求没有以说明书为依据的审查意见通知书。

那么，审查员的上述判断正确吗？要想正确回答这个问题，就必须掌握功能性特征的含义。

在《专利法》及其实施细则中没有涉及功能性特征的规定，在《专利审查指南 2010》中虽然对功能性特征的支持问题进行了规定，但没有对功能性特征进行定义。

为了对功能性特征所限定的范围进行研究，有学者对功能性特征提出了如下定义❶，即，如果一项产品权利要求中不是采用结构或者组合的技术特征来限定该产品，在一项方法权利要求中不是采用步骤或者操作方式的技术特征来限定该方法，而是采用产品的零部件或者方法的步骤在技术方案中所起的作用、功能或者所产生的效果来限定其发明创造，则称为功能性限定特征。

在上述定义中，作用、功能或者所产生的效果的特征被统一地纳入到了功能性特征中，但是其中并没有提及参数特征，而且也没有涉及功能性特征的本质。因此，通过该定义仍然难以判断参数特征是否是属于功能性特征。

那么该如何定义功能性特征呢，其概念的本质又是什么呢？究竟参数特征属不属于功能性特征呢？效果特征属不属于功能性特征呢？

由于结构或步骤的含义是确定的，能够很好地保证权利要求的公示性，因此也是专利审查指南中所鼓励使用的特征，而功能性特征、参数特征、效果特征这三者由于含义的不明确，也是专利审查指南中不鼓励的应当尽量避免使用的特征❷。因此，笔者提出了如下的定义功能性特征的思路，即，从该三者与结构或步骤之间的对应关系来得出。

首先，参数特征，其实质是结构或步骤本身所体现出来的性质。其次，功能性特征或效果特征，其实质是结构或步骤所要达到的目的。也即，参数特征的实质与功能性特征或效果特征的实质是不同的，其不应该适用功能性

---

❶ 尹新天. 中国专利法详解［M］. 北京：知识产权出版社，2011：587.

❷ 例如，在《专利审查指南 2010》第二部分第二章第 3.2.1 节中记载有"对产品权利要求来说，应当尽量避免使用功能或者效果特征来限定发明"、"只有在某一技术特征无法用结构特征来限定，或者技术特征用结构特征限定不如用功能或效果特征来限定更为恰当，而且该功能或者效果能通过说明书中规定的实验或者操作或者所属技术领域的惯用手段直接和肯定地验证的情况下，使用功能或者效果特征来限定发明才可能是允许的"，在第二部分第二章第 3.2.2 节中记载有"特殊情况下，当产品权利要求中的一个或多个技术特征无法用结构特征予以清楚地表征时，允许借助物理或化学参数表征"。

特征的判断方式进行判断。而功能性特征或效果特征的实质是一致的，两者可以采用相同的判断方式进行判断。

因此，笔者对功能性特征给出如下定义，即，功能性特征是指仅仅记载了功能而没有记载结构或步骤的特征，可以引申为不是结构或步骤但是通过结构或步骤所要达到的一种目的（功能和效果等）的特征，但是并不包括结构或步骤本身所具有的性质（物理或化学参数）的特征。

由此，笔者对上述审查意见的回答是，参数特征与功能性特征具有本质的区别，将参数特征适用功能性特征的判断方式进行判断是值得商榷的。

2. 功能性限定权利要求的保护范围

如上文所述，判断权利要求书是否以说明书为依据，也即是判断在由说明书记载的实施方式扩展到权利要求所包含的所有的实施方式时是否均能解决发明所要解决的技术问题。

因此，在判断权利要求是否以说明书为依据时，应该判断权利要求所包含的所有的实施方式，也即判断权利要求的保护范围。

关于功能性特征限定的权利要求的保护范围，在《专利审查指南 2010》中规定："对于权利要求中所包含的功能性限定的技术特征，应当理解为覆盖了所有能够实现所述功能的实施方式"，这符合其字面的含义，而且便于审查，也有利于公众掌握，能够保证权利要求的公示性。

但是，在最高人民法院的司法解释《最高人民法院关于审理侵犯专利权纠纷案件应用法律若干问题的解释》的第 4 条中，规定了"对于权利要求中以功能或者效果表述的技术特征，人民法院应当结合说明书和附图描述的该功能或者效果的具体实施方式及其等同的实施方式，确定该技术特征的内容"。该规定的本意是对专利权的保护应该相应于发明所作出的贡献，不能将保护范围定得过大而导致创新空间受到过度压缩，从而影响了产业的发展。但是，笔者想指出的是，在该司法解释中，阐明了"为正确审理侵犯专利权纠纷案件，根据《中华人民共和国专利法》、《中华人民共和国民事诉讼法》等有关法律规定，结合审判实际，制定本解释"，也即，该司法解释是为侵权判定而制定的，并没有提及是否适用于确权阶段，也即，并没有否定目前的《专利审查指南 2010》中的做法。

由此可见，在判断功能性限定权利要求的保护范围时，我国目前是两种观点并存，并且均是有效的，在不同的阶段需要适用不同的判断规则。

3. 功能性限定权利要求的支持的判断

如上文所述，《最高人民法院关于审理侵犯专利权纠纷案件应用法律若干问题的解释》是为侵权判定而制定的，并没有否定目前的《专利审查指南 2010》中的做法。因此，在功能性限定权利要求是否依说明书为依据的判断中，对于权利要求中所包含的功能性限定的技术特征，应当理解为覆盖了所有能够实现所述功能的实施方式。

更具体地，《专利审查指南 2010》中还进一步规定："如果权利要求中限定的功能是以说明书实施例中记载的特定方式完成的，并且所属技术领域的技术人员不能明了此功能还可以采用说明书中未提到的其他替代方式来完成，或者所属技术领域的技术人员有理由怀疑该功能性限定所包含的一种或几种方式不能解决发明或者实用新型所要解决的技术问题，并达到相同的技术效果，则权利要求中不得采用覆盖了上述其他替代方式或者不能解决发明或实用新型技术问题的方式的功能性限定。"

因此，在判断功能性限定权利要求是否依说明书为依据时，需要具体地判断权利要求中限定的功能是否是以说明书实施例中记载的特定方式完成的，所属技术领域的技术人员能否明了此功能还可以采用说明书中未提到的其他替代方式来完成；或者是判断所属技术领域的技术人员是否有理由怀疑该功能性限定所包含的一种或几种方式不能解决发明或者实用新型所要解决的技术问题，并达到相同的技术效果。

另外，《专利审查指南 2010》中还进一步规定："如果说明书中仅以含糊的方式描述了其他替代方式也可能适用，但对所属技术领域的技术人员来说，并不清楚这些替代方式是什么或者怎样应用这些替代方式，则权利要求中的功能性限定也是不允许的。另外，纯功能性的权利要求得不到说明书的支持，因而也是不允许的。"

因此，在判断功能性限定权利要求是否依说明书为依据时，需要具体地判断说明书中仅以含糊的方式描述的其他也可能适用的替代方式，对所属技术领域的技术人员来说能否清楚这些替代方式是什么或者怎样应用这些替代方式。另外，还要判断是否是纯功能性的权利要求。

三、问题与建议

1. 适用现状的问题

如上所述，在《专利审查指南 2010》中，对功能性限定权利要求是否依说明书为依据方面有着非常具体的规定，在专利审查或代理工作中可操作性非常强。但是，笔者在专利代理的实务工作中，发现上述规定存在一些问题，有必要进行深入的探讨。

（1）首先，《专利审查指南 2010》中规定："权利要求中限定的功能是以说明书实施例中记载的特定方式完成的，并且所属技术领域的技术人员不能明了此功能还可以采用说明书中未提到的其他替代方式来完成……则权利要求中不得采用覆盖了上述其他替代方式或者不能解决发明或实用新型技术问题的方式的功能性限定"。

对此，如上文所述，笔者认为，判断权利要求是否依说明书为依据，也即是判断在由说明书记载的实施方式扩展到权利要求所包含的所有的实施方式时是否均能解决发明所要解决的技术问题。

针对功能性限定的技术特征而言，要判断在由说明书记载的实施方式扩展到功能性限定所包含的所有的实施方式时是否均能解决发明所要解决的技术问题。而对于所属领域技术人员而言，解决发明所要解决的技术问题所利用的是该功能性特征所带来的功能，因此能够实现该功能也就能够解决发明所要解决的技术问题。因此，也就不存在在由说明书记载的实施方式扩展到功能性限定所包含的所有的实施方式时涵盖了不能解决发明所要解决的技术问题的技术方案的情形。

由此可见，不管说明书实施例中记载的方式是否是特定的，也不管所属技术领域的技术人员是否能够明了此功能还可以采用说明书中未提到的其他替代方式来完成，该功能性限定的技术特征均应该是得到说明书支持的。当然，如果对于所属技术领域的技术人员而言，有理由怀疑在由说明书记载的实施方式扩展到功能性限定所包含的所有的实施方式时，涵盖了现有技术中的技术方案或者是不能解决发明所要解决的技术问题的技术方案时，应该质疑其不具有新颖性或创造性，或者说明书公开不够充分，但质疑其没有以说明书为依据则是值得商榷的。

（2）其次，《专利审查指南 2010》中规定："所属技术领域的技术人员有理由怀疑该功能性限定所包含的一种或几种方式不能解决发明或者实用新型所要解决的技术问题，并达到相同的技术效果……则权利要求中不得采用覆盖了上述其他替代方式或者不能解决发明或实用新型技术问题的方式的功能性限定。"

如上文所述，对于所属领域技术人员而言，解决发明所要解决的技术问题所利用的是该功能性特征所带来的功能，因此能够实现该功能也就能够解决发明所要解决的技术问题。因此，笔者认为，无须要求在解决技术问题时所达到的技术效果是否相同。当然，如果能够解决发明所要解决的技术问题，但是达到的技术效果非常差，差到所属技术领域的技术人员容易想到，应该质疑其创造性，但质疑其没有以说明书为依据则是值得商榷的。

（3）再次，《专利审查指南 2010》中规定："如果说明书中仅以含糊的方式描述了其他替代方式也可能适用，但对所属技术领域的技术人员来说，并不清楚这些替代方式是什么或者怎样应用这些替代方式，则权利要求中的功能性限定也是不允许的。"

如上文所述，对于所属领域技术人员而言，解决发明所要解决的技术问题所利用的是该功能性特征所带来的功能，因此能够实现该功能也就能够解决发明所要解决的技术问题。因此，笔者认为，判断权利要求是否依说明书为依据，与说明书中描述的其他替代方式是否含糊以及所属技术领域的技术人员是否清楚这些替代方式是什么或者怎样应用这些替代方式无关。当然，如果对于所属技术领域的技术人员而言，说明书中描述的其他替代方式是含糊的，所属技术领域的技术人员不清楚这些替代方式是什么或者怎样应用这些替代方式，由此导致所属技术领域的技术人员不能够实施本发明，那么应该质疑说明书公开不够充分，但质疑其没有以说明书为依据则是值得商榷的。

（4）其次，《专利审查指南 2010》中规定"纯功能性的权利要求得不到说明书的支持，因而也是不允许的"。

如上文所述，对于所属领域技术人员而言，解决发明所要解决的技术问题所利用的是该功能性特征所带来的功能，因此能够实现该功能也就能够解决发明所要解决的技术问题。因此，笔者认为，只要说明书中公开了具体的实施方式，纯功能性的权利要求也是应该得到说明书的支持的。当然，如果对于所属技术领域的技术人员而言，其整个纯功能性的权利要求的含义是模糊的，或者根据说明书中公开的具体的实施方式并不能解决其技术问题，那么应该质疑权利要求不清楚，或者说明书公开不够充分，但质疑其没有以说明书为依据则是值得商榷的。

2. 专利审查指南修改建议

如上文所述，《专利审查指南 2010》中关于"功能性限定权利要求"的规定，存在一些问题，对此，笔者提出了如下的修改建议：

（1）在《专利审查指南 2010》第二部分第二章第 3.2.1 节中，添加"功能性特征是指仅仅记载了功能而没有记载结构或步骤的特征，可以引申为通过结构或步骤所要达到的一种目的（功能、效果）的特征，但是并不包括结构或步骤本身所具有的性质（物理或化学参数）的特征。"

（2）将《专利审查指南 2010》第二部分第二章第 3.2.1 节中规定的"如果权利要求中限定的功能是以说明书实施例中记载的特定方式完成的，并且所属技术领域的技术人员不能明了此功能还可以采用说明书中未提到的其他替代方式来完成，或者所属技术领域的技术人员有理由怀疑该功能性限定所包含的一种或几种方式不能解决发明或者实用新型所要解决的技术问题，并达到相同的技术效果，则权利要求中不得采用覆盖了上述其他替代方式或者不能解决发明或实用新型技术问题的方式的功能性限定"修改为"对于所属领域技术人员而言，解决发明所要解决的技术问题所利用的是功能性特征所带来的功能，因此能够实现该功能也就能够解决发明所要解决的技术问题。因此，不管说明书实施例中记载的方式是否是特定的，也不管所属技术领域的技术人员是否能够明了此功能还可以采用说明书中未提到的其他替代方式来完成，该功能性限定的技术特征均应该是得到说明书的支持的。但是，如果对于所属技术领域的技术人员而言，有理由怀疑在由说明书记载的实施方式扩展到功能性限定所包含的所有的实施方式时，涵盖了现有技术中的技术方案或者是不能解决发明所要解决的技术问题的技术方案时，需要审查其是否不具有新颖性或创造性，或者审查说明书是否公开不够充分。在审查功能性限定是否得到说明书的支持时，只需审查在由说明书记载的实施方式扩展到功能性限定所包含的所有的实施方式时是否均能解决发明所要解决的技术问题，无须要求在解决技术问题时所达到的技术效果是否相同。但是，如果能够解决发明所要解决的技术问题，而达到的技术效果非常差，差到所属技术领域的技术人员容易想到，需要审查其是否具有创造性。"

（3）将《专利审查指南 2010》第二部分第二章第 3.2.1 节中规定的 "此外，如果说明书中仅以含糊的方式描述了其他替代方式也可能适用，但对所属技术领域的技术人员来说，并不清楚这些替代方式是什么或者怎样应用这些替代方式，则权利要求中的功能性限定也是不允许的。另外，纯功能性的权利要求得不到说明书的支持，因而也是不允许的" 修改为 "此外，如果对于所属技术领域的技术人员而言，说明书中描述的其他替代方式是含糊的，所属技术领域的技术人员不清楚这些替代方式是什么或者怎样应用这些替代方式，并且由此导致所属技术领域的技术人员不能够实施本发明，需要审查说明书公开是否充分。如果对于纯功能性的权利要求，在说明书中公开了其具体的实施方式，也是可以得到说明书的支持的。但是，如果对于所属技术领域的技术人员而言，整个纯功能性的权利要求的含义是模糊的，或者根据说明书中公开的具体的实施方式并不能解决其所要解决的技术问题，需要审查权利要求的记载是否清楚，或者审查说明书的公开是否充分"。

四、结　论

本文中，笔者首先分析了功能性特征的含义，阐述了参数特征、功能性特征、效果特征之间的关系，并对功能性特征给出了定义。

其次，笔者对功能性限定权利要求的范围进行了探讨，分析了我国目前存在的两种观点，并且指出两者并不矛盾，有着各自起作用的空间。

再次，笔者还对功能性限定权利要求的以说明书为依据的判断规则进行了详细的探讨，认为目前在判断功能性限定权利要求是否以说明书为依据时，应按照《专利审查指南 2010》中的规定进行判断，但是，《专利审查指南 2010》中的有些规定是值得深入探讨的。

最后，笔者还对专利审查指南的相关部分提出了修改建议。

综上所述，若能够对功能性限定权利要求是否以说明书为依据的判断规则的完善有所裨益则幸甚。

鉴于笔者水平和经验有限，不妥之处敬请各位业界前辈、同仁批评指正。

浅析专利创造性判断中的"事后诸葛亮"*

张永康

一、引 言

在俗语中，事前无意见事后才高谈阔论并且自称有先见之明的人，我们称为"事后诸葛亮❶"。

在对专利有无创造性进行判断时，由于审查员是在已经阅读了涉案申请文件、并详细地理解了其发明内容的基础上来进行的，因此，实际上来讲审查员所作的分析、评价属于一种事后的行为，因而容易对发明的创造性评价偏低，从而犯"事后诸葛亮"的错误。

"事后诸葛亮"是专利创造性判断时容易发生的失误，在我国的《专利审查指南2010》第二部分第四章第6.2节中，针对"事后诸葛亮"的情形专门进行了特别的规定，以用来提醒审查员在审查发明的创造性时不要犯"事后诸葛亮"的错误。

但是，在《专利审查指南2010》中并没有针对"事后诸葛亮"进行详细的解释，也没有给出可供审查员参照的事例，因此，在实际的审查业务中，一方面，难以引起足够的重视，另一方面，在对"事后诸葛亮"的理解及掌握上也可能会千差万别，从而容易影响审查的公平公正，使申请人或专利权人的合法权益受到损失。

因此，笔者希望根据自身从事专利代理的实务经验对"事后诸葛亮"的产生原因进行详细剖析，通过一些案例更加直观地揭示出"事后诸葛亮"的表现形式，并对如何避免"事后诸葛亮"的错误提出一些解决思路，进而对专利审查指南提出修改建议，以能够供审查员在审查业务当中或专利代理人在专利代理业务当中尽可能避免犯"事后诸葛亮"的错误，更好地服务于审查工作或专利代理工作。

另外，值得说明的是，为了叙述方便，本文在行文中均是以发明专利为代表，但基本上同样适用于实用新型专利。

---

* 原文刊于知识产权出版社2012年1月出版的《专利法第22条——创造性理论与实践》一书中。

❶ 该定义摘自百度百科（http://baike.baidu.com/view/249737.htm，2011年5月21日访问）。

二、专利创造性判断中的"事后诸葛亮"

根据我国《专利法》第22条第3款的规定，在进行专利的创造性判断时需要判断是否具有如下两个要件，即，突出的实质性特点和显著的进步。根据专利审查指南中关于创造性判断的相关规定，在实际的判断过程中，通常只要发明具有有益的技术效果则认定为具有显著的进步❶，因此，创造性判断的核心在于是否具有突出的实质性特点。《专利审查指南2010》中对于突出的实质性特点的判断，采用的是按照如下所述的三个步骤来进行判断的"三步法"❷：

（1）确定最接近的现有技术；

（2）确定发明的区别特征和发明实际解决的技术问题；

（3）判断要求保护的发明对本领域的技术人员来说是否显而易见。

从上述3个步骤的判断顺序来看，笔者认为，该"三步法"其实就是在还原了发明人在进行发明时的过程的基础上，尽可能使审查员将自己设身于发明前的客观环境中判断发明的创造性的方法。

因此，采用此"三步法"进行判断，对于克服审查过程中的"事后诸葛亮"错误，统一审查标准具有重要意义。

1. "事后诸葛亮"的产生原因

笔者认为，在专利审查指南中对"三步法"的规定不够翔实具体，甚至存在可能会导致审查员误解的记载，更进一步说，笔者认为，在该"三步法"中存在滋生"事后诸葛亮"的错误的土壤。

首先，在"三步法"的第一步骤中，在确定最接近的现有技术时，专利审查指南通过列举的方式进行了如下规定❸：

最接近的现有技术，例如可以是与要求保护的发明技术领域相同，所要解决的技术问题、技术效果或者用途最接近和/或公开了发明的技术特征最多的现有技术，或者虽然与要求保护的发明技术领域不同，但能够实现发明的功能，并且公开发明的技术特征最多的现有技术。

笔者认为，对于一项发明而言，其应该是发明人在工作或生活等过程中发现了技术问题，然后开始在现有技术中寻找解决该技术问题的方法，在寻找不到令人满意的解决方法的情况下开始自行研发，然后完成了发明创造。由此，我们能够理解，最接近的现有技术实际上应当是发明人事先所掌握的知识储备，发明人是在该知识储备的基础上，作出了解决其面临的技术问题

---

❶ 《专利审查指南2010》第二部分第四章第3.2.2节，第175页。

❷ 《专利审查指南2010》第二部分第四章第3.2.1.1节，第172~174页。

❸ 《专利审查指南2010》第二部分第四章第3.2.1.1节，第172页。

的发明。

进一步来说，"隔行如隔山"。就发明人而言，通常来讲只在某些领域有所成就，而对另一些领域并不了解。退一步来说，即使对其他领域的技术知识有所了解也很难深刻理解并掌握，更不用说要运用该技术知识来作为发明创造的起点，然后想方设法解决该技术中的问题，从而完成发明创造了。

即在通常情况下，发明人并不能将与其研究领域不同的技术来作为发明创造的起点。当然，对于不具有创造能力的本领域技术人员❶而言更是如此。

但是，在实际的审查作业中进行创造性判断的审查员都是拥有本科、硕士、博士或博士后等文凭的高学历人群，而且，还有大量审查员同时具有企业研发的工作经验，应该说他们都是相应领域的技术专家而且所涉领域相当广泛。在这些所涉领域广泛的专家阅读了申请文件并了解了发明内容之后，通过事后判断的方式找到不同技术领域的现有技术，然后用来作为发明的起点是非常容易的。这样，可能会导致进行创造性判断的审查员不适当地扩大了能够选择的技术领域，对发明的创造性评价偏低，从而轻易地判断发明不具有创造性。因而犯了"事后诸葛亮"的错误。

其次，在"三步法"的判断方法的第三步骤中，专利审查指南进行了如下规定❷：

在该步骤中，要从最接近的现有技术和发明实际解决的技术问题出发，判断要求保护的发明对本领域的技术人员来说是否显而易见。在判断过程中，要确定的是现有技术整体上是否存在某种技术启示，即现有技术中是否给出将上述区别特征应用到该最接近的现有技术以解决其存在的技术问题（发明实际解决的技术问题）的启示，这种启示会使本领域的技术人员在面对所述技术问题时有动机改进该最接近的现有技术并获得要求保护的发明。

在该步骤中，规定了判断是否显而易见的关键在于，现有技术中是否给出启示，这种启示会使本领域技术人员在面对所述技术问题时有动机改进该最接近的现有技术并获得要求保护的发明。

也即，该步骤中的关键在于对"本领域技术人员"及"启示"的把握。

如果将"本领域技术人员"的水准定得过高，那么在其看来绝大多数区别都是容易想到的，绝大多数发明都是显而易见的，反之，如果将其水准定得过低，那么绝大多数区别都是难以想到的，绝大多数发明都是非显而易见的。

另外，如果认定现有技术中给出的启示需要足够明显，那么，就不容易

---

❶ 《专利审查指南 2010》第二部分第四章第 2.4 节，第 170~171 页。
❷ 《专利审查指南 2010》第二部分第四章第 3.2.1.1 节，第 173 页。

将现有技术之间进行结合从而得出发明人的技术方案，由此，具备创造性的发明就越多。如果认定现有技术中给出的启示无须过于明显即可，那么就容易将现有技术之间进行结合从而得出发明人的技术方案，由此，具备创造性的发明则极少。

虽然，在专利审查指南中为了尽量避免审查员主观因素的影响，对于"本领域技术人员"进行了定义❶，并且对于"启示"也给出了举例❷，然而，笔者认为，"本领域技术人员"与"启示"仍然是非常抽象的、难以确定的。

另外，如上文所述，在实际的审查作业中，进行创造性判断的审查员都是相应领域的技术专家而且所涉领域相当广泛，对这些专家来说，容易超越专利审查指南中给定的框框，站在比较高的角度对发明进行评价，从而对创造性估计偏低。而且，对这些专家来说，能够看到本领域技术人员所看不到的"启示"，而且，通过事后判断的方式，更容易将某些不能作为"启示"的记载或公开认定为"启示"。因而犯了"事后诸葛亮"的错误。

2. "事后诸葛亮"的表现形式

通过上节的分析，在专利创造性的审查中，"三步法"的第一步骤和第三步骤容易出现"事后诸葛亮"的错误。

下面，笔者根据该两个步骤，将从事专利代理实务中所出现的"事后诸葛亮"的情形分为两类并各选一个案例来进行分析探讨。

（1）最接近的现有技术选择不当

本案例的独立权利要求1是要求保护一种有机EL元件，在审查过程中，审查员找到了一篇涉及有机金属配位化合物的对比文件。

审查员据此认为，权利要求1限定了有机金属配位化合物是构成正负极之间有机薄膜层的物质并且形成有机EL元件，对比文件的有机金属配位化合物能够发射荧光，而有机EL元件正是利用化合物的这种特性，因此，在对比文件公开的有机金属配位化合物的基础上，本领域技术人员容易想到将对比文件的有机金属配位化合物用于有机薄膜层而形成有机EL元件。从而认定权利要求1不具有创造性。

但是，笔者认为，就本案而言存在如下事实：

本发明的发明对象为有机EL元件，而非有机金属配位化合物，对发明人来说，要解决现有技术中的问题、得出权利要求1的技术方案，需要完成如下三步。

第一步：在有机EL元件中究竟是什么样的技术特征与现有技术问题有关。也即，在该步骤中，需要得出有机金属配位化合物与现有技术问题有关，

---

❶ 《专利审查指南2010》第二部分第四章第2.4节，第170~171页。

❷ 《专利审查指南2010》第二部分第四章第3.2.1.1节，第173~174页。

然后，着手研究有机金属配位化合物。

第二步：上述技术特征采用什么样的实施方式能够解决上述技术问题。也即，在该步骤中，需要从不记可数的有机金属配位化合物中选择能够用于本发明的具体的有机金属配位化合物。

第三步：针对上述技术特征所采用的实施方式，该有机 EL 元件中的其他技术特征需不需要进行相应的改进以及该进行怎样的改进。

笔者认为，在本案中申请的发明对象为有机 EL 元件，而对比文件的对象是一种发荧光的有机金属配位化合物，两者属于毫不相同的两个领域，如果审查员不是在对本发明已经非常了解的基础上，很难从"有机金属配位化合物"入手，根据其能够发射荧光的特性，想到利用在有机 EL 元件上得到本发明的有机 EL 元件。

而且，在进行创造性的判断时，由于审查员对本发明已经非常了解，因此从结论入手反推过程，极易忽略影响发明的创造性判断的事实。相对于该发明的发明过程来说，审查员的判断仅仅是对上述第二步进行了判断而没有对整体进行判断，进而轻易地得出了权利要求 1 的技术方案不具有创造性的结论。

（2）显而易见性的判断不够客观

本案例的独立权利要求 1 是要求保护一种电解铜箔的制造方法，其采用了二聚体以上的五元环的二烯丙基二甲基氯化铵聚合物。在审查过程中，审查员找到了一篇对比文件，公开了一种电解铜箔的制造方法，该方法采用了二烯丙基二甲基氯化氨与二氧化硫的聚合物。

审查员据此认为，二烯丙基二甲基氯化氨与二氧化硫的聚合物和二烯丙基二甲基氯化铵聚合物的结构相似，其中，一个是二烯丙基二甲基氯化铵的均聚物，一个是二烯丙基二甲基氯化铵与二氧化硫的共聚物。对比文件公开的二烯丙基二甲基氯化氨与二氧化硫的聚合物具有降低电解铜箔的粗糙度的作用，本领域技术人员对二烯丙基二甲基氯化氨与二氧化硫的聚合物的发生作用原因通过常规的逻辑分析可知，该物质结构中含有两种基团，即二烯丙基二甲基氯化铵的部分和二氧化硫部分，其中，二氧化硫部分对整个聚合物的作用要么是协同二烯丙基二甲基氯化铵的部分要么是阻抑二烯丙基二甲基氯化铵的部分，因而二烯丙基二甲基氯化铵的聚合物可能比二烯丙基二甲基氯化铵与二氧化硫的共聚物具有更好的性能，这是本领域技术人员通过常规分析即可知道的，为了改进对比文件的相关发明，获得性能更好的性能的电解铜箔，本领域技术人员优先想到选择有可能比二烯丙基二甲基氯化铵与二氧化硫的共聚物具有更好性质的二烯丙基二甲基氯化铵的聚合物以获得本发明，无须付出创造性的劳动。

但是，笔者认为，就本案而言存在如下事实：

相对于对比文件，本发明实际要解决的技术问题是，获得一种采用不同于对比文件中采用的二烯丙基二甲基氯化氨与二氧化硫的聚合物的物质来制造电解铜箔的方法，并且根据该制造方法能够品质偏差小且效率高地制造相比于以往市场中供应的低轮廓电解铜箔轮廓更低且具有高强度机械特性的电解铜箔。

对于该不同的物质，在现有技术中并没有给出任何的启示，更没有给出其功能或作用与对比文件中的二烯丙基二甲基氯化氨与二氧化硫的聚合物相同的启示。

笔者认为，在进行创造性的判断时，由于审查员对本发明已经非常了解，因而对发明的创造性估计偏低，对现有技术中的"启示"判断不够客观，甚至有点凭空创造"启示"。

本案中，在现有技术中"没有给出作为区别特征的二烯丙基二甲基氯化铵聚合物"、"更没有给出二烯丙基二甲基氯化铵聚合物与二烯丙基二甲基氯化氨和二氧化硫的聚合物的作用相同"的基础上，直接对相区别的两者的作用进行推断，并且认为"两者之间的作用只有相同和不同两种，因此，能够容易地进行试验而得出"。显然地，审查员由于技术功底深厚，看到了本领域技术人员所看不到的"启示"，将显而易见性的判断标准放得过低了。

三、"事后诸葛亮"的克服策略

笔者认为，要避免犯"事后诸葛亮"的错误，应该把自己假定为正在进行涉案专利的发明创造的本领域技术人员，回溯到专利申请之时的现有技术状态下，参照正常的发明过程来评价发明人的技术方案。

需要说明的是，笔者并不是想否定"三步法"的判断方法，而是认为在进行"三步法"的判断时，若能够加上笔者所述的上述条件来进行判断，或许能够尽可能地避免犯"事后诸葛亮"的错误，更好地服务于审查工作或专利代理工作。

1. 假定为正在进行涉案专利的发明创造的本领域技术人员

本文中，正在进行涉案专利的发明创造的本领域技术人员是指，在专利申请作出前的现有技术状态下，面临该专利申请中记载的技术问题，并试图解决该技术问题以完成发明创造的本领域技术人员。

当审查员将自己假定为正在进行涉案专利的发明创造的本领域技术人员时，通过还原发明人进行发明的过程，能够尽量摈弃自己已经掌握到的说明书中的发明内容，更客观地体会到发明人在发明时所作的每一步是否是具有创造性。因此，能够尽可能避免事后分析评价所带来的容易对发明的创造性估计偏低的影响，从而避免犯"事后诸葛亮"的错误。

2. 参照正常的发明过程

笔者认为，正常的发明过程应该是，发明人在工作或生活等过程中，发现了技术问题，然后开始在现有技术中寻找解决该技术问题的方法，在其寻找不到令人满意的方法的情况下开始自行研发，然后得出了发明。

通过参照正常的发明过程，审查员能够尽量摒弃自己已经掌握到的说明书中的发明内容，从事后分析、评价的角色转换成事先分析、评价的角色，并且能够避免忽略影响创造性判断的发明步骤或过程。因此，能够更客观地评价发明的创造性，从而避免犯"事后诸葛亮"的错误。

四、《专利审查指南 2010》的修改建议

如上文所述，《专利审查指南 2010》中的"三步法"的规定不够翔实具体，甚至存在可能会使审查员误解的记载。

为了尽可能避免发生"事后诸葛亮"的错误，笔者给出如下的修改建议：

（1）在《专利审查指南 2010》第二部分第四章第 3.2.1.1 节"判断方法"中，将第一句话修改为"判断要求保护的发明相对于现有技术是否显而易见，审查员应该把自己假定为正在进行涉案专利的发明创造的本领域技术人员，回溯到专利申请之时的现有技术状态下，参照正常的发明过程，来评价发明人的技术方案，通常可按照以下三个步骤进行"。

（2）在《专利审查指南 2010》第二部分第四章第 3.2.1.1 节"判断方法"的"（1）确定最接近的现有技术"中，最后一句话修改为"应当注意的是，在确定最接近的现有技术时，应首先考虑技术领域相同或相近的现有技术，在考虑不同技术领域的情形时，要特别注意不要犯'事后诸葛亮'的错误"。

（3）在《专利审查指南 2010》第二部分第四章第 6.2 节"避免'事后诸葛亮'"的最后，加入下述语句："为了避免犯'事后诸葛亮'的错误，审查员应该把自己假定为正在进行涉案专利的发明创造的本领域技术人员，回溯到专利申请之时的现有技术状态下，参照正常的发明过程，来评价发明人的技术方案。"

五、结 论

本文中，笔者对"事后诸葛亮"的产生原因进行了详细的分析，指出在《专利审查指南 2010》中对"三步法"的规定不够翔实具体，甚至存在可能会导致审查员误解的记载，并且详细分析了在"三步法"的判断方法的第一个步骤及第三个步骤中容易产生事后诸葛亮的原因。

　　然后，笔者将"事后诸葛亮"的表现形式分成了两类，即，最接近的现有技术选择不当和显而易见性的判断不够客观，并且针对该两类各举出了一个在代理实务中遇到的案例，以供探讨。

　　然后，笔者还对要避免犯"事后诸葛亮"的错误，提出了解决思路，即，应该把自己假定为正在进行涉案专利的发明创造的本领域技术人员，设身于专利申请作出前的现有技术状态下，参照正常的发明过程，来评价发明人的技术方案。

　　最后，笔者还对《专利审查指南 2010》提出了修改建议。

　　本文若能在审查员的审查业务或专利代理人的专利代理业务当中，对尽可能避免犯"事后诸葛亮"的错误有一丝帮助，则笔者幸甚。

　　鉴于笔者水平和经验有限，不妥之处敬请各位业界前辈、同仁批评指正。

知识产权法律研究

论不可避免披露原则及其对我国商业秘密保护的启示[*]

论不可避免披露原则及其对我国商业秘密保护的启示[*]

论不可避免披露原则及其对我国商业秘密保护的启示[*]

程 稆

绪 论

随着现代社会科学技术的快速发展和市场竞争的日益激烈，企业之间的人才流动也越来越频繁，由此产生的商业秘密泄露问题也日益突出。尤其是掌握公司重要商业秘密的高级管理层的人员离职并且加盟到原雇主的竞争对手的时候，可能引发的商业秘密泄露问题更是值得人们关注。为防止商业秘密泄露问题的发生，雇主一般会与雇员签订竞业禁止合同和保密合同，以禁止雇员在任职期间和离职后一定时间内从事与其雇主相竞争的业务，要求雇员保守其所掌握的雇主的商业秘密。但是，如果雇主与雇员之间并未签订竞业禁止合同，或者即使签订了合同，之后被认定为无效或有漏洞时，雇主的商业秘密就很有可能受到侵犯。对于如何解决该问题，美国法院通过有关商业秘密的司法审判实践，逐步确立了"不可避免披露"原则，为我国在该问题的处理上提供了一定的借鉴。

一、不可避免披露原则的确立

不可避免披露原则是美国法院为保护商业秘密不被潜在披露侵害而逐步创立的禁令救济原则之一。一般来说，该原则用于禁止雇员在其专业领域内为其前雇主的竞争者工作：在这类案件中，被告大都是掌握原告重要商业秘密的前雇员，离职后准备或已经就职于原告的竞争对手，其新的工作将使其不可避免地依靠原告的商业秘密，因此原告请求法院发布禁令，禁止被告从事该项工作和侵占其商业秘密。[1]

关于不可避免披露原则的确立，最早可以追溯至 1902 年的 Harrison 案和 1919 年的 Kodak 案。进入 20 世纪 90 年代之后，该原则得到进一步完善。1995 年第七巡回法院审理的 PepsiCo 案真正标志着该原则发展到了一个成熟的阶段。在该案中，法庭明确适用了不可避免披露原则，并进行了充分的推

---

* 撰写论文时作者为中国人民大学学生，本文获 2013 年度隆天知识产权优秀论文奖。

[1] 彭学龙. 不可避免披露原则研究——美国法对商业秘密潜在侵占的救济 [EB/OL]. 中国民商法律网，http: //www. civillaw. com. cn/article/default. asp? id = 15078.

理，构建了该原则的基本框架。第七巡回法院对 PepsiCo 案的判决对商业秘密所有者迅速采取行动防止"潜在的"侵占提供了强有力的支持，并使伊利诺伊州和美国其他地方朝着加强商业秘密保护的方向迈进了一大步。此后，PepsiCo 案被美国法院频繁引用，该案几乎成了不可避免披露原则的同义语。

美国学者在归纳总结不可避免披露原则相关判例时，虽然对该原则的规定性要素的理解存在差异，但就总体而言都认同不可避免披露原则的证明标准包括以下要素：离职雇员是否拥有前雇主的商业秘密；新旧雇主之间是否存在竞争关系；雇员新旧工作职责之间的功能等同性或相似性。这 3 个要素是得到美国法院广泛认可的要素，但是还有两项存在争议性的要素。❶

第一个争议性的要素是前雇员是否缺乏坦诚和直率，即所谓的"恶意"要素。由于在 PepsiCo 案中，法庭未能清晰阐明"恶意"是否是不可避免披露原则的构成要件，或仅仅是支持发布禁令的诸多因素之一。为了防止这种不确定的情形继续下去，有的法院认为，如果披露真正达到了不可避免的程度，则雇员的善意已无关紧要，也就是说不将新雇主或者雇员的主观因素作为其考量因素之一。

另外一个争议点则是前雇员不可避免披露商业秘密的行为是否会给前雇主造成不可弥补的损害。在 PepsiCo 案中，法院发布禁令时并没有考虑不可弥补的损害这一要素。法院在这一要素上的态度被认为在先例上是一大突破，因为此前的判例在考虑不可避免披露禁令时，都要求原告证明不可弥补的损害。但也正是这种突破，潜在地减少了前雇主在不可避免披露诉讼程序中的举证负担。

二、关于不可避免披露原则的争议以及适用限制

虽然该原则为解决商业秘密保护问题开创了一条新的道路，但是不可避免披露原则由于其模糊性也让有关各方争论不休、褒贬不一。所以迄今既有适用该原则的案例，也不乏明确拒绝适用该原则的例子。例如，在 2002 年的 Whyte 案中，加州上诉法院拒绝适用"不可避免地披露"的理论，认为这个规则创设了一个事实上的"事后的竞业禁止合同"，产生了限制雇员流动的结果，因而违背了加州的法律和政策。在 2004 年的 LeJeune 案中，马里兰上诉法院也明确否定了不可避免地披露理论，认为不符合马里兰州采纳的《统一商业秘密法》。❷

美国学者詹姆斯·普尔在分析不可避免披露原则时指出即使没有发生实

---

❶ 祝磊. 不可避免披露原则的证明标准与适用限制——以美国商业秘密判例法为中心展开 [J]. 电子知识产权，2007 (9).

❷ 李明德. 美国的竞业禁止协议与商业秘密保护及其启示 [J]. 知识产权，2011 (3).

际的侵占商业秘密的行为，即使被告已经离职并发誓不会侵占雇主的商业秘密，滥用商业秘密之威胁也可导致法院对被告发布禁令。美国《统一商业秘密法》中的规定"实际或潜在的侵占可以采用禁令禁止"也使得美国法院在司法实践中适用不可避免披露原则时，常常引用该条款作为支撑。❶ 而审理 Whyte 案和 LeJeune 案的两个上诉法院拒绝适用该原则，是认为不可避免披露原则允许雇主在没有证明前雇员真实使用或者威胁使用商业秘密的情况下，仅仅推论该雇员在新职业上将不可避免使用其所知晓的商业秘密，从而禁止前雇员从事新的职业。其结果不仅是禁止使用商业秘密，而且限制了就业。❷

正因为该原则在适用过程中受到的诸多争议，而且该原则的适用有将天平倒向拥有商业秘密的雇主之嫌，所以美国法院在司法实践中对于该原则的适用持更为谨慎的态度，近年来对其适用进行了一定程度的限缩。一方面是在适用该原则时条件更为严格，雇员或新雇主是否存在恶意或者存在侵犯他人商业秘密的不诚信记录成为法院是否会颁发禁令的重要因素；另一方面则是美国各州法院更倾向于支持其他诉因，如以违反诚信义务、违反保密义务、共谋等来替代不可避免披露原则的适用。❸

三、不可避免披露原则与利益平衡

之所以不可避免披露原则会引起各方争议，以致在适用该原则时法院往往十分谨慎，是因为它牵涉到的是多种重要利益和权利的冲突，不仅涉及雇主保护商业秘密的权利，还有雇员的择业自由权甚至是自由竞争的市场秩序问题。

首先，一旦雇主的商业秘密在雇佣关系终止后就很有可能不由雇主独占，而雇主对此也不能从法律上得到救济，那么雇主对于投资研究或者改进现有的生产方法的积极性就会大打折扣。另外，由于现今经济发展下的公司模式，企业主不得不把越来越多地与技术开发有关的秘密信息也告知给适当的雇员。这就不能避免要将一些商业秘密告知给相关雇员，而因为企业间人才的流动，就可能会导致在该雇员离职时使雇主的商业秘密被其新雇主知悉。如果没有不可避免披露原则对雇主的商业秘密进行保护，那么一旦商业秘密被披露，其经济价值就将不复存在，因为很多情况下商业秘密的经济价值就是体现为一种竞争优势。

其次，对于雇员来说，不可避免披露原则的适用构成了对雇员自由择业

---

❶ 祝磊. 不可避免披露原则的证明标准与适用限制——以美国商业秘密判例法为中心展开 [J]. 电子知识产权，2007（9）.

❷ 李明德. 美国的竞业禁止协议与商业秘密保护及其启示 [J]. 知识产权，2011（3）.

❸ 范晓波，孙红玲. 美国不可避免披露原则的适用及其启示 [J]. 电子知识产权，2010（5）.

权这一基本人权的限制。一般能够知悉雇主商业秘密的雇员，其专业能力必定不低，但是正因为知悉雇主的商业秘密，他反而不如一般的雇员可以自由选择自己的去向，在其专攻的领域寻求更大的发展。而且，该原则的适用可能会导致对雇员的事后竞业禁止。而在事前未签订竞业禁止合同的情况下，法院在适用该原则时并没有竞业禁止条款约定的界限作为标准，而只能靠法官的职业素养对适用该原则的合理性进行判断。在这种情况下，对法官的要求是十分高的，因为他需要权衡各种利弊关系。如果法官自身素养不足以合理判断，那么对该原则的适用很有可能对雇员造成不公。

最后，关于自由竞争的市场秩序问题。很多时候，雇员在对新雇主忠诚时就不可避免地要违反对原雇主的诚实信用义务。如果说雇员在加盟新雇主之后确实将原雇主的商业秘密披露给了新雇主，那么此种行为就违反了商业上的诚实信用原则。此时若不对此行为进行否定，那么原雇主的合法权益就会受到侵害而得不到法律上的救济，这并不是一个健康的自由竞争市场中应该存在的现象。但是，另一方面，如果说原雇主要求对离职雇员适用不可避免披露原则是为了防止雇员以其自身在工作过程中获得的技能而展开与原雇主相竞争的业务，此时若支持原雇主的请求，那么对于竞争市场的健康发展也是十分不利的，会导致技术传播受到阻碍。

四、不可避免披露原则对我国司法的启示

虽然说不可避免披露原则在美国司法实践的适用过程中受到了较多的批评，对其适用也出现了一定的限缩趋势，但是至今该原则仍然是美国商业秘密侵权判定中的一个重要的规则，说明虽然其自身有一定的争议性，但是也不乏许多可取之处，有其存在的必要价值，所以对该原则进行研究必然能从中获益。

（一）不可避免披露原则在我国司法实践中的体现——"一得阁"案

我国司法实践中适用不可避免披露原则的案例很少，"一得阁"案是引入该原则的第一案，在我国的司法实践中具有一定的开创性，并且为其他类似案件的审判起到了一定的示范作用。

该案中北京一得阁工贸中心（以下简称一得阁）在 20 世纪 80 年代研制出了一得阁墨汁和中华墨汁，之后一得阁对这两种墨汁的生产技术进行了改进，并把改进后的生产技术作为一得阁的长期保密的秘密技术，包括墨汁的配方和生产工艺等。2002 年年底，一得阁从荣宝斋等处发现并购买了北京某文化艺术公司生产的三种墨汁产品，其质量和性能都和一得阁生产的一得阁墨汁及中华墨汁、北京墨汁、云头雁墨汁相仿。后一得阁查明，该文化艺术有限公司成立于 2002 年 1 月 9 日，是由知悉一得阁持有的秘密技术全部内容

的一得阁墨汁厂副厂长高某出资设立的。2003 年 5 月，一得阁与高某正式解除了劳动关系，并于同年 7 月，向北京市第一中级人民法院提起诉讼，要求高某及某文化公司停止侵犯其商业秘密，并赔偿经济损失，法院支持了原告的诉讼请求。

在本案中，某文化公司的股东中只有高某长期在一得阁担任高级管理人员，熟知原告墨汁配方。而高某出资成立的某文化公司在没有专门技术人员的情况下在短时间内就生产出高档的墨汁产品，没有现成的墨汁配方是不可能的。并且也通过证人王某、杨某的陈述证实高某曾向其告知一得阁中心的墨汁配方。高某作为原告的高级管理人员，负有保护企业商业秘密的义务。法院认为，高某违背了该义务，向其他人披露了其掌握的配方，并使某文化公司非法使用了该配方，所以高某和某文化公司侵犯了原告的商业秘密，应当承担停止侵害、赔偿损失的责任。之后，被告不服，向北京市高级人民法院提出了上诉。2005 年 5 月，北京市高院作出终审判决，维持原判。❶

在案件的审判过程中，法官的逻辑是这样的：由于高某的高级管理人员的身份，所以在其与他人成立的生产相同产品的企业中，高某不可避免地会将其掌握的商业秘密带到该企业，而要推翻这样一个推定，那么高某就有义务证明某文化公司生产的与一得阁相似的墨汁是有合法技术来源的，如果举证不能，那么推定成立，也即侵权成立。

虽然说一得阁案开创了我国适用不可避免披露原则的先河，但是必须注意，该案的情况与美国的不可避免披露原则还是有不同之处。美国的司法判例中，该原则的适用是在被告真正实施侵权行为之前，原告是在缺乏被告侵犯其商业秘密证据的情况下提起诉讼，适用该原则得出的结论并不是被告侵权成立，而只是通过法院提供禁令救济，改变这种可能会发生的侵害原告商业秘密的结果，并不会判令被告停止侵害并赔偿损失。也就是说，该原则的适用主要是用来证明商业秘密有被侵害的危险，从而采取对该可能发生行为的预防措施。而在一得阁案中，高某的侵权行为已经发生了，原告有一定的证据可以非直接地证明被告有泄露其商业秘密的行为。法院如果不适用不可避免披露原则，也可以依据其他的法律规定很好地解决问题。

（二）我国商业秘密保护制度中存在的问题

虽然一得阁案严格来说与美国的不可避免披露原则司法实践不同，但是其引入该原则，对我国的司法实践还是具有十分重大的意义。因为我国商业秘密的保护制度还存在一些不足，适用不可避免披露原则，可以更好地对商

---

❶ 龙文懋，李元. 从"接触加相似"到"不可避免披露"——从一得阁案看中国商业秘密侵权证明原则的进展［J］. 首都师范大学学报：社会科学版，2007（6）.

业秘密进行保护。

我国现在对商业秘密进行保护的法律主要有《反不正当竞争法》，其第 10 条规定了侵犯商业秘密的一些不正当手段以及第 25 条关于侵犯他人商业秘密的惩罚，然后在《民法则》、《合同法》、《劳动法》以及《刑法》中也有一些相关的规定。另外，国家工商行政管理局为了加强对商业秘密的保护，也曾在 1995 年发布实施了《关于禁止侵犯商业秘密行为的若干规定》。但是，以上法律或者相关规定规范的都是侵犯了商业秘密之后的事后救济措施，侧重点在于实际侵权行为。而对于侵犯商业秘密的行为尚未发生但是又存在发生的危险或者虽然已经发生但还未产生一定的损害结果的情形，并不能从法律的规定中寻求救济的依据。

实践中，为防止上述情形的发生，我国主要是利用竞业禁止合同进行规制。但是对于竞业禁止合同的内容，我国并没有明确的法律规范可以作为参考，所以就导致实践中存在竞业禁止合同对雇员执业自由在期限、地域、行业等方面的限制超过了合理限度的情况，剥夺了离职雇员的择业选择权。而在美国的司法实践中，法院通常不会支持禁止或者限制雇员竞争的竞业禁止合同。因为禁止或者限制离职雇员与原雇主展开竞争，不是一个自由竞争的市场经济所允许的。而只有当竞业禁止合同的条款和维护雇主的商业秘密存在一致的情况下，法院才会对该条款进行支持，而且此时对该合同的解释也是限定性的，使得其效力限定在为维护雇主的商业秘密的范围内。❶

（三）为完善我国商业秘密保护制度可为的改进

我国商业秘密保护制度存在不足，这导致在实践中就有可能发生商业秘密所有人因他人的侵害行为而受到损害，但却不能从法律上得到救济的情况。而商业秘密因其自身的特殊性，会使商业秘密侵权行为给商业秘密的享有者带来很大的危害，因此，为保护商业秘密享有者的合法权益，我国应当尽量完善该保护制度。

一方面，对于尚未发生但极有可能发生的侵犯商业秘密行为，可以通过引入不可避免披露原则对该情形进行禁令预防。我国是一个成文法国家，所以不可能像美国一样通过司法判例来确立不可避免披露原则，但是我国或许可以通过立法来实现这个目的。我国《民法通则》第 134 条规定当行为人将来的行为确实可能侵害他人的民事权利时，权利人可以通过要求适用"消除危险"这样一种责任方式来防止损害后果的发生。从这一点上，可以为立法上规定不可避免披露原则提供法律依据。同时通过深入研究美国判例法对该原则的解释，对该原则进行全面细致的解读，并借鉴美国《统一商业秘密法》

---

❶ 李明德. 美国的竞业禁止协议与商业秘密保护及其启示 [J]. 知识产权，2011（3）.

关于潜在侵权禁令救济的规定，在吸收国外相关法律精华的基础上，创造出适应我国具体国情同时在实践操作中不会引起诸多争议的法律规定，使得商业秘密的保护延伸至侵犯商业秘密尚未实际发生但极有可能发生的情形。

另一方面，不可避免披露原则也为我国竞业禁止制度的设计提供了较好的借鉴。在认定竞业禁止合同的有效性方面，可以借鉴美国法院的做法，以不可避免披露原则的适用条件来对竞业禁止条款以及竞业禁止合同的合理性进行衡量，考虑竞争程度以及职位的相似度，约束竞业禁止合同的效力边界，防止竞业禁止条款或者竞业禁止合同对雇员的限制超过合理的限度，侵犯雇员的择业自由权。❶ 通过对竞业禁止范围的缩小，使得离职雇员在选择职业时更为自由，从而促进人才的流动，进而有助于行业技术得到整体提高。

结　语

不可避免披露原则的发展、确立经过了一个漫长的过程，因为该原则的适用牵涉到多方的利益，所以至今仍然存在一定的争议。但是虽然有争议，却还是在实践中指导着美国的法院进行审判活动，说明该原则还是有其存在的必要价值。所以，如果想要将该原则引入到我国的司法活动中，完善我国的商业秘密保护制度，那么就必须对该原则进行全面的分析了解，特别是其受争议之处，这样才能将该原则更好地运用到我国的司法实践中。

---

❶ 范晓波，孙红玲. 美国不可避免披露原则的适用及其启示［J］. 电子知识产权，2010（5）.

我国著作权法上技术措施保护的完善[*]

罗明东

一、引　言

技术措施是著作权人保护自己权利的手段，其产生伴随着数字传媒的产生和普及。美国著名知识产权专家萨缪尔森（Pamela Samuelson）曾归纳了数字传媒的几个基本特点，这种归纳很好地突出了数字传媒与传统知识产权体制相关联的问题。根据她的观点，"六个数字传媒的特征会对法律带来重大的变化。"即：①易于复制；②易于传播并有多样的利用方式；③极强的可塑性；④数字格式作品的等价性；⑤数字传媒的紧凑性；⑥数字传媒的非线性（non-linearity）。[1] 实践证明，数字传媒环境下，作品的复制、传播更加便捷、质量更高、数量更多，这使得著作权权利人对作品的控制能力降低，权利实现陷入困境。为此，著作权人被迫采取一种自力救济的技术措施，在数字格式的作品上施加密码、反连续复制、电子水印、激活链接等技术障碍，使得著作权人能在事实上控制作品的复制和传播，阻止他人对作品的非法使用。[2]

就技术措施本身而言，包括插销（keyplugs）、智能卡（smart card）、密码（password）、水印（watermark）、连续复制管理系统（serial copy management system）、加密（encryption）、计算机程序如电子信息扰频系统（content-scrambling system）等。[3] 技术措施从功能角度大致可以分为：①控制访问（access control）[4] 作品的技术措施，用以禁止他人未经许可访问作品。例如，收费网站、收费频道设置的密码，只有支付了使用费的用户才能够登录网页、收看节目；②权利保护的技术措施（right control），用以控制他人对作品的使用和制止他人的侵权行为。例如，连续复制管理系统（The Serial Copy Management System，SCMS），只允许直接来自原件的复制，复制件

---

[*] 撰写论文时作者为中国人民大学学生，本文获 2013 年度隆天知识产权优秀论文奖。

[1] PAMELA SAMUELSON. Digital Media and the Law［M］. 34 Communications of the ACM，1991：23.

[2] 李琛. 知识产权法关键词［M］. 北京：法律出版社，2006：220.

[3] 章中信. 著作权法制中科技保护措施与权利管理信息之探讨［J］. 网络法律评论，2002（1）.

[4] access control 在大多数著述中都将其翻译为"接触控制"，"接触"包括浏览、阅读等行为，从抽象意义上来说，可以与复制、下载、传播等行为相区分。但是，这里的 access control 是在数字传媒的语境下产生的，并且本身就有"访问"之意，因此，将 access 翻译为"访问"，其含义更加准确。

不可被继续复制。❶

技术措施的确为著作权人实现自己的权利提供了有效的途径，在知识产权领域，尤其是著作权领域，技术保护措施被立即采用，法律措施也以前所未有的速度迅速准备着。❷ 然而，通过使用规避技术，这些技术措施常常可以被规避掉。事实上，技术措施出现之后，相应地就出现了解密措施等规避技术措施的技术和装置，旨在消除技术措施的防范功能。❸ 基于这一原因，新的知识产权规则已经囊括了额外的法律保护，尤其是针对技术保护措施，造成了一种加强了的双重保护效果，一重保护给予享有著作权的电子信息（content）❹，另一重则给予了对其进行保护的技术措施。❺ 这条道路上最重要的决定当属世界知识产权组织（WIPO）的两个重要条约，即 1996 年《世界知识产权组织版权条约》（WCT）和《世界知识产权组织表演与录音制品条约》（WPPT）。❻ 紧接着是各国主动跟进的立法。❼

目前，几乎所有发达经济体和大型经济体都有保护技术措施的相关条款可以适用。当然我国也不例外，我国《著作权法》第 48 条第（六）项规定"禁止未经著作权人或者与著作权有关的权利人许可，故意避开或者破坏权利人为其作品、录音录像制品等采取的保护著作权或者与著作权有关的权利的技术措施。法律、行政法规另有规定的除外"。《信息网络传播权保护条例》（以下简称《条例》）进一步作出了具体规定，《条例》第 26 条对技术措施有所界定，并且禁止三类规避技术措施的行为：第一类是避开或者破坏技术措施的行为；第二类是制造、进口或者向公众提供主要用于避开或者破坏技术措施的装置或者部件的行为；第三类是为他人避开或者破坏技术措施提供技术服务的行为。❽

传统著作权的一大特点是权利与限制并存。技术措施不是作品，在著作

---

❶ 李琛. 知识产权法关键词 ［M］. 北京：法律出版社，2006：220.

❷ NICOLA LUCCHI. Digital Media & Intellectual Property ［M］. Berlin：Springer-Verlag，2006：41.

❸ 李琛. 知识产权法关键词 ［M］. 北京：法律出版社，2006：220.

❹ content 一般被翻译为"内容"，ICP 被翻译为"网络内容提供商"，与 ISP"网络服务提供商"相对应，理解上不会有偏差。但根据英汉大词典的解释，content 也有"电子信息"之意，在数字传媒语境下，content 应当被还原其最精准的含义，即"电子信息"。

❺ NICOLA LUCCHI. Digital Media & Intellectual Property ［M］. Berlin：Springer-Verlag，2006：43.

❻ 另外，《伯尔尼公约》和 TRIPS 协议是另外两个重要的国际条约，都旨在协调各国的著作权法。WIPO 的两个条约被认为是经过仔细斟酌和平衡考虑过的应对数字时代的条约。但也有人批评该条约代表着进一步的美国化。PAMELA SAMUELSON . Challenges for the World Intellectual Property Organization and the Trade-related Aspects of Intellectual Property Rights Council in Regulating Intellectual Property Rights in the Information age ［J］. Europe Intellectual Property Review，1999（21）：578.

❼ PAMELA SAMUELSON. The U. S. Digital Agenda at WIPO ［J］. Virginia Journal of International Law，1997：369.

❽ 参见《著作权法实施条例》第 18 条第（二）项和第 19 条第（一）项的规定。

权法上不存在"技术措施权"一说。但是技术措施作为保护著作权，特别是保护信息网络传播权的有效技术手段，被规定在著作权法当中，在立法技术上没有太大问题。❶ 所以，技术措施保护仅仅是法律赋予权利人享有的利益，但这种利益保护实际上却产生了对于信息网络传播权的双重保护效果，❷ 加之技术措施被滥用的案例频繁发生，迫切需要我们对技术措施反规避条款进行再思考。

二、我国技术措施反规避规定及其不足

（一）我国技术措施反规避规定

我国是 WCT 和 WPPT 两条约的缔约国，所以我国的技术措施规范首先受到这两个条约的限制。依据上述两条约的要求，我国著作权法应当为作者、表演者以及录音制品制作者使用的有效技术措施加以保护，但 WCT 和 WPPT 对缔约国的要求仅限于这一程度，对于是否必须通过知识产权立法给予保护，是否应该对技术措施保护做进一步的限制等并无更为明细的规定。我国在2001 年修订的《著作权法》中已经执行了 WIPO 两条约的规定，《著作权法》第 48 条就是我国的反规避条款。❸ 依据该条款，规避技术措施的人不仅应当承担民事责任，而且还有可能承担行政和刑事责任，可以说，在著作权法领域，这样的保护强度和责任力度应该是很强的。但令人遗憾的是《著作权法》中并没有对技术措施做进一步解释或界定，也没有规定规避技术措施的例外或限制，更没有规制技术措施滥用的相关规则。只有回到本法的一般性规定，才可以寻找到一般性的限制，❹《侵权责任法》对侵权行为的一般性规定也是该类侵权行为的一般性限制。

---

❶ 刘春田. 知识产权法［M］. 4 版. 北京：中国人民大学出版社，2009：83. 也有学者认为，不宜把技术措施放入著作权法内规定，WCT 只要求成员国为技术措施提供充分的保护，有效的救济就可，并不要求将规避技术措施行为定性为侵害著作权的行为。用行政法或是刑法治裁更为恰当。参见：李琛. 知识产权法关键词［M］. 北京：法律出版社，2006：220. 就著作权法保护技术措施的正当性问题，还可以进一步参照：王迁. 版权保护技术措施的正当性［J］. 法学研究，2011（4）.

❷ NICOLA LUCCHI. Digital Media & Intellectual Property［M］. Berlin：Springer-Verlag，2006：42.

❸《著作权法》第 48 条规定："有下列侵权行为的，应当根据情况，承担停止侵害、消除影响、赔礼道歉、赔偿损失等民事责任；同时损害公共利益的，可以由著作权行政管理部门责令停止侵权行为，没收违法所得，没收、销毁侵权复制品，并可处以罚款；情节严重的，著作权行政管理部门还可以没收主要用于制作侵权复制品的材料、工具、设备等；构成犯罪的，依法追究刑事责任；……（六）未经著作权人或者与著作权有关的权利人许可，故意避开或者破坏权利人为其作品、录音录像制品等采取的保护著作权或者与著作权有关的权利的技术措施的，法律、行政法规另有规定的除外……"

❹ 即《著作权法》第 4 条："著作权人行使著作权，不得违反宪法和法律，不得损害公共利益。国家对作品的出版、传播依法进行监督管理。"

对技术措施反规避条款的进一步细化和限制，在时隔 5 年之后颁布实施的《信息网络传播权保护条例》（以下简称《条例》）当中方见端倪，❶《条例》第 4 条第 1 款："为了保护信息网络传播权，权利人可以采取技术措施。"接着《条例》第 4 条第 2 款将《著作权法》第 48 条规定的规避行为具化为："任何组织或者个人不得故意避开或者破坏技术措施，不得故意制造、进口或者向公众提供主要用于避开或者破坏技术措施的装置或者部件，不得故意为他人避开或者破坏技术措施提供技术服务。但是法律、行政法规规定可以避开的除外。"在责任承担上，"故意避开或者破坏技术措施"的视情形承担民事、行政和刑事责任。而"故意制造、进口或者向他人提供主要用于避开、破坏技术措施的装置或者部件，或者故意为他人避开或者破坏技术措施提供技术服务的"应视情况承担行政或刑事责任。❷

对技术措施保护的限制条款可以见诸《条例》当中，《条例》第 12 条第 2 款规定了可以避开技术措施的 4 种情形：①教学、科研例外；②为盲人提供作品的例外；③执行公务的例外；④安全性能测试的例外。其中第一、二项还增加了对象人群的限制以及作品只能通过信息网络获取的要件。该条第 1 款还限制"不得向他人提供避开技术措施的技术、装置或者部件，不得侵犯权利人依法享有的其他权利。"可见《条例》中规定的避开技术措施的免责情形之少，限制之多。

但是，《著作权法》和《条例》中均没有技术措施滥用的相关规定。

（二）我国技术措施反规避规定的不足

1. 对技术措施的规定过宽，未作合理限制

对技术措施的规定过宽，其结果是我国《著作权法》对技术措施的保护范围过大。这首先体现在对技术措施的界定上，《著作权法》没有对技术措施进行界定，而是在《条例》第 26 条第 2 款中规定："技术措施，是指用于防止、限制未经权利人许可浏览、欣赏作品、表演、录音录像制品的或者通过信息网络向公众提供作品、表演、录音录像制品的有效技术、装置或部件。"可见，技术措施的对象包括作品、表演及录音制品和录像制品，而 WPPT 中仅及于录音制品。录音制品（phonograms）在 WPPT 中的定义为："除并入电影或其他视听作品中的固定外，表演的声音或其他声音的固定或展现。"❸ 我

---

❶ 其实早在 2002 年 1 月开始施行的《计算机软件保护条例》中便有了计算机软件著作权领域的技术措施规避规则，只是新颁布的《信息网络传播权保护条例》已经很好地吸纳和覆盖了原《计算机软件保护条例》的相关规定，故后所称《条例》一律指《信息网络传播权保护条例》）。

❷ 详见《信息网络传播权保护条例》第 18 条第（二）项、第 19 条第（一）项。

❸ WPPT Article 2 Definitions（b）.

国法律中的录音、录像制品对应的表达应当为 sound recording 和 video recording,❶ 其中,后者是被 WPPT 明确排除在录音制品之外的。上述条款的差异实际上体现了著作权体系与版权体系的相关差别。❷ 也就是说,录像制品中的机械式录制等不具备最低原创性而只体现录制者劳动和投资的作品不是 WPPT 中技术措施的对象,但在我国著作权法规定下却是。造成的结果便是,针对该部分录像制品采取的技术措施在国外并未提供保护,而国内却要受到反规避条款的庇佑。

2. 未区分控制访问技术措施与权利保护技术措施

虽然美国 DMCA 中将技术措施区分为控制访问的技术措施和权利保护技术措施的做法并没有收到大大优于他国的效果,❸ 但只有将控制访问的技术措施和权利保护的技术措施相区分才更为符合法律本身的逻辑。因为与针对控制访问技术措施的规避行为相比较而言,针对权利保护技术措施的规避行为不可避免地具备侵犯他人著作权的故意,可以在现有著作权侵权规则下进行处理,并且可以适用现有著作权法合理使用的限制,立法上再将其界定为侵权行为不仅多余,反而还会造成著作权人实际上享有"技术措施权"的假象。而针对控制访问的技术措施的规避行为,才是传统著作权法及侵权规则尚未触及的领域,另外,控制作品访问的技术措施正是需要重点限定和规制的。

3. 缺乏对技术措施滥用行为的规制,对利益平衡的考量不足

《信息网络传播权保护条例》第 12 条是我国著作权法中规定的反规避规则的唯一例外条款。首先,从量上来看,4 项例外远远不够,甚至都未达到美欧的水平。再从质上看,上述 4 项例外首先受到一般性的限制,即"不得向他人提供避开技术措施的技术、装置或者部件,不得侵犯权利人依法享有的其他权利",技术措施的种类包括插销、智能卡、密码、水印、连续复制管理系统、加密等,❹ 针对这些技术措施的解密、解码等规避措施、装置或部件比技术措施本身更加专业、复杂,上述 4 项例外情形中,除计算机系统安全测试者外,其他主体一般并不掌握规避技术措施的技术,在法律禁止他人提供

---

❶ PETER K. YU. From Pirates to Partners(episode ii):Protecting Intellectual Property in Post-WTO China [J]. American University Law Review, 2006 (11).

❷ WCT 和 WPPT 规则根本上是美国等发达国家推动的,一定程度上体现的是这些国家的意志。在版权法体系中,并没有录像制品的规定,而是将部分录像制品纳入了"电影和其他视听作品"中,而版权法中的"电影和其他视听作品"相当于我国著作权法中的"电影和以类似摄制电影的方法创作的作品"。根据美国版权法和相关判例,电影和其他视听作品的原创性要求非常低,只要求具备最低的创造性,而著作权法要求以类似摄制电影方法创作的电影必须达到"体现作者精神状态或人格印迹"。

❸ JOANNA PERRIT. Protecting Technology over Copyright:A Step Too Far [J]. Entertainment Law Review, 2003:14.

❹ 章中信. 著作权法制中科技保护措施与权利管理信息之探讨 [J]. 网络法律评论, 2002 (1).

避开技术措施的技术、装置或部件的情况下，上述主体几乎无法独立实施技术措施的规避行为，那么，上述例外规定也就成了一纸空文。其次，第一、第二两项还仅限于通过信息网络，虽然信息网络是数字时代最主要的传媒，但权利人采用技术措施时并不限于在信息网络环境下，上述两项的限制极大削弱了相关例外的效果。

历史的经验告诉我们，对某种权利，尤其是知识产权的保护，必须立足于现实国情，而非一味地加强保护，造就法律上的空中楼阁。不具备一定的社会条件，"徒法不能自行"。❶ 国际上，由近代自由资本主义向现代垄断资本主义演进的过程中，民法上出现了从"个人本位"思想向"社会本位"思想的转变。到了 20 世纪，"社会本位"已成为各国私法立法的主导思想和重要原则。❷ 国内情况来看，我国仍是发展中国家，知识的迅速、广泛传播对国计民生尤为重要，我国与以美国为首的发达国家之间就知识产权问题展开的长期、艰苦的谈判，已经说明了问题。然而，正是在这种背景下，我国著作权法对用于阻碍知识有效传播的技术措施却给予了远高于欧美等发达国家的保护，虽然很大部分原因是迫于美国的强力施压，❸ 但这的确是对国情的背离。即便是美国学者也承认，"对技术措施的保护应该进一步考虑公共政策目标，包括发展目标和技术目标。应该使最不发达国家能够建立健全的和切实可行的技术基础。还应该有助于促进技术发明及其交易、传播，有助于以利于社会和经济福利的方式实现知识制造者和使用者相互的利益。这些目标都不可能要求给发展中国家狭窄的选择。"❹

可见，对技术措施超强的保护是我们有限而无奈的选择。这种超强的保护表现在：首先，我国著作权法中技术措施的规则与欧美，尤其是 EUCD 模式较为相似，都是先一般性地确认规避技术措施的行为侵权，再基于公共利益的考量添加限制或例外规则。❺ 若不考虑法律执行的因素，这样的立法模式在对技术错的保护上是非常强有力的。其次，我国对技术措施的保护，还远

---

❶ 周大伟. 佟柔民法讲稿 [M]. 北京：北京大学出版社，2008：54.

❷ 李双元，邓杰，熊之才. 国际社会本位的理念与法院地法适用的合理限制 [J]. 武汉大学学报：社科版，2001（5）：517.

❸ PETER K. YU. From Pirates to Partners（episode ii）：Protecting Intellectual Property in Post-WTO China [J]. American University Law Review，2006：7.

❹ PETER K. YU. From Pirates to Partners（episode ii）：Protecting Intellectual Property in Post-WTO China [J]. American University Law Review，2006：10.

❺ 著作权法保护技术措施的模式，总结起来有：WCT、WPPT 的模式；美国 DMCA 和欧盟的 EUCD 模式；澳大利亚模式。以上模式各有特点，其中 WCT、WPPT 模式最为灵活，美国 DMCA 和欧盟 EUCD 模式对技术措施保护最强，澳大利亚模式下对技术措施保护的例外限制最多。我国《著作权法》上对技术措施保护的规定与欧盟 EUCD 模式最为接近，而限制较之甚少，因此保护甚强。罗明东. 著作权领域技术措施的滥用及对策 [D]. 西南大学，2012：35-37.

强于即便是采用同样模式的国家和地区，主要表现在 3 点：①对技术措施的保护过宽；②规避技术措施的例外和限制过少；③对规避技术措施例外本身的限制过多。❶

三、我国技术措施反规避条款的完善

（一）细化技术措施有关规定

1. 在《条例》已有的粗略限制上，增加技术措施本身的限定

首先，技术措施是否有效常常是案件中双方争议的焦点之一，❷ 因此有必要对"有效性"作出具体化的限定。这点可以借鉴 EUCD 相关规定，EUCD 第 6 条第（三）项："当受保护的作品或其他客体由权利人通过所使用的访问控制或保护程序，如对作品或其他对象进行加密、扰频或其他改变、控制复制机制实现保护目标时，技术措施被视为'有效'。"同样，美国 DMCA 也是从实际效果的角度来界定"有效"，而且更进了一步，即对控制访问技术措施而言，是"在正常的操作中，需要获得著作权人授权的应用信息或处理程序以获取对作品的访问。"❸权利保护技术措施的有效性则指"在正常操作中，阻止、限制或限定对著作权人权利的行使。"❹

其次，对于何为《信息网络传播权保护条例》第 4 条、第 18 条和第 19 条中的"避开或破坏"技术措施的行为，以及何为《计算机软件保护条例》第 24 条第 1 款第（三）项的"避开或破坏"也应当予以明确。这点也可以参照 DMCA 的相关规定，该法案将规避技术措施的行为界定为"未经著作权人许可的，解码扰频作品、解密加密作品，或其他避开、越过、移去、取消或破坏技术措施的方法。"❺

另外，有必要在著作权法中明确并非技术措施的情形，有效预防权利人滥用技术措施，以防止权利人以保护作品著作权为名，行损害使用人利益、进行不正当竞争甚至垄断或危害社会公共利益之实。也可以对使用人和公众提供明确的法律指引，避免受到不当的限制。澳大利亚版权法在对技术措施本身的限制性条款中，已经吸纳了禁止利用技术措施进行市场控制或限制消

---

❶　分别参见《信息网络传播权保护条例》第 26 条和《信息网络传播权保护条例》第 12 条。

❷　例如在 Lexmark International 诉 Static Control Components 案中，被告方就以"验证技术"并不是一种能够对作品的使用进行"有效控制"的"技术措施"为理由抗辩。王迁．滥用"技术措施"的法律对策——评美国 Skylink 案及 Static 案．电子知识产权，2005（1）：44．

❸　DMCA1201（a）（3）（B）．

❹　DMCA1201（b）（1）（B）．

❺　DMCA1201（a）（3）（A）．

费者使用的规则，这是对技术措施滥用非常有效的限制。❶ 我国《著作权法》第 48 条明确规定采取技术措施是"为了保护作品、表演或录音录像的著作权或相关权利"，《条例》第 4 条也规定保护信息网络传播权是采用技术措施的唯一目的，那么非基于这一目的的技术措施，如为了垄断市场、垄断商品派件或售后等，就应当被排除在著作权法保护的技术措施之外。

2. 明确不得采用技术措施之对象

明确不得采用技术措施之对象，严禁对公共领域之作品或对象采用技术措施。无论是 EUCD 还是 DMCA，在技术措施反规避条款中都强调依据法令或指令享有的权利及权利人。❷ 这样的表述保证了采用技术措施的单位或个人是依法仍享有著作权或相关权利的人。而我国《著作权法》以及《条例》中，都回避了这一原则，许多并不享有信息网络传播权或已经丧失该权利的公共领域作品或对象，常被无权者利用技术措施进行控制，阻碍知识的传播。因此有必要明确，著作权法保护的技术措施，必须是以依法仍享有著作权或相关权利的作品、录音录像为对象，排除针对处于公共领域之对象而采用的技术措施，防止技术措施被滥用。具体应从两方面着手，一方面，不保护此类技术措施；另一方面，还应当作出保障性的规定，要求权利人在著作权或相关权利保护期限届满后主动移除技术措施，否则承担相应的民事、行政责任，保证已被采用技术措施的作品或对象在著作权保护期届满之后能够顺利进入公共领域。期限届满权利人未主动移除的，社会公众有权对该技术措施进行规避、破坏，为他人规避、破坏此类技术措施提供技术、装置、部件或服务的行为也应当免于承担民事、行政和刑事责任，并应受到法律的保护。

3. 区分控制访问技术措施与权利保护技术措施

避开或破坏权利保护技术措施的行为，依据传统著作权法及侵权行为理论可以认定为著作权侵权行为，同样，也可以援用合理使用等免责事由。而避开或破坏控制访问技术措施的行为，并不能断定其有侵犯著作权权利的意图或后果，不能依据传统著作权法及侵权规则认定为侵犯著作权。这才需要法律在著作权法规则之外规定控制访问技术措施的保护规则。

法律是第二性的，必须适应第一性的生产力的变迁。如今，随着数字传媒迅猛发展，使不得不依赖于知识产权之上的付费访问（access contracts）和

❶ 澳大利亚版权法就在"技术措施"的定义下附加了技术措施的排除性规定，1968 年的《澳大利亚版权法案》第 10 条（1）"技术保护措施"条款规定："技术措施并不包括如下范围的装置、产品、技术或部件：……（iii）如果作品或其他对象为摄制的电影或计算机程序（保护计算机游戏）时，通过阻止从国外合法获取的作品或其他对象的非侵权复制品在国内的重放，控制市场的地理细分。（iv）如果作品是植入一个机械或装置中的计算机程序，限制对商品（而非作品）或与机械或装置有关的服务的利用。"

❷ EUCD. Chapter3. Art. 6. 3.

大众市场许可（mass-market licences）成为数字环境下知识产品利用领域最普遍的商业模式之一，对该项利益的保护必须另外寻求有效的途径。❶ 反映到第二性的法律上，则利用合同法来保护控制访问技术措施似乎更为合理，在合同法领域，采取技术措施的权利人与作品的使用者就是付费访问合同关系的双方当事人，使用者未经权利人许可规避、破坏技术措施的行为视其具体情况可以被认定为违反诚实信用、恶意磋商的缔约过失行为或违约行为，相应地承担缔约过失责任或违约责任。

在这种模式下为他人规避、破坏控制访问技术措施提供技术、设备、部件或服务的行为也应当从著作权法体系内剥离。在付费访问和大众市场许可情形下，上述行为本质上属于第三人侵犯他人合同利益的行为，当然不属于违约行为，也不能被认定为《合同法》第 121 条规定的"当事人一方因第三人的原因造成违约"的情形，❷ 不能纳入合同法体系规制。由于我国法律也未赋予著作权及相关权利人以绝对性权利——"访问权（access right）"，其只是法律赋予权利人的相关利益。所以为他人规避、破坏控制访问技术措施提供技术、设备、部件或服务的行为不具备侵犯他人著作权的故意。但依据新颁布实施的《侵权责任法》第 2 条："侵害民事权益，应当依照本法承担侵权责任"，可将保护技术措施的利益作为财产利益而适用侵权责任法，❸ 但由于与侵权规则相比较存在公示性、确定性上的劣势，也由于权利人在个案中寻求救济的成本太高，故而这类行为应当同时被纳入行政管理规范和刑事规范中规制。事实上，为他人规避、破坏控制访问技术措施提供技术、设备、部件或服务的行为，往往涉及众多的利用者，参与破坏他人技术措施也绝不限于个别或较少的权利人，也绝不限于较少次数的破坏，其侵害的不仅是权利人的私人法益，而且侵害了整个权利人群体依法所享有的法益，故而利用行政法和刑法不仅可行，而且正当。

（二）加强对技术措施的限制

合理使用制度是国际公约和各国著作权法中最为重要的制度之一，是著作权限制的最重要表现。❹ 一般作品著作权的行使须受到《著作权法》第 22 条合理使用规则的限制，多达 12 项，但是技术措施并不是一项权利，不能适用该规定。《条例》第 12 条是避开技术措施的免责规定，共列举了 4 种情形，也就是说，在技术措施领域适用的免责事由，得援用《条例》第 12 条之规

---

❶ RAYMOND T. NIMMER. UCITA and the Continuing Evolution of Digital Licensing Law [J]. Computer & Internet Law, 2004: 10.

❷ 《中华人民共和国合同法》第 121 条。

❸ 《中华人民共和国侵权责任法》第 2 条第 1 款，以及第 2 款有关民事权益的解释。

❹ 冯晓青. 著作权合理使用制度之正当性研究 [J]. 现代法学, 2009 (4): 29.

定，而不是《著作权法》第 22 条之适用。通过比较《著作权法》第 22 条和
《条例》第 12 条的规定可以看出，技术措施领域合理使用的免责情形被大大
缩减。❶ 可见，在技术措施问题上，立法上采用了远窄于合理使用规则的免责
事由，而这种过窄的免责事由并不适应数字传媒环境的实际情况。故应当扩
大规避技术措施的免责事由，达到《著作权法》上合理使用的标准。

（三）建立技术措施滥用行为的救济制度和责任规则

前述几项立法对策都旨在预防技术措施被滥用，对滥用技术措施行为的
规制也理应以预防规则为主，但对滥用技术措施行为的救济措施和责任制度
在预防和制裁技术措施滥用行为上也起着更为直接的作用。依据我国《著作
权法》第 48 条，规避技术措施的行为不仅可以被认定为民事侵权行为，而且
可以被认定为犯罪，其责任从停止侵害、消除影响、赔礼道歉、赔偿损失等
民事责任，到没收违法所得，处以罚款的行政责任，直至刑事责任，其保护
相当之强。然而，目前著作权法中仅规定了规避、破坏技术措施应承担的民
事、行政和刑事责任，并没有技术措施滥用的相关救济措施和责任制度。

技术措施滥用行为首先侵害的是作品使用者合理使用的利益，然而，在
传统传媒下，著作权人尚不具备主动排除合理使用的能力，因其无法有效控
制作品的复制和传播，故传统著作权法中也并无规制这种规避行为的必要。
而在数字传媒环境下，技术措施使得著作权人有能力对作品进行事实上的排
他性控制，作品使用者合理使用的利益被著作权人主动侵犯已成为现实，所
以，相应的救济措施和责任制度的构建便势在必行。这一点上，EUCD 已经为
我们提供了有益探索和较好的指引，EUCD 第 6.4 条规定"为防止权利人滥用
技术措施，包括在自主协商，或政府干预的框架下，任何用以实现合理使用
的技术措施都应获得法律保护。"❷ 指令为防止权利人滥用技术措施，损害使
用者合理使用的利益；授权使用者采取相应的技术措施，实现合理使用的利
益，并且将这种技术措施纳入了法律的强制保护范围。值得庆幸的是，欧盟
这一规定当中指引性或授权性的表述，可以被我国立法很好地克服，因为我
国国内不存在欧盟那样复杂的内部法制关系，在法律适用的效果上会理想
得多。

另外，技术措施滥用行为，更多的是破坏市场竞争秩序、侵害消费者权
益、侵害公共利益，所以，必须同时适用公法（如行政法和刑法）和经济法

---

❶ 具体表现在以下情形中：①为个人学习、研究或欣赏的免责；②为介绍、评论之免责；③图
书馆、档案馆、博物馆、美术馆等的免责；④免费表演的免责；以及⑤将汉族文字作品翻译成少数民
族文字之免责。详见《中华人民共和国著作权法》第 22 条。

❷ Directive 2001/29/EC of the European Parliament and of the Counci ［J］. Official Journal（L 167），
2001：Art. 6.4（3）.

（如反不正当竞争法、反垄断法、消费者权益保护法等）的救济措施和责任制度，如此也才能将技术措施滥用行为之责任与规避技术措施行为之责任相等同。

（四）强化对消费者权益的保护

在数字传媒时代，当数字化权利完全被计算机软件掌控之后，对使用者权利的管理变得异常困难，基于合理使用原理下的例外也难以实现。❶ 数字传媒环境下，我们不得不承认，目前正发生的经济上的转型趋势 ［从传统的著作权授权向不依赖于知识产权之上的付费访问（access contracts）和大众市场许可（mass-market licences）商业模式的转变］与立法秩序相悖，立法未能迅速地与社会的变迁相适应，我们也不得不接受合同已成为立法创新和立法标准化的主要来源的事实。❷ 一般说来，技术保护措施的使用可能提升权利人针对使用者设置过分条件的能力，而合同与技术保护措施的结合，又可能表征着一种强力的"力量混合物"（mixed power），这种混合物是电子信息安全复制、权利管理、使用监测和费用支付的全自动系统。❸ 这种技术措施的使用后果是，消费者依据著作权法所享有的任何权利都有可能被一个商业契约所取代，而这种技术控制下的契约所产生的糟糕后果便是阻碍著作权人利益与使用人及社会公众利益之间平衡的实现。❹ 所以，在目前的知识产权法之下，消费者实现合法权利，实现合理使用的可能性被大大压缩，因此，我们必须将精力集中于消费者权益保护和合同条件的合理性方面。❺ 为避免对消费者享用数字传媒的选择和竞争之减损，电子信息的授权合同或者其他标准化的数字化电子信息转移，必须被纳入与其他合同一样的立法限制当中。消费者权益保护措施可以在恢复知识产权人和使用者之间的利益关系上扮演重要角色。

具体而言，应当首先概括性地规定技术措施的采用不得侵犯消费者的合法权益，其次向著作权人施以技术措施披露义务，尤其是披露付费访问及许可合同的相关条款，坚决摒除"隐形条款"（invisible contract terms）的存在，以保障消费者知情权。禁止技术捆绑以保障消费者的选择权，禁止采用技术措施不当地限制消费者合法获得的使用权。将付费访问合同、大众市场许可

❶ TOM W. BELL. Fair use v. Fared Use：the Impact of Automated Rights Managements on Copyright's Fair Use Doctrine ［J］. N. Carolina L. Rev. , 1998（76）：557.

❷ MARGARET J. RADIN. Online Standardization and the Integration of Text and Machine ［J］. Fordham L. Rev. , 2002（70）：1125.

❸ P. BERNT HUGENHOLTZ. Copyright and Electronic Commerce：Legal Aspects of Electronic Copyright Management Kluwer Law ［M］. The Hague, London Boston. , 2000：1, 2.

❹ NICOLA LUCCHI. Digital Media & Intellectual Property ［M］. Berlin：Springer - Verlag, 2006：100.

❺ NICOLA LUCCHI. Digital Media & Intellectual Property ［M］. Berlin：Springer-Verlag, 2006：99.

合同等所有有关电子信息转移使用的合同，都纳入我国现有民商、经济相关法律法规规范下，尤其注重《合同法》相关原理、规则的适用。坚决查处和打击利用有失公正的格式合同来不正当地限制消费者权利，不正当地免除或减轻己方责任的行为。另外，介于大多技术措施专业、复杂的特点，在是否存在滥用技术措施情形的举证上，应当由采取技术措施的权利人承担证明责任。

四、结　语

目前，我国《著作权法》的第三次重大修订正进入关键时期，从已公布的两稿《著作权法（草案）》来看，已经将技术措施和权利管理信息单列一章，吸收了绝大部分《信息网络传播权保护条例》的合理规定，在体系上使得技术措施反规避条款更加科学化、系统化，这足以反映立法者对技术措施保护条款的重视。在实体内容上，《草案》将录像制品排除在了技术措施保护对象之外，进一步与 WPPT 的规定相一致，在技术保护措施的限制上增加了加密研究和反向工程的例外。但除此之外，没有更多实质性的改动。总体上看，《草案》在技术措施反规避规则上并没有走太远，对于技术措施本身的限制仍然不足，对技术措施滥用行为的预防和处理也没有新的对策，因此技术措施保护规则仍需要我们进一步的讨论、研究和呼吁。

大数据时代的挑战：互联网环境中隐私权的保护

——以美欧的隐私政策为例*

一、引言：大数据商业使用与个人隐私的潜在冲突

作为近年来信息产业界频繁使用的热词，大数据（Big Data）已经成为理论界和实务界所广泛关注的焦点，然而却尚未形成权威性的定义。依维基百科的介绍，大数据又被称为巨量资料、海量资料，指的是所涉及的资料量巨大到无法透过目前主流软件工具，在合理时间内达到撷取、管理、处理、并整理成为帮助企业经营决策的资讯。❶从这一简短的说明可以看出，大数据的核心内涵是数量巨大的数据背后所蕴含的重大信息。而这些信息可以帮助各类主体在面对纷繁复杂的问题时作出最为科学、最为合理的选择，从而为其带来意想不到的收益。

大数据所附带的重大价值已经逐渐被人们发现并重视。美国麦肯锡全球研究所发布了《大数据：下一个创新、竞争和生产力的前沿》，指出"大数据的时代已经到来，数据正成为与物质资产和人力资本相提并论的重要生产要素"。美国政府在2012年3月宣布通过"大数据的研究和发展计划"提高对大数据的收集与分析能力。❷而为了获取这些数量庞大的数据供己所用，政府机构以及各类市场主体便会借助互联网的帮助。与十几年前对互联网的利用方式不同的是，人们不再仅仅扮演着接受由互联网公司提供各类信息的角色，还会通过各种方式创造着不同种类的信息；而与此同时，人们在进行网络购物、浏览信息、沟通交流甚至在借助搜索工具寻找自己想要了解的资料时，与个人信息相关的数据就会轻而易举地为网络服务提供商获得。这些信息看似没有任何价值，但是对于提供相关服务的市场经营者来说则极其重要。通过对这类数据的处理与分析可以得知某人的个性偏好，从而投其所好地为之提供服务。不仅如此，大数据还能够提供与人们行为趋势密切相关的信息，

---

* 撰写论文时作者为中国人民大学学生，本文获2013年度隆天知识产权优秀论文奖。

❶ [EB/OL].（2013-05-23）[2013-06-10]. http://zh. wikipedia. org/wiki/% E5% A4% A7% E6% 95% B0% E6% 8D% AE.

❷ 张杰，王慧，吴成良. 大数据：价值何在 [N]. 人民日报，2013-06-16：23.

从而帮助经营者预测市场需求，甚至预测疾病与犯罪的发生。

网络服务提供者为了抢占商机获取海量数据，必须对网络使用者的各种信息进行搜集，并能将这些信息汇集成数据库，供市场研究和预测使用。而此种搜集并保留各种信息的行为给网络使用者带来了很大的困扰，人们在网络上的私人活动因为此种行为而变成了一种公共活动：❶ 个人不愿为人知晓的信息被保留下来并且存在被利用之可能。人们因大数据时代的到来而产生了这样一种不安：大数据的发展将进一步扩大信息的开放程度，个人的隐私数据或敏感信息面临着被他人得知甚至是泄露的危险。❷ 由于网络服务提供商对于个人信息的收集与利用，互联网环境中的隐私权亟待保护。

二、互联网环境中的个人隐私

（一）隐私与隐私权的概念辨析

隐私与隐私权的概念在很多民法学者的著作之中都可得见。有学者认为：所谓隐私，是指不愿告人或不为人知的事情，而隐私权就是个人信息、个人私事和个人领域不受他人侵犯的权利。❸ 但按照这种定义方式，关于"什么是隐私"的判断标准就显得过于主观：只要主张某种信息是自己不愿别人知道的，则该种信息就会被认定是隐私。这种定义模式扩大了隐私的范围，并赋予了自然人过于宽泛的隐私权。

与个人公开的信息相对，隐私应该是自然人有意隐瞒、不想被不特定多数人知道的与个人身份、生活有关的信息。❹ 因而隐私应当是个人信息的下位概念，个人信息中已经被公开给不特定多数人的信息并不能被认定为隐私。在这种判断标准之下，对于那些已然公开并为不特定多数人所获知的个人信息，该个体并不能够主张其为隐私；个人信息一旦经个人同意而公开，也就不得再重新成为隐私。

在确认隐私之内涵的基础上，仍需明确其所指涉的外延所包含何种范围的信息。举例来说，甲的住宅地址是 A 小区 B 房间，甲曾经在某网站上购买了 C 产品，则甲之住宅地址以及曾经购买商品的记录是未曾对不特定多数人公开且甲不愿将之公开的个人隐私。但是，如果做如下这种去个人化的处理，即将上述信息改变为一个人住在 A 小区 B 房间、一个在某网站购买了 C 产品并将这些处理过的信息与千千万万的去个人化的信息汇集在一起，以使单个

❶ 向淑君. 敞开与遮蔽——新媒介时代的隐私问题研究［M］. 北京：知识产权出版社，2011：107.

❷ 郭三强，郭燕锦. 大数据环境下的数据安全研究［J］. 科技广场，2013（2）.

❸ 刘凯湘. 民法总论［M］. 北京：北京大学出版社，2006：149.

❹ 马骏驹. 人格和人格权理论讲稿［M］. 北京：法律出版社；2009：260.

人信息的分离不具有任何意义时，上述改变之后的信息就不应当被认为是个人隐私。隐私必定与个人身份相联系，必定与人身属性密不可分。❶ 因此，不能与单个自然人对应的个人信息不应作为隐私权保护的对象。

不仅如此，一些去个人化的信息是与公共利益密切相关的。比如，不同的自然人在某特定时期特定范围内借助网络搜索引擎查询同一种症状或疾病，那么这一时期内该地区就存在爆发大规模公共卫生事件的较大可能性。因而此时自然人主张自己的浏览记录是隐私而拒绝去个人化处理后的使用显然是对社会公共利益的损害。因而判断什么是隐私的关键应该是该类信息是否能够对应自然人的身份与人格特质。

根据我国《侵权责任法》第 2 条的规定，隐私权作为民事利益的一种受到法律的保护。但法律对于隐私权之客体——隐私并没有作出明确的定义。而根据上文提及的论述，我们通过概念分析的方法对隐私的定义予以厘清：即自然人未被公开且与其身份与人格特质紧密联系的个人信息。

（二）互联网环境中个人隐私保护的困难

在大数据时代，由于存在巨大商业利益的诱惑，网络服务提供商当然愿意搜集并存储互联网用户提供的个人信息；而随着科学技术的进步，海量储存并分析数据又并非难事，因而想要网络服务提供商自觉地不去搜集能够产生如此附加价值的个人信息是不现实的。❷ 在这些因素的共同作用之下，设法保护互联网环境中的个人隐私具有一定的困难。具体来说，这些困难主要体现在如下两方面：

1. 大数据时代网络服务提供商的运营模式

与借助黑客工具侵犯他人隐私、获取他人秘密数据、划取账户金额等违法活动不同，大数据时代的网络服务提供商一般并没有想要窃取他人隐私的意图，其主要想借助新兴的科学技术搜集并储存大量用户的海量数据，从而为其进一步商业发展提供指导和帮助。以电子商务为例，这种搜集、存储并利用用户个人信息的商业运营模式主要可以分为如下 3 种：

第一，网络服务提供商从用户处获取注册时需要的电子邮箱以及该用户浏览网站商品的记录，从而"投其所好"，向用户提供个人化的定制服务，精确地定位用户的偏好与个人信息，定期或不定期向该邮箱发送与用户浏览过的商品相关商品的推荐邮件。❸ 这种模式并未对用户信息做去个人化处理，其针对的就是用户个人的喜好，通过预测该用户可能的需求而作出相应的引导

---

❶ 张新宝. 隐私权的法律保护 [M]. 2 版. 北京：群众出版社，2004：12.

❷ 理查德·斯皮内洛. 铁笼，还是乌托邦——网络空间的道德与法律 [M]. 李伦，等，译. 北京：北京大学出版社，2007：157.

❸ 胡凌. 网络安全、隐私与互联网的未来 [J]. 中外法学，2012（2）.

与推荐，从而招徕该用户在其网站上购买相应商品或服务。不仅如此，该网络服务提供商也可能会将与其有"互帮互助"关系的其他网络服务提供商的商讯发送给该名用户。此种模式是较为常见的。

第二，与上一种模式类似，只不过搜集信息的网络服务提供商将此类个人信息转给其他的网络服务提供商，从而便于后者利用这些信息为注册用户提供服务。这种服务模式的核心在于将用户的个人信息提供给了其他的服务商，而这种提供信息的行为一般是未经用户同意的，从而存在泄露个人信息之可能。

第三，网络服务提供商将获取的全部用户的个人信息做去个人化处理，仅保留一些基本信息，例如用户所在地以及最近一段时间所需求的产品。通过搜集并分析这些数据能够获取某一地区或某个时间段的用户更需求何种商品或服务，从而在该地区调配更多的商品、服务人员或者在该时段的网页上放置此类商品或服务的信息。这种模式所需的技术手段较为复杂，其想实现的目的是利用海量数据针对不特定的全部可能浏览网页的用户进行有目的的广告宣传，从而尽最大可能促使浏览者消费。

网络服务提供商对于用户信息的其他利用方式与大数据的问题无关，因此在本文中不予考虑。针对上述 3 种模式，实际上都存在网络服务提供商利用个人数据获取商业收益的行为。因而都面临着侵犯他人隐私的风险。

2. 互联网环境中个人隐私的特点

互联网环境中个人隐私与现实生活中的个人隐私存在很大的不同，从而也是使前者的保护更为困难的重要原因。❶ 而除去互联网本身技术上的特点以外，网络环境中的个人隐私一般存在如下几个特点：

（1）个人隐私的非自愿性告知

现实生活中的隐私一般是非自愿就可以不被任何人知晓的。但是在网络环境下，我们为了在互联网上完成某事项，一般不得不将自己的隐私告知或公开给特定的网络服务提供商。如果任何公司或个人想要获得此类信息必须经该个体同意，那么信息的存储、流通与利用将充满障碍，因而在互联网时代，个人隐私会存在着被非自愿告知的可能。而这种非自愿告知一般以网络服务提供商与用户之间签订的协议为前提，换言之，通过这种协议，用户将个人信息告知给网络服务提供商。而对于此种信息的利用方式与分析方式则视不同网站管理者的选择而有所不同。但是，由于此类协议的存在，用户一般会选择告知网络服务提供商自己的个人信息，从而使个人隐私被泄露的可能性增大。

---

❶ 向淑君. 敞开与遮蔽——新媒介时代的隐私问题研究［M］. 北京：知识产权出版社，2011：91.

（2）个人隐私包含内容的扩大❶

现实生活中的隐私包含的内容较小，一般都是与个人身份或活动领域有关的信息。但是网络环境下的个人隐私还包括各式各样的非身份性的信息，比如用户的浏览记录、购买记录、聊天内容、网络存储空间中保留的资源等。这些信息的公开很可能造成用户的困扰与不便，用户一般也不希望别人能够获取此类信息。因此，用户在互联网之上的行为都会成为其个人隐私，从而使法律对其保护变得较为困难。

（3）具有人格权与财产权的双重属性❷

现实生活中的隐私权一般仅具有人格属性，对于某人隐私的侵犯一般也是造成精神损害而非经济损害。而在网络环境下，个人隐私一般会与财产权利密切相关，比如网上银行的密码，支付宝的密码等。不法分子如果获得此类个人隐私，则必然能够利用其获取经济上的不法收益。因而在互联网环境下更可能出现侵犯个人隐私的情形。

总而言之，基于互联网环境的介入以及对于大数据的广泛需求，个人隐私的内涵与外延发生了本质的变化，从而使个人隐私的保护问题亟待解决。同样的，网络环境下的个人隐私也越来越需要法律为其提供更为合适的保护模式。

三、各国互联网隐私政策的比较研究

（一）对我国隐私政策❸立法实践的分析

如何在网络环境下保护个人隐私权在我国一直是处于争议之中的问题。2012 年年底全国人大常委会发布的《关于加强网络信息保护的决定》以及2013 年 4 月工信部公布的《电信和互联网用户个人信息保护规定（征求意见稿）》（下文简称《征求意见稿》）代表了我国在个人信息保护领域的最新立法动向。本文将这两份法律文件的核心内容归纳为以下两点：

第一，界定保护对象的范围。《关于加强网络信息保护的决定》第 1 条将其保护对象表述为"个人电子信息"，并且以"能够识别公民个人身份"和"涉及公民个人隐私"两个并列条件进行限定。《征求意见稿》第 4 条虽然将保护对象表述为"个人信息"，但由于其已经限定了电信和互联网领域，因而

---

❶ 倪铁宝. 网络隐私权研究——以"人肉搜索"和"艳照门"为视角 ［D］. 山东大学法学院，2012.

❷ 向淑君. 敞开与遮蔽——新媒介时代的隐私问题研究 ［M］. 北京：知识产权出版社，2011：94.

❸ 隐私政策（privacy policy），规定各实体有关个人信息收集和利用的实践，以及保护个人隐私的措施。参见：FRED H. CATE. 常见术语定义 ［G］//周汉华. 个人信息保护前沿问题研究. 苏苗罕，译. 北京：法律出版社，2006：420.

可以认为与"个人电子信息"具有相同内涵；但在限定条件上则只有能够识别用户一个方面并进行了姓名、账号等不完全列举，并无"涉及公民个人隐私"的要求。

这两份法律文件对保护对象范围的界定存在以下问题：首先，形式上最为明显的问题在于两份文件的保护范围不同。《征求意见稿》理应符合人大常委会发布的《关于加强网络信息保护的决定》，然而却把该决定中明确表述的"涉及公民个人隐私"的限定条件舍弃了，看似是扩大了对公民的保护范围，实则另一方面则是对网络服务提供商的行为加以不合理的限制：能够识别公民身份却不涉及个人隐私的信息不属于《关于加强网络信息保护的决定》规定的保护范围。其次，出现了"个人隐私"的表述但尚未明确其内涵。或许这也是《征求意见稿》将这个方面舍弃而将识别公民个人身份方面加以列举式细化的原因之一，由于所谓隐私的内容并不明确，将会导致实践中执法标准的不统一。最后也是最为本质的问题在于，这两份文件的表述反映出我国学界和实务界对个人信息保护对象的认识不统一。是应当广义地保护个人信息，甚至专门立法创设个人信息权，❶ 还是应当保护狭义上的隐私？结合前文对隐私权内涵外延的学理分析，作者认为通过对隐私权的保护，实际上就能实现个人对于保护自身信息的需求。

对于公民而言，那些与其个人身份识别无关，或是虽然与身份识别有关但已经向不特定多数人公开的信息并不具有特别保护的价值；而对网络服务提供商而言，这些非隐私的个人信息通过大数据技术处理将会产生巨大的商业价值。因此经过利益衡量，不应对非隐私的个人信息加以过高保护。虽然《关于加强网络信息保护的决定》第1条并未明确何为隐私，但通过两方面的界定仍然体现出了狭义保护的倾向。如果能将原文表述为"能够识别公民个人身份并未被公民自愿公开的个人电子信息"，则更为恰当。

第二，确定网络服务提供商搜集数据的方式为"明示同意"。根据《关于加强网络信息保护的决定》第2条和《征求意见稿》第9条的规定，网络服务提供商使用用户个人信息的时候必须明确地征询并取得同意，同时负有"告知用户收集、使用信息的目的、方式和范围，留存信息的期限，查询、更正信息的渠道以及拒绝提供信息的后果等事项"的义务。

如果说狭义的保护公民的隐私信息是赋予网络服务提供商更多利用数据的机会，那"明示同意"的使用规则无疑则是对其行为加诸的限制。对于网络服务提供商而言，由于相关数据未对不特定多数人公开，因此网络服务提供商每次使用隐私信息都要得到明确同意，而对每个用户进行重复、显著、

---

❶ 关于设立个人信息权的建议，参见：王利明．论个人信息权在人格权法中的地位［J］．苏州大学学报：哲学社会科学版，2012（6）．

详细的意向征询，并等待其回应意味着服务成本的大量增加。而更为深刻的考虑在于，我们设置个人隐私信息搜集和保护模式时的立场倾向：在大数据时代，隐私信息不仅仅是一种被消极保护的人格权客体，更是可能会带来商业价值、增进公共利益的重要生产要素。如何在这两种属性的倾向间作出抉择？他山之石可以攻玉，为了澄清这个问题，本文试图着力介绍美国以及欧盟的隐私政策，希望从比较研究中探寻解决之道。

（二）美国的隐私政策

虽然在美国并不存在专门保护个人隐私的法律，但是却有相当多的部门法、州法对网络环境中的个人隐私提供保护，例如金融服务现代化法、健康保险转移与责任法、驾驶员隐私保护法、公平信用报告法、儿童在线隐私保护法、联邦贸易委员会法、消费者保护法、电子通信隐私法、电讯法等。但美国隐私政策的核心部分却不是这些法律。美国对网络隐私权的保护是市场主导模式，以行业自律为主，其通过从事网络服务的主体自行制定的行业行为规范来说明服务提供商们在网络隐私问题上的立场、态度和具体的保护措施，并以这些规范来约束网络从业者的行为。❶

在法律规范和行业规范的双重指导下，美国隐私政策的内容主要体现为如下几个方面：

1. 网络用户的隐私由联邦行政机关与网络服务提供商共同保护

根据美国一直以来保护隐私权的实践，联邦行政机关提供保护的方式主要是进行监督，即督促网络服务提供商在网站之上公布符合法律要求以及符合该网站真实经营模式的隐私政策并对其进行检查。根据《联邦贸易委员会法》的第五节禁止"商业上或影响商业的不公平的或欺骗性的做法"之授权，❷ 美国联邦贸易委员会对于未按照法律规定公布隐私政策的网站可以进行调查并提起指控。

但实际上，真正担负起保护用户隐私指责的主体仍旧是网络服务提供商。这些网络中的经营者必须按照法律的要求公布适于本网站的隐私政策，而且只能按照公布之隐私政策对相关用户的个人信息加以搜集和利用，不能超出公开政策的范围采取措施或行动。与此同时，对于经用户同意获取的个人隐私，网站也必须承担保护用户信息不被盗用或泄露的义务。因此在美国，隐私的保护由联邦行政机关和网络服务提供商共同进行，且后者为主要保护者。

---

❶ 向淑君. 敞开与遮蔽——新媒介时代的隐私问题研究［M］. 北京：知识产权出版社，2011：112.

❷ FRED H. CATE. 美国的隐私保护［G］//周汉华. 个人信息保护前沿问题研究. 苏苗罕，译. 北京：法律出版社，2006：84.

2. 法律及行业规范提供的保护针对的是用户的个人隐私

法律及行业规范所明确保护的是用户的个人隐私，而非用户所有的个人信息。如前文所说，用户在网站上公开的可以被任何浏览网页的不特定的网络使用者获取的信息并不是保护的对象。换言之，由用户个人自愿公开到网络之上的信息是不能算作隐私的，自然也就不受到隐私政策的保护。而事实上，对于这部分信息提供保护也是没有必要的。

3. 网络服务提供商以"默示同意"的方式取得用户的个人信息

以促进网络服务的便利与快捷为目标，美国的隐私政策采取了默示同意的原则，即网站即使未经信息主体明确同意，只要在接到相关通知后用户没有明确表示拒绝，则视为其默示同意对其个人信息进行搜集和使用。❶ 网站在搜集或使用用户的个人信息时，会通知相关用户或在网页之上作出提示，用户无视通知继续浏览网页或接受相关服务的应当视为已经同意网络服务提供商的搜集或使用行为。用户的"默示同意"意味着只要网络服务提供商按照其说明的方式搜集或利用个人数据，则用户不能再推翻之前的允诺。

4. 主要通过行业隐私政策明确网络服务提供商对于用户个人信息的搜集及利用方式

网络服务提供商在其网站之上必须按照法律公布隐私政策，而这一政策的核心内容就是其对于用户个人信息的搜集及使用的方式。以谷歌公司的隐私政策❷为例："我们的隐私权政策解释了以下几个方面的问题：我们搜集那些信息，以及搜集这些信息的原因；我们对这些信息的使用方式；我们为您提供的选择，包括如何访问和更新信息。"通过网站上公开的隐私政策用户可以知晓自己的个人信息何时以怎样的方式被搜集或利用，也能够作出适当的选择：是继续接受该网站提供的网络服务或者是为了保护隐私而放弃接受服务。这种模式要求用户尽到一定的注意义务，要求其了解网络服务提供商的搜集并利用个人信息的方式。而实际上，只有用户有权决定自己的哪些信息以何种方式可以被网络服务提供商利用。而一般的网站隐私政策也会指出，用户拒绝其进行信息搜集和使用工作也不会影响用户享受网站提供的基本服务。

综上所述，美国的隐私政策倾向于强调保证网络服务提供商对于个人信息的正常搜集和使用。❸ 自然人个人有权决定自己的隐私能够被搜集与利用，

---

❶ 姚朝兵. 个人信用信息隐私保护的制度构建——欧盟及美国立法对我国的启示 [J]. 情报理论与实践，2013（3）.

❷ [EB/OL].（2012-07-27）[2013-06-11].http：//www.google.com.hk/intl/zh-CN/policies/privacy/.

❸ 郭瑜. 个人数据保护法研究 [M]. 北京：北京大学出版社，2012：53.

而只要权利人不明示拒绝，且对于个人隐私的搜集与利用方式是合法并合理的，网络服务提供商就不承担侵犯隐私权的责任。所以，美国的隐私政策尊重个人信息的正常使用，并且不排斥网络服务提供商利用这些包括个人隐私的信息获取一定的商业利益。总而言之，对于自然人隐私权的保护，其在法律的支持下高度依赖市场力量和个人行动，❶ 从而适应了大数据时代对于个人信息的需求。

（三）欧盟的隐私政策

与美国隐私政策的出发点存在着明显的不同，欧盟的隐私政策对于自然人隐私权的保护问题是非常重视的。根据《欧洲人权公约》第 8 条的规定：每个人都有权要求其私人和家庭生活、住宅和通信受到尊重。因此在欧洲，个人的隐私权被看作是人权的一项而被予以大力保护。欧盟的隐私政策主要由数个具有法律拘束力的指令组成，包括《欧洲议会和欧盟理事会 1995 年 10 月 24 日与个人数据处理有关的个人保护以及此类数据的自由流动指令》、《欧洲议会和欧盟理事会 2002 年 7 月 12 日关于电子通信领域个人数据处理和隐私保护的指令》、《欧洲议会和欧盟理事会 2006 年 3 月 15 日关于保留公用电子通信服务或公共通信网络中处理或生成的数据以及修改指令》。在这些指令之下，各成员国都制定了与之相符且配套的本国法律来推进个人隐私的保护工作。由于成员国的法律与这些指令的要求基本一致，因此本文着重分析的是欧盟整体的隐私政策，即分析上述这些指令的相关内容。

与美国的隐私政策相比，欧盟所指定的规则并没有赋予行业规范以很高的效力，主要想通过具有强制力的法律条文对与互联网环境下用户隐私的各类问题作出明确、具体的规定，具体可以从如下几个方面窥知一二：

1. 个人隐私主要由欧盟数据保护机构、欧盟成员国的数据保护机构提供保护

能够为网络用户的隐私提供保护的欧盟机构有很多，这其中就包括负责制定三大指令的欧盟议会，负责监督欧盟成员国落实三大指令的欧盟委员会，负责解释法律并对相关争议进行裁决的欧盟正义法院，以及负责专门解释文件做咨询工作的"第 29 条工作委员会"以及负责检查欧盟的相关立法是否与指令相符的欧盟数据保护署。❷ 欧盟数据保护机构的工作主要是监督三大指令的落实情况，对欧盟成员国的相关法律文件进行审查，并对与指令不符的地方作出指明和纠正，从而保证各个国家都对互联网环境下用户的隐私权提供

---

❶ FRED H. CATE. 美国的隐私保护 ［G］//周汉华. 个人信息保护前沿问题研究. 苏苗罕，译. 北京：法律出版社，2006：102.

❷ 各机构的具体职责参见：CHRISTOPHER KUNER. 欧盟的隐私和数据保护 ［G］//周汉华. 个人信息保护前沿问题研究. 温珍奎，译. 北京：法律出版社，2006：29-30.

保护。

按照指令的要求，欧盟的每个成员国必须设立国家统一的数据保护机构。欧盟成员国必须制定保护用户个人隐私的法律，并且按照指令中明确的 6 大原则——合法原则、终极原则、透明原则、合适原则、保密和安全原则及监控原则❶对个人信息提供保护。因此欧盟数据保护机构保证各国法律为个人隐私提供保护，而各国的数据保护机构则保证相关法律能够得到落实，欧盟的隐私政策是由这两个主体密切配合共同协作才得到很好的贯彻与执行的。

2. 指令提供的保护及与特定或可特定的自然人有关的所有信息❷

与本文之前提出的建议不同，欧盟的隐私政策对与特定或可特定的自然人有关的所有信息提供保护。三个指令在保护对象上同时使用了个人数据与隐私，实际上就赋予了非隐私的个人信息以同等的权利。这就好比我们向不特定的人公开了自己的电子邮件，而如果其中任何一个知道邮件地址的人若想将其再转述给别人就可能侵犯了我们的权利。因此，指令的保护对象是非常宽泛的，这一规定反映出了欧盟隐私政策在应对大数据时代到来的问题上可能存在严重不足，从而影响欧洲各国网络服务产业的发展。

3. 指令采取赋权的方式保护用户的隐私权，非经"明示同意"即为侵权

欧盟委员会在通过指令的声明中指出：该指令为数据主体赋予了一系列重要权利，包括有权获取数据，有权知道数据源自何处，有权要求纠正不准确的数据，有权对不法处理数据者诉诸法律，甚至有权在某些情形下收回其允许使用数据的许可等。❸ 而任何被认为是个人信息的数据只有在征得权利人同意的前提下，网络服务提供商才可以按照指令的要求对这些数据进行收集和利用。因此，指令以赋予权利的方式对用户的个人隐私提供了保护，这也就必然导致对于个人隐私的搜集和利用需经过权利人的明示同意。这与欧盟将个人隐私权作为一种人权的观念是一脉相承的。任何自然人所享有的人权必定是一种不可让渡性的权利，其不同于财产规则与责任规则下的权利，别人对其隐私的利用不仅必须征得同意，而且权利人可以在任何情况下不再同意。这实际上是非常不利于大数据时代网络服务提供商对于信息的获取与利用的，也就使得相较于信息的交流与传播来说，隐私权具有更为强势的地位。

---

❶ 具体内容参见：CHRISTOPHER KUNER. 欧盟的隐私和数据保护 [G] //周汉华. 个人信息保护前沿问题研究. 温珍奎, 译. 北京：法律出版社, 2006：32.

❷ 向淑君. 敞开与遮蔽——新媒介时代的隐私问题研究 [M]. 北京：知识产权出版社, 2011：111.

❸ 约纳森·罗森诺. 网络法——关于因特网的法律 [M]. 张皋彤, 等, 译. 北京：中国政法大学出版社, 2003：222-223.

4. 指令明确规定网络服务提供商可以搜集并使用个人信息的条件、内容、方式

在基本原则的指导下，指令还明确了网络服务提供商在何种前提下以何种方式利用哪些个人信息。以网络通信为例，除了公共安全的需要，网络服务提供商只能为指定的、明示的、合法的目的而搜集，这种目的需得到当事人同意；网络服务提供商只可以利用数据拨打广告电话、发送广告传真、发送电子邮件、留存与通信有关的各类数据。对于除此之外的任何用途，指令都没有提及或认可。因此，欧盟的隐私政策只能解决当前大数据时代的问题，并不适用于现代网络服务提供商的运营模式，也就最终制约了这些网站提供相应服务的可能。

四、机遇与挑战：大数据时代、隐私权保护与利益衡量

如前所述，在大数据时代个人信息已经成为具有商业价值的资源，我们不能片面地阻止所有搜集或利用个人信息的行为。根据各国的立法经验，互联网环境下的个人隐私权主要是指"公民在网络上享有的私人生活安宁与私人信息依法受到保护，不被他人非法侵犯、知悉、搜集、复制、公开和利用；也指禁止在网上泄露与个人有关的敏感信息"。● 以此为准，法律所应当制止的侵害隐私的行为主要是针对恶意搜集并使用个人信息，主要包括非经权利人同意不得将个人隐私公开、转卖、泄露。

美欧两地的隐私政策存在着根本的不同，但对于网络用户隐私的保护效果是相差无几的。因为在现实中，网络服务提供商没有必要恶意搜集或使用用户的个人隐私，其所关注的无非对于这些信息进行商业化使用所带来的利益。而对于任何的恶意侵犯用户隐私的行为——例如贩卖个人隐私、盗取用户密码等实际上都会被美欧的隐私政策予以规制。个人信息的交易（包括个人隐私的交易）毕竟是市场行为，市场主体通过合意是可以使信息资源的分配达到最优的。法律只需明确信息归属，而对于信息的利用方式完全可以交给网络行业的自治性规章来解决。网络用户对于信息搜集与利用行为的反感和排斥可以通过"用脚投票"的方式予以解决。不仅如此，网络服务提供商搜集信息的目的就是为了"投其所好"，以用户的需求为出发点提供服务，其必定可以在市场经营的过程中调节自己的行为以满足网络用户对于个人隐私保护的需求。

因此，我国未来出台的"个人信息保护法"应当将出发点放在应对大数据时代带来的机遇与挑战上，在对现实发生的问题进行有效回应的同时避免

● 刁胜先. 论网络隐私权之隐私范围［J］. 西南民族大学学报，2003（2）.

造成过分限制网络服务提供商搜集及利用个人信息的结果发生。事实已经证明，数据作为一类资源其价值已经在不断地发掘之中。如果我们对于这类资源予以过分的保护，禁止其被商业利用的可能必定使我国网络服务业，甚至高新技术业的发展落后于世界发达国家的水平。隐私对我们个人很重要，但信息时代的好处更重要，良善的法律关注的是信息的有害滥用，并且能够给相关经营者指明自我管理、避免有害滥用的方向。❶ 从这个角度出发，以行业自治为基础辅以强制性法律保证的互联网环境下的隐私政策才更为适宜。

在当前的大数据时代中，个人和社会通过市场前所未有地紧密结合起来，但同时两者之间的对立和紧张关系却也同步加剧。传统上作为个人主体性地位之重要保障的隐私信息，由于技术的飞速进步而成为增进社会公共利益的利器，并因之带有了巨大的商业价值。个人隐私的保护以及信息资源的利用在大数据时代成为一对看似不可调和的矛盾，但事实上制定一个良好而完善的隐私政策不仅能够对个人隐私提供足够的保护，还能够促进社会对于信息资源的搜集与利用。

我们无须在个人本位与社会本位的立场间抉择不定，而应把目光放在个人、网络服务提供商与社会三者的现实利益关系当中。良善的隐私保护政策应当将以下 3 组关系的动态平衡视为设计目标：维持个人与网络服务提供商相对平等的市场地位和谈判能力，使个人对隐私的维护与企业对信息的获取处于相互制衡之中；政府应当在保障网络服务提供商之市场活动自由的同时引导企业避免信息资源的有害滥用；在满足人作为主体之尊严的前提下，个人隐私权应有所限制以促进公共利益的增加和科技水平的提高。

法律在现代作为社会控制的主要手段，有可能为最大多数人做最多的事情，❷ 而法律制度的设计者们则位于现在和未来的十字路口之上，时刻在对现实的维护和对未来的期望之间顾盼游移。面临大数据时代的机遇和挑战，法律和政策应当更多地着眼于未来、立足于社会的进步，为人类探索美好明天努力提供制度性的保障。

---

❶ MARTIN E. ABRAMS. 新兴数字经济时代的隐私、安全与经济增长［G］//周汉华. 个人信息保护前沿问题研究. 温珍奎，译. 北京：法律出版社，2006：25.

❷ 罗斯科·庞德. 通过法律的社会控制［M］. 沈宗灵，译. 北京：商务印书馆，2010：37-39.

我国知识产权领域反垄断问题研究*

赵 雪

一、知识产权法与反垄断法关系概述

就知识产权与反垄断之间的关系而言，二者既有矛盾的一面，亦有相通的一面。

首先，从表面上看，二者是相互矛盾的。"正如美国法院在 1981 年 United States 诉 Westinghouse Elec. Corp. 一案中所指出的那样：一种法律创立和保护垄断的权利，而同时另一种法律则力求禁止这样的垄断权。"❶ 不难看出，知识产权法的法律功能旨在保护权利人的独占使用，确立并保护合法"垄断"——知识产权，而反垄断法的功能则在于保护市场自由竞争，反对垄断。

其次，二者的最终目的或者说是实施效果是一致的，即推动技术的发展和增进消费者的福利。就知识产权而言，知识产权的存在本身就是为了鼓励发明和创造，尤其是在著作权和专利权领域，通过给予权利人相关的权利，使其获得精神上或者物质上的回报，从而达到鼓励发明创造、创作的目的，再通过合理使用、法定许可等一系列的制度，促进知识和技术的传播，使更多的人受益。就商标而言，通过商标制度的实施，既有助于保障消费者的合法权益，又有利于提升相关企业的商誉以及消费者的认可度，在消费者和商家之间建立互信机制，促进高质量的产品流通市场，保护消费者的合法权益。反垄断法则是通过保护市场的自由竞争，对卡特尔、滥用市场支配地位等现象警醒规制，最终促成自由市场竞争，使消费者从竞争市场中获益。

最后，知识产权法和反垄断法在激励创新方面是殊途同归的，反垄断法用竞争的"大棒"（不创新的企业就要遭到淘汰）来促进鼓励初始创新的市场结构；知识产权法则用有限专有性及由此获得的利益的"胡萝卜"来鼓励初始创新。反垄断法通过保护在专有性的知识产权以外的竞争机会来促使后续创新；知识产权法则通过要求初始创新的公开以及为后续创新者提供"合

---

* 撰写论文时作者为中国人民大学学生，本文获 2013 年度隆天知识产权优秀论文奖。
❶ 转引自：吴汉东. 知识产权基本问题研究［M］. 2 版. 北京：中国人民大学出版社，2009：164.

理使用"和不受知识产权"滥用"的权利来促使后续创新。❶

二者之间的关系在实践中也是表现得惟妙惟肖,作为现代反垄断法的发源地美国在处理知识产权和反垄断之间的关系方面也经历了一个由冲突转向互补的过程。从 20 世纪 30 年代到 70 年代,美国反托拉斯法在限制知识产权方面充当了积极的角色,法院亦倾向于将知识产权特别是专利与垄断联系在一起,认为知识产权很少能成为反托拉斯法的例外。❷ 在 20 世纪 80 年代之后,随着美国芝加哥学派经济自由主义和社会达尔文主义的新经济结构理论的提出,美国反托拉斯法的实施发生了重大的变革,主要表现在"合理原则"分析方法的采用以及"本身违法原则"适用范围的缩小。这主要反映在美国 1988 年和 1995 年的反托拉斯指南当中,1995 年指南更是鲜明地强调了知识产权法和反托拉斯法存在推动技术和增进消费者福利的共同目的。❸

从总体上说,知识产权法与反垄断法是一种既对立又统一的关系。知识产权在本质上构成一定的垄断,而反垄断法的规制对象则是一定的垄断行为,从立法旨趣来说,两者似乎存在着冲突之处。但是,在一国法律体系中,二者的最终目标是相同的,同时在规制知识产权滥用方面具有互动和协调的功能。反垄断法所规制的是知识产权的滥用,而知识产权的滥用构成了知识产权保护和反垄断审查的连接点。❹

我国《反垄断法》第 55 条规定:"经营者依照有关知识产权的法律、行政法规规定行使知识产权的行为,不适用本法;但是,经营者滥用知识产权,排除、限制竞争的行为,适用本法。"该条前半句表明通过知识产权获得的单纯垄断状态或者市场支配地位本身并不违反《反垄断法》,是对合法行使知识产权行为适用除外的规定,知识产权权利人可以以该条文抗辩,但基于"谁主张,谁举证"的原则,知识产权权利人应当承担举证责任,证明其权利行使未超越合法行使的边界。

《反垄断法》第 55 条后半句则表明违反《反垄断法》的行为即使发生在行使知识产权的过程中仍然要受《反垄断法》的规制,是对滥用知识产权限制竞争行为的禁止规定。知识产权的滥用是一种权利滥用,并因排除、限制竞争而构成《反垄断法》所规制的垄断行为。如果知识产权行使超越了法律规定的权利边界,并且排除或者限制了竞争,则构成《反垄断法》意义上的权利滥用,将受到《反垄断法》的规制。

---

❶ 王先林. 知识产权与反垄断法——知识产权滥用的反垄断问题研究 [M]. 北京:法律出版社,2001:84-85.

❷ 宁立志. 美国反托拉斯法中的专利权行使 [J]. 法学评论,2005.(5).

❸ 吴汉东. 知识产权基本问题研究 [M]. 2 版. 北京:中国人民大学出版社,2009:165.

❹ 吴汉东. 知识产权基本问题研究 [M]. 2 版. 北京:中国人民大学出版社,2009:168.

二、滥用知识产权的认定

由于知识产权被视为合法的垄断，在 20 世纪反垄断法兴起时，各国对知识产权无一例外地适用除外的规定。然而，建立在市场驱动机制基础上的知识产权制度带来的知识产权保护的异化，对创新和公平竞争带来了巨大的阻碍作用。由于利用知识产权进行限制竞争的行为越来越普遍，各国对知识产权的规制态度开始发生转变，从绝对豁免转向相对豁免，陆续在反垄断法中确立知识产权滥用行为的规制标准和前提。反垄断法对知识产权滥用的规制在于维护有效竞争，使得社会个体的知识产权行使行为不至损害社会的整体利益。反垄断法的限制主要运用公权力介入的方式，通过政府的干预实现对宏观利益的维护。❶

知识产权的滥用，是相对于知识产权的正当行使而言的，意指权利人在行驶其知识产权时超出了法律所允许的范围或正当的界限，损害他人利益和社会公共利益的情形。❷ 滥用知识产权的行为并不导致知识产权本身无效。但是，滥用知识产权却会导致公法和私法上的违法。就违反私法而言，知识产权的滥用会导致权利人丧失依其知识产权专有权请求救济的可能。

根据《反垄断法》第 55 条以及知识产权滥用的规制实践，构成《反垄断法》下的滥用知识产权需要满足下列条件：①滥用知识产权的经营者应当享有知识产权；②经营者实施了达成垄断协议、滥用市场支配地位、经营者集中等滥用知识产权的行为；③经营者滥用知识产权的行为限制或排除了公平竞争。三者缺一不可。

首先，享有知识产权的经营者一般是知识产权所有人或者是通过独占许可或者合同约定的方式而享有知识产权权利人的全部权利之人。但是，有学者指出对于下列情形的经营者而言，虽然其权利存在瑕疵，但仍然可能构成滥用知识产权：①通过欺骗或不正当手段获得了权利并进行滥用；②利用知识产权制度的设计而获得本不该获得的权利，例如，专利授权制度中对实用新型和外观设计不进行实质性审查即授权。❸

其次，经营者实施了滥用知识产权行为。根据《反垄断法》对垄断行为的规定，这类滥用知识产权，排除或者限制竞争行为包括：①通过达成垄断协议来滥用知识产权；②通过滥用市场支配地位来滥用知识产权；③进行具有排除和限制竞争效果的经营者集中。

---

❶ 吴敬琏，江平. 洪范评论（Journal of Legal and Economic Studies）：知识产权——法律与基本政策的反思 [M]. 北京：生活·读书·新知三联书店，2012：75.

❷ 吴汉东. 知识产权基本问题研究 [M]. 2 版. 北京：中国人民大学出版社，2009：168.

❸ 反垄断法实务指南 [EB/OL]. 威科先行.

最后，该滥用知识产权的行为限制或排除了公平竞争。经营者实施的滥用知识产权的行为如果并未造成限制或排除竞争的后果，则一般不受《反垄断法》的规制，但可能受到《专利法》、《商标法》等知识产权法律的规制。经营者滥用知识产权的行为一般应具有排除或限制竞争的故意。❶ 但是，需要注意的是，我国《反垄断法》没有将主观意图作为认定构成垄断行为的要件。

在知识产权滥用的判断上，垄断地位的判断和排除、限制竞争的效果的判断是比较复杂而且重要的。而是否具有垄断地位主要是看相关市场的界定和市场份额的判断。就相关市场的界定而言，依据我国国务院反垄断委员会《关于相关市场界定的指南》的有关规定进行判断，如在"奇虎360诉腾讯"一案中，法官也是以此来界定相关市场的，这包括对"假定垄断者测试"的运用。当然，遇到具体案例还是要具体分析。就排除和限制竞争的效果而言，在民事案件中主要体现的是双方当事人的举证责任。根据《最高人民法院关于审理因垄断行为引发的民事纠纷案件应用法律若干问题的规定》（以下简称《反垄断民事诉讼司法解释》），在横向垄断协议的情形下，实行举证责任倒置，即被告应举证证明协议的存在不具有排除、限制竞争的作用；而在纵向垄断的情形下，则仍然是"谁主张，谁举证"，这在最近的"锐邦诉强生"二审判决里亦有所体现。

三、我国滥用知识产权的相关规定梳理

从立法上而言，我国《反垄断法》第 55 条只是从宏观上肯定了滥用知识产权的行为将受到《反垄断法》的规制，对于哪些行为可能构成具有排除和限制竞争效果的滥用知识产权的行为，并没有具体规定。对滥用知识产权的限制行为进行规制的相关规定散见于其他法律法规当中。以下作简要梳理。

首先，涉及滥用知识产权规制的法律有：（1）《合同法》第 329 条规定，非法垄断技术、妨碍技术进步或者侵害他人技术成果的技术合同无效；第 343 条规定，技术转让合同可以约定让与人与受让人实施专利或者使用技术秘密的范围，但不得限制技术竞争和技术发展。（2）《对外贸易法》第 30 条规定：对于下列滥用知识产权的限制竞争行为，国务院对外贸易主管部门可以采取必要的措施消除危害：①阻止被许可人对许可合同中知识产权的有效性提出质疑；②进行强制性一揽子许可；③在许可合同中规定排他性返授条件；④其他滥用知识产权的限制竞争行为。很明显这是参照了 TRIPS 协议的相关内容。

其次，涉及滥用知识产权规制的行政法规有：《中华人民共和国技术进出

---

❶ 反垄断法实务指南［EB/OL］. 威科先行.

口管理条例》。该条例第 29 条列举了技术合同中不得含有的 7 种限制性条款，这也可以视为对于滥用知识产权行为的限制，具体包括：① 搭售；②专利权有效期限届满或专利权无效后的义务；③限制改进技术；④限制技术来源；⑤限制购买；⑥限制产量、品种、价格；⑦出口限制。

最后，涉及滥用知识产权规制的司法解释有：（1）《最高人民法院关于审理因垄断行为引发的民事纠纷案件应用法律若干问题的规定》。这部司法解释规定了起诉、案件受理、管辖、举证责任分配、诉讼证据、民事责任及诉讼时效等问题，建立了我国反垄断民事诉讼的基本框架。在举证责任分配方面，司法解释区分不同的垄断行为类型，明确了当事人的举证责任分配。（2）《最高人民法院关于审理技术合同纠纷案件适用法律若干问题的解释》。其中第 10 条对《合同法》第 329 条作出了解释，规定了"非法垄断技术、妨碍技术进步"所包括的 6 种具体情形：①限制技术研发和限制使用或不对等交换改进技术；②限制技术来源；③限制技术实施；④搭售；⑤限制购买；⑥不主张专利权。

TRIPS 协议仅列举了 3 项滥用知识产权的行为：①独占性的返授条件；②禁止对有关知识产权的有效性提出异议的条件；③强制性一揽子许可。根据 TRIPS 协议，各国可以对什么是滥用知识产权进行广泛的定义。

四、知识产权领域垄断案件的分析

在知识产权领域的反垄断案件，当属微软一案为全球最有影响力的案件。以欧盟反垄断机构对微软调查与处罚为例（见下表），反垄断对于知识产权的规制越来越成为一种规制知识产权权利人滥用知识产权、维护市场有效竞争和消费者权益的重要手段。

欧盟反垄断机构对微软调查与处罚大事记❶

2013 年	欧盟反不当竞争监管机构因微软未能遵守 2009 年有关网页浏览器选择的承诺，对该公司罚款 5.61 亿欧元
2012 年	根据微软的上诉，欧盟第二最高法庭将 2008 年的罚款从 8.99 亿欧元降低至 8.60 亿欧元
2009 年	微软与欧盟就 2008 年有关浏览器选择的调查达成和解，提出允许用户访问竞争对手的产品
2008 年	欧盟委员会向微软罚款 8.99 亿欧元，因其再次未能遵守欧盟在 2004 年发出的命令

---

❶ 中国反垄断网.

续表

2008 年	欧盟监管机构展开两项新调查，一项是互操作性问题，另一项是浏览器选择
2006 年	欧盟委员会再向微软罚款 2.805 亿欧元，因其未向竞争对手提供数据，没有遵守欧盟 2004 年发出的命令
2004 年	欧盟监管机构因为微软未能向竞争对手提供数据并且将 Media Player 与其操作系统绑定，对该公司罚款 4.97 亿欧元
2000 年	欧盟委员会开始对微软将 Media Player 与其操作系统绑定进行调查
1998 年	由于太阳微系统对微软提出申诉，欧盟委员会对后者展开调查，以了解操作系统的互操作性问题

但在我国，知识产权领域的反垄断案例并不多见。在检索相关法律数据库后发现，就知识产权领域反垄断法民事诉讼案例而言：在万律（Westlaw）仅有 20 个，在北大法宝仅有 13 个，威科先行法律数据库中仅有 5 个相关案例。剔除 3 个数据库中的重复案件、合并相同案件的一审和二审之后，最终有判决书可查的案例不到 15 个。

其中值得一提的是"3Q 大战"即"奇虎 360 诉腾讯滥用市场支配地位"一案。在该案中，奇虎 360 以腾讯滥用市场支配地位为由，请求法院判令腾讯立即停止滥用市场地位，停止实施 QQ 软件用户不得与原告交易并捆绑搭售安全产品等行为，赔偿经济损失 1.5 亿元，并公开道歉。最终，广东省高级人民法院对本案作出了一审判决，驳回奇虎 360 公司的全部诉讼请求，腾讯公司不构成垄断。据悉，这是国内首个在即时通信领域对垄断行为作出认定的判决。另外，2013 年 8 月 1 日，也即在《反垄断法》实施 5 周年的纪念日当天，上海市高级人民法院对全国第一起纵向垄断协议案件（锐邦诉强生案）作出终审判决，判决上诉人（原告锐邦）胜诉，被上诉人强生应在判决生效之日起 10 日内赔偿上诉人锐邦经济损失人民币 53 万元。本案也是迄今为止第一起二审法院撤销一审判决并判决原告胜诉的反垄断民事案件。❶ 在本案中，强生经销合同中限定最低转售价格的条款最终被认定为具有排除、限制公平竞争的作用。

在我国，垄断争议除了可以通过民事诉讼的方式来解决之外，与之共存的是行政解决方式，即我国反垄断的双轨制。目前，垄断争议由国务院反垄断执法机构（包括商务部下设的反垄断局、国家发展和改革委员会下设的价格监督检查司、国家工商行政管理总局下设的反垄断与不正当竞争执法

---

❶ 宁宣凤，尹冉冉，刘佳. 第一起纵向垄断协议民事诉讼案件：锐邦诉强生固定转售价格案简析 [J/OL]. 中国法律期刊，2013（8）.

局）解决。其中，国家工商行政管理总局的主要职责包括负责垄断协议、滥用市场支配地位、滥用行政权力排除限制竞争方面的反垄断执法工作（价格垄断行为除外）；国家发展改革委员会的主要职责是查处涉及价格因素的滥用知识产权的行为；商务部则主要负责依法对经营者集中行为进行反垄断审查，各部门分工明确，俨然形成三足鼎立之势。

《反垄断法》实施至今确实有很大收效。例如，中国商务部今年 5 月 23 日公布数据，截至今年 3 月 31 日，商务部共收到经营者集中反垄断申报 698 件，立案 627 件，审结 579 件。在审结案件中，无条件批准了 562 件，占 97.1%，附加限制条件批准 16 件，禁止 1 件。国家发改委近年因市场垄断行为对企业处罚也在不断加强，这包括最近的 6 家奶企因价格垄断被罚 6.68 亿元；茅台和五粮液因实施价格垄断行为将被合计罚款 4.49 亿元；三星等 6 家境外企业因液晶面板价格垄断被罚 3.53 亿元等。这些数据一方面凸显出了我国对反垄断法执行的力度在不断加强，也从侧面反映出在知识产权领域做好反垄断工作是十分重要的。

五、对我国知识产权领域反垄断规制的建议

我国《反垄断法》实施 5 年多来，可谓硕果累累。但同时，随着科技的迅猛发展，知识产权领域越来越复杂化，如通过网络侵犯著作权、抢注域名等案件量迅速飙升。对知识产权领域的反垄断规制越发显得重要。而且，我国在知识产权领域的反垄断立法和实践都处于一个初步的阶段，很多问题需要立法和司法进一步明确。在此过程中，我们要不断地去研究国外的法律以及相关著作，进一步探讨中国知识产权领域反垄断的改革与发展思路。

首先，基于知识产权法本身对权利行使的限制和《反垄断法》对知识产权的限制，可采取双管齐下的策略。如在专利中，滥用专利权的行为构成垄断的，行为人在承担《反垄断法》规定的法律责任的同时可以依照《专利法》的规定给予强制许可，这样可以更好地维护公平的市场竞争和消费者的权益。两部法律彼此配合，可以更为充分地消除滥用知识产权行为带来的不良后果。

其次，由于知识产权本身的特性，使得知识产权领域垄断的判断更为复杂。而我国又没有相关的详细立法，这造成了实践中《反垄断法》对知识产权的规制无具体章法可循，这也是国家工商行政管理总局《关于知识产权领域反垄断执法的指南（草案）》（第五稿）产生的原因。该指南很明显比《反垄断法》和我国其他法律法规中的知识产权垄断规制的规定要更详细、更明确。但是距该指南第五稿发布已经过去 1 年多的时间，相关部门仍然未出

台具有法律效力的指导文件。虽然，该指南对学术研究和司法实践会有一定的影响，但是，尽快将其上升为有法律效力的文件必将为知识产权的反垄断规制司法活动提供良好的指引。

最后，由于我国反垄断实行双轨制，即行政执法和民事诉讼同步，那么就有必要妥善处理行政调查和民事诉讼之间的启动与衔接问题。我国《反垄断法》并未明确行政执法程序为民事诉讼的前置条件。《反垄断民事诉讼司法解释》进一步明确了反垄断民事诉讼无须以反垄断执法机构的行政执法为前置条件。当反垄断行政调查和民事诉讼同时进行时，目前的立法尚无明确规定。在当事人一方面向法院提起民事诉讼，另一方面向行政机关举报涉嫌违法行为的情况下，行政机关和司法机关应当怎样处理以及分别会以怎样的态度处理呢？《反垄断民事诉讼司法解释》第 2 条规定，"原告直接向人民法院提起民事诉讼，或者在反垄断执法机构认定构成垄断行为的处理决定发生法律效力后向人民法院提起民事诉讼，并符合法律规定的其他受理条件的，人民法院应当受理。"即在反垄断执法机构尚未作出生效行政决定之前，人民法院依然可以受理案件。那么，这两个程序之间的关系怎么处理，是同时进行还是一个程序需要先中止，等待另一个程序有结论后再继续进行？这些问题，我国目前的法律都没有给出答案。据悉，《反垄断民事诉讼司法解释（草案）》第 16 条曾规定，"反垄断执法机构对被诉垄断行为进行调查的，在确有必要时，人民法院可以根据案件具体情况，决定中止诉讼。"但该条并没有被纳入最终发布的《反垄断民事诉讼司法解释》当中。❶ 一般而言，在此种情形下，行政执法机构和司法机关有权在各自的职权范围内进行调查和审理。但是，如果两个程序"双轨"并行，在实践中可能导致行政和司法的处理结果不一致。为了避免这种情况，行政机关和法院可能会制定相关规定，或者在实践中采取一些措施。例如，不排除在特定情况下，法院援引《中华人民共和国民事诉讼法》第 150 条规定的兜底条款中止审理，等待行政调查的结果。❷

六、结　语

知识产权与反垄断虽处于两个领域，但却有诸多交集。《反垄断法》明确其对滥用知识产权的规制，是二者间最直接的联系。知识产权和其他民事权利一样，是有限度的一种专有权，一旦超出了必要限度，必然要遭到知识产权法、《反垄断法》等的规制和惩处。本文通过对我国目前知识产权领域反垄

❶❷ 彭荷月，刘佳，萧达莎.《反垄断法》的双轨制——行政执法与民事诉讼的互动（［EB/OL］. 威科先行）.

断的法律法规梳理、相关实践状况的分析，发现了一些我国反垄断制度在知识产权领域有待改进的点，并提出了自己的建议。本文从知识产权与反垄断之间的关系入手，对我国的知识产权反垄断立法、司法状况作出探究，旨在将我国知识产权领域的反垄断制度更加明晰化。

中外专利法比较研究

——以中外专利法之修改超出原始公开的范围规定为例[*]

贺 兰

一、专利法概述

（一）专利法的缘起

我国《专利法》1984 年通过，经过了 1992 年、2000 年、2008 年共 3 次修正。中国第一部专利法典是 1944 年 5 月 29 日由中华民国政府公布的，到 1949 年 1 月 1 日才实施，目前适用于我国台湾地区。《中华人民共和国专利法》于 1984 年 4 月 1 日开始实施，即我们常说的《专利法》。《专利法》主要是规制专利权之法，专利权（Patent Right），简称"专利"，是发明创造人或其权利受让人对特定的发明创造在一定期限内依法享有的独占实施权，是知识产权的一种。我国《专利法实施细则》对有关事项作了具体规定。

（二）专利权的性质

（1）排他性。也称独占性或专有性，是专利权人对其拥有的专利权享有独占或排他的权利，未经其许可或者出现法律规定的特殊情况，任何人不得使用，否则即构成侵权。这是专利权最重要的法律特点之一。专利权是指就一项经依法审查并公开的发明所享有的一定期限内的排他性权利。专利权是排他性、有期限的绝对财产性权利。专利权作为私权，也即技术发明成为私权的对象。专利权的私权属性，其本质不是专利权属于私权抑或公权，而是专利权作为私权才具有正当性。❶

（2）时间性。指法律对专利权所有人的保护不是无期限的，而是有限制的，超过这一时间限制则不再予以保护，专利权随即成为人类共同财富，任何人都可以利用。这是考虑到促进社会进步和公共利益等方面的因素，对专利权人的权利内容作出严格的限制。

（3）公开性。在专利制度的诸多属性中，"公开"是极为重要的一个。具体表现为：

---

* 撰写论文时作者为中国人民大学学生，本文获 2012 年度隆天知识产权优秀论文奖。

❶ 张新锋. 技术私权化的路径研究［J］. 中国知识产权评论，2011（4）：237.

第一，权利范围公开，通过权利要求书予以描述。

第二，技术内容公开，通过说明书予以体现。例外规定是《专利法》第4条对于国防专利、保密专利仅内部公开。专利权的保护范围不包含任何技术秘密。

二、对我国《专利法》第33条的理解

（一）我国立法规定

《专利法》第33条是审查质量标准化和规范化的体现。修改文件是否超范围在实质审查中历来是一个很难把握的条款。授权的专利如果不符合《专利法》第33条的要求，是一个很严重的质量问题。因此，专利审查必须严格以法律为依据，确保准确、无误，也是为了避免实践中的纷争。

对于专利申请文件的修改，我国现行《专利法》第33条规定，申请人可以对其专利申请文件进行修改，但是，对发明和实用新型专利申请文件的修改不得超出**原说明书**和**权利要求书**记载的范围，对外观设计专利申请文件的修改不得超出**原图片**或者**照片**表示的范围。

《专利审查指南2010》（以下简称《审查指南》）对此条内容的适用有进一步的规定。

《审查指南》第二部分第八章第5.2.1.1节规定，原说明书和权利要求书记载的范围包括原说明书和权利要求书文字记载的内容和根据原说明书和权利要求书文字记载的内容以及说明书附图能直接地、毫无疑义地确定的内容。

《审查指南》第二部分第八章第5.2.3节规定，如果申请的内容通过增加、改变和/或删除其中的一部分，致使所属技术领域的技术人员看到的信息与原申请记载的信息不同，而且又不能从原申请记载的信息中直接地、毫无疑义地确定，那么，这种修改就是不允许的。其中的关键是如何判断"直接地、毫无疑义地确定"。

《审查操作规程·实质审查分册》中又规定，"直接地、毫无疑义地确定的内容"是指虽然在申请文件中没有明确的文字记载，但所属技术领域的技术人员根据原权利要求书和说明书文字记载的内容以及说明书附图唯一可以确定的内容。该规程中还规定，即使根据原权利要求书和说明书文字记载的内容可以判断出增加的内容属于公知常识中多个并列选项的一部分，但由于存在多种可选项，该增加的内容也不属于"直接地、毫无疑义地确定的内容"。

一般来说，所属技术领域的技术人员是指普通技术人员，这个人应该具备3个特征：①只具有所属技术领域的一般知识，不具有超出平均水平的能力；②具有一个技术人员所应当熟悉的邻近或相关领域的知识；③缺乏创造

能力，只有认识和了解现有和过去知识的能力。❶

（二）对我国专利立法的理解

《专利法》第 33 条赋予了申请人对其申请文件进行主动修改的权利，但同时也对该权利的行使进行了适当的权利限制，以防止申请人滥用权利而损害公众的利益。然而，在实践中，就如何适用《专利法》第 33 条往往会在审查者与申请人之间产生矛盾。审查者倾向于采取严格的做法以限制申请人主动修改的范围，而申请人往往宽泛地理解该条款，以尽可能地扩大自己的权利。很显然，无论哪种态度都不利于该条款的正确适用，也无法达到《专利法》的立法初衷。

对于本条所述"**权利要求书记载的范围**"的含义，有学者提出，《专利法》有关规定涉及与权利要求有关的两个范围：一是本条所述的权利要求书"记载的范围"；二是《专利法》第 59 条所述的权利要求的"保护范围"，两个"范围"的含义显然不同。前者是指权利要求书通过其文字已经明确记载的内容，因此权利要求书记载的技术特征越多，其记载的范围就越大。后者正好相反，凡是权利要求中没有记载的技术特征均被认为是其要求保护的发明或者实用新型技术方案中可有可无的技术特征，被控侵权人实施的技术方案即使包括权利要求没有记载的其他技术特征也仍然落入该权利要求的保护范围之内，因此权利要求记载的技术特征越少，其保护范围就越大。显然，在判断申请人对其专利申请文件的修改是否符合本条规定的修改原则时，不能以权利要求的保护范围为准。❷

所谓不得超过"**原说明书（包括附图）和权利要求书记载**"的范围，是指不得以增添、删节或者替换等修改方式导致或者事实上造成修改后申请文件中增加在本领域技术人员看来是原说明书（包括附图）和权利要求书所没有记载，而且又不能从中直接和毫无疑义地导出有关发明目的、构成和效果等方面的内容。❸

应该注意的是：①对明显错误的更正，不能被认为超出了原说明书和权利要求书记载的范围。所谓明显错误，是指不正确的内容可以从原说明书、权利要求书的上下文中清楚地判断出来，没有作其他解释或者修改的可能。②对于附图中明显可见并没有唯一解释的结构，允许补入说明书并写入权利要求书中。❹

---

❶ 刘春田. 知识产权法 [M]. 4 版. 北京：中国人民大学出版社，2009：205.

❷ 尹新天. 中国专利法详解 [M]. 北京：知识产权出版社，2011：412.

❸ 参见专利复审委员会第 123 号复审决定（1990 年 12 月 6 日，高炉喷煤支管流量调解装置案）。

❹ 冯晓青，刘友华. 专利法 [M]. 北京：法律出版社，2010：155.

三、需要考虑的几个原则

（一）利益平衡原则

实际上，在理解《专利法》第 33 条时应该把握我国《专利法》的立法宗旨和目的，在适用该条款时采取利益平衡原则，以达到专利权人的利益和社会公众利益之间的平衡。所谓利益平衡原则或者利益均衡原则，它是在一定的利益格局和体系下出现的利益体系相对和平共处、相对均衡的状态，也就是要考虑到知识产权法律关系中最基本的主体即知识产权人和知识产品的使用者之间利益的平衡，以及它们自身权利和义务之间的平衡。一方面，知识产品私权性赋予知识产权人对知识产品以独占性的专有权，以禁止或限制各种侵权行为，鼓励知识创新。另一方面，知识产品的生产具有相当强的社会性，知识产品的生产离不开对人类已有的"公共领域"知识的借鉴和利用，因此需要对这种独占性的专有权进行限制，以此来平衡知识产权人和社会公众之间的利益关系。

另外，要保护他人的信赖利益。对信赖利益的保护一方面要充分尊重和保护专利申请人的合法权益，申请人在撰写申请文件时难免会出现某些偏差或过错，应该允许申请人在后续申请程序中对其申请文件进行完善，同时这也是对社会公众负责任的表现。法律应该赋予申请人改正错误或者完善权利的机会，以产生良好的专利权。但是，另一方面对这种权利的行使也应该进行限制，保护社会公众基于申请人原始公开的内容而产生的信赖利益，这种信赖利益往往会产生一定的法律效果。

（二）先申请原则

我国的专利制度采用的是先申请原则。《专利法》第 9 条第 2 款规定，两个以上的申请人分别就同样的发明创造申请专利的，专利权授予最先申请的人。

申请人对申请文件的修改存在一个重要的限制条件，即修改不得超过原申请文件记载的范围。对于其立法目的，国家知识产权局条法司在《新专利法详解》中提到："之所以规定不得超过原说明书和权利要求书记载的范围，是因为我国专利制度采用的是先申请原则。如果允许申请人对申请文件修改超过原始提交的说明书和权利要求书记载的范围，就会违背先申请原则，造成对其他申请人来说不公平的后果。"❶

修改之所以不得超出这个范围，是因为《专利法》采用先申请原则，新颖性和创造性是参照申请日前的现有技术审查的，修改后的申请仍然保留原

---

❶ 尹新天. 新专利法详解［M］. 北京：知识产权出版社，2011：228.

申请日，所以修改后的申请必须保持在申请日原来公开的水平上，不能增加新的内容。❶

（三）禁止反悔原则

禁止反悔原则是指专利权人在专利申请期间或者维持阶段通过对权利要求、说明书的修改或者意见陈述放弃了某特定权利要求或者对专利保护范围进行限缩性的说明，则在专利侵权诉讼中不得将专利保护扩及其曾经放弃了的领域。

我国司法解释对此有明确的规定。《最高人民法院关于审理侵犯专利权纠纷案件应用法律若干问题的解释》第6条规定，专利申请人、专利权人在专利授权或者无效宣告程序中，通过对权利要求、说明书的修改或者意见陈述而放弃的技术方案，权利人在侵犯专利权纠纷案件中又将其纳入专利权保护范围的，人民法院不予支持。禁止反悔是英美法中的一项衡平法原则，一方当事人已经作出了某种行为，并且被他人所信赖，该当事人以后就不能再否认该行为以损害他人的利益。

《专利法》第26条第3款和第4款规定："说明书应当对发明或者实用新型作出清楚、完整的说明，以所属技术领域的技术人员能够实现为准……""权利要求书应该以说明书为依据，清楚、简要地限定要求专利保护的范围。"这些规定体现了充分公开的要求，目的是要保证权利要求所描述的发明方案能够为熟练技术人员所实现。这一要求更多关注的是权利要求和说明书之间的关系。而申请修改限制是为了防止申请人事后将新的内容加入申请，而沿用先用的申请日。在我国司法实践中，法院对专利申请修改限制采用下列标准：如果熟练技术人员基于先前申请能够自然获得的认识可以在修改申请时加入。在这一意义上，充分公开与申请修改限制所采用的标准基本一致。本质而言，前者主张说明书的文本的实际含义很清楚，无须添加诉争的文字说明；后者同样主张申请的文本的实际含义很清楚，添加诉争文字不过是使之更明确。❷

四、其他国家的立法参考

1. 欧洲专利局对专利申请或专利的修改的类似规定

《欧洲专利公约》第123条第2款规定：欧洲专利申请或欧洲专利的修改，其主题不得超出原始申请的内容。欧洲专利局审查指南规定：《欧洲专利公约》第123条第（二）项的法律含义是，不允许专利申请人通过加入未在

---

❶ 汤宗舜．专利法教程［M］．北京：法律出版社，2003：123.
❷ 崔国斌．专利法原理与案例［M］．北京：北京大学出版社，2012：378.

原始申请文件中记载的主题来完善其发明，否则将赋予申请人不正当的权利，并且也会损害对原申请文件有所依赖的第三方的利益。

2. 日本的规定

日本特许厅审查指南在"修改限制制度的主旨"中规定：为了顺利进行各项程序，希望最初就能提交完整内容的说明书等文件，如果申请时说明书、权利要求书及附图很完整，就没有必要对说明书等进行补正。

关于修改超范围的判断，日本审查基准给出了更具体、更详细的基本要点，使得修改是否超范围的审查实践更具操作性。对于基于附图的修改是否超范围，日本具体规定为：

（1）根据原始申请文件的记载，无须任何证明而明白的内容；

（2）接触该原始申请的本领域普通技术人员，按照申请日时的技术常识进行判断；

（3）对于公知惯用技术，仅仅根据其技术本身为公知惯用技术的事实，增加它的修改是不允许的；

（4）从本领域普通技术人员来看，结合原始申请文件的多项记载进行判断。

从上述国家/地区专利局的立法宗旨来看，对申请文件的修改内容加以限制的基本出发点都是为了平衡申请人与公众之间的利益。

3. 美国的做法

多年来，美国对专利侵权诉讼中应当如何适用禁止反悔原则一直存在争议，主要体现在两个问题上：①专利申请人在专利审批过程中的哪些修改和意见陈述将导致禁止反悔原则的使用；②一旦认定应当禁止反悔原则，将使专利权保护范围受到何种程度的限制。美国最高法院于2002年对Festo一案作出了重要判决。体现在：①扩大了会导致适用禁止反悔原则的修改和意见陈述的范围，明确了凡是与授予专利权的实质性条件有关的限制性修改或者意见陈述都将导致禁止反悔原则的适用，而不再是仅仅与避开现有技术有关的修改或者意见陈述；②增强了禁止反悔原则对专利权人的限制作用，一旦认定适用禁止反悔原则，除非专利权人能够提出合理的反对理由，否则就推定对适用该原则所涉及的技术特征不能适用等同原则，只能按照其字面含义来确定专利权保护范围……在该判决的影响下，申请人必须一开始就尽量提交保护范围适当、符合专利法各项规定的原始申请文件，尽可能地避免在审查过程中修改其申请文件和进行意见陈述。这相当于敦促广大申请人更加自觉地遵守美国专利法的各项规定，有利于减轻专利局审查员的负担，提高授

权专利的质量，克服美国专利制度所存在的问题。❶

五、对我国的借鉴意义

综上所述，对《专利法》第 33 条产生的纷争从来没有停止过，结合我国相关立法规定，借鉴国外发达国家的立法经验，完善其理论框架、增强可操作性才是最重要的。

（1）基于上述利益平衡原则的分析，在具体操作制度设计上，可以将《专利法》第 26 条第 4 款与《专利法》第 33 条结合起来适用，以使得《专利法》第 33 条更具有可操作性。即是在现行的专利法律制度框架下，在适用《专利法》第 33 条时考虑《专利法》第 26 条第 4 款的内容，以达到专利申请人/专利权人与社会公众之间的利益平衡的效果。

具体来说，在考虑申请人的修改内容是否超出原始公开范围时，可以考虑《专利法》第 26 条第 4 款"权利要求书应当以说明书为依据，清楚、简要地限定要求专利保护的范围"，以这一判断准则来确定申请人所做的修改内容是否可以得到说明书的支持。如果该修改内容可以得到说明书的支持，则可以认为该修改内容符合《专利法》第 33 条的规定，可以允许。如果修改内容不能够得到说明书的支持，则认为该修改内容根本不符合《专利法》第 33 条的规定，是不允许的。在现行的实践中，修改内容是否可以得到说明书的支持仅仅是修改不超出原始内容公开范围的必要条件，而不是充要条件。采用上述建议的判断原则，显然使得对《专利法》第 33 条的适用更加具有可操作性，而且也适当地扩大了申请人的权利。这只是在现行的法律框架条件下把《专利法》第 26 条第 4 款作为适用《专利法》第 33 条的一个判断手段，以使得上述的利益平衡原则更具有可操作性。

对《专利法》第 26 条第 4 款规定"权利要求书应当以说明书为依据，清楚、简要地限定要求专利保护的范围"，《审查指南》第二部分第二章（第 2~27 页）做了进一步的解释：在判断权利要求是否得到说明书的支持时，应当考虑说明书的全部内容，而不是仅限于具体实施方式部分的内容。如果说明书的其他部分也记载了有关具体实施方式或实施例的内容，从说明书的全部内容来看，能说明权利要求的概括是适当的，则应当认为权利要求得到了说明书的支持。

关于权利要求与说明书的支持问题，应该理解为权利要求旨在描述一种技术方案，具有概括性（包括上位概括）特点，因此其描述方式会与说明书不一致，如果本领域的技术人员能够从说明书中理解和实施这种概括的技术

---

❶ 尹新天. 美国专利政策的新近发展动向［G］//刘春田. 中国知识产权评论（第三卷）. 北京：商务印书馆，2008：261-262.

方案,则可以认为这样的权利要求得到了说明书的支持,是《专利法》所允许的。

(2) 具体运用——以"墨盒"案为例。案情简介❶——精工爱普生株式会社是名称为"墨盒"的发明专利申请的申请人。2002 年 11 月,国家知识产权局就该申请发出第一次审查意见通知书,指出"存储装置"和"记忆装置"修改超范围。针对该通知书,精工爱普生于 2003 年 5 月 9 日提交了意见陈述书,对原权利要求作出修改,将原权利要求 23 修改为新权利要求 1。针对审查员提出的"修改超范围"问题,精工爱普生在意见陈述书第 2.2 项指出:权利要求 23 涉及附图 6 和附图 7,申请人解释,"存储装置"是指图 7 (b) 所示的"半导体存储装置 61";在意见陈述书第 3.1 项指出:申请人首先希望解释,该权利要求及其后的权利要求中所述的"记忆装置"是指说明书及附图中记载的电路板及设置在其上的半导体存储装置。对于"记忆装置"是否超范围,基本不存在争议,而对于"存储装置"是否存在修改超范围的问题,有着不同观点。

笔者认为,《专利法》第 33 条赋予了申请人对其专利申请文件进行主动修改的权利,但同时也对该权利的行使进行了适当的权利限制以防止申请人滥用权利而损害公众的利益,充分体现了利益平衡的原则。然而,在实践中往往会产生矛盾,审查者倾向于限制申请人主动修改的范围,而申请人往往尽可能地扩大自己的权利。《审查指南》对该条款做了进一步的规定,要求根据原说明书和权利要求书文字记载的内容以及附图能够直接地、毫无疑义地确定内容的范围。

结合中国《专利法》第 33 条的立法目的,可以说该条规定是民法中的诚实信用原则的体现,本条的立法本意是保障先申请原则和禁止反悔原则。在专利授权程序中,法律已经赋予了申请人修改专利申请文件的权利,只要这种修改不超出原说明书和权利要求书记载的范围,禁止反悔原则在该修改范围内就无适用余地。结合本案,只要所推导出的内容对于所属领域普通技术人员是显而易见的,就可认定该内容属于原说明书和权利要求书记载的范围。具体到本案,对所属领域普通技术人员而言,通过综合第 780 号专利申请公开的说明书、权利要求书和附图,很容易联想到可以用其他存储装置替换半导体存储装置,并推导出该技术方案同样可以应用于使用非半导体存储装置的墨盒。所以,涉案公司主动将原权利要求书中的"半导体存储装置"修改为"存储装置",并未引入新的技术内容,没有违反《专利法》第 33 条。涉

---

❶ 本案情根据专利复审委员会作出的第 11291 号专利无效宣告请求审查决定、北京市第一中级人民法院作出的 (2008) 一中行初字第 1030 号行政判决及北京市高级人民法院作出的 (2009) 高行终字第 327 号行政判决改编而成。

案专利应维持有效。

中国目前是专利申请大国，但还不是专利强国。中国专利制度的领导人在展望未来时，还非常明显地混淆了量与质的标准。❶ 严格把握专利审查标准，必须从每个审查员严格把关开始，只有这样才能产生出更多的优质专利技术。

---

❶ 安守廉. 窃书为雅罪 [M]. 李琛，译. 北京：法律出版社，2010：92.

中日专利法之专有权比较及我国专利制度的发展与完善初探[*]

赵 雪

一、专利制度概述

"专利"一词可追溯到二千年前《国语》中"荣公好专利",是指一个人把"利"独占之意,跟目前"专利"的含义相去甚远。专利制度是国际上通行的一种利用法律手段推动科学技术进步的管理制度。这种制度的基本内容是:依据专利法,对申请专利的发明创造经过审查和批准授予专利权,同时把申请专利的发明创造公诸于世,以便于进行发明创造信息交流和有偿技术转让。[❶]专利制度从其产生开始,就与一国的科学技术发展状况,以及由新技术引起的市场竞争和专利权人的权利紧密地联系在一起,彼此促进,共同发展,使各国技术得以迅速发展。

专利制度的内容主要有以下 3 个层次:首先,以法律手段保障专利权人的排他性权利。一项专利的问世离不开权利人的辛勤创作,通过制定专利法来授予发明人对发明享有的独占权,通过国家强制力来为发明保驾护航,是鼓励发明创造的基本保障。其次,公布专利内容,提高专利利用的效率。将专利的内容公布于众,一方面可以提供该领域研究的最新成果,促进科技交流,避免重复研究;另一方面可以为专利投入市场起到广而告之的作用,为专利的许可使用、转让等发布信息。最后,有效促进专利的转化和运用,提高经济效益。一项发明创造只有运用于社会生产实践即被转化为现实生产力,才能显示出其实用价值,使专利权人和社会公众都能从发明创造的使用和推广中受益,进而推动科技进步与经济发展。总之,专利制度的核心就是依靠专利法律,鼓励发明创造,促进专利转化,实现经济利益。[❷]

专利制度的核心就是专有权,专利制度中存在的其他制度概莫都是为专有权的实现服务的。在专利概念的统摄下,可以说有专利主体制度、专利客体制度、专有权制度、专利许可转让制度、专利侵权救济制度。其中,专利主体制度就哪些人享有专利申请权及专利权进行规定,专利客体制度则是就

———————————

   [*] 撰写论文时作者为中国人民大学学生,本文获 2013 年度隆天知识产权优秀论文奖。

   ❶ 包桂荣.专利制度与促进技术创新问题探析 [J].科学管理研究,2002 (5):46.

   ❷ 王正志.中国知识产权指数报告 2011 [M].北京:知识产权出版社,2011:149.

可以申请专利的客体范围进行规定，在我国就是发明、实用新型、外观设计。专有权制度则是就专利权人所享有的专利权内容进行规定。专利权许可转让制度则是对于专利权的许可使用进行了可操作性规定。专利侵权救济制度则是就专利权受到侵害后的权利人的救济途径作出阐释。除上述制度以外，专利法中还涉及专利的排除。

总之，随着全球经济的不断发展，全球范围内的专利申请量和授权量持续攀升，专利许可费用迅速增长，专利对于新建立的公司在前沿技术领域的作用越来越重要。专利在经济上的重要性变得越来越显著。专利法规也相应地应当与时俱进，不断发展完善，只有这样，才能更好地保护和促进专利的发展，从而促进国家产业经济的发展壮大，最终提升国家经济实力。

二、中日专利法关于专有权规定的差异

关于专有权，我国《专利法》第 11 条明确规定了专有权的范围。该条规定：

"发明和实用新型专利权被授予后，除本法另有规定以外，任何单位和个人未经专利权人许可，都不得实施其专利，即不得为生产经营目的制造、使用、许诺销售、销售、进口其专利方法以及使用、许诺销售、销售、进口其专利产品，或者使用其专利方法以及使用、许诺销售、销售、进口依照该专利方法直接获得的产品。

外观设计专利权被授予后，任何单位或者个人未经专利权人许可，都不得实施其专利，即不得为生产经营目的制造、许诺销售、销售、进口其外观设计专利产品。"

就日本专有权的规定而言，日本专利法制度包含日本专利法、日本实用新型法、日本外观设计法三部分。其体例与我国不同，我国是将三部分全部放到《专利法》中。日本专利相当于我国《专利法》中的发明创造。就日本专利的规定而言也相应地由三部分构成。

通过对比可以发现，中日专有权的规定差异主要体现在以下几个方面：

首先，立法模式不同。我国采用大专利法立法模式，《专利法》包含了发明、实用新型、外观设计的有关规定，而日本采用的是分别立法，由日本特许法对发明专利进行规定，由日本实用新型法对实用新型专利进行规定，由日本意匠法对外观设计专利进行规定。另外，就专有权的实施而言，日本专利法将其明确分为产品发明、方法发明以及制造产品的方法发明三类来分别进行规定，我国《专利法》则相对较为笼统，直接杂合在一起，但仔细看来也是分为此三类的。

其次，专有权的实施方式不尽相同。我国专利权的实施分为发明和实用新型之实施和外观设计之实施，与日本专利制度中的专有权的实施相比较，二者的区别表现在以下几方面：

（1）就发明专利而言。①发明专利的产品专利的实施，中国《专利法》中是指：为生产经营目的制造、使用、许诺销售、销售、进口该专利产品的行为。日本专利制度下发明专利之产品专利的实施则是指制造、使用、转让等（包括转让、出租、出借）、出口、进口或为转让等而提出（包括实施转让而做的展示）该产品的行为。②就发明专利之制造产品的方法发明的规定则有所不同，日本专利法指使用、转让、出口、进口或为转让等而提出根据该方法制造产品的行为。中国《专利法》则是指使用、许诺销售、销售、进口依照该专利方法直接获得的产品。

（2）就实用新型专利而言。我国实用新型专利分为产品实用新型、方法实用新型、产品制造方法实用新型三类。而日本专利法未对此作出分类，其"实用新型"是指利用自然法则进行的技术思想的创作，其对实用新型的实施与日本发明专利之产品专利的实施一致。那么日本实用新型专利是否只限于产品专利呢？

（3）就外观设计专利而言。我国外观设计专利之实施是指：为生产经营目的制造、许诺销售、销售、进口其外观设计专利产品。日本外观设计专利之实施则是指：制造、使用、转让、出借或为转让、出借而提供有关外观设计产品的行为。

最后，有关进口、出口的规定不尽相同。

（1）关于出口的行为。我国《专利法》对于专利产品未经许可而出口的行为未加限制。日本专利法则明确规定了对于发明专利、实用新型专利未经许可出口行为的限制。可见日本专利法下的专利权人享有更为广泛的专利权。

（2）平行进口的问题。平行进口（parallel imports）一般是指未经专利权人授权的进口商，将由权利人自己或经其同意在其他国家或地区投放市场的产品，向专利权人或独占被许可人所在国或地区的进口。与专利平行进口密切相关的一个概念是专利权权利用尽（exhaustion doctrine）原则。由于专利权权利用尽包含国内用尽和国际用尽两种理解与可能，因而平行进口是否需要被禁止也就有两种不一样的处理方式。就中国而言，我国现行《专利法》第69条规定，当专利产品被售出以后，任何单位或个人进口产品的行为将不视为侵犯专利权，这说明我国在专利权用尽问题上采用的是"专利权国际用尽"的立场。因而，将通过合法途径获得的来源于我国专利权人或经许可人的专利产品进口到我国并不构成对我国专利权人的专利权侵害。其法律基础在于我国《专利法》第69条的规定，但其深层次原因则是因为专利权人已经从该专利产品上获得了相当的合理回报。至于来自国外合法专利权人的相同专利产品是否构成对本国专利权人的侵权则相对较为复杂，在此不作说明。就日本而言，日本专利法并未涉及专利权权利用尽和专利产品平行进口的问题，其实践准则主要是在司法判例过程中形成和发展的，其中日本最高法院 1997 年 7 月 1 日终审判决 BBS 案采用默示许可理论，判定专利产品不构成侵权，该判决是与国际用尽原则相一致的。通过日本判例可以看出：如果专利权人或独占被许可人在其专利作品上作出"产品不得销往日本"的明确标示，就可以阻止平行进口。相反，如果未作出明确标示，则平行进口并不构成对专利权人的侵害。同时，日本专利法还对诸如独占进口分销商为了控制产品价格水平而阻止平行进口的行为等属于不平等的交易活动，规定为平行进口的不合理阻止。此时，独占进口分销商的禁止平行进口的行为不受法律保护。

三、我国专利制度的发展分析

我国专利制度的发展是一个从无到有、从粗糙到不断完善的发展过程。总体而言，我国专利制度的建立与发展脉络如下：1980 年 3 月中国专利局正式成立；1984 年 12 月《专利法》被批准并于 1985 年 4 月 1 日正式实施，这标志着中国专利制度的建立；1992 年 9 月 4 日，第七届全国人民代表大会常务委员会第二十七次会议，通过并颁布了《关于修改〈中华人民共和国专利法〉的决定》，定于 1993 年 1 月 1 日起施行，对《专利法》进行了第一次修正；1994 年国家知识产权局成为 PCT 组织的 ISA 和 IPEA 成员；2000 年 8 月 25 日，第九届全国人民代表大会常务委员会第十七次会议通过了《专利法》的第二次修正案，修正后的《专利法》于 2001 年 7 月 1 日生效；2008 年 12 月 27 日，第十一届全国人民代表大会常务委员会第六次会议通过了《关于修改〈中华人民共和国专利法〉的决定》，对《专利法》进行了第三次修正。

专利制度和其他法律制度一样，其发展是受国家经济、政策、政治背景、文化以及国际环境的影响的。就我国的专利制度而言，国家经济的发展不足、引进外商投资的迫切需要、国家法律制度的初建即对国外法律制度的借鉴、移植等都是促使我国专利制度产生及发展的重要因素。

四、对我国专利制度存在的问题以及专利制度发展的建议

我国的专利制度还处在一个发展的阶段，随着社会经济的日益复杂化，专利制度中难免会存在一些缺陷与不足，一些问题亟待解决。以下是笔者对自己所洞悉到的专利制度中的问题的分析及解决建议：

（一）关于平行进口的问题以及我国应采取的态度

平行进口（parallel import），是指在国际贸易中，未经进口国知识产权人或独占实施许可持有人的同意，第三人进口并销售其持有的合法制造并通过

合法渠道的知识产权产品的行为。

对于平行进口问题，不同国家或区域采取的是不同的处理方法。美国专利法规定，在美国的专有实施权人可以依据专有实施权请求制止平行进口，而专利权人在国外许可他人实施或自行销售专利产品时，如果在许可实施合同或买卖合同中对专利产品的再销售未加以限制，专利权人即无权行使专利权禁止平行进口。❶ 欧共体对此问题的处理则是，实行欧共体范围内的权利穷尽原则，坚持贸易自由的原则，但该原则不适用于最初来源于欧共体以外的商品，即使这些商品已经合法地被进口到欧盟的某个国家。对于来自欧盟以外的第三个国家的平行进口，则由各国国内法规定。依据欧共体范围内的权利穷尽原则，在共同体内，只要首次投放市场是经专利权人同意的，即使被进口产品在出口国价格受到限制，或被进口产品在出口国不能得到专利保护，或被进口产品在出口国既不能受到专利权的保护又受到价格控制，专利权都视为在共同体内权利穷尽。若进口产品在出口国不能得到专利保护，且首次投放市场是未经专利权人同意的，或被进口产品在出口国是经颁布强制许可证而制造的，则专利权没有在欧共体范围内穷竭。❷ 日本 1992 年的 BBS 铝制车轮案中，法官采用了"有条件的国际用尽论"，即买卖双方未作保留，即声明禁止向某国出口，专利权被视作国际用尽。也就是说，双方没有在买卖合同中明确禁止向某一国出口，就意味着卖方默许了买方向该国的出口行为（也就是平行进口行为）。

我国《专利法》第 11 条在对专利权人专有权进行规定时赋予了专利权人进口权，即专利权人有权许可或禁止他人从国外进口权利要求书中所说的专利产品，至于该产品在其制造国和出口国是否享有专利保护以及从哪国运来均不影响专利权人的进口权，因为他国的专利法对我国不发生效力。❸ 据此分析，似乎我国对于专利的平行进口态度明朗，然而理论界则持多种观点。我国理论界多数观点认为，应当限制平行进口，认为《专利法》第 11 条规定条款就有限制平行进口的作用。但笔者认为对我国《专利法》第 11 条的理解还主要依据对我国的权利用尽原则的解释。该条中"许可"若采用专利权的国内用尽原则，那么在一国的许可不得适用他国，则该条可以起到阻止平行进口的作用。若适用于专利权国际用尽原则，则该条只可以禁止未经专利权人许可制造的产品进口的行为，对于那些经权利人许可制造的产品通过合法途径获得专利产品的人而言，他们实行平行进口的行为是专利权人无权过问和苛责的。由此可见，规定了进口权不等于禁止平行进口。同时，仅仅依据该

---

❶❷　刘筠筠，熊英．知识产权国际保护基本制度研究［M］．北京：知识产权出版社，2011：111.

❸　刘筠筠，熊英．知识产权国际保护基本制度研究［M］．北京：知识产权出版社，2011：93.

条款解决实践中各种平行进口问题仍然是不明确和全面的，可见，我国《专利法》在平行进口问题上存在待完善之处。

然而，《专利法》中并未明确我国之权利用尽到底是国际用尽还是国内用尽，这是解决平行进口问题的首要问题。到底应该采用哪种权利用尽原则则是与我国现状息息相关的。因为《保护工业产权巴黎公约》和 TRIPS 协议对于权利用尽原则作了回避，将其下放到各个国家的国内法来予以解决，因而，每个国家都会依据自身发展的需要来采用相关原则。我国当然也不例外。笔者认为，我国作为发展中国家宜采用专利权国际用尽原则。原因在于我国主要属于技术输入国，国内研发能力不足，而且国内所申请的多数发明专利技术为外国人拥有。如果《专利法》对于专利权人赋予过于强劲的保护，反而会对技术的研发造成相当大的限制，无法达到《专利法》促进产业发展的目的。因此，在专利产品平行进口问题上，宜采取保护专利权人的进口权以及专利权国际用尽的立法原则和司法保护。故我国《专利法》应当明确规定专利权的国际用尽原则，从而更好地解决平行进口问题，最终既保护专利权人的利益，又能促进国家的产业发展和经济发展。

（二）专利侵权之将"非生产经营目的"改为"私人方式且无商业目的"更为适宜

我国《专利法》对于专利权的侵害是以"生产经营目的"为前提的。但是当被控侵权人以非生产经营目的抗辩时会产生以下几个问题：①该抗辩人是否包括单位，以及自发性团体。对此，《北京专利侵权判定若干意见》第94条规定，单位不能以"非生产经营目的"进行抗辩，那么自发性团体是否可以以此进行抗辩呢？②怎么看待营利主体的非营利行为以及非营利主体的非营利行为。一般而言，营利主体都是以生产经营为目的的，而国家机关、社会团体、非营利性单位等的行为不具有为生产经营为目的的性质。③我国《专利法》第69条规定：专为科研及实验和为医疗行政审批而未经许可实施专利的，不视为侵犯专利权。这一规定是对"非生产经营目的"的进一步细化还是根本否定了这两种行为与"非生产经营目的"之间存在关联。笔者认为将"非生产经营目的"改为"私人方式且无商业目的"更为适宜。这不仅明确了该抗辩适用的主体范围，而且"非商业目的"可以覆盖营利主体的非营利行为。

（三）专利审查制度存在的问题及完善

专利审查是保障专利之专有权的基础，专有权保护的具体客体范围是由审查中所涉及的权利请求书等内容所决定的。审查制度从侧面意义上具有确保专利合法有效，在不造成对他人专利的侵权方面起到一定的保障作用。要真正做到专利权的保护，做好审查工作也是一个前提性步骤。

1. 专利审查标准的进一步完善

我国专利制度依据专利的 3 种类型设定了相应的审查标准：对发明专利的审查相对较为严格，要进行新颖性、创造性、实用性的实质审查；实用新型和外观设计专利申请只进行形式审查，也就是只要专利行政部门进行初步审查，其申请条件完备并符合法律规定的形式就可以获得专利权。而对于已经取得专利的实用新型和外观设计专利，在不符合《专利法》规定的取得专利须具备的实质条件时，可以通过专利复审和专利无效宣告程序来进行纠正。这种形式审查所带来的不良后果就是大量的无效专利、垃圾专利充斥市场，造成市场专利泡沫。这同时也是国家行政资源、司法资源的浪费。

专利审查的质量直接制约着专利的质量，要不断提高我国专利的质量水平就必须对我国专利审查制度进行改革与完善。对于专利审查制度的完善首先要从专利审查标准着手。只有建立起合理的专利审查标准，才能从根本上提高专利的水准，减少无效专利、垃圾专利等的产生，从而有效抑制"专利灌木丛"的出现。同时，合理的审查标准也能够鼓励创新、减少国家资源的浪费。其次，还需要规范专利审查人员的管理，不断提高审查质量。我国专利审查中存在着审查人员少、专利申请量大、审查人员主观性强等问题，因而，我们要不断提高审查人员的业务素质，加强对专业审查人员的培养。最后，由于专利往往涉及一些较为专业的领域，我们的审查部门在审查时可能会不知专利申请文件之所云，于是便无法顺利地进行审查工作。在面对诸如此类困境的时候，我们的专利审查部门不妨仿效国外委托专业机构来进行专利的实质审查，如荷兰海牙国际专利研究所。这样一来可以有效地对专利申请进行审查并得出中肯的结果。

2. 专利简易审查制度的创建

依据我国《专利法》的规定，发明专利申请的审查包含了受理、初审、公布、实质审查、授予专利 5 个阶段。实用新型和外观设计专利申请则由受理、初审、授权 3 个阶段组成，时间相对较短。由于专利本身具有为专利权人带来经济效益的特点，而且伴随着科学技术的发展，专利保护的及时性需求不断增强，要推动战略性新兴产业的创新主体在较短的时间内获得经济收益，适当缩短诸如新能源、节能减排等新技术申请获得专利权保护的时间是十分必要的。对此，我们可以通过立法简化相应的审批程序、缩短受理时间，最终提高审查效率。

（四）专利期限延长制度的建立

专利期限的延长可见诸于日本专利法等外国专利法中，然而我国并未有任何有关此项制度的规定。在当今科技时代，专利技术对于一个国家的经济发展而言至关重要，因而适当借鉴和引入专利期限延长制度是具有实际意义的。如日本专利法第 67 条之 2 所规定的专利期限的延长。专利期限延长的适用一方面能够延长专利权人的专有权，使其获得更多的投资回报，国家通过税收等也会从中获益；另一方面对于一些特殊的领域如医药行业而言，由于这个行业的发展好坏直接关系到公共健康问题，通过专利期限延长制度，能够更好地鼓励有关企业进行研发，从而有助于科技的发展与进步。

五、结　语

专利制度的进一步完善与发展是专利目的实现的基本保障。我国《专利法》第 1 条明确规定了专利的目的在于保护专利权人的合法权益，鼓励发明创造，推动发明创造的运用，提高创新能力，促进科学技术进步和经济社会的发展。只有专利制度得到进一步完善与发展，才能够有效确保专利从申请到授权以及涉及侵权等各个方面出现和存在的问题得到有效解决，专利才能真正发挥作用。

通过本文的分析和阐述，我国专利制度的发展不仅要积极响应诸如 TRIPS 协议、《巴黎公约》等国际性条约的规定，充分借鉴其他国家专利的先进制度，同时更应该充分考虑到我国专利的基本状况，有所针对地制定相关政策法律，唯此才能真正有效地促进我国专利制度的发展，才能有效地实现专利的功能，促进社会经济的发展。

论部分外观设计的保护[*]

柴耀田

一、导　语

在市场经济条件下，企业之间的竞争集中体现在产品之间的竞争。随着消费者需求水平的不断提高和市场竞争的日益深化，产品的升级换代也围绕着专利制度的两大组成部分持续展开。一方面，企业对产品的"质"不断精益求精，以专利和实用新型抢占市场先机或构建防御战略，追求更先进的产品性能；另一方面，为了满足消费者的审美要求，许多企业也将大量资金投向产品"形"的研究，致力于制造出集艺术性与实用性于一体的产品。特别是对于一个产业内的若干领先企业而言，在产品功能较为相近的情况下，令人耳目一新的外形设计往往成为争夺消费者的关键。

外观设计保护制度为企业创新提供了重要激励，通过赋予一定期限的垄断权，给予企业研发和生产的回报。然而，对于一些较为成熟的产业，其产品外观改进的空间已经很小，创新主要体现在产品部分设计的改进上，如微波炉的门把手、冰箱的显示控制部分等。根据我国目前专利法律法规中关于外观设计授权条件的规定，以及司法实践中侵权判定的原则，这类产品局部的外观设计难以得到我国《专利法》的保护。这一现状不仅打击了企业的创新热情，纵容了剽窃者，影响了实质上的公平竞争，而且不利于我国外观设计专利整体水平的提高。因此，为从根源上解决部分外观设计保护缺失的问题，亟待从比较法的角度寻找我国立法的表面缺陷及深层根源。

二、我国关于部分外观设计立法的缺失

（一）我国立法的缺失

根据我国现行《专利法》的定义，外观设计必须依附于一定的产品，[❶]是美感与工业实用性的结合。《专利审查指南 2010》（以下简称《审查指

---

[*] 撰写论文时作者为中国人民大学学生，本文获 2012 年度隆天知识产权优秀论文奖。
❶ 《专利法》第 2 条第 4 款：外观设计，是指对产品的形状、图案或者其结合以及色彩与形状、图案的结合所作出的富有美感并适于工业应用的新设计。

南》）对此又做了进一步的限定，在不授予外观设计专利权的情形中排除了产品的不能分割或者不能单独出售且不能单独使用的局部设计，例如袜跟、帽檐、杯把等。❶

虽然这一规定并没有将外观设计的授权范围明确限定为最终产品的整体，但根据《审查指南》可以推断出，只有能够拆卸、单独出售或使用的零部件等才可能获得外观设计专利。严格意义上的部分外观设计是指对产品某一部分的形状、图案、色彩、位置关系或者其中几项的结合进行的新设计，是产品不可分割的组成部分，不是指对零部件进行的设计，因而难以满足这一独立存在的要求。❷

由此可见，我国现行立法排除了对产品部分外观设计的保护。

（二）与相关国家立法的比较

与我国形成鲜明对比的是，众多欧美发达国家在立法中均明确允许对产品的局部提供外观设计专利保护，在申请实践中，则通过设计图中虚线和实线的不同运用来区别公知设计和请求保护的部分。

1. 美国

美国专利法第 171 条第 1 款规定：就产品而发明的任何新的、原创性的和装饰性的外观设计，其发明者可依据本法的规定和要求获得专利。❸ 审查指南第 1502 条对此作了进一步的细化：外观设计是指包含于或应用于工业品或其一部分的设计，而非工业品本身。❹

由此可见，美国明确在立法中允许对部分外观设计提出专利申请。在申请中，附图的虚线部分表示产品的公知部分，通常伴有不属于保护范围的声明（the portions of the drawings shown in broken lines form no part of the claimed design）。如果使用了虚线，申请人就必须描述视图中不被视为外观设计的部分。❺

---

❶ 参见《专利审查指南 2010》第一部分第三章第 7.4 节。

❷ 刘桂荣. 对部分外观设计保护的探讨［G］//程永顺. 外观设计专利保护实务. 北京：法律出版社，2005：103.

❸ 35 U.S.C. 171 Patents for designs：Whoever invents any new, original, and ornamental design for an article of manufacture may obtain a patent therefor, subject to the conditions and requirements of this title.

❹ MPEP 1502 Definition of a Design［R-2］：In a design patent application, the subject matter which is claimed is the design embodied in or applied to an article of manufacture (or portion thereof) and not the article itself. Ex parte Cady, 1916 C.D. 62, 232 O.G. 621 (Comm'r Pat. 1916). "［35 U.S.C.］171 refers, not to the design of an article, but to the design for an article, and is inclusive of ornamental designs of all kinds including surface ornamentation as well as configuration of goods." In re Zahn, 617 F. 2d 261, 204 USPQ 988 (CCPA 1980).

❺ 史蒂芬·皮特森.［N］. 中国知识产权报，2012-10-09，18：30. 转引自：国家知识产权局网站. http：//www.sipo.gov.cn/wqyz/gwdt/201101/t20110127_571958.html.

2. 欧洲

欧盟的共同体外观设计独立于专利单独立法，由欧洲内部市场协调局（OHIM）负责，建立起与欧洲各国国内法平行的授权模式。1998 年 10 月 13 日通过的欧洲议会与欧盟理事会关于外观设计的法律保护指令（98/71/EC）❶及 2001 年 12 月 12 日通过的欧盟理事会共同体外观设计条例（6/2002/EC）❷均将共同体外观设计定义为产品的全部或部分外观，由线条、轮廓、色彩、形状、质地、和/或产品本身的材料和/或产品的装饰等的特点而形成，涵盖了产品的部分外观设计。

除欧盟统一立法外，主要的欧洲国家对外观设计也都采取了独立于专利的保护模式，且无一例外地在立法中承认部分外观设计。如德国的外观设计法将外观设计定义为：产品整体或部分的平面或立体的外观，由产品线条、轮廓、颜色、外形、表面结构或产品本身的材料或产品的装饰的特点所构成。❸ 在申请中，申请人一般除提交若干相近似的局部设计外，另外还同时提交使用该局部设计的产品的立体图作为参考图。

法国的外观设计法将外观设计定义为：产品或其一部分的外观，由产品的线条、轮廓、颜色、形状、质地或材料等的特点构成。这些特点既可以来自产品本身，也可以来自产品的装饰。❹ 在申请中也以虚线和实线来区分要求保护的部分和公知部分。

英国注册设计法于 1949 年制定，1988 年修改，于 2001 年 12 月 9 日为与欧盟指令 98/71/EC 再次进行协调修改。现行的注册设计法规定，外观设计是指由产品全部或部分的外观，由特别是产品本身或其装饰的线条、轮廓、颜

---

❶ Directive No. 98/71/EC of the European Parliament and of the Council of 13 October 1998 on the Legal Protection of Designs. Article 1 (a): "design" means the appearance of the whole or a part of a product resulting from the features of, in particular, the lines, contours, colours, shape, texture and/or materials of the product itself and/or its ornamentation.

❷ Council Regulation (EC) No 6/2002 of 12 December 2001 on Community designs (OJ EC No L 3 of 5.1.2002, p. 1). Article 3 (a): "design" means the appearance of the whole or a part of a product resulting from the features of, in particular, the lines, contours, colours, shape, texture and/or materials of the product itself and/or its ornamentation.

❸ Geschmacksmustergesetz (GeschmMG) § 1 Begriffsbestimmungen: Im Sinne dieses Gesetzes 1. ist ein Muster die zweidimensionale oder dreidimensionale Erscheinungsform eines ganzen Erzeugnisses oder eines Teils davon, die sich insbesondere aus den Merkmalen der Linien, Konturen, Farben, der Gestalt, Oberflächenstruktur oder der Werkstoffe des Erzeugnisses selbst oder seiner Verzierung ergibt.

❹ Code de la propriété intellectuelle. Livre V: Les dessins et modèles. Art. L511-1: Peut être protégée à titre de dessin ou modèle l'apparence d'un produit, ou d'une partie de produit, caractérisée en particulier par ses lignes, ses contours, ses couleurs, sa forme, sa texture ou ses matériaux. Ces caractéristiques peuvent être celles du produit lui-même ou de son ornementation.

色、形状、质地或材料构成。❶ 出于其判例法的特点，只有产品的部分可以单独制造或使用时，其部分外观设计才可以注册，否则只能作为未注册外观设计享受普通法上的保护。❷ 在 Sifam v. Sangamo Weston❸ 案中，法院裁决电表正面的外观设计不可以注册。尽管电表的正面可以由零件商出售给组装者，但"是否可以单独出售"这一标准应以设计时的意图为准，即设计者是否旨在设计一个具有单独存在价值的物品，其实用性不依赖于组装为整体商品。否则任何工业制品的一部分都有可能单独出售，从而可以注册，这与注册设计法的宗旨相违背。

3. 亚洲

亚洲的主要国家长期以来没有部分外观设计保护制度，但日本和韩国都已率先修改法律，在立法中承认了部分外观设计。1999 年，日本开始实施的新的意匠法其第 1 章第 2 条规定：本法所称的外观设计是指对产品（包括产品的一部分，除第 8 条外）的形状、图案、色彩或者其结合所作出的通过视觉引起美感的设计。在申请中，提交六面视图时，要求以实线表示要求保护的局部设计，以虚线表示产品的整体外形，并在简要说明中对要求保护的局部外观设计予以说明。而且其优先权必须是部分外观设计专利申请，即包含该部分外观设计的整体产品的外观设计不能作为部分外观设计的优先权基础。❹ 韩国也于 2001 年 7 月实施了新的部分外观设计保护制度。❺

三、我国部分外观设计保护缺失带来的问题

由上文讨论可以得知，与欧美主要发达国家和亚洲其他经济强国相比，我国的立法中没有部分外观设计存在的空间。这一立法缺陷已经给我国的授权审查、侵权判定等行政、司法实践带来了许多问题。

（一）授权审查中的问题

目前的《专利法》只对产品整体的外观设计进行保护，成熟产品局部后续改进型的外观设计很容易被判定与在先的整体设计相近似。但由于外观设计专利申请没有实质审查，有的申请人为了以新颖的产品外观吸引更多的消

---

❶ Registered Designs Act 1949 (c. 88). (1) Registration of designs: (2) In this Act "design" means the appearance of the whole or a part of a product resulting from the features of, in particular, the lines, contours, colours, shape, texture or materials of the product or its ornamentation.

❷ CHRISTINE FELLNER. Industrial Design Law [M]. London: Sweet&Maxwell, 1995: 22, 108.

❸ [1973] R. P. C. 899.

❹ BRIAN W. GRAY, EFFIE BOUZALAS. Industrial Design Right-An International Perspective [J]. International Bar Association, 2001: 191-192.

❺ 刘桂荣. 对部分外观设计保护的探讨 [G] //程永顺. 外观设计专利保护实务. 北京：法律出版社, 2005: 102-105, 103.

费者，增强市场竞争力，同时防止他人将略作改动的外观设计进行使用或抢先注册，不得不将相近似的几项部分外观设计同时作为产品整体外观设计提出专利申请。● 然而，即使通过了初步审查并获得授权，这样的外观设计专利权仍然存在下述问题。

首先，由于此类部分外观设计是借助于产品整体的外观设计获得授权的，其权利范围也限制在申请文件中指定的产品上。如一件牙刷的外观设计专利只能保护该牙刷的整体，即牙刷柄与牙刷头的结合，其范围远远小于一件牙刷头的外观设计应用于各种牙刷柄的情形。侵权人仍然可以模仿创新的牙刷头设计，而通过采用不同的牙刷柄以逃避侵权指控。

其次，即使此类部分外观设计借助于产品整体获得了授权，其保护范围也不容易确定。由于外观设计专利没有权利要求书来明确界定专利范围，其保护范围是以图片或者照片为准，简要说明中记载的设计要点只是起解释作用，在确定外观设计专利的创新部分时，往往会对公知部分或惯常设计的范围产生争议。在目前的申请实践中，有的申请人用实线表示产品的设计要部，虚线表示产品的轮廓，这样既突出了主要设计部位，又展示了所使用该外观设计的产品整体，为明确外观设计的保护范围提供了极大的便利。但在目前的审查规则下，审查员一般会要求申请人将表示局部的虚线改成实线，结果也就难以判断设计要部的位置了。●

最后，即使申请人提出的几项相近的部分外观设计均作为整体外观设计通过了初步审查并获得了授权，其权利也是不稳定的。根据单一性原则和先申请原则，这些外观设计专利日后被宣布无效的风险很高。权利人往往被迫只能选择其中的一件专利予以保留，而在设计中和申请中付出的大量的资金和人力都付诸东流。

（二）优先权授予中的实质不公平

由于我国不保护部分外观设计，也就没有部分优先权。在申请人首先在国外提出部分外观设计专利申请，而后在我国请求优先权的情况下，附图中的虚线往往被审查员要求改为实线。然而，修改后产品的类别和名称也会相应地发生变化，通常被认为不是相同主题，不符合授予优先权的条件。如申请人在国外提交牙刷刷毛的外观设计专利申请，并在附图中用实线和虚线表示出完整的牙刷。在优先权期限内，在中国提交申请时，即使附图相同，但一方面虚线改为了实线，另一方面，外观设计的名称由牙刷刷毛图案改为牙

●● 蔡民军，杨文泉. 对外观设计的部分保护——专利法中亟待解决的问题［G］//程永顺. 外观设计专利保护实务. 北京：法律出版社，2005：106-112.

刷后，根据现行《审查指南》对优先权申请的规定，❶ 由于产品不同，难以认定属于相同主题，不符合享有优先权的条件。

有的学者认为，无论是要求保护整个外观设计的申请，还是要求保护部分外观设计的申请，首次外观设计申请的主题均是该申请所披露的整个设计内容。对于部分外观设计申请，附图表示的是整个设计，而申请人要求保护的是其中的一部分。因此，对于部分外观设计而言，请求保护的主题是申请主题的一部分。在后申请虽然将虚线改为了实线，在没有改变设计内容的情况下不能得出申请主题不相同的结论。

该观点区分了申请的主题和要求保护的主题，认为只要申请主题相同就符合了优先权的要求。然而，根据目前《审查指南》的规定和审查实践来看，"相同主题"的含义实际为同一产品的同一项相同的外观设计，而产品是指要求保护的外观设计应用的产品。因此在外观设计所应用的产品或其部分名称变化的情况下，难以认定是相同主题。

因此，我国对部分外观设计保护的缺失导致申请人不能享有相应的优先权，可能会造成对抄袭者的纵容，是不公平的。

（三）无效程序和侵权判定中的困难

虽然部分外观设计在我国目前可以借助于产品整体的外观设计获得专利保护，但根据《审查指南》❷ 和相关司法解释❸的规定，在外观设计专利无效程序和侵权判定中都遵循整体观察、综合判断的原则。虽然法释〔2009〕21号第11条中规定，授权外观设计区别于现有设计的设计特征，即设计要部，对外观设计的整体视觉效果更有影响，但设计要部的作用仍要服从于整体印象，结合整体观察、综合判断的原则来判断。正如北京高院在"小型摩托车"

---

❶ 《专利审查指南2010》第四部分第五章第9.2节"外观设计相同主题的认定"：外观设计相同主题的认定应当根据中国在后申请的外观设计与其在外国首次申请中表示的内容进行判断。属于相同主题的外观设计应当同时满足以下两个条件：（1）属于相同产品的外观设计；（2）中国在后申请要求保护的外观设计清楚地表示在其外国首次申请中。

❷ 《专利审查指南2010》第四部分第五章第5.2.4节"整体观察、综合判断"：对比时应当采用整体观察、综合判断的方式。所谓整体观察、综合判断是指由涉案专利与对比设计的整体来判断，而不从外观设计的部分或者局部出发得出判断结论。

❸ 《最高人民法院关于审理侵犯专利权纠纷案件应用法律若干问题的解释》（法释〔2009〕21号）第11条：人民法院认定外观设计是否相同或者近似时，应当根据授权外观设计、被诉侵权设计的设计特征，以外观设计的整体视觉效果进行综合判断；对于主要由技术功能决定的设计特征以及对整体视觉效果不产生影响的产品的材料、内部结构等特征，应当予以考虑。下列情形，通常对外观设计的整体视觉效果更具有影响：（一）产品正常使用时容易被直接观察到的部位相对于其他部位；（二）授权外观设计区别于现有设计的设计特征相对于授权外观设计的其他设计特征。被诉侵权设计与授权外观设计在整体视觉效果上无差异的，人民法院应当认定两者相同；在整体视觉效果上无实质性差异的，应当认定两者近似。

外观设计专利无效案❶中指出的，应根据外观设计的具体对象，采取要部判断或者整体观察、综合判断的方法。这两种判断方法并非互相排斥。对于外观设计产品简单、消费者关注的设计要部明显的，一般可以采用要部判断的方法；对于外观设计产品复杂、消费者关注的设计要部较多，一般可以先进行要部比较，再进行整体观察、综合判断。因此，虽然可以将工业品局部的设计看成是该工业品的设计要部，❷ 但除非产品局部外观的改进能够影响到整体印象，包含在后创新部分外观设计的整体外观设计极易被判定与在先设计相近似，从而导致被宣告无效或被认定侵权。这对后续改进创新型的部分外观设计的设计人而言是极不公平的，专利制度在此失去了其对研发创新的激励作用。

另外，在整体观察、综合判断原则下，对产品局部外观的差异对整体外观设计影响的评判是因人而异的，容易导致司法的不确定性。如在本田汽车外观设计无效纠纷案❸中，专利复审委员会和一审、二审法院均认定涉案专利在前大灯、雾灯、前护板、格栅、侧面车窗、后组合灯、后保险杠、车顶轮廓等装饰性较强的部位与在先设计存在差异，但都以该差别属"细微差别"为由，将该部分的设计特征从汽车外观设计的"整体"中排除。而最高法院在再审中认为这些局部外观的差异对于一般消费者而言是显而易见的，对于涉案外观设计的整体视觉效果具有显著的影响，与在先设计相比，不属于相近似的外观设计，最终作出了相反的判决。

四、部分外观设计立法缺失的根源

我国立法中部分外观设计保护的缺失对部分外观设计的研发者造成了实质的不公平，不仅影响到其专利权的获取和优先权的享有，也容易造成侵权认定的错误。但这一缺失绝不仅仅是立法疏忽造成的空白，而是我国外观设计专利制度的整体功能定位错误而导致的。

从本质上说，外观设计虽然是对产品外形的创新，与专利、实用新型分属不同的创造进路，但都是智力创造的产物。虽然世界各国对外观设计采取了专利法、专门立法和专利、版权双重保护等不同的立法模式，在外观设计更类似于专利抑或版权这一问题上也态度不一——如1949年，英国制定专门的注册外观设计法，而1968年外观设计版权法则是该国为划定工业产权和版

---

❶ （2003）高行终字第 15 号。
❷ 林柏楠. 外观设计专利若干问题研究［G］//程永顺. 外观设计专利保护实务. 北京：法律出版社，2005：48.
❸ （2010）行提字第 3 号。

权之间的界限而徘徊多年的产物。❶ 但各国都毫无例外地将其归入智力成果权，与商业标记权相对应。从《巴黎公约》、TRIPS 协议等主要国际公约的分类也可以看出这一点。

因此，外观设计制度的本质功能在于通过一定期限的垄断权来鼓励对产品外形作出的创新设计这一智力创造，从而从整体上推动产品外观的不断美化，给消费者带来美的享受。然而，我国的外观设计制度并不是定位于保护智力创造成果，而是定位于防止产品外观的混淆，与商标法的功能混同。《审查指南 2001》规定外观设计相同和相近似的判断原则为混同原则，即如果一般消费者仅凭其购买和使用所留印象而不能见到被比外观设计的情况下会将在先设计误认为是被比外观设计，即产生混同，则被比外观设计与在先设计相同或者与在先设计相近似；否则，两者既不相同，也不相近似。这一原则注重的是产品外观对消费者购买的影响，将产品外观的功能等同于商标。现行《专利审查指南 2010》修改为显著影响原则，❷ 更倾向于从设计本身进行判断，强调差别的存在及其质的要求，即要求对整体视觉效果具有显著的影响，而把混同、误认当作不具有显著影响的一个例证，更接近于外观设计保护的立足点。❸ 但是，这一原则仍然立足于外观设计是否会使一般消费者产生误认，即外观设计的识别功能，而不是其保护智力创造的功能。

因此，考虑到制度整体定位的错误，就不难理解为何我国外观设计制度中缺失了对部分外观设计的保护。因为产品的部分难以实现产品的区分功能，防止消费者发生混淆的只能是产品的整体，我国外观设计的客体才定位为产品，排除了产品的部分。实际上，外观设计制度整体定位错误带来的问题远不止部分外观设计保护的缺失，还涉及创造性要求是否必要、授权判断主体的"专业技术人员"与"普通消费者"之争、产品相同或相近似的判断原则、产品比较的判断方式等。

在长期使用中，产品的外观设计有时确实会发挥区别商品来源的作用，成为事实上的立体商标。但在这种情况下，也只是外观设计专利和商标权在同一个对象——同一产品的外观上发生了重叠，并不代表这两种性质不同的知识产权融为了一体。商标权保护的是该产品外观设计的区分功能，目的在于防止消费者发生混淆，对商品生产经营者培育品牌、提高商品质量的行为进行回报。而外观设计专利保护的是该产品外观设计中的创新成分，目的在

---

❶ 郑成思. 知识产权保护实务全书［M］. 北京：中国言实出版社，1995：15.

❷ 《专利审查指南 2010》第四部分第五章第 6.1 节"与相同或者相近种类产品现有设计对比"：如果一般消费者经过对涉案专利与现有设计的整体观察可以看出，二者的差别对于产品外观设计的整体视觉效果不具有显著影响，则涉案专利与现有设计相比不具有明显区别。

❸ 张广良. 外观设计的司法保护［M］. 北京：法律出版社，2008：32.

于避免开发者研发的外观设计被他人剽窃，从而促进产品外观的不断美化，使消费者获得实用性与艺术性相统一的产品。由此可见，即使外观设计发挥了商标的作用，外观设计专利仍然有独立于商标权的功能。我国外观设计制度定位于产品外观的区分作用是错误的。

另外，外观设计制度的目的固然在于促进艺术与工业的结合，使艺术服务于产品，但对部分外观设计的否定已经超越了产品对外观设计的应有限制。作为一种工业产权，外观设计只有与一定的产品相结合才能受到专利权的保护，这也正是其与版权区分的界限。❶ 部分外观设计虽然是产品部分外观的改进，但并不意味着其脱离了产品。但同时也应注意到，产品对于外观设计专利权的限制仅仅应该体现在：①外观设计必须应用在产品上；②外观设计专利权仅仅应该限制在设计者打算用这个设计的产品上。❷ 超出了这两点限制，就构成了对创造者智力成果应享有权利的不当剥夺。部分外观设计只要应用在设计者制定的产品种类上，其权利范围仅与其应用的产品以及与其相类似的产品有关，就符合产品对外观设计的正当限制。一些观点认为对该部分外观设计授权后，应用于任何产品、任何位置上都将得到保护。这种担心是不必要的，因为进行外观设计专利申请的前提首先是要确定使用该外观设计的产品，部分外观设计的载体也必须是产品。❸ 同时，只有使用的部分外观设计构成了另一产品的显著特征，即另一产品对这一部分外观设计的使用是实质性的，才有可能构成侵权。❹

因此，只有回归外观设计制度的本旨，才能真正发挥这一制度对产品外观不断进步的推动作用。既然外观设计制度的原意是确认并保护产品外观中的创新成分，那么产品局部外观的创新也应当受到保护。

---

❶ 目前学术界对此存在两种不同的观点。一种观点认为，外观设计是产品的外观设计，不能脱离产品而存在；脱离具体产品的外观设计是不能获得外观设计专利权的。专家学者从我国《专利法》及其实施细则的明确规定中寻找依据，并且进一步认为，尽管发达国家有两者分离的立法趋势，但我们应当考虑国情不应盲目地跟在发达国家背后亦步亦趋，而应当强调外观设计与产品相结合。另一种观点认为，外观设计可以与产品脱离，即外观设计不必一定是产品的外观设计，其可以脱离产品而得到专门保护。持该观点的学者认为我国专利立法的宗旨是保护外观设计而不是产品，并不要求外观设计必须与产品相结合才能得到专利法保护。例如欧盟对外观设计的保护就强调外观设计必须具备新颖性和创造性，而不是外观设计的产品必须具备新颖性和创造性。[胡充寒. 我国外观设计定义之应然性重构 [J]. 科技与法律，2009（6）：69]本文认为根据目前欧美主要国家的立法和司法实践，外观设计应当与一定的产品相结合，否则只是普通的美术作品。

❷ 应振芳. 外观设计研究 [M]. 北京：知识产权出版社，2008：169.

❸ 刘桂荣. 对部分外观设计保护的探讨 [G] //程永顺. 外观设计专利保护实务. 北京：法律出版社，2005：104.

❹ CHRISTINE FELLNER. Industrial Design Law [M]. London：Sweet&Maxwell，1995：110.

五、修改立法中外观设计定义的建议

我国部分外观设计保护的缺失不符合外观设计制度的应有之意，在实践中挫伤了产品外观的开发者的积极性。有的企业为了保护自己产品局部的外观设计，不得不重叠申请产品整体和产品一部分（作为零部件来申请）的外观设计专利，造成了企业知识产权保护成本的浪费。❶ 对于不满足零部件要求的产品局部，其部分外观设计则无法得到现行《专利法》的保护。产品局部的外观设计被迫借助于零部件这一中间平台来获得保护，本身就说明了我国现行立法中外观设计的概念不能自洽，因为有着足够张力的抽象概念正是现代知识产权法在法律美学上的要求。❷ 另外，专利审查人员在执行《审查指南》的过程中，标准也并不统一，对产品部分外观设计专利的申请，有的已经获得了批准，有的则未被批准，❸ 从而造成了授权中的不公平。

因此，我国《专利法》中有关外观设计的规定亟待进行修改。在 2008 年《专利法》第三次修改后，简要说明的提供与设计要点的说明有利于部分解决因整体保护而产生的不利影响，❹ 但并没有从根本上解决部分外观设计保护缺失的问题。《专利法》中外观设计的定义应当首先进行修改，将外观设计的范围拓展到产品的部分。建议修改后的定义如下："外观设计，是指对产品或其部分的形状、图案或者其结合以及色彩与形状、图案的结合所作出的富有美感并适于工业应用的新设计。"

当然，在我国外观设计制度整体定位存在偏差的情况下，仅仅修改外观设计的定义是远远不够的，最根本的措施应当是将外观设计制度的立足点还原于保护智力创造成果，同时系统调整外观设计的其他规则进行配合。在法律尚未修改的情况下，仍应严格按照现行法律标准予以判断，不能随意将保护水平提高，将部分相同或者相近似，而整体观察并不相同、不相近似的相关对比物认定为侵犯外观设计专利权。❺ 同时，也可以充分发挥司法的能动性，在坚持整体观察、综合判断的前提下，注意产品局部外观创新对整体印象的影响，最高人民法院在本田汽车外观设计专利无效纠纷案再审中的意见值得借鉴。

---

❶ 应振芳. 外观设计研究［M］. 北京：知识产权出版社，2008：169.

❷ 布拉德·谢尔曼，莱昂内尔·本特利. 现代知识产权法的演进——英国的历程（1760~1911）［M］. 金海军，译. 北京：北京大学出版社，2012：88.

❸ 程永顺. 中国专利诉讼［M］. 北京：知识产权出版社，2005：450. 根据专利检索，已获权的部分外观设计有：玩具娃娃躯干——专利号：993110592；牙刷头——专利号：98309560.4。

❹ 蔡民军，杨文泉. 对外观设计的部分保护——专利法中亟待解决的问题［G］//程永顺. 外观设计专利保护实务. 北京：法律出版社，2005：112.

❺ 程永顺. 中国专利诉讼［M］. 北京：知识产权出版社，2005：451.

六、结　语

从根本上说，外观设计的保护水平是由社会的经济发展程度决定的。市场竞争越激烈，消费者的需求水平越高，某类产品的外观设计也会越成熟，越向产品的局部发展。外观设计立法如果滞后于产业的发展，就无法发挥其激励创新的作用。外观设计作为专利制度的组成部分，对于我国创新型国家的建设将起到重要的支撑作用。我国应合理借鉴世界其他国家和地区的法律规定，将部分外观设计纳入我国外观设计保护制度中，激励企业不断对产品的外观作出改进，以美观实用的产品不断丰富我国消费者的物质文化生活。

中美发明专利创造性比较研究[*]

史 兆 欢

随着经济一体化的发展，中美两国之间的交往日益深入，我国许多企业申请美国专利以期获得美国专利法的保护；同样，美国的许多企业也在我国大量申请专利。因此，发明专利的授权条件是各国申请者十分关注的问题。在授予发明专利的实质性条件中，最为重要的是新颖性、创造性和实用性，其中创造性的判断是"三性"审查中的重点和难点。在美国，专利不具备创造性进而导致专利无效也是专利侵权案件中的重要抗辩理由。从我国建立专利制度的历史来看，许多具体制度的设计都从美国借鉴而来。本文试就中美两国发明专利的创造性进行比较研究，进而从中总结出值得我国借鉴之处，为我国发明专利创造性判断提供建议。

一、中国发明专利创造性概述

我国《专利法》第 22 条第 3 款对"创造性"进行了界定：创造性，是指与现有技术相比，该发明具有突出的实质性特点和显著的进步，该实用新型具有实质性特点和进步。尽管法律就"创造性"给出了明确的定义，但是就发明专利而言，对于客观判断什么是"突出的实质性特点"和"显著的进步"依然困难重重。有学者指出，如果发明是所属领域的技术人员"在现有技术的基础上通过逻辑分析、推理或者有限的实验可以得到的，则该发明是显而易见的，也就不具备突出的实质性特点"；"发明有显著的进步，则是指发明与最接近的现有技术相比能够产生有益的技术效果"。[1] 我国《专利审查指南 2010》也有此种类似规定。[2] 虽然这种论述将判断标准进一步明确，但是对于判断发明是否具有创造性仍然缺乏可操作性的步骤。

实际上，在实际审查工作中，《专利审查指南 2010》具有可操作性的判断方法。我国在 2001 年的《审查指南》中首次规定了"判断要求保护的技术方案相对于现有技术是否显而易见"的 3 个步骤。[3] 2006 年和 2010 年的《审

---

[*] 撰写论文时作者为中国人民大学学生，本文获 2012 年度隆天知识产权优秀论文奖。

[1] 王迁. 知识产权法教程 [M]. 北京：中国人民大学出版社，2007：381.

[2] 参见《专利审查指南 2010》第二部分第四章第 2.2 节、第 2.3 节（第 170 页）。

[3] 石必胜. 中美专利创造性判断方法的比较研究 [J/OL]. 中国知识产权（网络版），2012（5）.

查指南》专门对"突出的实质性特点的判断"作出规定。❶ 语言的详尽描述总是起着双重的作用，一方面，它使问题简单化，使判断创造性更具有可操作性；另一方面，它也使问题不断复杂化，不得不用其他语言来解释用于描述其他语言的词句。依照这样的逻辑，现在对"是否具有突出的实质性特点"的判断转变为对"相对于现有技术是否显而易见"的判断。

《专利审查指南 2010》也不能免于陷入此种两难困境之中，紧接着即规定了"是否显而易见"的判断步骤：①确定最接近的现有技术；②确定发明的区别特征和发明实际解决的技术问题；③判断要求保护的发明对本领域的技术人员来说是否显而易见。其中，第三步的判断又明确指出判断过程中，要确定的是现有技术整体上是否存在某种技术启示，这种启示会使本领域的技术人员在面对所述技术问题时，有动机改进最为接近的现有技术并获得要求保护的发明。如果存在这种启示，则发明是显而易见的，不具有突出的实质性特点。❷

对于"显著的进步"的判断，《专利审查指南 2010》则以列举的方式举例说明何种情形属于"具有显著的进步"。通常情况下，应当认为发明具有有益的技术效果，具有显著的进步：①发明与现有技术相比具有更好的技术效果，例如，质量改善、产量提高、节约资源、防治环境污染等；②发明提供了一种构思不同的技术方案，其技术效果能够基本上达到现有技术的水平；③发明代表某种新技术发展趋势；④尽管发明在某些方面有负面效果，但在其他方面具有明显积极的技术效果。❸

判断发明的创造性是一件非常复杂的工作。为了尽量减少审查员主观因素的影响，通常采用一些客观标准予以补充。如果发明具有开拓性，或者解决了长期以来渴望解决的技术难题，或者克服了技术偏见，或者取得了预料不到的技术效果等，则可认定该发明具备创造性。❹《专利审查指南 2010》对这些辅助因素也有规定，除此之外，《专利审查指南 2010》还将"商业上获得成功"作为判断发明是否具备创造性的依据。由于审查员是在了解发明内容之后才对是否具有创造性作出判断，因此为避免主观性对审查员的影响，

---

❶ 《专利审查指南 2010》规定："判断发明是否具有突出的实质性特点，就是要判断对本领域的技术人员来说，要求保护的发明相对于现有技术是否显而易见。如果要求保护的发明相对于现有技术是显而易见的，则不具有突出的实质性特点；反之，如果对比的结果表明要求保护的发明相对于现有技术是非显而易见的，则具有突出的实质性特点。"参见《专利审查指南 2010》第二部分第四章第 3.2.1 节（第 171~172 页）。

❷ 参见《专利审查指南 2010》第二部分第四章第 3.2.1.1 节（第 172~173 页）。

❸ 参见《专利审查指南 2010》第二部分第四章第 3.2.2 节（第 175 页）。

❹ 张玉敏. 知识产权法学［M］. 2 版. 北京：法律出版社，2011：211.

《专利审查指南 2010》特别提醒审查员要避免犯"事后诸葛亮"的错误。❶

由于法律位阶因素的存在，虽然《专利审查指南 2010》规定了创造性的判断方法和步骤，但是在法律位阶层次上只属于部门规章，人民法院并不需要遵守，不能直接引用其内容作为判决的依据。人民法院如何判断创造性，法律或行政法规并无规定，也无相关司法解释。但在司法实践中，法院一般依照《专利审查指南 2010》确立的标准和步骤来判断创造性。

二、美国发明专利非显而易见性的历史演变

美国与中国的创造性相对应的概念为非显而易见性（non-obviousness）。非显而易见性的要求在美国发明专利的授权条件中经历了漫长的历史演变，最初美国的专利授权条件并不要求具备创造性，只要该申请确实"足够重要"就能获得授权。❷ 直到 1952 年美国修改专利法，才在第 103 条首次将非显而易见性作为专利授权的法定条件之一。❸ 美国专利法第 103 条（a）款规定：一项发明，虽然并未在第 102 条所述的情形中被完全一致地描述或公开，如果其整体与现有技术的差别甚微，该发明在完成之时，对于该领域的普通技术人员而言是显而易见的，那么将不被授予专利。❹

（一）第 103 条之前最高法院的"非显而易见性"尝试

在第 103 条之前，美国专利法中并没有规定非显而易见性。但是实际上，在最高法院的司法判例中不断改变着以往的授权条件，在普通法上长期运用"发明"（invention）这一要求，与第 103 条的"非显而易见性"十分类似。❺ 1851 年的 Hotchkiss v. Greenwood 案开启了向第 103 条迈进的进程。该案涉及一种在球形装置上固定杆形手柄的方法，其中固定技术和陶瓷球形把手都是公知技术，涉案专利使用了黏土制成的把手。在此案中，法院首次陈述只有"发明"（invention）才具有可专利性，为此一项新技术必须超越一个熟练技工的日常努力。❻ 法院在判决中陈述道，球形把手并非新技术，金属手柄和固

---

❶ 参见《专利审查指南 2010》第二部分第四章第 5.1 节、第 5.2 节、第 5.3 节、第 5.4 节、第 6.2 节（第 181~183 页）。

❷ Patent Act of 1790. §1, 1 Statutes at Large 109. reprinted in P. J. Federico.

❸ ROCHELLE COOPER DREYFUSS, ROBERTA ROSENTHAL KWALL. Intellectual Property: Trademark, Copyright and Patent Law [M]. 2nd ed. Foundation Press, 2004: 666.

❹ 35 U. S. C., §103 (a). A patent may not be obtained though the invention is not identically disclosed or described as set forth in section 102 of this title, if the differences between the subject matter sought to be patented and the prior art are such that the subject matter as a whole would have been obvious at the time the invention was made to a person having ordinary skill in the art to which said subject matter pertains.

❺ EDMUND KITCH. Graham v. John Deere Co: New Standards for Patents, 1966 S. Ct. Rev. 303.

❻ MARTIN J. ADELMAN, RANDALL R. RADER, JOHN R. THOMAS. Patent Law [M]. 3rd Edition: 289.

定轴也是公知技术，用来固定的楔形榫头同样如此，用来将它们固定连接起来的方法亦是如此；所有这些东西都是众所周知的，唯一的新颖之处是将连接所用的门把手换做了另一种材料。法院进一步指出，本案中材料的选择和替换仅仅是出于商业目的而非其他目的，这一差别是普通的，独创性或发明成分是不充分的。换言之，这一改进是一个熟练技工的工作，而非发明者的创造。❶

在随后的案件中，最高法院不断肯定或延续 Hotchkiss 案中确立的"非显而易见"的要求。在 1883 年 Atlantic Works v. Brady 一案中，美国最高法院要求授予专利的主题必须是"发明人的创造性工作"，并认为"专利法不会将专利权授予以专利垄断为目的的投机者"，如果该发明"对于本领域普通技术人员来说是不重要的设备、浅显易知的思想、自然而然出现的事情"，❷ 那将不被授予专利。1941 年的 Cuno Engineering Corp. v. Automatic Devices Corp. 一案重申 Hotchkiss 案所确立的原则，认为"如果一项进步要获得专利特权，应当比普通技术人员的技能更具有创造性"，"必须有天才灵光的闪现，而不只是只有技能"。❸ 1944 年的 Goodyear Rubber and Tire Company v. Ray-O-Vac Company 一案将"商业上的成功"作为判断是否具有创造性的依据之一。❹ 1950 年 Great A&P Tea Company v. Supermarket Equipment Corporation 一案中，法院认为"申请人并没有对公有知识作出贡献，仅仅是将现有技术中的元素组合在一起，以期获得组合体的独占权"，并运用了"创造性天才的灵光"（Flash of Genius）标准作为判断创造性的标准。❺

"天才的灵光标准"产生一个问题，即基于并非灵光闪现，而是经过长期努力取得的发明是否具有可专利性。答案显然是肯定的，因此 1952 年通过新专利法时在第 103 条中指明，发明的专利性不能因发明完成方式的不同而予以否认。❻ 至此，第 103 条最终形成，"创造性天才的灵光"不再被用于判断专利的创造性上。

（二）Graham 要素与 TSM 测试法

第 103 条制定以后，美国最高法院在 Graham v. John Deere 案中第一次对其适用作出解释，促使发明专利造性判断的客观化。在 Graham 案中，最高法

---

❶ Hotchkiss v. Greenwood. 52 U. S. （11 How）248，267，13 L. Ed. 683（1851）.

❷ Atlantic Works v. Brady. 107 U. S. 192，200（1983）.

❸ Cuno Engineering Corp. v. Automatic Devices Corp. ，314 U. S. 84，90（1941）.

❹ Goodyear Rubber and Tire Company v. Ray-O-Vac Company，321 U. S. 275（1944）.

❺ Great A&P Tea Company v. Supermarket Equipment Corporation，340 U. S. 147（1950）.

❻ 35 U. S. C. ，§ 103（a）. "Patentability shall not be negatived by the manner in which the invention was made".

院提出了一个判断显而易见性的四步骤测试，即"Graham 测试标准"或"Graham 要素"。法院指出，需要分析以下要素来判断创造性：①现有技术的范围和内容；②现有技术与要求保护的发明之间的不同之处；③技术领域的一般技术水平；④辅助性考量因素，例如商业上的成功、长期存在但尚未解决的需求、他人的失败等。❶

在如何推理出所申请发明具有初步显而易见性这个问题上，联邦巡回上诉法院一直运用著名的"教导—启示—动机"（Teaching - Suggestion - Motivation，TSM）测试法：只有在现有技术文献、本领域技术人员的知识或者所要解决技术问题的性质中，发现某种结合现有技术教导的动机或启示，才能证明该发明是显而易见的。❷上述"启示"主要来源于参考文献本身、本领域的知识，包括特定领域的某些公开或参考文献及所要解决的问题，引导发明人去查找解决问题方法的相关文献。❸根据这一判断准则，当创造性的判断需要多份对比文献组合起来时，只有当这些文献中给出了明确的建议、教导，使普通技术人员有动机将它们组合起来，才允许以这些对比文献的组合来否定申请发明的创造性。❹

TSM 测试法有其优点，可以防止审查员犯"事后诸葛亮"的错误，减少主观因素的影响。但是缺陷也是十分明显的，很少会有撰写者会直接在文献中写出明确、清楚的提示语句。从另一方面来讲，即便专利文献中并没有明确记载上述启示内容，但是也不能证明所申请的发明就具有非显而易见性。TSM 测试法低估了普通技术人员的技术水平，容易对那些十分显而易见却没有明确"教导—启示"的发明授予专利。包括一些大公司在内的许多机构认为 TSM 准则背离了美国联邦最高法院对专利法第 103 条的法律解释，实质上

---

❶ "Under § 103, the scope and content of the prior art are to be determined; differences between the prior art and the claims at issue are to be ascertained; and the level of ordinary skill in the pertinent art resolved. Against this background the obviousness or nonobviousness of the subject matter is determined. Such secondary considerations as commercial success, long felt but unsolved needs, failure of others, ect., might be utilized to give light to the circumstances surrounding the origin of the subject to be patented." 参见 Graham v. John Deere，383 U. S. 1（1966）。另需指出的是，有人将 Graham 要素总结为 3 点或者 5 点，但是均包含以上要素，只是各研究者总结习惯或划分断句喜好上的差异。

❷ 方慧聪. KSR 案与美国专利审查指南的最新修改［G］//国家知识产权局条法司. 专利法研究（2007）［M］. 北京：知识产权出版社，2008：60.

❸ 蔡萍. 解读美国专利法的非显而易见性［J］. 中国发明与专利，2007（8）.

❹ 尹新天. 美国专利政策的新近发展及对我国知识产权制度的有关思考［G］//国家知识产权局条法司. 专利法研究（2007）. 北京：知识产权出版社，2008：1。美国专利商标局也曾指出，只有"教导"或"启示"是"明确、肯定、清楚"（Specific，Definitive and Clear）的情况下，才可以否定显而易见性。

降低了创造性标准，导致了专利权过多过滥，阻碍了技术创新。❶

总体言之，Graham 案确立了创造性判断的事实依据，而非显而易见判断是基于这些事实依据之上的法律问题。第 103 条是判定显而易见性的法律依据，实际操作中则通过 TSM 测试法审查 Graham 要素来判定非显而易见性。Graham 案明确了判定非显而易见性需要确定的内容；TSM 则体现 Graham 要素分析内容的内在联系、判定步骤和方法，是一个定性标准。❷

（三）KSR 案对非显而易见性审查的改变

KSR 案在美国专利创造性审查上具有里程碑意义，该判决对其后的类似案件以及美国专利商标局对创造性的审查都产生了重大影响。原告 Teleflex 拥有一项"带有气节门电子控制装置的可调油门踏板"，被告 KSR International 公司是一家生产包括踏板系统在内的汽车部件的加拿大公司。Teleflex 公司控告 KSR 侵犯其专利权，但是 KSR 公司并没有对侵权是否成立进行抗辩，而是主张该专利权利要求 4 不具备创造性，因而是无效的。

一审法院根据 Graham 要素对涉案专利进行了分析，认定其与现有技术几乎没有什么区别，仅仅是现有技术的简单组合，并根据 TSM 测试法检测对比文件，得出现有技术公开的因素能够指引普通技术人员发明出涉案专利，同时没有认同专利权人提出的被控侵权人采用该技术获得商业上的成功可以作为该发明具有创造性的证据，因此涉案专利是显而易见的，不具备创造性。

Teleflex 公司不服判决，上诉至美国联邦巡回上诉法院（CAFC）。CAFC 认为，TSM 标准需要地方法院有确定的事实依据和证据表明，除非现有技术准确地提到了专利权人所要解决的问题，否则该问题本身不会使一个发明人去查看这些现有技术。易言之，CAFC 认为，地方法院并没有严格适用 TSM 准则对事实进行认定，从而来表明通过现有技术的启示可以在可调控踏板上安装电子控制系统，因此否定了一审法院的判决。

KSR 公司不服，将案件上诉至最高法院。最高法院认为，即使是有助于判断创造性的规则，也不应僵化或千篇一律，假使如此，TSM 测试法就不符合最高法院的判例。创造性的判断不能局限于表达教导、启示或者动机的文字上，也不能过分强调公开文献和授权专利的字面表达的重要性。如果法院将一项普遍原则变成一种僵化的规则来禁锢创造性的判断，正如 CAFC 所为，那便是错误的。❸ 因此，最高法院否定了 CAFC 的判决。

最高法院对 KSR 案的判决，实质上提高了创造性审查的标准，但是同时

---

❶ 何伦健，唐国政. 美国专利制度中的非显而易见性判断及其对我国创造性审查的启示［G］//国家知识产权局条法司. 专利法研究（2007）. 北京：知识产权出版社，2008：49.

❷ 关健. 美国非显而易见性判定实践的五区和难点［J］. 知识产权，2012（7）.

❸ KSR International Co. v. Teleflex Inc. 550 U. S. 398（2007）.

却牺牲了判断标准的客观性，通过赋予普通技术人员一定的创造力，增加了创造性判断中的主观因素。虽然 KSR 案具有重大意义，但是并没有推翻 TSM 测试规则，仅仅是对其进行了调整，使这一规则更符合专利法的本意。

三、中美发明专利创造性概括比较

我国专利制度多有借鉴美国，因此两国创造性判断上的差距并没有想象中那么大，这也能从《专利审查指南 2010》中体现出来。例如，我国《专利审查指南 2010》中直接运用了美国的"显而易见"这一表述；关于发明过程不应影响创造性的判断也在我国《专利审查指南 2010》中有所规定，与美国专利法第 103 条一致；我国《专利审查指南 2010》中对避免审查员犯"事后诸葛亮"错误的提醒，也与美国对"事后眼光"（Hindsight）的顾虑相一致，并都规定了一些辅助因素。❶

美国 Graham 要素确定了 3 项事实要素，与 TSM 测试法对显而易见性的判断构成了美国专利创造性判断的完整过程。比较我国创造性审查的"三步法"与美国 TSM 测试法，实质上存在诸多相同之处，二者均需要确定现有技术的范围、区别特征以及确定本领域的普通技术水平，进而对是否具备创造性进行判断。详细观之，我国三步法的前两步以及美国 Graham 要素的确定均属于事实上的判断，比较客观，受主观性因素影响最大的是对于是否"显而易见"的判断。这一步中包含了两个较为抽象的概念，掌握起来有较大的伸缩余地：一是如何确定所属领域的普通技术人员的技术水准；二是如何判断现有技术是否提供了将最接近现有技术与其他技术以及技术常识结合起来的教导或启示，使人相信普通技术人员有理由、有动机会想出要求保护的发明或实用新型。❷ 美国在专利制度的发展历程中对于这些因素的判断经验，对我国都有较好的借鉴意义。

四、美国非显而易见性判断之于我国的有益启示

虽然中美两国关于创造性的制度实质上差距不大，但是在美国修正创造性判断的历程中不断发现的专利制度中存在的问题，我国在今后的发展中同样也会面临。我们应当从中得到启示，作为前车之鉴。

（一）审查方式的逆向性

我国专利创造性的审查方式是一种逆向性的。根据《专利法》的规定，判断创造性采取以现有技术为坐标，从后向前比较的方式，即与"申请日前"

---

❶ 《专利审查指南 2010》第二部分第四章第 170~184 页。
❷ 尹新天. 中国专利法详解［M］. 北京：知识产权出版社，2011：265.

已有的技术相比。美国专利法规定的"非显而易见性"这一表述即表明创造性判断的预测性，是以现有技术为坐标，自前向后比较的，即"发明能否从现有技术中明显得出"或"是否显而易见"。我国的比较方式十分容易引起"事后诸葛亮"的错误。判断主体很难避免申请日以后的技术以及所公布的技术方案对发明本身创造性判断的影响。❶

虽然我国《专利审查指南2010》中采用了"显而易见"性判断的表述方式，但是并没有上升为法的高度，法院并无必须遵守的义务，因此容易导致在授权程序中与司法程序中关于创造性判断标准不一的情形。因此，宜在《专利法》中引入"显而易见"表述方式。实质上，这不仅仅是法律用语上的不同，更体现的是一种思维逻辑方式的不同。

（二）对"本领域技术人员"的界定

我国《专利法》没有明确规定发明创造性的判断主体，导致在理论界和实务界长期对判断主体的争议。在创造性审查中，曾一度将专利审查员作为本领域的普通技术人员。在司法实践中则会选择法官作为创造性的判断主体。这就极易导致创造性标准的不一。

除此之外，我国《专利审查指南2010》对审查主体作出如下规定：所谓技术领域的技术人员，也可以称为本领域的技术人员，是指一种假设的"人"，假定他知晓申请日或者优先权日之前发明所属技术领域所有的普通技术知识，能够获知该领域中所有的现有技术，并且具有应用该日期之前常规实验的能力，但他不具有创造能力。❷

很明显，我国将一个虚拟的"人"作为创造性的判断主体，然而其本身并无任何创造性能力。实际上，在具体判断之时，审查员只能最大限度地接近法律虚拟的"普通技术人员"，其间的误差不可避免地存在。❸ 不赋予普通技术人员一定的创造力，则极易导致几乎没有创造性的发明获得专利。美国法院对KSR案的判决客观上赋予了普通技术人员一定的创造力。从实质上说就是要让过去那种完全杜撰的"普通技术人员"朝现实生活中的"普通技术人员"回归，摒弃过去所采用的对组合对比文献过于严格和僵硬的限制，提高创造性标准的判断门槛，减少不该授予的"问题专利"的数量。❹

---

❶ 牛强. 专利"创造性"判断中否认"事后诸葛亮"：兼评我国《专利法》第22条及《审查指南》中相关规定 [J]. 知识产权，2009（7）.

❷ 《专利审查指南2010》第二部分第四章第2.4节（第170~171页）.

❸ 崔国斌. 专利技术的等同比较 [G] //郑胜利. 北大知识产权评论（第一卷）. 北京：法律出版社，2002：46.

❹ 尹新天. 美国专利政策的新近发展及对我国知识产权制度的有关思考 [G] //国家知识产权局条法司. 专利法研究（2007）. 北京：知识产权出版社，2008：20.

因此，基于以上分析，我国应在《专利法》中明确创造性的判断主体。虽然采取何种创造性标准与各国的科技发展水平以及国家政策直接相关，依照现在的创造性标准，我国必然存在大量的垃圾专利。因此，在将来必要的时候应当提高创造性的标准，赋予普通技术人员一定的创造力，对那些显而易见的发明不授予专利，从长远来看于国于民都是有利的。概言之，建议将《专利审查指南 2010》中"但他不具有创造能力"的限定删除，将创造性的判断主体向生活中的"人"转变。

（三）重视辅助判断因素

我国《专利审查指南 2010》中也规定了创造性判断的辅助因素，其目的在于最大限度避免审查员犯"事后诸葛亮"的错误，减少主观因素对创造性判断的影响。当然，这些因素只是判断是否具有创造性的辅助因素，并不能起决定作用。《专利审查指南 2010》中也对此有所告诫：应当强调的是，当申请属于以下情形时，审查员应当予以考虑，不应轻易作出发明不具备创造性的结论。[1]

但是，我国对于专利创造性判断中辅助因素的重视还不够，很少有判决直接依据辅助因素判断创造性。辅助性判断因素在美国司法判例中经常用到，在著名的 KSR 案中权利人也以"商业上的成功"作为支持专利有效的抗辩之一。在我国司法实践中，这样的案例十分少见。就笔者观察所见，最新的一个运用"商业上的成功"这一辅助性因素来判断外观设计创造性的是胡颖上诉案。[2] 因此，在司法实践中，我国应当重视辅助因素对创造性判断的作用，使法律法规的规定能真正发挥作用。

（四）司法机关应对专利有效性判定有一定的裁量权

从美国的显而易见性判定的程序中可以看出，不仅美国专利商标局对发明创造的显而易见性有判定的权利，而且在侵权诉讼中，美国的法院对专利是否有效也有裁量权。而在我国，法院并没有审查专利有效性的权利。在专利无效案件中，如果法院撤销了专利复审委员会的决定，只能由专利复审委员会重新作出裁决，而不能直接裁决专利有效或者无效。这可能导致马拉松式的专利无效诉讼——请求人提出无效宣告请求，专利复审委复审决定，起诉，一审，二审，专利复审委重新决定，再起诉，一审，二审，专利复审委再重新作出决定……理论上，这一循环可以无休无止。[3] 在侵犯专利权的案件中，

---

❶ 《专利审查指南 2010》第二部分第四章第 5 节（第 181 页）。

❷ 商业成功能佐证实用新型专利的创造性——胡颖与专利复审委员会实用新型专利权无效行政纠纷上诉案［EB/OL］.［2012-09-18］. http：//www. shipa. org/ip_litigation_show. asp？id＝321.

❸ 崔国斌. 专利法：原理与案例［M］. 北京：北京大学出版社，2012：410.

如果当事人提出专利无效抗辩，法院不能直接判断专利是否有效，只能中止诉讼，等待复审委的决定。当然有些案件法院可以不中止诉讼，❶ 那么这就极易产生法院与复审委关于专利有效性判定不一的情况。

我国存在的上述情况，从微观层面来看，容易导致专利创造性标准的不统一，使专利制度设计本身存在矛盾；从宏观层面来看，造成了司法资源和行政成本的浪费。目前法院没有对专利有效性审查权的状况，与我国目前司法队伍的结构有关。在现在条件下，我国的法官队伍中还没有大量存在既懂技术又懂法律的专业人员，知识结构的偏差导致了上述情形。赋予法院判定专利有效性的权限是理所当然的，不存在法理上的障碍，只存在客观情形的限制。但是，随着我国法官队伍和相关专家制度的不断发展完善，这一客观因素也将会消除。

五、结 论

我国专利制度建立只有几十年的时间，经验还十分缺乏。美国专利制度有长达数百年的历史，发展过程中遇到的种种问题通过自身的不断完善得到解决，创造出了适合本国的专利制度。我国可能同样会遇到美国遇到的各种问题，可以从美国的经验中获得启示，根据我国实际情况制定出符合我国国情的专利制度和政策。实际上，随着经济全球化的深入发展，中美两国之间专利制度的差距正在逐渐缩小。美国 AIA 法案的通过，也最终使美国放弃了"先发明制"（First-to-file），改为了"发明人先申请制"（First-inventor-to-file），力图"与世界保持和谐"（Harmony with the rest of word）。❷

---

❶ 《最高人民法院关于审理专利纠纷案件适用法律问题的若干规定》（2001）第 9 条规定：人民法院受理的侵犯实用新型、外观设计专利权纠纷案件，被告在答辩期间内请求宣告该项专利权无效的，人民法院应当中止诉讼，但具备下列情形之一的，可以不中止诉讼：（一）原告出具的检索报告未发现导致实用新型专利丧失新颖性、创造性的技术文献的；（二）被告提供的证据足以证明其使用的技术已经公知的；（三）被告请求宣告该项专利权无效所提供的证据或者依据的理由明显不充分的；（四）人民法院认为不应当中止诉讼的其他情形。

❷ TOSHIKO TAKENAKA. Harmony with the Rest of World? The America Invents Act［J］. Journal of Intellectual Property Law & Pratice，2011.

Insider's Look:

Exploring the Intricacies of Chinese IP Law

Claim Definitions Undergoing Change[*]

By: Xiaoying Wu & Zongliang (Stephen) Zou

An invention is defined by patent claims, which are often compared to the recitation of property lines in a deed for land because both show upon the property that the owner has the right to exclude others from trespassing on or infringing. The construction (i. e. , giving the meaning) of patent claims plays a critical role in nearly every patent case. It is central to the evaluation of infringement and validity, and can affect or determine the outcome of other significant issues such as enablement and remedies. During the last few years, the Chinese Supreme People's Court has worked on standards for delineating patent claims.

This article discusses a recent court decision for construing a closed−ended transitional phrase in a pharmaceutical patent claim, as well as provides guidance on the best practices for drafting and prosecuting a patent application.

1. Defining Transitional Phrases: U. S. Practice

A transitional phrase, in U. S. patent law, is a phrase that links the preamble of a patent claim to the specific elements set forth in the claim which define what the invention itself actually is. The transitional phrase acts as a limitation on the claim, indicating whether a similar device, method or composition infringes the patent if it contains more or fewer elements than the claim in the patent. [1] In the U. S. , the transitional phrases "comprising", "consisting essentially of" and "consisting of" define the scope of a claim with respect to what un−recited additional elements or steps, if any, are excluded from the scope of the claim. [2]

Specifically, regulations as well as the corresponding prejudicial decisions provided in the *Manual of Patent Examining Procedure* (*MPEP*) define these transitional phrases. The transitional term "comprising", which is synonymous with "including", "containing" or "characterized by" is inclusive or open−ended and

---

[*] First published at China IP Focus 2014, Managing Intellectual Property, United Kingdom, 2014.
[1] http: //en. wikipedia. org/wiki/Transitional _phrase.
[2] Section 2111, Chapter 2100, *Manual of Patent Examining Procedure* (*MPEP*).

does not exclude additional, unrecited elements or method steps. The transitional phrase "consisting of" excludes any element, step or ingredient not specified in the claim, particularly as "closing the claim to the inclusion of materials other than those recited except for impurities ordinarily associated therewith". The transitional phrase "consisting essentially of" limits the scope of a claim to the specified materials or steps "and those that do not materially affect the basic and novel characteristic (s)" of the claimed invention. A "consisting essentially of" claim occupies a middle ground between closed claims that are written in a "consisting of" format and fully open claims that are drafted in a "comprising" format. ❶

2. Undergoing Evolution: Definitions in Patent Examination in China

The *Guideline for Patent Examination 2001* (the "*Guideline 2001*") ❷, specifies three transitional phrases, the section of which is reproduced below. See the *Guideline 2001*, Section 3. 2. 1, Chapter 10, Part II.

There are three formats of presentation for a claim: open - ended, closed - ended, and semi-open-ended. The open-ended format means that the composition does not exclude those components that are not recited in the claim. The closed-ended format means that any of the other components that are not recited in the claim shall be excluded. The semi-open-ended format is somewhere between the two formats. The three formats of presentation are different in scope of protection sought. The commonly used wording is as follows.

(1) Open-ended format: wording such as "comprising", "including", "containing", etc. All indicate that some other components which are not indicated in the claim may be further included in the composition, though the former may take quite a great proportion in content.

(2) Closed-ended format: wording such as "consisting of", etc. , all indicate that the composition claimed is composed of the indicated components only, without any other components to be included in. However, there could be impurities, and the impurities may take only normal proportion in content.

(3) Semi-open-ended format: wordings includes, such as "essentially consisting of"... The scope of protection of the claims presented in this format is between

---

❶ Section 2111, Chapter 2100, *Manual of Patent Examining Procedure* (*MPEP*), Eighth Edition, Latest Revision August 2012.

❷ The patent has a filing date of July 21, 2004, and thus the *Guideline for Patent Examination 2001* is applicable.

that of the open−ended format and the close−ended format. It makes the close−ended format claim open only to the components that are not mentioned in the claims and these components may take any proportion in content on condition that they have no substantial effect on the basic feature (s) or the new feature (s) of the components already mentioned.

However, in the *Guideline for Patent Examination 2010*, (the "*Guideline 2010*"), only two formats are specified: open−ended and closed−ended, where the open−ended format refers to the wordings such as " comprising" ... " essentially consisting of" , etc. , indicating that some other components which are not recited in the claim may be further included in the composition, though the former may take quite a great proportion in content. ❶❷

Deleting the semi−open−ended format, the *Guideline 2010* defines "essentially consisting of" functionally as "comprising", i. e. , open to those unrecited elements. Nevertheless, it is unclear whether such definitions would be applicable for patent infringement cases.

3. Setting the Scene: Opinions from the Supreme People's Court

In Hu Xiaoquan v. Shanxi Zhendongtaisheng Pharm. Corp. et al, (2008) −Jinan−Civil−First Instance−No. 4, Hu Xiaoquan, owner of a patent entitled "Lyophilized Dry Powder Of Adenosine Disodium Triphosphate And Magnesium Chloride For Injection And The Preparation Method Thereof" (Chinese patent No. : ZL 200410024515. 1, the "patent") , filed a complaint against Shanxi Zhendongtaisheng Pharm. Corp. for patent infringement on the ground that claim 2 of the patent treads on a product manufactured by Shanxi Zhendongtaisheng Pharm. Corp.

Claim 2 reads: Lyophilized dry powder of adenosine disodium triphosphate and magnesium chloride for injection, characterized in that, consisting of adenosine disodium triphosphate and magnesium chloride with weight ratio of 100mg : 32mg.

The accused infringing product manufactured by the defendant, in the trade name of adenosine disodium triphosphate and magnesium chloridefor injection, is a lyophilized dry powder consisting of adenosine disodium triphosphate, magnesium chloride, sodium bicarbonate and arginine.

---

❶ Section 4. 2. 1, chapter 20, part II, *Guideline* for *Patent Examination 2010* (English version).

❷ Since 2006, there are some changes to the *Guideline 2001*, where semi−open−ended mode has been deleted. The current *Guideline 2010* has only two modes, open−ended mode and close−ended mode. There exists no middle ground.

The issue in dispute is whether the accused infringing product falls into the scope of claim 2.

In the first instance, Jinan City Intermediate People's Court opined, the accused infringing product, a lyophilized dry powder for injection with the main components of 100mg adenosine disodium triphosphate and 32mg magnesium chloride, has the same features as claim 2 and therefore falls into the scope thereof. As to the two other components, sodium bicarbonate and arginine, the court treated them as pharmaceutical adjuvants instead of main components, and they have no influence on both of the composition of the claimed product and the weight ratio of the main components. Accordingly, an infringement was found.

On appeal, Shandong Province High People's Court affirmed the lower court's decision ((2010) −Shandong−Retrial−Civil−No. 33). The court further opined that, a claim shall be construed in light of the specification and the state of the art. As to the two other components, sodium bicarbonate and arginine, according to the specification of the alleged infringing products, they are adjuvants instead of major components. Adding adjuvants is common practice in the manufacture of a medicament. Referring to the specification of the patent at issue, in the preparation of the claimed product, sodium hydroxide is added to adjust pH before lyophilization, which means that certain adjuvants are also actually contained in the claimed product in addition to the two major components. Accordingly, even if the product claim is drafted in close−ended, the pharmaceutical adjuvants cannot be excluded. The court stated it was improper to construe the close transition, defined as "without any other components to be included in" to exclude adjuvants. As a result, the accused infringing product falls within the scope defined by claim 2.

The Supreme People's Court reversed all the lower courts' decisions during retrial ((2011) −Supreme Court−Retrial−Civil−No. 183), and construed claim 2 in accordance with the provisions stipulated in the Guidelines, supra. ❶

The Supreme People's Court articulates that, to maintain the public's reliance and certainty on the scope of a patent claim, when construing the claims in infringement litigation, the provisions and the claim languages governing the patent allowance shall be generally followed, i. e. , the court shall take the same position as the patent office. As for a claim with a closed−ended transitional phase, the provisions regarding the protection scope in the Guidelines have never changed since

---

❶ There are no regulations as to how to construe a claim with a transition phrase in both of the *Patent Law of China* and the *Implementing Regulations* thereof.

1993, and the public knows that such a claim excludes any other components or steps. Turning to claim 2, the claimed product only consists of adenosine disodium triphosphate and magnesium chloride with weight ratio of 100mg : 32mg and no other components are included apart from some possible impurities with usual contents. Accordingly, the accused product with other components does not fall within claim 2.

4. Construing the Close Transition: Equity for Patentee and Interests for Public

The first instance and appellate courts ignored the difference between the transitional phrases "consisting of" and "consisting essentially of" as prescribed in the Guidelines, and unreasonably interpreted "consisting of" recited by claim 2 as "consisting essentially of" .

Such a claim interpretation brings on a tense between the patent grant proceedings and litigation proceedings, resulting in that the protection scope in litigation was different from that the public or even the patentee would have anticipated. As pointed by the Supreme People's Court, the meaning and the scope of the transitional phrase "consisting of" in a claim have never changed since 1993. How to draft a claim and use which transitional phrase is the applicant's own option. When the applicant pursues a claim with such a transitional phrase, he or she would know the scope of the claim. When a claim with such a transitional phrase is issued, the public would anticipate the scope. However, if the court construed the transitional phrase of "consisting of" differently from the long established provisions in the patent granting proceedings, the public and even the patentee would lose their reliance on the patent granting and protection system, and the public would lose guidance in his business activity in light of an issued claim.

A scope of a claim delimits a boundary for patent protection. Only if the boundary is clear and certain, can the public know the limits of the boundary and try to avoid trespassing. A stable and foreseeable claim construction from the patent office to the court will provide good guidance, both for the patentee and the public and will also be beneficial to maintain the balance of the interests between the patentee and the public.

5. Looking to Best Practice: Claims Drafted and Prosecuted with Specificity

In the *Guidelines 2010*, the semi-open-ended format has been deleted. For a claim with "essentially consisting of", its scope is open to any other unrecited elements. In view of this, it is different from the U. S. practice.

The difference should be considered when an application is drafted to enter both China and the U. S.. Depending on the contribution of the invention over the state of the art and different practices, the applicant needs to select a proper drafting format from various options, for example, open-ended transition, close-ended transition, close to active ingredients, close to partial components or even include various options in one application. For instance, for an invention novel to some specific active ingredients, when drafting a composition claim, the claim may be drafted as close to active ingredients. Considering the difference between China and the U. S., we suggest drafting one claim by incorporating the wordings like "active ingredients consisting of" in a clause following "comprising" transitional phrase, rather than solely drafted as the semi-open-ended format with "essentially consisting of" transition phrase.

Chinese Practice on Design Freedom Degree/Design Room for Design Patents

By: Yan Huang

The patent system for designs was significantly adjusted under the 3rd amendment to *Chinese Patent Law* (effective on October 1, 2009), including an increased bar for patentability. While Chinese design patents are granted without substantive examination, a patentability review in comparison between a prior design (made available to the public before the effective filing date of a patented design) and the patented design would mainly be made during an invalidation proceeding based on the principle of "overall observation and comprehensive judgment" from the perspective of an ordinary consumer, which refers to a fictional "person" as prescribed by the *Guidelines for Patent Examination*. Viewing the ordinary is not an average, Chinese patent practice applies a concept of "design room" in some cases recently to elevate the ordinary consumer to one who is technically capable and discriminatory. Below, we would like to discuss the degree of design freedom analyzed in a case before OHIM and the design room referred to some opinions issued by the Supreme People's Court, together with our thoughts and practical tips.

1. An OHIM Case

In comparing with any prior design, it has been established in the European Union that a community design may be protected if it is novel and has individual character. Specifically, a design is novel if there is no identical prior design and prior design whose features differ only in immaterial details; and a design has individual character if the overall impression it produces on an informed user differs from the overall impression produced on such a user by any prior design taking the degree of freedom of a designer into consideration, where the more the designer's freedom in developing a design is restricted, the more likely minor differences between the designs in issue will be sufficient to produce a different overall impression on the informed user.

In the Decision of the Invalidity Division ICD 8611 made by the Office for Harmonization in the Internal Market ("OHIM"), OHIM affirms the validity of the registered Community design No. 001600560-0001 ("the concerned design"), entitled "watches (part of -)", over three prior designs and further elaborates the consideration of "the degree of freedom of a designer".

The drawings of the concerned design:

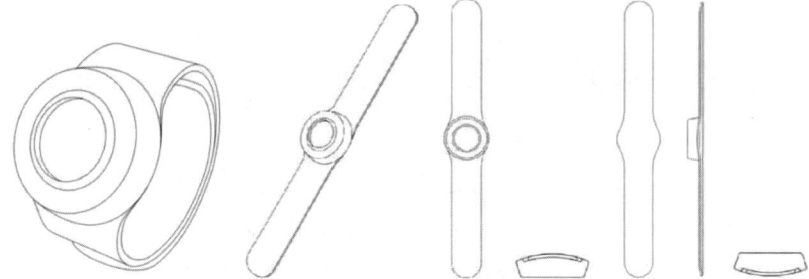

Prior design 1 is the FR design registration No. 042596-004:

Prior design 2 is the U. S. Design patent No. D455,356 S:

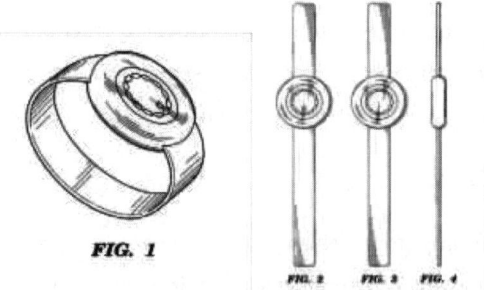

FIG. 1

The prior design 3 is the International Design No. DM/063479:

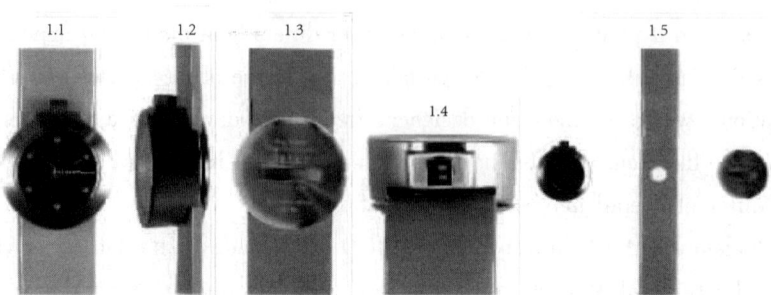

OHIM makes a comparison between the concerned design and the prior art designs respectively.

Regarding the overall impression produced on an informed user, OHIM considers, the informed user is familiar with the basic features of the products to which the concerned design relates, and is aware that the degree of freedom of a designer of wristwatches is almost unlimited since the features of a wristwatch such as the watch case or straps can take different shapes, patterns and materials. The only limitation for the designer consists in that wristwatches must include some sort of a watch dial to show the time and have a means to attach the watch to the wrist. However, the more crowded the market (which is the case of wristwatch market), the more differences may contribute to the individual character of the concerned design. ❶

OHIM also thinks, the concerned design and the prior designs share some basic features, namely the round dial and case, which are common features and therefore have less weight in the overall impression produced on the informed user. However, the large, protruding case and wide bezel in addition to its wide strap of the concerned design give the impression of a more robust, heavier watch that departs significantly from the overall impressions produced by the prior designs, which are more in line with traditional wristwatches with less bulky.

It appears that OHIM will give attention to the basic functional design of the wrist watches, such as the watch dial and the case, when considering the degree of freedom of a designer, during the determination of whether the overall impression of the concerned design differs from the prior art references. And OHIM's opinion about the degree of freedom of a designer is that, the larger the design freedom degree is, the less the common features produce in the overall impression on the informed user. After that, OHIM judges whether the several different visual features between the concerned design and the prior designs are sufficient to notably influence the general appearance of the product.

In the decision, OHIM confirms the relative range that the design freedom de-

---

❶ It is prescribed in Council Regulation (EC) No 6/2002 of 12 December 2001 on Community designs (OJ EC No L 3 of 5. 1. 2002, p. 1), Article 6 "Individual character": 1. A design shall be considered to have individual character if the overall impression it produces on the informed user differs from the overall impression produced on such a user by any design which has been made available to the public: (a) in the case of an unregistered Community design, before the date on which the design for which protection is claimed has first been made available to the public; (b) in the case of a registered Community design, before the date of filing the application for registration or, if a priority is claimed, the date of priority. 2. In assessing individual character, the degree of freedom of the designer in developing the design shall be taken into consideration.

gree may be extended after considering which designs belong to the designs for achieving the basic functions of the product. That is, excluding at least the design features only for playing a role in technical function and effect, other designs will fall in the scope of the design freedom degree, in which some are only immaterial details and cannot bring significant impression to the informed user, while others are able to provide significant impression to the informed user.

2. Chinese Practice

While Chinese Patent Law does not require a design to possess an individual character for a patent grant, the law does specify that any design for which a patent right may be granted shall be notably different from the prior design or a combination of the features of the prior design. The law, however, is silent upon the definition with respect to "notably different", the judicial interpretations from Supreme People's Courts requires that an alleged infringing design shall be considered from the view of an ordinary consumer based on the principle of overall observation and comprehensive judgment. Such a principle, practically, is applied in assessing the patentability of a design for a patent right.

Recently, the concept of "design room" is introduced in the Chinese design patent practice, which is different from the provision "the degree of freedom of the designer in developing the design shall be taken into consideration" in Art. 6 of Council Regulation (EC) No 6/2002, at least to the extent that the judgment subject for determining same/similar designs is an ordinary consumer❶ in China.

Even so, the ideas of the degree of freedom of a designer in EC design protection system still have a certain reference for the Chinese patent practice.

Since "an ordinary consumer" is a fictional person, when judging whether there are notable differences between the patent design and prior art reference (s), a problem that must be faced is how to objectively acknowledge the level of the knowledge and cognitive capability of an ordinary consumer, which is always hard to

---

❶ As prescribed in *Guidelines for Patent Examination*, the judgment of some/similar designs shall be made according to the knowledge and cognitive capability of an ordinary consumer of the product incorporating the patent concerned, and an ordinary consumer of a certain category of product incorporating a design shall have the following characteristics: (1) common knowledge of the designs and commonly used design methods (including design transformation, mosaic, replacement, etc.) incorporated in the same or similar products as that incorporating the patent concerned before its filing date; (2) certain capability of distinguishing the differences in shape, pattern and colour between design patent products, but without notice to the minor differences in shape, pattern or colour of products.

separate from the subjective factors and causes the differences of judgment ways and results. This is one reason that the design room is introduced gradually into the determination of same/similar designs in recent years in China, so as to obtain an objective, fair and correct conclusion.

In the invalidation cases (ZL200630110998. 7 and ZL200730112575. 3) included in the *Supreme People's Court Annual Report on IP Cases 2010*, the concept of design room is introduced by the courts. In the two cases, the Supreme People's Court points out that " design room" refers to the degree of freedom of a designer when developing a design of a specific product.

The Supreme People's Court gives an opinion, that the degree of freedom of a designer in a specific product area is usually constrained and influenced by various factors such as prior design, technology, law and conception and so forth. The size of design room for a specific product closely relates to the determination about the knowledge and cognitive capability of an ordinary consumer of the same or similar kind of products. For the product area with a large design room, the degree of freedom of development is higher, and the designs in the product area have inevitably various forms, styles and splendors, such that an ordinary consumer of the design products is not easy to pay attention to the relatively minor design differences. On the contrary, in the product area with a considerably restricted design room, there are inevitably more same or similar features due to the relatively narrower design room for development, such that an ordinary consumer of the design products will normally notice some minor differences between various designs.

From the explanation of the Supreme People's Court and the case under OHIM, both provide the judgment basis of same or similar designs from different perspectives by adopting the design room/the degree of freedom of a designer, even though both concern the overall visual effect. From the perspective of OHIM, the more crowded the market, the more differences may contribute to the individual character of the design concerned; whereas from the perspective of the Supreme People's Court, the bigger the design room, the more the forms of designs appear, and thusly the tiny different details will not be concerned by a normal consumer.

Actually, the Supreme People's Court clarifies that in the judgment of same or similar designs between the design patent and the prior art reference (s) , it is allowable to consider the design room or the degree of freedom of a designer, so as to determine exactly the knowledge and cognitive capability of an ordinary consumer. When considering the factor of design room, it should be acknowledged that the size of the design room is a relative concept. In the meantime, for the design room of the same product, the size of the design room may change. Thus, the consideration of the design room in the patent invalidation procedures should be based on the state on the filing date.

3. Conclusion

It should be mentioned that the detailed interpretation from the Supreme People's Court may be a guide in the future and is a useful supplement to the principle of comparison of designs through approach of overall observation and comprehensive judgment. However, when concerning "design room", a designer, a new group of people which is different from an ordinary consumer in the sense of *Chinese Patent Law*, will be introduced. A designer and an ordinary consumer are not equivalent and cannot be confusedly used during the judgment of same or similar designs. "Design room" should be primarily used to accurately determine the level of the knowledge and cognitive capability of an ordinary consumer. And, the extendable range of the design room should be considered from different aspects, and should not be limited to one view.

In brief, during the judgment of same/similar designs, whatever the concept of "design room" is introduced, the design room for an industrial design objectively exists and may be considered from different aspects. However, the legal attribute of an ordinary consumer cannot be changed by considering design room of a designer. In addition, the extendable range of the design room should be determined under recognizing design features for only playing functional and/or effective roles. For this, a party is recommended to provide sufficient evidence to prove the size of the design room.

Expedited Patent Examination in China:
Options and Practical Tips

By: Yan Wei & Xiangyun Jin

Some companies, particularly those in industries whose products have a relatively short shelf life, those trading patent rights for investment or licensing opportunities, and/or those regarding patent rights as an important defensive tool against infringers, prefer to obtain a patent as soon as possible. In China, a patent for utility model or design can be directly granted without proceeding any substantive examination within a short period of time. ❶

In this communication, we introduce how to expedite patent prosecution for a patent for invention in China.

1. General Procedure of a Patent for Invention from Filing to Granting

Firstly, time required by a Chinese patent for invention from filing to granting will be described with reference to Fig. 1.

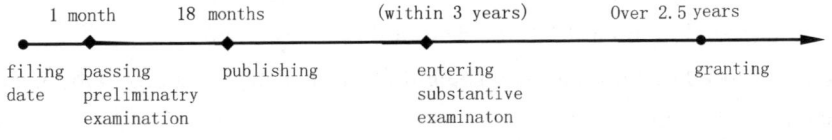

Fig. 1

It is prescribed by Article 34 and Article 35 of the *Chinese Patent Law*: "Where, after receiving an application for a patent for invention, the Patent Administration Department Under the State Council, upon preliminary examination, finds the application to be in conformity with the requirements of this Law, it shall publish the application promptly after the expiration of eighteen months from the date of filing. upon the request of the applicant, the Patent Administration Department Under the State Council publishes the application earlier. " and "upon the request of

---

❶ The *Chinese Patent Law* is the *Patent Law of the People's Republic of China* which was amended for three times and entered into force on October 1, 2009.

the applicant for a patent for invention, made at any time within three years from the date of filing, the Patent Administration Department Under the State Council will proceed to examine the application as to its substance. "

As shown in Fig. 1, the prosecution of an invention patent application has following steps: filing an application, passing preliminary examination, publishing, proceeding substantive examination, and granting. As described above, the *Patent Law* provides that the patent application for invention shall be published promptly after the expiration of eighteen months from the date of filing, and enter a procedure of substantive examination upon the applicant's request within three years from the date of filing. In practice: passing preliminary examination is made within one month from the date of filing an application; the PCT national phase entry is published in Chinese within four months from the date of passing the preliminary examination; the substantive examination is made within one month from the latest one of publishing date and the date for requesting substantive examination; a First Office Action is issued after three months from the date of entering the substantive examination. In general, an average pendency for a patent application for invention is about 2.5 years from the filing date to be granted a patent right.

Hereinafter, how to be speed up the procedures of granting a patent right will be illustrated.

As shown in Fig. 1, a patent for invention from filing an application to being granted a patent right mainly has three procedures, namely:

(1) a procedure from the filing date to the publishing date;

(2) a procedure from the publishing date to the date of entering substantive examination;

(3) a procedure of making substantive examination.

Obviously, if by advancing the starting date of the two procedures (for example, filing date, publishing date) or shortening length of the third procedure, the patent application will be probably granted a patent right as soon as possible.

The ways of advancing the filing date, the publishing date and shortening the substantive examination procedure will be respectively introduced.

2. Process of Advancing the Filing Date

Advancing the filing date is performed mainly by using priority right.

It is prescribed by Article 29 of the *Chinese Patent Law* that: "Where, within twelve months from the date on which any applicant first filed in a foreign country an application for a patent for invention or utility model, or within six months from the date on which any applicant first filed in a foreign country an application for a patent for design, he or she files in China an application for a patent for the same subject matter, he or she may, in accordance with any agreement concluded between the said foreign country and China, or in accordance with any international treaty to which both countries are party, or on the basis of the principle of mutual recognition of the right of priority, enjoy a right of priority. "

For a patent for invention filing a first application in a foreign country, as shown in Fig. 2, complying with relevant provisions of the *Paris Convention*, an actual filing date of filing an application before the Chinese Patent Office is able to be advanced to the date of filing a first application in a foreign country, by advancing at most one year.

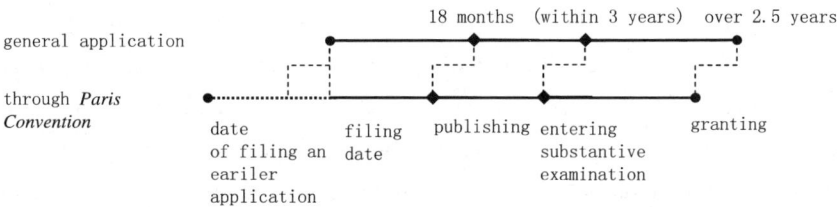

Fig. 2

For a patent for invention that is filed a first application in China, as shown in Fig. 3, actual filing date of the patent application will be also advanced according to domestic priority, by advancing at most one year.

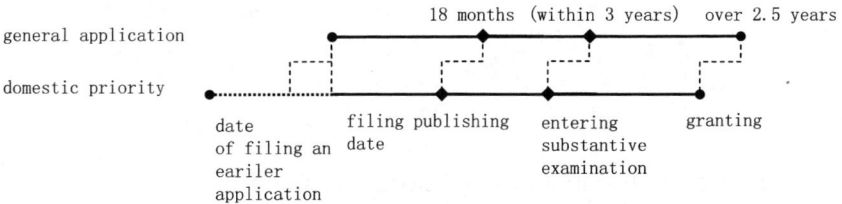

Fig. 3

Using a foreign priority or a domestic priority mentioned above, the actual filing date could be advanced to the date of filing the first application.

For an example of using the domestic priority, as shown in Fig. 4, in a phase that the invention – creation does not enter into the actual R&D process but has a complete conceive, a patent application for the invention—creation is filed firstly in a form of a utility model or an invention, and after supplementing and perfecting the filed invention-creation through specific R&D activities, the filed application for the invention-creation may serve as an previous application to claim the priority, and thereby the actual date of filing the patent application can be advanced to a large extent. Wherein, an object of claiming a previous application is to acquire the filing date and application number of the previous application but not require to pay any fee to the patent office. And also, such method is adapted to the circumstance of claiming the foreign priority.

Truly, the contents newly added into a subsequent application mentioned above but not included in the previous application cannot claim the priority of the previous application. As prescribed by the provisions, the contents newly added into the subsequent application are scarcely different from a general patent application filed by the application. Nevertheless, for those skilled in the art, it is possible to gain some value❶ to claim the domestic priority in such a manner. Generally, judging whether claim for the priority of a patent application is established or not, the examiner only examines whether the claim is satisfied with the formal condition but scarcely takes substantive difference between the previous application and the subsequent application for consideration. Therefore, in the phase of filing a new application, such claiming for the priority are probably approved so as to accelerate granting.

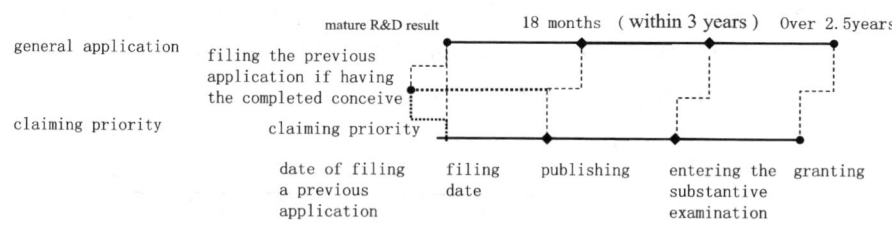

Fig. 4

3. Process of Advancing the Publishing Date

Advancing the publishing date mainly employs a principle of publishing the application earlier.

In accordance with Article 34 of the *Chinese Patent Law*, supra, Rule 46 of

---

❶ YIN XINTIAN. Introduction of the Patent Law of China [M]. Beijing: Intellectual Property Publishing House, 2011: 393.

the *Implementing Regulations*❶ provides that "Where the applicant requests an earlier publication of his or her application for a patent for invention, a statement shall be made to the patent administration department under the State Council. The patent administration department under the State Council shall, after preliminary examination of the application, publish it immediately, unless it is to be rejected. "

As shown in Fig. 5, a patent application for invention, if adopting the above earlier publication, allows the publication date to be earlier by 6−8 months than the general patent for invention.

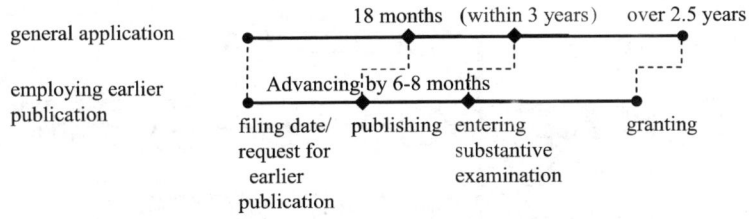

general application

employing earlier publication

Fig. 5

4. Process of Shortening the Substantive Examination

Shortening the substantive examination mainly employs a patent prosecution highway (hereinafter referred to as PPH) and a priority examination.

(1) Using the Patent Prosecution Highway

The Chinese Patent Office has a number of bilateral PPH agreements with various foreign patent offices. Under PPH, if the office of first filing (OFF) rules at least one claim or more than one claim is patentable, the applicant may request that the office of second filing (OSF) fast track the examination of corresponding claims in the corresponding applications filed in the OSF.

Fig. 6❷ shows three basic circumstances of filing a request for PPH.

---

❶ It refers to *Implementing Regulations of the Patent Law of the People' Republic of China* that was amended for three times and entered into force on February 1, 2010.

❷ EXAMINATION DEPARTMENT OF THE STATE INTELLECTUAL PROPERTY OFFICE OF THE PEOPLE'S REPUBLIC OF CHINA. User's Manual of PPH [M]. Beijing: Intellectual Property Press House, 2012: 2.

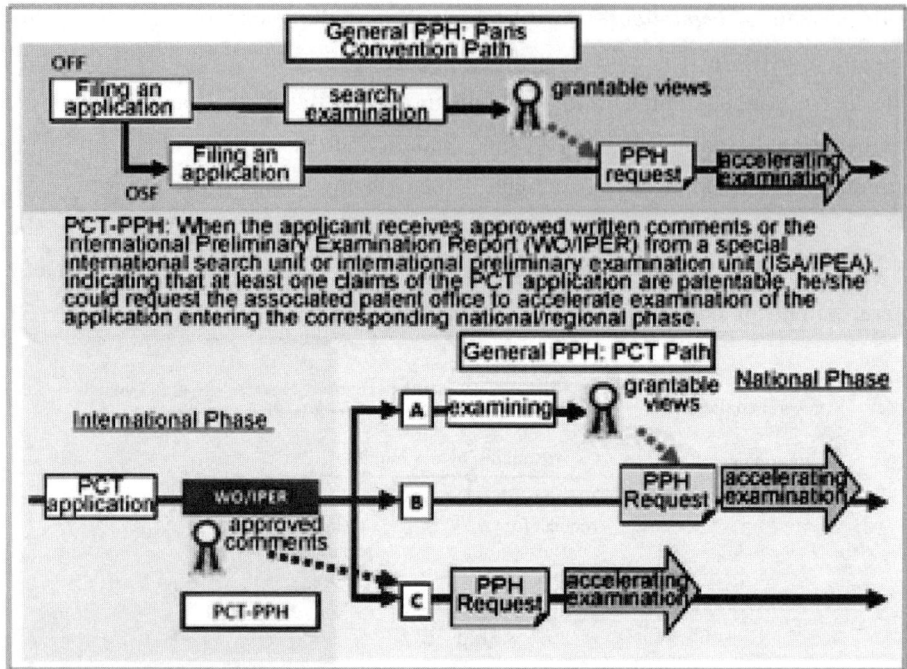

Fig. 6

Under PPH, as shown in Fig. 7, a First Office Action is issued earlier significantly, generally within 1-1.5 months (which data is obtained through practical experiences) from receipt of requesting PPH, so that the phase of the substantive examination can be shorten largely so as to accelerate the granting.

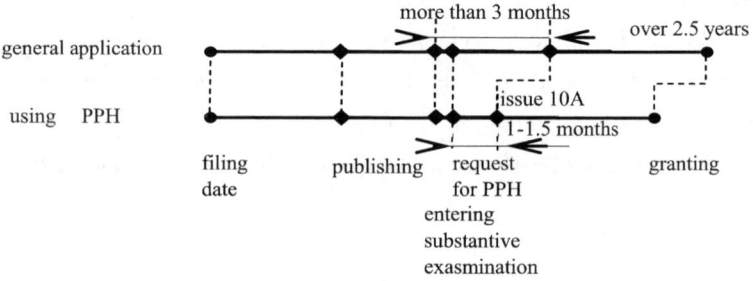

Fig. 7

(2) Using Priority Examination

By using the priority examination based on *Administrative Measures on Priority*

Examination of Invention Patent Applications❶, as shown in Fig. 8, a First Office Action is issued within 30 working days from approval of a request for the priority examination (Article 9) and the case is closed within one year (Article 2) such that the phase of the substantive examination will be shorten largely.

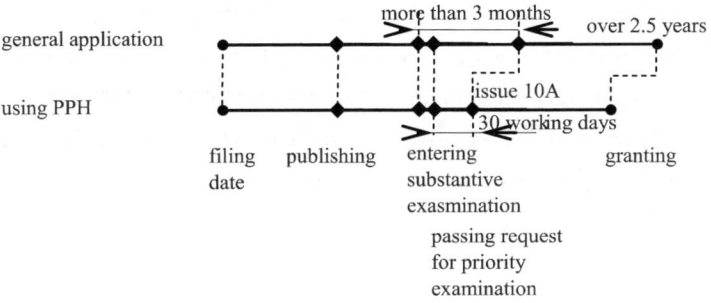

Fig. 8

Article 7 of *Administrative Measures on Priority Examination of Invention Patent Applications* provides that "Applicants applying for priority examination shall submit the following materials: 1) a *Request Form for Priority Examination of Invention Patent Application* examined by the State Intellectual Property Office of the province, autonomous region or centrally–administered municipality which bears a signed–off opinion and is affixed with the official seal; 2) a search report which satisfies the stipulated format issued by an organization which satisfies patent search criteria, or a search report issued by the patent examination authorities of another country or region and the examination findings and the Chinese translation thereof."

It can be seen that the relevant provisions of the priority examination has some details to be perfected, for example, if a foreign applicant intends to use the priority examination, it is not prescribed clearly which office seal is affixed onto the Request Form for Priority Examination of Invention Patent Applications. For this reason, at present most of foreign applicants employ the PPH rather than the priority examination.

(3) Other matters

Besides of the processes mentioned above, some well–known processes can be adopted to shorten the substantive examination phase of the patent application, for

---

❶ Promulgated by *Decree No. 65 of the State Council of the People's Republic of China*, and effective as of August 1, 2012.

example:

Removing the claims that have effects indicated by the Office Action and are not anxious for granting a patent right to file a divisional application to as to accelerate granting of the rest claims;

Flexibly making shrinkage limit modification without serious problem to shorten the substantive examination accordingly so as to accelerate granting.

In conclusion, in order to acquire a patent right of the patent for invention as soon as possible, various mechanics may be used to advance the filing date and the publishing date or shorten the substantive examination. Of course, a best effect will be achieved by combining the various processes properly.

Issues and Tips Relating to Software-Related Inventions to Be Patented in China *

By: Yuyue Zhang

Most countries place some limits on the patenting of invention involving software, but there is no legal definition of a software patent. This short article focuses on the patent eligibility of software-related inventions and certain limitations on patenting these inventions in China.

1. Patent Eligibility

The first issue is whether a software-patent should be allowed, and if so, where the boundary should lie. Like in the U. S. where an abstract idea is non-statutory subject matter, *Chinese Patent Law*, in Article 25. 2, explicitly excludes scientific discoveries and rules/methods for mental activities from patent eligibility.

For example, a claim directed to a pure business method, i. e. a claim not reciting applications of any machine such as a computer, intelligent terminal or network, both the American and Chinese patent practices have clear negative attitudes that it is not patentable. For example:

Case 1 [Bilski vs. Kappos (2010)]

"1. A method for managing the consumption risk costs of a commodity sold by a commodity provider at a fixed price comprising the steps of:

(a) Initiating a series of transactions between said commodity provider and consumers of said commodity wherein said consumers purchase said commodity at a fixed rate based upon historical averages, said fixed rate corresponding to a risk position of said consumer;

(b) Identifying market participants for said commodity having a counter-risk position to said consumers; and

(c) Initiating a series of transactions between said commodity provider and said market participants at a second fixed rate such that said series of market participant

* First published on Outstanding Essays of *Patent Applications With High Quality* 2013, ACPAA.

transactions balances the risk position of said series of consumer transactions. "

While Case 1 is deemed too abstract, the U. S. Supreme Court's Bilski case established that a tie to a machine is a clue to patent eligibility.

For example, if the title of subject matter of Case 1 be amended as "[a] method for managing the consumption risk costs of a commodity sold by a commodity provider at a fixed price with the aid of a computer terminal", it is named as Case 2 for short.

Despite a legal assumption that software running on a computer, maybe as Case 2, is patentable subject matter in the U. S., a U. S. appeals court recently has ruled that an abstract idea is not patentable simply because it is tied to a computer system. See CLS Bank v. Alice (decided on May 10, 2013). Specifically, one camp of five judges led by Judge Lourie supported invalidating the patents based on the view that the computer limitation as merely "insignificant post-solution activity relative to the abstract idea..."

While in China, Case 2 may not be considered as belonging to circumstances not eligible for patent protection under Article 25. 2 of *Chinese Patent Law*, but needs to be judged whether it belongs to patentable subject matter required by Article 2. 2 of *Chinese Patent Law* for applications for invention patents with a "3-factor-test" (i. e. solving technical problem, using technical means as well as achieving technical effect) provided by Chapter 9 in the "Guidelines for Patent Examination" (the "GPE").

If the title of subject matter of Case 2 be further amended as "[a] method for managing the consumption risk costs of a commodity sold by a commodity provider at a fixed price with the aid of a computer terminal, the computer is programmed to perform the steps of the method", it is named as Case 3 for short.

In the U. S., in many judges' view, viewing the software and hardware together (as Case 3) as a new machine was sufficient to overcome the objection that the patent was too abstract. However, in the CLS Bank case, half of the en banc Federal Circuit judges took a sensible view that running a program on a computer does not transform the computer or render software less abstract.

But in China, Case 3, similar to Case 2, although may pass the barrier set by Article 25. 2, will be determined as patentable subject matter required by Article 2. 2 only after passing the above "3-factor-test".

It is significant to note that all the three factors in "3-factor-test" must be satisfied. The "3 - factor - test" concentrates on testing whether, for a claimed invention, an innovation in term of technology exists, regardless an innovation in term of business mode. Technology innovation means, for instance, application of some software that enlarges storage space, improves die forming process of rubber by preventing over-vulcanization and under-vulcanization of rubber or improves quality of an image (Chapter 9, the "GPE").

In other words, it is not correct to say all inventions related to business mode innovations cannot be granted in China. Specifically, besides a new business mode, if a claimed invention also comprises some technological innovation, it is a patentable subject matter in China.

2. Limitations on Patentability

Another issue to be addressed here is the prosecution of a software-related invention application in China. One important difference about patent prosecution between the U. S. and China is related to a product claim directed to a product such as a computer, intelligent terminal or the like only involving into improvement of software. In brief, the difference is in "intangible" product in China and "tangible" product in the U. S.

The "GPE", Chapter 9 provides a way of drafting a product claim defined by a group of software functional modules on the basis of a computer program flow described in the specification or on the basis of a method claim reflecting the computer program flow. Such a claim may be called "intangible-style" product claim by the author of this article, and the claimed product is an abstract, virtual device realized mainly through the computer program described in the specification, rather than an entity device realized mainly through hardware. When a Chinese examiner examines whether such "intangible-style" product claim is supportive by the specification and whether it is clear under Article 26. 4 of *Chinese Patent Law*, he or she will consider, directly based on the above provision of Chapter 9, the "GPE", the protection scope of such claim just covers a solution realized by software, and thus is supported by the specification and clear. The author of this article calls this examination manner "special manner" dedicated to an "intangible-style" product claim.

In contrast, the USPTO emphasizes tangibility of a claimed product, and carefully examines whether there exists functional and structural relationship between the claimed product and software, algorithm and etc. Such a claim claiming a tangible product is called "tangible-style" product claim by the author of this article.

However, in China, such a "tangible-style" product claim often faces some examination opinion that is not easily understood by the applicant.

Case 4 [claim 19 of U. S. Patent No. 7,469,381 in the case Apple v Samsung]

"A device, comprising:

a touch screen display;

one or more processors;

memory; and

one or more programs, wherein the one or more programs are stored in the memory and configured to be executed by the one or more processors, the programs including:

instructions for displaying a first portion of an electronic document;

instructions for detecting a movement of an object on or near the touch screen display;

instructions for translating the electronic document displayed on the touch screen display in a first direction to display a second portion of the electronic document, wherein the second portion is different from the first portion, in response to detecting the movement;..."

Case 5 [amended from Case 4]

"A device, comprising:

a touch screen display;

one or more processors;

memory; and

one or more programs, wherein the one or more programs are stored in the memory and configured to be read by the one or more processors in order to execute:

step of displaying a first portion of an electronic document;

step of detecting a movement of an object on or near the touch screen display;

step of translating the electronic document displayed on the touch screen display in a first direction to display a second portion of the electronic document, wherein the second portion is different from the first portion, in response to detecting the movement;..."

Case 6 [amended from Case 5]

"A device, comprising:

a touch screen display;

one or more processors;

memory, wherein the one or more programs are stored in the memory;

wherein the one or more processors comprising:

means for displaying a first portion of an electronic document;

means for detecting a movement of an object on or near the touch screen display;

means for translating the electronic document displayed on the touch screen display in a first direction to display a second portion of the electronic document, wherein the second portion is different from the first portion, in response to detecting the movement;..."

Because the claimed product in any of Cases 4-6 is not drafting the way completely corresponding to the flow of the computer program required by Chapter 9, the "GPE", the claimed product will be deemed as an entity device, not an abstract and virtual product. In face of such a claim to assess whether the protection scope of the claim is supported by the specification and whether the claim is clear, the examiner will not follow the above "special manner" under Chapter 9, the "GPE", instead, he or she will follow the general manner provided in Chapter 2, the "GPE".

In detail, Cases 4-5 may be rejected for lack of clarity under Article 26. 4 of Chinese Patent Law with a rationale by the Chinese examiner that limitations such as program, instruction, etc. don't belong to structural or method features used for defining the structure of a processor.

Case 6 may be rejected for not being supported by the specification under Article 26. 4 of *Chinese Patent Law*, due to its functional definitions such as "means for displaying a first portion of an electronic document" . The rationale is the function means considered as covering all modes realizing the function such as "displaying displaying a first portion of an electronic document" , while the specification only discloses specific mode (s) using a computer program to realize the function, therefore one with ordinary skill in the art cannot reasonably predict using other equivalent mode (s) such as hardware mode not described in the specification to realize the function.

As a result, in China a product claim, directed to a product such as computer, intelligent terminal or the like only involving improvement of software, needs be drafted as a product claim only consisting of a group of virtual software functional modules completely corresponding to steps of the computer program flow disclosed in the specification or corresponding to steps of a method claim reflecting the computer program flow. Such a product claim can avoid or overcome the above examination opinion. Herein Case 4 is taken for example to illustrate one way of amending.

Case 7 [amended from Case 4]

"A device used in an intelligent communication terminal, the terminal comprising: a touch screen display; one or more processors; memory, wherein the one or more programs are stored in the memory;

wherein the device comprises:

means for displaying a first portion of an electronic document;

means for detecting a movement of an object on or near the touch screen display;

means for translating the electronic document displayed on the touch screen display in a first direction to display a second portion of the electronic document, wherein the second portion is different from the first portion, in response to detecting the movement;…"

Trademark Coexistence: Issues and Practice in China[*]

By: Xiaomin Liang

Trademark coexistence, the coexistence of identical/similar trademarks held by different entities, has been recognized in Chinese trademark practice. While the likelihood of confusion test has not been codified in the law, the issues regarding the legitimacy to preserve coexistence, the standard to determine infringement, and the consequence to present coexistence agreement have arisen. This article, with recent case studies and practical considerations, will discuss these issues.

1. The concept and characteristics of trademark coexistence

In practice, trademark coexistence has been recognized as a condition that identical/similar trademark is legally used on identical/similar goods/services by different entities without causing consumer's confusion. While the coexistence may be found between registered marks, unregistered marks, registered and unregistered marks, in addition to good faith, the following characters shall exist:

a. The trademarks of coexistence are identical or similar.

In the process of trademark registration, the same or similarity will be determined in the aspects of phonetics, constitution, connotation and etc, according to *The Guidelines for Trademark Examination* issued by the Chinese Trademark Office (CTO) and the Trademark Review and Adjudication Board (TRAB). In courts, the strength of the mark at issue and the general understanding of the public will also be considered. In the event of trademark coexistence, these factors should all be included in the criteria of judging trademark similarity for comprehensive consideration.

b. The trademark is designated/used on same or similar goods/services.

Considering similar goods/services, in addition to *The Classification System of Similar Goods/Services* adopted in China, it should be related to the real life and comprehensively consider the function of goods/services, sales channels, relevant

---

* First published on *Chinese Trademark*, July 2013.

consumers and other pertinent factors.

c. Trademarks are held by different owners.

In the event of trademark coexistence, the coexisted trademarks should be held by different owners.

d. The coexistence of trademarks will not cause confusion.

Trademarks used to identify the source of goods/services and avoid confusion are the basis of trademark protection.❶ Accordingly, avoiding consumer confusion is also a premise of trademark coexistence.

2. Likelihood of confusion should be the core factor in defining whether trademarks could legally coexist

Likelihood of confusion refers to the possibility that the consumers will be confused or mistaker regarding... the sources of or relationships between two goods/services, when two similar or identical trademarks exist in the market. The core factor of judging whether similar trademarks coexisting are legal or constitute trademark infringement is the likelihood of confusion.

In practice, it is easy to mix similarity with confusion and think similarity will lead to confusion, which is indeed an absolute viewpoint. The so-called similarity refers to two marks that are similar in the font, pronunciation and meaning of words, the composition and color of devices or the overall structures of word and device combination, which is an objective description of the characteristics of a trademark; the so-called confusion is generated by the general public to the source of the goods/services, which is an objective consequence caused by the consumers. Therefore, similarity is not equivalent to confusion, and similarity does not mean infringement, either. Only in the condition that the trademarks are both similar and easily lead to consumer confusion does the infringement occur. Otherwise, if it is only similar but there is no likelihood of confusion, the legitimacy of similar marks on same or similar goods/services should be recognized.

In fact, the likelihood of confusion doctrine is regulated as a standard in many international conventions and trademark laws of other countries. For example, the Article 16 of *TRIPS Agreement* specifies: The owner of a registered trademark shall have the exclusive right to prevent all third parties not having the owner's consent from using in the course of trade identical or similar signs for goods/services which

---

❶ MU HANDONG. Basic Researches on Intellectual Property Rights [M]. 2nd ed. Beijing: China Renmin University Press, 2009.

are identical or similar to those in respect of which the trademark is registered where such use would result in a likelihood of confusion. In case of the use of an identical sign for identical goods/services, a likelihood of confusion shall be presumed. *The American Lanham Act* also clearly regulates that causing confusion to the public is a main factor to constitute trademark infringement. In the introduction of CTMR, it stresses that "The likelihood of confusion is a special condition to trademark protection".

Learning from the successful experience of foreign countries, I believe the Chinese Trademark Administrative Organs and Judicial Offices should pay attention to the following points in the process of judging the likelihood of confusion:

a. In judging similarity of marks, comparisons should focus on overall expression in addition to the aspects of the sound, font and meaning of word part, the composition of device part, as well as other aspects. Additionally, the comparison should be carried out in an isolated manner;

b. In determining the likelihood of confusion, multiple factors such as the mark's distinctiveness, reputation, prior usage, the degree of consumers' recognition, the subjective intent of the defendant, should be considered;

c. It should proceed from the general attention of the related public. The so-called "relevant public" should include all people that should be affected in the use of trademark, including but not limited to buyers, potential buyers and so on; and

d. It should be decided case by case. As underlined facts of each case are different, it should analyze specific issues, and not simply apply mechanically the previous similar cases or the opinions formed in similar cases.

As one of the *2010 China Top Ten Cases of Intellectual Protection* issued by IPR Courts, the trademark dispute between "Singapore Crocodile" and "French Crocodile" is a typical case where the Supreme Court has flexibly and comprehensively judged the likelihood of confusion in trial by combing various factors: ❶

In the judgment of that case, the Supreme Court approved the legal coexistence of the two "crocodile", and it also created a new principle. Namely, judging the trademark similarity in the case of trademark infringement, it should not only generally consider the degree of similarity in the trademark composition, but also, according to specific circumstances, comprehensively consider other factors such as the subjective intent of the alleged infringer, the usage history and current status of both

---

❶ Reference to the Judgment " (2009) Min San Zhong Zi No. 3" by the Supreme People's Court.

the registered mark and the disputed trademark. It should judge whether the disputed mark would cause confusion or not based on all the above mentioned factors. Undoubtedly, this is a clear standard in judging confusion in the case of trademark infringement, which is significant to Chinese trademark judicial practices.

3. The application and perfection for the theory of confusion in the practice of trademark coexistence in China

It is provided both administrative and judicial protections to the exclusive rights of registered trademark in China. Regardless of the TRAB or the courts, the current *Chinese Trademark Law* is the primary basis in hearing trademark disputes/infringement cases. Meanwhile, for judging a large number of cases in practice whether they are trademark coexistence or infringement, it is somewhat limited if only the *Chinese Trademark Law* is applied. Therefore, the TRAB or the courts has also issued some specific examination rules or judicial interpretation for reference or guidance when judging such cases.

In the 24th commission meeting of the TRAB in 2007, the TRAB Conducted... a study on the "coexistence agreement" filed by the applicant in the refusal review. The TRAB considers the trademark disputes as disputes of private rights, so that a coexistence agreement between two parties should be considered. However, it should also consider the following two factors in judging whether the coexistence would cause confusion to the consumers: 1) the similarity of goods, the similarity of the marks, and the reputation of two parties; 2) the reputation of two parties' marks.

In one case, company A applied for registration the mark "LOWEPRO & device" (referred as the below mark 1). The CTO rejected the mark 1 on the ground that it was similar to the prior registered mark (referred as the below mark 2) owned by Company B on related goods. During the review process, two companies submitted a notarized and legalized coexistence agreement. The TRAB reversed the CTO's decision not to register the mark 1 in considering the agreement and the difference between those two marks.❶

---

❶ Reference to the decision on the refusal review "Shang Ping Zi 2010 No. 36429" by the TRAB.

Mark 1

Mark 2

From the above case, we note the TRAB begins to conditionally accept the coexistence agreement signed by two parties in refusal review. However, whether the two marks and the goods covered by the two marks are similar is still the primary factor considered by the TRAB in judging whether it would cause confusion and whether they could coexist. As to the reputation of marks, the applicant of this case did not mention. Thus, the TRAB judges whether it would cause confusion mainly from the aspect of the similarity degree of two marks. From this case, we could conclude the similarity degree of marks is a decisive factor in judging the likelihood of confusion by the TRAB in the process of trademark registration. As to the mark's actual usage in the market and the recognition degree of the related customers, they are not essential conditions in judging the likelihood of confusion.

The courts have also introduced the theory of confusion in trying cases related to confirming trademark rights or trademark infringement. The Paragraph 1 of Article 11 of *Interpretation of the Supreme Court on the Law Applicable to a Number of Cases of Trademark Civil Dispute* regulates: The phrase "similar goods" under item (1) of Article 52 of the *Chinese Trademark Law* means goods that have identical functions, uses, production entities, sales channels, target consumers, etc., or goods that the relevant public would normally consider to have a certain connection and thus easily cause confusion. The Paragraph 2 of Article 9 of that interpretation regulates: The phrase "similar trademarks" under item (1) of Article 52 of the *Chinese Trademark Law* means where the suspected infringing trademark is compared with the plaintiff's registered trademark and the font, pronunciation or meaning of the words or the composition or coloring of the device are similar, or the overall structure of its combined main elements is similar, or where its three-dimensional shape and combination of colors are similar thereby easily leading the relevant public to mistake the source of the products or to believe that their source has a certain connection to products using the plaintiff's registered trademark. That is to say, "similar goods/services" and "similar trademarks" are also defined by the standard of whether or not it would cause confusion to the relevant public. This standard gets a specific development in the *Interpretation of the Beijing High Court on the Law Applicable to Cases of Trademark Civil Dispute*: Being sufficient to cause confusion and mistake to the relevant public is an essential condition for constituting trademark similarity. If word parts or device parts of trademarks are only similar, but not enough to cause confusion and mistake to the relevant public, it does not constitute trademark similarity. It should accord with whether it would cause confusion and mistake to the relevant public while judging trademark similarity.

In another case, German BASF SE (hereinafter referred to as BASF) applied the mark "狮马牌" (the cited mark, the below Mark 3) for registration in China in 1987. Hubei Xiang Yun (Group) Chemical Co., Ltd. (hereinafter referred to as the Xiang Yun) created the mark "红狮犸 & device" (the disputed mark, the below Mark 4) in 1999 and registered it in 2005. In March 2010, the mark "红狮犸 & device" was recognized as a "Famous Mark of Hubei Province".

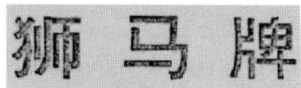

Mark 3   Mark 4

The BASF filed a dispute application with the TRAB by claiming the Xiang Yun's mark "红狮犸 & device" was a deliberate imitation of "狮马牌" which the BASF prior applied for registration and owned exclusive trademark rights, and it would cause confusion to the public. Then, the TRAB ruled to cancel the Xiang Yun's mark "红狮犸 & device" on the goods "fertilizer, compound fertilizer, phosphate fertilizer (manure) and chemical fertilizers" for the reason the word part of the two marks constituted similarity on similar goods. The Xiang Yun was not satisfied with the TRAB's decision and then instituted the administrative lawsuit to the Beijing First Intermediate People's Court (hereinafter referred to as "the Court"). After hearing the case, the Court considers for those disputed marks which has been used for a long time, has established a high reputation in the market and has also drawn some relevant public groups, it should accurately hold the legislative spirit of *Chinese Trademark Law*, which is aimed to protect prior trademark rights and coordinated with maintaining the market in order, and to fully respect the fact some relevant public has already objectively distinguishes relevant trademarks in market and to defend the stable market order. Though the "狮犸" and "狮马" are identical in pronunciation and similar in font, the disputed mark "红狮犸 & device" has a significantly distinctive device part and it is strongly differentiated from the cited mark in overall visual appearance. When judging whether it could identify the source of goods, the TRAB does not comment on those evidences concerning the usage and publicity of the disputed mark, such as brochures, sales invoices, etc, provided by the Xiang Yun, which belongs to leaking-trial. Accordingly, the Court rules to quash the TRAB's decision and requires the TRAB to make a new decision on the disputed mark "红狮犸 & device" with the Reg. No. 3783811❶.

The above case reflects the criterion of confusion the Court adopts in judging the trademark similarity, and also reflects the different scales held in judging the trademark confusion by the administrative organs and judicial offices. When judging whether it could cause confusion or not in the processes of trademark registration, the administrative organs often simply apply to *The Guide of Trademark Examination*. And when judging whether trademarks are similar, the administrative organs largely remains to compare two marks mechanically in pronunciation, font and meaning, which is also used as an important basis for judging whether it could cause confusion.

While for the court, it focuses more on the nature of trademark and adheres to the principle of examining case-by-case. In addition to the comparison of main composition elements of trademarks, the court also considers the specific circumstances of the disputed mark's usage in the market. As long as the similarity of two marks is insufficient to cause confusion to the public, the two marks could be allowed to coexist.

As a matter of fact, it is an extremely complex process to judge whether marks are similar and could cause confusion. Although the confusion theory has already been progressively introduced into the Chinese trademark examination and judicial practices, the current Chinese Trademark Law does not explicitly take the "likelihood of confusion" as a standard to judge the trademark infringement, so the "confusion" as a core standard in judging trademark infringement has not been clearly regulated in legislation yet. Trademark coexistence, as an objective common phenomenon, should be paid high attention to in legislation. In the time of the third revision of *Chinese Trademark Law*, the Chinese legislature should clearly mark the central position of the concept of trademark confusion in judging trademark infringement, and take the likelihood of confusion as the standard for judging trademark infringement, so as to create a reasonable condition for the

---

❶ Reference to the Judgment " (2010) Yi Zhong Zhi Xing Chu Zi No. 2047" by the Beijing First Intermediate People's Court.

trademark legal coexistence. Additionally, the two parties generally reach coexistence through signing the coexistence agreement in practice, so it could make stipulations on trademark coexistence through the trademark law or relevant judicial interpretation, which would in law accept the coexistence agreement which is reached by two parties, as long as it does not violate mandatory provisions of laws and without prejudice to the public interest.

Amendment to Claims in Invalidation Proceedings

By: Zixuan Kan

In recent years, the number of invalidation proceedings has increased significantly, due to greatly increased patent applications filed in the Patent Office together with the increased awareness of patent rights. The Chinese Patent Reexamination Board (PRB)❶ has sole jurisdiction over patent validity issues, regardless of whether there is a parallel patent infringement proceeding. The PRB is required to adhere to the laws and to base its decision upon the facts in the records. The principles adopted by the PRB in invalidation proceedings are governed by the *Chinese Guidelines for Patent Examination 2010* (*Guidelines*), which provide the main ways for amending patent claims during an invalidation proceeding, and moreover, some criterions have also observed in our practice. This newsletter will elaborate these criterions in combination with the specific examples.

Under Article 45 of the *Patent Law*, starting from the date of the announcement of the grant of the patent right by the Patent Office, any entity or individual, who considers that the grant of the patent right is not in conformity with the relevant provisions of the *Patent Law*, may request the PRB to declare the patent right or certain claims invalid.

In accordance with the *Guidelines*, any amendment to a patent for invention or utility model shall be limited to the claims only in an invalidation proceeding, and principles and manners of the amendments of the patent also be regulated in the *Guidelines*.

According to the *Guidelines*, any amendments to the patent documents in the invalidation procedure shall follow the following principles:

(1) The subject matter of the original claims cannot be changed;

(2) Broadening amendments are not permitted;

(3) The amendment shall not go beyond the scope of disclosure contained in the initial description and claims; and

---

❶ The PRB is independent from the Patent Office.

（4）Addition of disclosed but unclaimed technical features is generally not allowed.

Further, the *Guidelines* specify three permissible amendments to claims:

（1）Deleting one or more claims;

（2）Deleting one or more technical solutions; and

（3）Combining one or more claims.

Furthermore, the patentee, i. e., the respondent, has an opportunity to amend the claims in the following sifuations:

（1）When responding to the request for invalidation;

（2）When responding to supplemental submissions of the request for invalidation; and

（3）When responding to the grounds for invalidation or evidence not mentioned by the petitioner but introduced by the PRB.

EXAMPLE Ⅰ

Now, the three permissible amendments to claims in an invalidation proceeding will be illustrated by reference to a specific example.

Assuming the claims in a granted patent are:

1. An A, characterized in B.

2. The A according to claim 1, characterized in C.

3. The A according to claim 1 or 2, characterized in D.

4. The A according to claim 1, characterized in E.

5. The A according to claim 4, characterized in F or G.

（i）Amending the claims in the granted patent by way of deleting claim（s）

Deletion of claim means one（or more）claim, including independent claim or dependent claim, is removed from the claims.

For example（1）, in case that the dependent claim 5 is to be removed from the claims, the amended claims are as follows:

1. An A, characterized in B.

2. The A according to claim 1, characterized in C.

3. The A according to claim 1 or 2, characterized in D.

4. The A according to claim 1, characterized in E.

As a general disposal during invalidation, one may delete the dependent claim （s）which is deemed not being clearly defined.

For example（2）, in case that the independent claim 1 is to be removed from the claims, the amended claims are as follows:

1. An A, characterized in B+C.
2. The A according to claim 1, characterized in D.
3. The A according to claim 1, characterized in E.
4. The A according to claim 3, characterized in F or G.

Generally, in case that an independent claim is rejected for lack of essential technical feature (s), lack of novelty/inventiveness, or not being supported by the description, one may delete this independent claim.

(ii) Amending the claims in the granted patent by way of deleting technical solution (s)

Deletion of technical solution means to remove from the same claim one or more parallel technical solutions which is/are pointed out invalid in the procedure. In the patented claims above, for instance, the dependent claim 5 comprises two parallel technical solutions, only which may be amended by way of deleting technical solution.

For example 3, in case that the technical solution comprising the feature F is to be removed from the dependent claim 5, the amended claims are as follows:

1. An A, characterized in B.
2. The A according to claim 1, characterized in C.
3. The A according to claim 1 or 2, characterized in D.
4. The A according to claim 1, characterized in E.
5. The A according to claim 4, characterized in G.

Generally, in case that one or more of technical solutions of one claim is/are deemed not being clearly defined or not having inventiveness, the technical solution or solutions may be deleted from this claim.

(iii) Amending the claims in the granted patent by way of combining claims

Combination of claims means to combine two or more dependent claims which are dependent on the same independent claim and not dependent on each other. Under this circumstance, all the technical features of the combined dependent claims form a new claim. The new claim shall contain all the technical features of each of the dependent claims thus combined. Under the *Guidelines*, such combination shall not be allowable in case that the independent claim they depend on is not amended. In other words, the amendment in combination manner can only be used to the dependent claims, and can only be adopted in condition that the commonly independent claim is amended.

For example 4, in case that the independent claim 1 is to be deleted (independent claim be amended), the dependent claims may be amended according to the following formats:

(1) The original dependent claim 2 can be rebuilt into a new independent claim.

(2) The original dependent claim 3, which is dependent on the claim 1 can be reconstructed into a new independent claim.

(3) The original dependent claim 4 can be rebuilt into a new independent claim.

(4) The original dependent claims 2 and 3 which are dependent on the original independent claim 1 may be combined into a new independent.

(5) The original dependent claims 2 and 4, which are dependent on the original independent claim 1, may be combined into a new independent.

(6) The original dependent claims 3 and 4 which are dependent on the original independent claim 1 may be combined into a new independent.

(7) The original dependent claims 2, 3 and 4 which are dependent on the original independent claim 1 may be combined into a new independent.

(8) The original dependent claim 5, which is dependent on the original dependent claim 4 can be reconstructed into a new dependent claim.

(9) The original dependent claim 3, which is dependent on the claim 2 can be reconstructed into a new dependent claim. However, the new dependent claim is deleted since the protection scope of the new dependent claim is the same as that of the amended independent claim combined the original claim 2 and 3.

Amended claims are as follows:

1. An A, characterized in B+C.

2. The A, characterized in B+D.

3. The A, characterized in B+E.

4. The A, characterized in B+C+D.

5. The A, characterized in B+C+E.

6. The A, characterized in B+D+E.

7. The A, characterized in B+C+D+E.

8. The A according to any one of the claim 3, 5, 6 and 7, characterized in F or G.

The three manners for amending claims exemplified above are provided in the Guidelines. However, we will face more complicated situations in the practice, for example, in case that the independent claim and one of its dependent claim are deleted, whether those dependent claims, which are dependent on the deleted dependent claim, may be amended in the combination manner? The answer will be made with reference to an invalidation proceeding which was handled at our firm.

EXAMPLE II

For the convenience of reading and comprehension, the claims are simply exemplified as follows:

Claims as in the granted patent:

1. An A, characterized in B.
2. The A according to claim 1, characterized in C.
3. The A according to claim 1 or 2, characterized in D.
4. The A according to claim 2, characterized in E.
5. The A according to claim 4, characterized in F or G.

Amended claims are as following:

1. An A, characterized in B+C+D.
2. The A, characterized in B+C+E.
3. The A, characterized in B+C+D+E.
4. The A according to claim 2 or 3, characterized in F or G.

In above amendment, the original independent claim 1 and its dependent claim 2 are deleted. The original dependent claims 3 and 4, which are directly dependent on the original dependent claim 2, are combined together to rebuild a new independent (reference to amended independent 3). Such manner for amending claims during invalidation procedure is not described in the *Guidelines*. In the invalidation case, however, the PRB allowed such amendment to the claims. According to our understanding, the existing stipulations about the amendment to the claims tend to forbid those technical solutions which are not described directly or indirectly in the granted claims.

As seen, the permissible amendment to claims of granted patent, indeed, is very limited, the Supreme People's Court of PR China, however, showed the willingness to relax the limitation. In PRB v. Jiangsu Xianshen Pharm Co Ltd et al. (Case No. Zhixingzi 17/2011), the Court held that a patentee may amend a claim in a manner other than that provided in the *Guidelines*, rejecting the PRB's rigid application of law. Nevertheless, China is not a case law country, and the PRB still applies the *Guidelines* with respect to the amendment to claims of granted patents.

We believe more will see, in light of the holding, the PRB may do comprehensive examination to determine whether claims amended in invalidation proceedings meet all the statutory requirements for granting a patent.

Assessing Inventiveness in China: Whether the Specification Passes a Threshold of Disclosing Enough [*]

By: Xiaoying Wu, Qinghong Xu

Inventiveness, inventive step, and non-obviousness refer to the same patentability requirement present in most patent law, according to which a patentable invention must be inventive or non-obvious. The underlying principle for this requirement is to avoid granting patents for inventions that are not sufficiently distant beyond the state of the art, in order to ultimately achieve a proper balance between providing an incentive to promote innovations and limiting monopoly rights costs to society. Although the principle is roughly the same, the assessment for this requirement varies from jurisdiction to jurisdiction. Many applicants seeking patent protection of life sciences inventions in China have found that the threshold for sufficient disclosure (e. g. , the requirement of experimental data) is high. But few may become aware that the standard is also high when Chinese patent practice imposes disclosure requirements in assessing inventiveness. This article will focus on the later by introducing a selection of cases from the Patent Reexamination Board and people's courts in order to provide patent practitioners with some guidance.

1. Laying the Foundation: Legal Justification of China

One of conditions for granting a patent right is an invention shall possess inventiveness. It is stipulated in Article 22, third paragraph (Art. 22. 3) of *Chinese Patent Law*, inventiveness means that, compared with the prior art, the invention possesses prominent substantive features and indicates remarkable advancements, and the utility model possesses substantive features and indicates advancements.

Like in the European Patent Office, a three-step problem-and-solution approach for assessing inventiveness has been used in China, where a technical problem may be reformulated as the most pertinent item of prior art comes to light af-

---

[*] First published at China IP Focus 2013, Managing Intellectual Property, United Kingdom, 2013.

ter search which is often "closer" to the invention than the prior art originally taken into account when the claimed subject – matter was drafted by the applicant. The *Guideline for Examination* (the *Guideline*) specifies the legitimacy of the reformulation as part of the problem–and–solution approach and further states that any technical effects may be used as a basis for reformulating a technical problem as long as such a technical effect could be recognized by one skilled in the art from the technical contents described in the description. See, Part II, Chapter 2, § 3. 2. 1. 1.

2. Setting the Scene: Opinions from the Board and People's Courts

To argue that the claimed solution to the reformulated problem is inventive in view of the closest prior art, one would point to certain technical effects achieved by the claimed solution, which, sometimes, cannot be considered by Chinese Patent Office, the Reexamination Board (the Board) or people's courts due to lack of sufficient disclosure of the pointed technical effects. The cases below illustrate such sufficiency requirement in Chinese patent practice.

In Boehringer v. the Board, a granted patent (patent No. 01817143. 5), entitled "Crystalline monohydrate, processes for the preparation thereof and the use thereof for preparing a pharmaceutical composition" and owned by Boehringer Ingelheim Heim Pharma Gmbh & Co. KG (Boehringer), was challenged for validity in an invalidation proceeding before the Board in 2008. Claim 1 in dispute was directed to crystalline tiotropium bromide monohydrate with specified parameters. To traverse the ground for lacking inventiveness required by Art. 22. 3, Boehringer argued that the claimed crystalline has an unexpected technical effect in meeting the stringent requirements imposed on pharmaceutically active substances as provided in the description, together with a submission of experimental data during the invalidation proceeding.

The Board denied claim 1's validity on the ground of non–inventiveness reasoning that: the argued technical effect is only disclosed but not verified in the description, and therefore cannot be relied upon for assessing inventiveness. Moreover, the Board refused to take the submitted experimental data into consideration as they were provided after the filing date.

Boehringer appealed to Beijing First Intermediate People's Court, who upheld the Board's decision. On appeal to Beijing High People's Court ((2010) No. 751), the invalidity was further affirmed where the court expressed the position that there is not enough evidence in the description to make it plausible that unexpected technical effects have been achieved by the claimed crystalline, as, based on Boehringer's admission, the purity and stability (among the unexpected effects Boehringer emphasized in the arguments) were not expected to one skilled in the art.

In Weale v. the Board, a granted patent (patent No. 97108942. 6), entitled "A composite of antibiotics for inhibiting β-lactamase" and owned by Weale Man Pharmaceutical Limited (Weale), was challenged for validity before the Board in 2002. The patent has one claim (claim 1) reading as, "A composite of antibiotics for inhibiting β-lactamase, consisting of Sulbactam and Piperacillin or Cefotaxime, mixed at a ratio of 0. 5-2 : 0. 5-2," which, according to the description, aims to produce enhanced antibacterial activity and enlarge antibacterial spectrum. Evidence 1, submitted by the petitioner, has disclosed that Sulbactam in combination with Piperacillin (0. 5 : 2) or Cefotaxime (1 : 2) can achieve better antibacterial effect and resistance in β-lactamase, as well as can broaden antibacterial spectrum. The Board declared the patent invalid for lack of inventiveness over Evidence 1 because one skilled in the art would readily arrive at the invention based on the above teaching.

Weale appealed to Beijing First Intermediate People's Court, and the court ((2006) No. 786) maintained the Board's decision. On appeal, Beijing High People's Court overturned the lower court's ruling ((2007) No. 146) for the reason that no evidence showed it would be easy for one skilled in the art to readily produce a composite by admixing Sulbactam and Piperacillin or Cefotaxime. In rehearing, Weale submitted evidence of experimental data with respect to long term and acute toxicity of Sulbactam and Cefotaxime, and general pharmacological studies on them to show inventiveness in the respect that a composite used for humans must be safe, effective and stable which can only be determined by experiments and could not be deduced by one skilled in the art. The Supreme People's Court ((2011) No. 8) opined that such evidences were unacceptable and could not be considered for assessing inventiveness since they have not been disclosed in the documents as originally filed, based on which, the invalidity decision was affirmed. Specifically, Weale argued that, to solve the reformulated technical problem regarding safety, effectiveness and stability, they produced and submitted those experimental data. To answer this, the Court articulated that such technical contents could not demonstrate that the patent made inventive contribution to the prior art due to that they have not disclosed in the originally filed documents and thus could not be used for evaluating inventiveness.

Additionally, Weale argued that the description has complied with the sufficiency patentability requirement, and it is unnecessary for those submitted data to be described in the description to ascertain inventiveness. The Court denied Weale's arguments, and stated it is only the minimal requirements for the description to sufficiently disclose an invention therein. Furthermore, the Court stated that the patentee has the right to disclose the technical contents to the extent they want and keep some technical knowhow unrevealed, but he should take the possibly adverse consequences, even though the description meets the requirements of sufficient disclosure.

3. Discussing the Significance: Sufficiency of the Disclosed Technical Effect

It can be seen from the cases above, Chinese Patent Office, the Board and people's courts are of the same opinion that an invention should be disclosed sufficiently with respect to technical effects in order to argue against non-inventiveness.

Without citing any legal basis for such requirement, the *Guideline* specifies that in accordance with the problem-and-solution approach to assess inventiveness, any technical effect may be used as a basis for reformulating a technical problem as long as such a technical effect could be recognized by one skilled in the art from the technical contents described in the description. Chapter 10, § 2.1.2.2. However, the *Guideline* has not made it clear what "could be recognized by one skilled in the art". In practice, Chinese Patent Office asks for submission of post-filing experimental data to support inventiveness where the data should direct to the technical effects that have been described and verified by experiments in the originally-filed description. Assertory conclusions alone without necessary data to support in the description would not suffice, nor be relied upon for submission of post-filing data to support inventiveness before Chinese Patent Office and the Board. While patentees/applicants in all fields must meet this requirement, the life sciences fields are effectively held a heightened standard that can be challenge to meet as they are treated as unpredictable arts or experimental sciences.

Similarly, people's courts hold the same position that the invention in dispute should disclose sufficiently the technical effects for establishing inventiveness. Specifically, in the decision of (2011) No. 8 of the Supreme People's Court, the Court made the point, without any provision of a definite legal basis on which the opinion relied, that "[a] patent right is a legal exclusive right which can be obtained after examined by Chinese Patent Office based on the invention published to the public. The documents as originally filed are not only a basis for examination but also a basis for public to understand, transmit and utilize the technology disclosed in the invention. Thus, any technical solutions and technical effects undisclosed in the documents as originally filed by applicants cannot be a basis for assessing the patentability of the invention to avoid of against the first to file principle used in China and contradicting the essential attribution of a patent, i. e. , granting a patent right for an invention as a quid pro quo for disclosure of the invention. "

Practically, a technical problem of a patent (application) will usually be reformulated with a newly identified closest prior art document after search during either the substantive examination procedure or an invalidation proceeding. Based on the reformulated technical problem, inventiveness will be assessed from the point of view of one skilled in the art. Under current Chinese patent practice, it is required that the technical effect to be used for establishing inventiveness should meet the requirements of sufficiency in the originally filed description.

Arguably, criteria for determining the closest prior art have not been established, which, however, will not affect the fact that the closest prior art is always changing when an examiner identifies a new reference document at the procedure of substantive examination or a petitioner locates a new reference document at the invalidation procedure. At the time of drafting a patent application, it might be unlikely for an applicant to obtain the same prior art documents with those identified at later procedures. It is the reason that a technical problem is allowable to be reformulated in applying the problem-and-solution approach. Nevertheless, Chinese Patent Office, the Board, and people's courts impose a high threshold for applicants or patentees to prepare an application document with consideration of all possible prior art documents before filing. In view of the current Chinese patent practice, it is advantageous for applicants or patentees, before drafting, to conduct a thorough prior art searches, and incorporate the necessary experimental data in the drafting based on the located prior art documents. Relying on such an originally filed document, the applicants or patentees would have opportunities to provide some comparison data for any unexpected technical effects verified in the description with the closest prior art used in later procedures to argue against non-inventiveness.

In conclusion, by introducing Chinese patent practice with respect to disclosure requirement in assessing inventiveness, we encourage patent practitioners to conduct thorough prior art searches and provide more examples and data in the application description, where in particular life sciences inventions are sought to be patented, and not rely on post-filing evidence to supplement an alleged inventive invention.

Rights of Joint Patent Owners in China[*]

By: Yunling Ren & Yan Hong

Introduction

Prior to the *Third Revision of the Chinese Patent Act*,[1] issues relating to patent ownership were partly dealt with by the Chinese courts under the *General Principles of Chinese Civil Law* (*General Principles*),[2] *Contract Law*,[3] and *Property Law*.[4] Recognizing the special attributes of intellectual property, the Chinese legislature codified prior judicial practice and interpretations in the area of patent ownership by adding Article 15 to the *Chinese Patent Action* response to the growing demands in technology innovation and transfer. [5]

---

[*] First published at *The John Marshall Review of IP Law*, the U. S. A, 2012.

[1] *The Chinese Patent Act* was first adopted at the Fourth Session of the Study Committee of the Sixth National People's Congress on March 12, 1984, and became effective on April 1, 1985. PETER GANEA, THOMAS PATTLOCH, CHRISTOPHER HEATH. Intellectual Property Law in China, § I. 2 (2005). The law was thereafter amended in 1992, 2000, and 2008. PHILIPP BOEING. The Chinese Patent System [J] . China Bus. & Res. , 2011 (1): 1-2. *The third Amendmentof the Chinese Patent Act* was approved by the National People's Congress on December 27, 2008 and took effect on October 1, 2009. *Id.*

[2] The *General Principles of the Civil Law of the People's Republic of China* (*General Principles*) were implemented in 1986, which was the first Chinese civil legislation, where the basic legal principles and judicial process concerning civil disputes among citizens were described. *See General Principles of the Civil Law of the People's Republic of China* (promulgated by the Nat'l People's Ct. , Apr. 12, 1986, effective Jan. 1, 1987), art 118. It consists of three parts: The Civil Principles, The Civil Rights, and The Civil Responsibilities. *Id.* The Civil Rights include the property rights, the intellectual property rights, the debtors' rights, and the inheritance rights, etc. The General Principles form the foundation for the later *Civil Law* legislation including the individualized legislations of Chinese Contract, Property Law, Patent, Trademark and Copyright Law.

[3] Adopted at the Second Session of the Ninth National People's Congress on March 15, 1999. *See* ZHANG YUQING, HUANG DANHAN. The New Contract Law in the People's Republic of China; UNIDROIT. Principles of International Commercial Contracts: A Brief Comparison, 63 Unif. L. Rev. 429, 429 (2000).

[4] Adopted at the FifthSession of the Tenth National People's Congress on March 16, 2007. *See* BRAD HERROLD. An Overview of Property Development in China, 1 S. G. L. A. L. J. 1, 1 (2008).

[5] EU-China Ipr 2, European Patent Office. Third Revision of China's Patent Law: Legal Texts and Documents on the Drafting Process 2006-2008, 4 (2009) [EB/OL]. http: //www. ipr2. org/images/eu _ patent _ law-090805-7-final. pdf. .

Article 15 of the Patent Actintroduces the concept of joint patent ownership into law. ❶More specifically, it defines the rights associated with such owner-ship. ❷However, this provision has been criticized as resulting in more questions than answers to the patent ownership issue. ❸A majority of the questions remain widely open as of today. This article is not meant to find solutions to those open ques-tions. Rather, the authors wish to provide a glimpse into the development of Chinese law in the area of patent ownership based on their observations.

1. An Overview

Since the first legislation in 1984, Chinese patent law has been evolving mostly in parallel to China's economic reform, which began in the early 1980s and was notably accelerated in the early 1990s. ❹In 1992, China and the United States (U. S.) jointly signed a *Sino-U. S. Memorandum for Protection of Intel-lectual Property*❺, triggering the *First Amendment of the Chinese Patent Act.* ❻The 1992 Amendments made several important improvements, including: (ⅰ) expanding patent protection to the technological fields of pharmaceutical products, foods, bev-erages, flavorings, and substances obtained through chemical processes;❼ (ⅱ) ex-tending the patent term for inventions from fifteen to twenty years, and for utility

---

❶ MAARTEN ROOS, PENG KAI. The 3rd Amendment to the PRC Patent Law [J]. China IP Bull. , 2009 (4): 1, 3.

❷ XIAOQING FENG. The Interaction Between Enhancing the Capacity for Independent Innovation and Patent Protection: A Perspective on the Third Amendment to the Patent Law of the P. R. China [J]. 9 U. Pitt. J. Tech. L. & Pol'y 1, 2009 (41).

❸ *Id.*

❹ Boeing, *supra* note 286, at 2.

❺ *See* LAURENCE P. HARRINGTON. Recent Amendments to China's Patent Act: The Emperor's New Clothes? [J]. 17 B. C. Int'lL. & Comp. L. Rev. , 1994: 358, 337 n. 8, 371~374.

❻ LEI FANG. Chinese Patent System and Its Enforcement [M]. 2005: 1, 2 nn. 1-2 (Sutherland Asbill & Brennan LLP).

❼ PATENT LAW OF THE PEOPLE'S REPUBLIC OF CHINA. (promulgated by the Standing Comm. Nat'l People's Cong. , Mar. 12, 1984, amended Sept. 4, 1992) [hereinafter *1992 Chinese Patent Act*]. The 1992 Amendments had been harmonized with international standards to remove the restriction and recognize the patentability of both chemical processes and chemical substances. *Id.* ; FANG, *supra* note 296, at 1, 2 nn. 1-2; Chinese Patent Act (2001), art. 11.

models and designs from five to ten years; ❶ and (iii) narrowing the grounds under which a compulsory license may be granted. ❷During the same period, the State initiated the process of privatization of State owned properties. ❸Althoughthe concept of private property ownership appeared in the "General Principles" of 1987, which states that "a citizen's personal property shall include the lawfully earned income, housing, savings, articles for daily use, objects of art, books, reference materials, trees, livestock, means for production permitted by law, and any other lawful property", it was not until the 1990s that the private property ownership became meaningful. ❹Yet, China's intellectual property law that began to address substantive proprietary rights was first passed by the Chinese People's Congress in 2007, about twenty years after the introduction of the private property ownership concept. ❺

Neither the General Principles, nor the *Chinese Patent Act* of 1984 and its 1992

---

❶ *See* FANG, *supra* note 296, at 1, 2 nn. 1-2; *Patent Law of the People's Republic of China* (promulgated by the Standing Comm. Nat'l People's Cong. , Mar. 12, 1984, amended Aug. 25, 2001), art. 11 [hereinafter *2001 Chinese Patent Act*]; *Patent Law of the People's Republic of China* (promulgated by the Standing Comm. Nat'l People's Cong. , Mar. 12, 1984, amended Dec. 27, 2008, effective Oct. 1, 2009) [hereinafter *2009 Chinese Patent Act*] . Chinese Utility Model patents, similar to the invention patents, have a shorter term and less stringent patentability requirements. The *Chinese Patent Law* provides that Utility Model patents, relating to improvements on shapes, structures, or a combination thereof, are merely granted without substantive examination once they are found to comply with formalities. While particular subject matter required for utility model protection, other patentability requirements regarding novelty, inventiveness, support and sufficient disclosure are applicable to Utility Model patents. The validity of Utility Model patents can be challenged after granting in invalidation proceedings before the Reexamination Board of State Intellectual Property Office. A principal disadvantage of Utility Model patents is their ten-year term from the filing date, rather than the twenty-year term enjoyed by the invention patents. But inventions relating to electronics or to those experienced a limited period of being fashionable or new are excellent Utility Model patent candidates.

Chinese Design patents provide protection for new designs that create aesthetic feelings and are fit for industrial application. Similar to Chinese Utility Model patents, Design patents have a ten-year term from the filing date and are granted without substantive examination. The validity of Design patents can be challenged after granting in invalidation proceedings.

❷ It has been interpreted that compulsory license provisions, are commonly used in some other countries, especially developing countries, as a limit on the exclusive patent right to exploit an invention, while retaining the economic incentive for invention. *See* HARRINGTON, *supra* note 295, at 337, 368.

❸ *See* HARRINGTON. *supra* note 295, at 344 n. 44, 368, 368 n. 221. This process is officially referred to as "ownership structural reform" . *Id*.

❹ "A citizen's personal property shall include the lawfully earned income, housing, savings, articles for daily use, objects of art, books, reference materials, trees, livestock, means for production permitted by law, and any other lawful property. " *General Principle of the Chinese Civil Law*, art. 75.

❺ KAI WANG. Whatever-ism with Chinese Characteristics: China's Nascent Recognition of Private Property Rights and Its Political Ramifications [J]. 6 U. Pa. E. Asia L. Rev. , 2011: 43, 64.

Amendment made the connection between patents and proprietary rights and interests, leaving the patent ownership issue silent in the *Chinese Patent Act*. There was an assumption at the time that all patent rights resulting from any inventions belong to the State. ❶ The individual inventor's rights were limited to the right to apply for, and receive, certificates of honors, bonuses, or other awards" from the States. ❷ For example, the General Principles provide that "a discoverer shall have the "right to apply for and obtain a certificate of discovery, a bonus, or other commendation", and citizens who make inventions or other achievements in scientific and technological research shall have the "right to apply for and obtain a certificate of honor, a bonus or other commendation".❸

The second *Amendment of the Chinese Patent Act* was a product of China becoming a member of the World Trade Organization (WTO) in 2000. ❹ To meet the standards and requirements of the international community, China made many significant changes to its patent system to conform with the provisions of the TRIPS Agreement❺ in 2001. Among the changes was a provision to grant individual inventors the right to prohibit a third party from unauthorized making, using, offering to sell, and selling patented inventions. ❻ The 2001 *Amendment of the* Chinese Patent Act unambiguously set forth the legislature's intent to promote the progress of technology and innovation. ❼ After this Amendment, the notion of patent co-ownership was born and

---

❶ In the prototype of the *Chinese Patent Act*, "Provisional Regulations on the Protection of the Invention Right and the Patent Right" (1950) and subsequent enabling rules promulgated in 1963, state ownership of novel inventions was mandated. *See* HARRINGTON, *supra* note 295, at342.

❷ WHITMORE GRAY, HENRY RUIHENG ZHENG. Principles of Civil Law of the People's Republic of China [G] // 52 Law and Contemporary Problems, The Emerging Framework of Chinese Civil Law 27 (EDITOR, 1989); General Principles of the Civil Law, art. 97.

❸ *Id.*

❹ *See* Backgrounds and Major Reforms Associated with Two Amendments to the Patent Act [EB/OL]. St. Intell. Prop. Off. of the P.R.C., http://www.sipo.gov.cn/zxft/zlfdscxg/bjzl/200804/t20080419 _ 383845.html.

❺ Several of the 1992 amendments were already made to reconcile the Patent Act with the Agreement on TRIPS. The 2000 amendment took a further step signifying its attention to meet the requirements of the TRIPS Agreement. *See* Y. HU. Three Amendments and TRIPS Agreement [EB/OL]. China Intell. Prop. Rights News (Apr. 2, 2007), http://www. cipnews. com. cn/showArticle. asp? Articleid=4163.

❻ *See* FENG. *supra* note 292, at 44.

❼ *See 2001 Chinese Patent Act*, art. 1 (stating that the purpose of the Patent Act to encourage the introduction and use of new inventions, to promote the progress of science and technology and to bolster the socialist economy).

slowly but surely matured. ❶

The third Amendment of the *Chinese Patent Act* marked the maturation of the Chinese patent system, which is a very important step for China to play a role in the international intellectual property community. Before this Amendment of the *Chinese Patent Act*, the State Council issued a document entitled *The Outline of the National Intellectual Property Strategy* (The *Outline*).❷ The *Outline* is a major strategic initiative by the State Council to focus on China's technology innovation, manifested as the transformation from "made in China" to "invented in China."❸ The *Guideline* sets the direction for the intellectual property related legal framework in China. It states:

By 2020, China will become a country with a comparatively high level in terms of the creation, utilization, protection and administration of IPRs. The legal environment for IPRs is much better, market entities are much better at the creation, utilization, protection and administration of IPRs, the public awareness of intellectual property is increased greatly, the quality and quantity of the self−relied intellectual property are able to effectively support the effort to make China an innovative country, the role of the intellectual property system in promoting economic development, the culture prosperity and social progress in China become very apparent. ❹

The *Outline* also emphasizes the importance of improving intellectual property law by expressly pointing out:

[1] aws and regulations concerning IPRs need to be improved. Special intellectual property laws, such as the *Patent Law*, *Trademark Law* and *Copyright Law*, and related regulations need to be promptly revised. Legislation concerning genetic resources, traditional knowledge, folklores and geographical indications should be formulated as needed. The uniformity and coordination of intellectual property legislation need to be strengthened to improve the practicability of laws and regulations. Intellectual property−related provisions contained in statutes and regulations concerning unfair competition, foreign trade, science and technology and national defense

---

❶ Joint patent ownership in the Chinese Patent Act includes the right to jointly apply for a patent and the joint right to own a patent. *See* 2001 *Chinese Patent Act*, art. 8 (indicating that the joint ownership of patent applications or patents may arise by operation of law or be created by express agreement).

❷ *See generally*, *Outline of the National Intellectual Property Strategy* St. Council of the People's Republic of China (June 5, 2008), http://gov. cn [hereinafter *Outline*].

❸ *See* THOMAS E. VOLPER. TRIPS Enforcement in China: A Case for Judicial Transparency, 33 Brook. J. Int'l L. 309, 323−334 (2007).

❹ *See Outline*, *supra* note 311, at Part II. 2 ¶ 6.

need to be improved. ❶

The *Chinese Patent Act* (2009) is the first amended intellectual property law af-ter the *Outline* was issued in 2008, demonstrating the Chinese government's good faith intent to carry out the *National Intellectual Property Strategy.* ❷In this Amend-ment, the Chinese legislature started to recognize that not only patent rights should be proprietary rights, but also patent owners could have economic interests derived from their rights in the patent, as any other property owners. ❸ Such rights include the right to make, use, offer to sell, and sell the patented invention. ❹Thus, a sig-nificant improvement of the Chinese patent law in 2009 was to add Article 15 to the *Chinese Patent Act.* ❺The language of "co-owners" of the inventions or patents ap-peared in the 2009 Amendment:

[w] here co-owners of an invention have a preexisting agreementwith respect to the rights in and to a patent or patent application, the agreement controls. Absent such agreement, each of the co-owners shall have the right to practice or grant a non-exclusive license to others, provided that any profits resulting from the non-ex-clusive license shall be distributed among the co-owners.

Exercise of any rights relating to a patent or a patent application shallbe agreed upon by all co-owners of such patent or patent application except for the provision provided above. ❻

2. Article 15 of the *Chinese Patent Act* (2009) and Some Recent Practice

As discussed above, article 15 of the *Chinese Patent Act* (2009) speaks for the first time about the issues relating to jointly owned patents. It sets forth the following principles with respect to patent co-ownership:

First, article15 specifies that agreements among co - owners take preced-ence. ❼This principle encourages the co-owners of the patent to engage in arm's-

---

❶ *See id.* at Part III. 1 ¶ 8.

❷ *See* FENG. *supra* note292, at 49-50.

❸ *See id.* at 38-39.

❹ FANG. *supra* note 296, at 2 nn. 1-2; *2001 Chinese Patent Act*, art. 11.

❺ *See* St. Intell. Prop. Off. of the P. R. C. Backgrounds of the Third Amendment [EB/OL]. http://www. sipo. gov. cn/zxft/zlfdscxg/bjzl/200804/t20080419 _383848. html .

❻ *2009 Chinese Patent Act*, art. 15.

❼ *Id.* (If there are agreements regarding the exercise of rights by the co-owners of the right to apply for the patent or of the patent right, the agreements shall prevail).

length negotiations regarding their respective interests and responsibilities. ❶ Each of the co-owners will have the opportunity to decide whether they want to be an owner by shares, a joint owner, a mixture of the two, or any other forms of ownership. ❷

The courts normally treated the agreements between parties with deference. For example, in Deng Xiandeng v. Chongqing Qianhong Elecs. Co. , ❸ two co-owners, Mr. Deng and Mr. Mao, of a patent on a magnetic engine had an agreement, which stipulated that neither of them could use the patented invention without the consent of the other. ❹They later licensed their patent to Chongqing Hengda Magnetic Materials Co. , where Mr. Mao agreed in a Confidentiality Agreement that he would not manufacture any patented products anywhere other than Chongqing Hengda Magnetic Materials during the patent term. ❺Thereafter, Mr. Mao unilaterally licensed the patent to Chongqing Qianhong Electrics in violation of his agreement with Mr. Deng and the Confidentiality Agreement with Chongqing Hengda Magnetic Materials. Mr. Deng sued Chongqing Qianhong Electrics for patent infringement. ❻Holding in favor of Deng, the court stated that Mr. Mao had no right to license the patent to Chongqing Qianhong Electrics because of his prior agreement with the co-owner of the patent. ❼

Second, article 15 makes a patent co-ownership a joint ownership and sets up ownership-by-shares as an exception to joint ownership. ❽The concepts of patent ownership-by-shares and joint ownership in the patent law were derived from the

---

❶ *Id.* (If there are agreements regarding the exercise of rights by the co-owners of the right to apply for the patent or of the patent right, the agreements shall prevail).

❷ *See General Principles of Civil Law*, art. 78.
Property may be owned jointly by two or more citizens or legal persons. There shall be two kinds of joint ownership, namely co-ownership by shares and common ownership. Each of the co-owners by shares shall enjoy the rights and assume the obligations respecting the joint property in proportion to his share. Each of the common owners shall enjoy the rights and assume the obligations respecting the joint property. Each co-owner by shares shall have the right to withdraw his own share of the joint property or transfer its ownership. However, when he offers to sell his share, the other co-owners shall have a right of preemption if all other conditions are equal.

❸ *See Final Written Civil Judgment No. 154* (2005), by Chongqing Higher People's Court.

❹ *Id.*

❺ *Id.*

❻ *Id.*

❼ *Id.*

❽ *See 2009 Chinese Patent Act*, art. 15 (In the absence of such agreements, the co-owners may separately exploit the patent or may, in an ordinary manner, permit others to exploit the said patent.); FENG, *supra* note 292, at 41-42 (noting that "co-owners can exploit separately or permit others to exploit the patent in the form of common license, excluding permitting others to exploit the patent exclusively").

General Principles of the *Chinese Civil Law*❶ and the *Chinese Property Law*. ❷It provides in the General Principles that the property may be owned jointly by two or more citizens or legal persons. ❸There shall be two kinds of joint ownership, namely co-ownership by shares and joint ownership. ❹Each of the co-owners by shares shall enjoy the rights and assume the obligations concerning the joint property in proportion to his share. ❺Each of the joint owners shall enjoy the rights and assume the obligations respecting the joint property. ❻Each co-owner by shares shall have the right to withdraw his own share of the joint property or transfer its ownership. However, when he offers to sell his share, the other co-owners shall have a first right of refusal if all other conditions are equal. ❼It also provides in the *Property Law* that a home or chattel may be co-owned by two or more entities or individuals. Co-ownership includes co-ownership by shares and joint ownership❽. However, thepatent co-ownership issue was never mentioned anywhere in the Statutes priorto the third Amendment (2009), ❾ even though it had become an issue of recurrence. To resolve disputes, the Chinese courts and the State Intellectual Property Office (SIPO) routinely relied on relevant provisions of the General Principles of the *Chinese Civil Law*, the Chi-

---

❶ *See* The General Principles of *Civil Law*, art. 78.

Property may be owned jointly by two or more citizens or legal persons. There shall be two kinds of joint ownership, namely co-ownership by shares and common ownership. Each of the co-owners by shares shall enjoy the rights and assume the obligations respecting the joint property in proportion to his share. Each of the common owners shall enjoy the rights and assume the obligations respecting the joint property. Each co-owner by shares shall have the right to withdraw his own share of the joint property or transfer its ownership. However, when he offers to sell his share, the other co-owners shall have a right of preemption if all other conditions are equal. *Id.*

❷ *See Property Law of the People's Republic of China* (promulgated by the Nat'l People's Cong., Mar. 16, 2007, effective Oct. 1, 2007), art. 93 (2007) [hereinafter *Chinese Property Law*] (Immovables or moveables may be co-owned by two or more units or individuals. Co-ownership consists of shared ownership and joint ownership).

❸ *See General Principles of Civil Law*, art. 78.

❹ *Id.*

❺ *Id.*

❻ *Id.*

❼ *Id.*

❽ *See Chinese Property Law*, art. 93.

❾ *See* CUI, GUOBIN. 中国专利共有制度述评 (上) (Study on Jointly-Owned Patents in China, Part I) [J]. 6 Elec. Intell. Prop., 2010 (12): 15-17; XIANGJUN SI, STEPHANIE C. WANG. Chinese Patent Law and Implementation Amendments Bring Key Changes, Interpretive Challenges [J]. 23 Intell. Prop. & Tech. L. J. 2011: 17, 19 (noting "[c] o-owners' rights to a patent were not covered in the *2000 Patent Law*").

nese Contract Law, and the *Chinese Property Law* to find solutions. ❶

The General Principle of the *Chinese Civil Law* sets forth two types of property co-ownership: ownership-by-shares❷ and joint ownership,❸ determination of which defines how the co-owned property is to be controlled, used, divided, or transferred, how the property right is to be enforced when infringement occurs, and what duty and responsibility each co-owner is to take. ❹

It has been debated among Chinese legal scholars whether the nature of patent co-ownership is an ownership-by-shares or a joint ownership absent an agreement. ❺Most of the scholars are reluctant to treat patents in the same way as to treat other conventional properties on the basis that intellectual property is "intangible" in nature. ❻Some even argue that since the intellectual property rights covered by provisions separate from those covering other conventional properties in the General Principles of the *Chinese Civil Law*, it must be something different from the conventional properties. ❼Thus, the prevailing view favors the belief that the conventional notion of property ownership-by-shares❽ cannot be applied to patent co-ownership due to the difficulties in the measurement of the rights in intangible properties. ❾

Not surprisingly, article 15 of the *Patent Act* sets co-ownership of a patent to

❶　FENG. *supra* note 292, at 116 n. 202 (explaining that in the context of invention-creation by an individual "using the material and technical means of the entity to which he belongs", ownership under the *2001 Chinese Patent Act* "seems to be unclear").

❷　General Principles of *Civil Law*, art. 78 (Each of the owners by shares shall enjoy the rights and assume the responsibilities with respect to the co-owned property in proportion to his/her share).

❸　*Id.* (Each of the joint owners shall jointly enjoy the rights and assume the responsibilities with respect to the co-owned property).

❹　Comparison between shared ownership and joint ownership is thoroughly explained in Chinese textbooks of civil law, which will not be discussed in this article.

❺　*See* CUI, GUOBIN. *supra* note 337, at 15–17.

❻　*Id.*

❼　*Id.*

❽　*Chinese Property Law*, art. 103 (stating that if "co-owners fail to reach an agreement either on shared or on joint ownership of the immovables or movables, or the agreement reached is indefinite in this respect, the ownership shall be deemed to be shared ownership, unless the co-owners are of a family or have other relations").

❾　*See* the *Contract Law of the People's Republic of China* (promulgated by the Nat'l People's Cong. , Mar. 15, 1999, effective Oct. 1, 1999), art. 341 [hereinafter *Chinese Contract Law*]; *Interpretation of the Supreme People's Court Concerning Some Issues of Law for the Trial of Cases on Disputes over Technology Contracts* (promulgated by the Sup. People's Ct. , Dec. 16, 2004, effective Jan. 1, 2005) (China). art. 21.

be joint ownership❶ absent any agreement, contrary to the basic principle of the *Chinese Property Law*, where ownership-by-shares according to each owner's contribution is presumed absent any agreement among co-owners. ❷

Under the *Chinese Property Law*, joint property owners are not permitted to unilaterally license their rights to a third party without consent of other joint owners. ❸However, article 15 made an exception to the presumed patent joint ownership to the extent that a joint patent owner may practice the invention alone or grant non-exclusive license to a third party. ❹Why did the Chinese legislature make an exception to the joint ownership in the patent law? The conventional property is usually not measured by terms and the property value does not change over the years. ❺A patent has a term of ten or twenty years from the filing date. ❻The term becomes even shorter if calculated from the date the patent is granted, and the value of the patent is inversely proportional to the length of its term. ❼Significantly, a patent normally has no market value unless it is commercialized before its term expires. ❽In other words, a patented invention could quickly depreciate if it is not commercialized.

---

❶ *See 2009 Chinese Patent Act*, art. 15; *See also* CHENG, YONGSHUN. 中国专利诉讼（Chinese Patent Litigation）, 170 5th ed. （May 2005）; *see also* FENG, XIAOQING. 专利权共有若干问题之我见（My View On Issues of Patent Right Co-ownership）, J. Cent. Leadership Inst. Pol. & L., Feb. 1997, at 28.

❷ *2007 Chinese Property Law*, art. 103.
The ways for protecting real right as prescribed in the present Law may apply either independently or jointly in light of the specific situation of an injury of real right. In addition to assuming civil liabilities, any entity or individual infringing upon a real right shall assume the administrative liabilities where it/he violates any provision on administrative regulation; in case any crime is established, it/he shall assume the criminal liabilities.

❸ *Id*. art. 97（Disposing of... co-owned immovables or movables shall be subject to agreement reached by the co-owners who possess two-thirds or more of the totalshares or by all of the joint owners, except where the owners agree otherwise）.

❹ *2009 Chinese Patent Act*, art. 15.

❺ *See generally Chinese Property Law*, art. 108（stating that "［a］fter a bona fide transferee acquires a piece of movables, the rights previously attached to the said piece shall extinguish", from which it may reasonable inferred that the attached property rights would not automatically expire.）.

❻ *2009 Chinese Patent Act*, art. 42.（stating that "［t］he duration of the invention patent right shall be twenty years and that of the utility model patent right and of the design patent right shall be ten years respectively, all commencing from the date of application"）.

❼ *See generally* JANICE M. MUELLER. An Introduction to Patent Law 17（2d ed. 2006）（explaining that "the term, or enforceable life, of a patent does not begin until the date the patent is *issued*（i. e., on the "issue date"）..."）（emphasis in original）.

❽ *See* JONATHAN A. BARNEY. A Study of Patent Mortality Rates: Using Statistical Survival Analysis to Rate and Value Patent Assets, 30 AIPLA Q. J. 317, 326-327（2002）（noting that "［l］ike stocks, bonds, and other intangible assets, patents possess no inherent or intrinsic value", but instead are "valued based on what they can produce or provide to the holder of the asset in terms of a future return on investment"）.

Any licensing activity that requires consent of all joint patent owners would inevitably slow down the process of commercialization. It also sometimes may be impossible for all joint patent owners to agree on certain transactions. Thus, the "consent" requirement proves to be counter-productive and would be contrary to the legislative intent of promoting technology and innovation.

Having recognized the need for commercialization of valuable technologies and innovations, the Supreme Court of China in 2004 made an exception to the general principles of *Chinese Property Law* by permitting a joint patent owner to unilaterally grant a non-exclusive license to a third party without consent of other joint owners. ❶This exception made by the Supreme Court of China was codified into the third Amendment of the *Chinese Patent Act* (2009).❷

This principle has been applied by the courts. For example, in Jiangxi Yongxin Magnetic Tools v. Nanchang Yongwang Magnetics Co. ,❸ the parties' settlement agreement in a prior dispute specified only on the terms of assignment of the patent but was silent with respect to how to use the patent or to grant license to a third party. ❹Relying on article 15, the court held that Nanchang Yongwang Magnetics, a joint patent owner, may unilaterally practice the invention or grant a non-exclusive license to a third party without the consent of the other joint owner. ❺

Third, article 15 clarifies the rights of a joint patent owner to the extent that a joint patent owner can do two things without the consent of other joint patent owners: (1) to make and use the patented invention by the joint owner alone; and (2) to grant a non-exclusive license to a third party, provided other joint patent owners have the right to accounting. ❻Any other acts requires the consent of all joint patent owners. ❼

However, article 15 of the *Patent Act* (2009) adds, but by no means ends, the ambiguities in the already murky area of the joint patent ownership discussion. Ownership-by-shares is likely a result of a contractual relationship among the co-owners in the patent law, where the co-owners acquire their portions of the respective interests

---

❶ *See* CUI, GUOBIN. *supra* note 337, at 43.

❷ *2009 Chinese Patent Act*, art. 15 (In the absence of [controlling agreements between co-owners], co-owners may separately exploit the patent or may, in an ordinary manner, permit others to exploit the said patent).

❸ *See Final Written Civil Judgment No. 35 (2009)*, by Jiangxi Higher People's Court.

❹ *Id.*

❺ *Id.*

❻ *2009 Chinese Patent Act*, art. 15.

❼ *Id.*

in the patent, by an arm's-length negotiation. ❶The issues arise when the patent co-owners fail to negotiate a contract, thereby becoming, or sometimes forced to become, joint patent owners by operation of the law, whose rights and interests in the patent are not wholly defined by the statues. ❷

3. The Rights of Joint Patent Owners in China

Having ownership of a patent gives the owners the fundamental rights to exclude others from engaging in certain activities reserved exclusively to the owners of patents. ❸The rights of a patent owner in China include the right to control, practice, license, and enforce the patented invention. ❹For patent co – owners in China, execution of these rights, absent any agreement, more or less depends on contributions made by each of the joint patent owners and the relationship between them, even though the statute generally defines the nature of the patent co-ownership as a joint ownership. ❺

In contrast, patents have the attributes of personal property in the U. S. ❻Each of the joint patent owners will have an undivided interest in the whole patent under the U. S. patent law absent an agreement, regardless of the contributions made by

---

❶ *2009 Chinese Patent Act*, art. 15.

❷ *Id.*

❸ *Id.* at art. 11. After the patent right is granted for an invention or a utility model, unless otherwise provided for in this Law, no unit or individual may exploit the patent without permission of the patentee, i. e. , it or he may not, for production or business purposes, manufacture, use, offer to sell, sell, or import the patented products, use the patented method, or use, offer to sell, sell or import the products that are developed directly through the use of the patented method. After a design patent right is granted, no unit or individual may exploit the patent without permission of the patentee, i. e. , it or he may not, for production or business purposes, manufacture, offer to sell, sell or import the design patent products.

❹ *Id.* ; *see also*, *id.* , art. 12 (Any unit or individual that intends to exploit the patent of another unit or individual shall conclude a contract with the patentee forpermitted exploitation and pay the royalties. The permittee shall not have the right to allow any unit or individual not specified in the contractto exploit the said patent) ; *see also id.* at art. 59 (For the patent right of an invention or a utility model, the scope of protection shall be confined to what is claimed, and the writtendescription and the pictures attached may be used to explain what is claimed. For the design patent right, the scope of protection shall be confined to the design of the product as shown in the drawings or pictures, and the brief description may be used to explain the said design as shown in the drawings or pictures).

❺ FANG. *supra* note 296, at 42.

❻ 35 U. S. C. § 261 (2006) (Subject to the provisions of this title, patents shall have the attributes of personal property).

each owner, respectively. ❶Further, each of the joint patent owners may make, use, offer to sell or sell the patented invention without consent of and without accounting to the other owners. ❷However, joint patent owners' rights may be limited in the event of litigation, which will be discussed below. ❸

A. Inventorship versus Ownership

Chinese patent law generally does not differentiate between inventions and patented inventions, nor between patents and patent applications when dealing with patent ownership issues. ❹In comparison, joint inventorship and joint patent ownership are governed by separate statutory provisions in the U. S. ❺A significant difference between inventorship and ownership in the U. S. is that the ownership of a patent can be transferred but the inventorship cannot. ❻There is no Statute in China that is directed solely to patent inventors. ❼In the U. S. , inventors have a presumption of patent ownership, and those patentees may transfer the ownership by assignment to any individuals or entities and may in fact be under a legal duty to do so by virtue of a contractual or other obligation. ❽This presumption is not applicable in China. ❾Under Chinese law, an employer is the presumed owner of the inventions, patent applications, and patents absent any agreements. ❿The employee‒inventors

---

❶　*Id.* (In the absence of any agreement to the contrary, each of the joint owners of a patent may make, use, offer to sell, or sell the patented invention within the United States, or import the patented invention into the United States, without the consent of and without accounting to the other owners).

❷　*Id.*

❸　*See* Ethicon Inc. v. U. S. Surgical Corp. , 135 F. 3d 1456, 1468 (Fed. Cir. 1998) (stating that "as a matter of substantive law, all co‒owners must ordinarily consent to join as plaintiffs in an infringement suit," meaning that "one co‒owner has the right to impede the other co‒owner's ability to sue infringers by refusing to voluntarily join in such a suit").

❹　HARRINGTON. *supra* note 295, at 353.

❺　*See* 35 U. S. C. § § 116, 261 (governing inventorship and ownership).

❻　*See* Beech Aircraft Corp. , v. EDO Corp. , 990 F. 2d 1237, 1248 (Fed. Cir. 1993); 35 U. S. C. § 116 (stating that inventorship cannot be transferred) *cf.* 35 U. S. C. § 261 (stating thatownership can be transferred).

❼　*See* JUSTIN MCCABE. Enforcing Intellectual Property Rights: A Methodology for Understanding the Enforcement Problem in China, 8 Pierce L. Rev. 1, 8‒9, 17‒18 (2009).

❽　*See* 35 U. S. C. § 261; 8 Donald S. Chisum, Chisum on Patents § 22. 01 (2011).

❾　*See* JUDITH EVANS, DAVID HILL. Chinese Patent Law: Recent Changes Align China More Closely with Modern International Practice [J]. Geo. Wash. J. Int'l L. & Econ. , 1993‒1994 (27): 359, 366, 367.

❿　*See 2009 Chinese Patent Act*, art. 6. An invention‒creation, made by a person in execution of the tasks of the entity to which he belongs, or made by him mainly by using the material and technical means of the entity is a service invention‒creation. For a service intention‒creation, the right to apply for a patent belongs to the entity. After the application is approved, the entity shall be the patentee absent an agreement. *Id.*

do not own the rights to the inventions, patent applications, or patents, other than the rights of being rewarded,❶ remunerated,❷ and named. ❸Since a majority of inventions are service inventions in China, i. e., inventions made by inventors during their employment, the employer automatically owns the invention, whether it is patentable or not. ❹In the case of a non-service invention, the individual inventor is the presumed owner of the invention absent any agreement. ❺Thus, inventorship and ownership of a patent are often mixed concepts in China. ❻While the law does not include any provisions on inventorship, the ownership of patents and patent applications are defined under Article 6❼ and article 8 of the Chinese Patent Act (2009).❽ Because inventorship is not the focus of this article, it will not be further discussed.

B. The Right to Control the Patented Invention

The rights for a patent owner to control the patented invention in China include the right to assign a patent to a third party, to take a mortgage on a patent, and to invalidate one or more claims in a patent or the entire patent through the invalidation proceeding. ❾Under article 15, such control requires the consent from

---

❶ *Id.*, art. 16 (The entity that is granted a patent right shall award to the inventor or creator of a service invention-creation a reward...).

❷ *Id.* ([U] pon exploitation of the patented invention-creation, [the entity that is granted a patent] shall pay the inventor or creator a reasonable remuneration based on the extent of spreading and application and the economic benefits yielded).

❸ *Id.*, art. 17. (The inventor or creator has the right to be named as such in the patent document. The patentee has the right to affix a patent indication on the patented product or on the package of that product).

❹ *Id.*, art. 6.

❺ *Id.*

❻ *Id.*, arts. 6, 8.

❼ *Id.*, art. 6. An invention-creation, made by a person in execution of the tasks of the entity to which he belongs, or made by him mainly by using the material and technical means of the entity is a service invention-creation. For a service invention-creation, the right to apply for a patent belongs to the entity. After the application is approved, the entity shall be the patentee. For a non-service invention-creation, the right to apply for a patent belongs to the inventor or creator. After the application is approved, the inventor or creator shall be the patentee. In respect of an invention-creation made by a person using the material and technical means of an entity to which he belongs, where the entity and the inventor or creator have entered into a contract in which the right to apply for and own a patent is provided for, such provisions shall apply. *Id.*

❽ *Id.*, art. 8. For an invention-creation jointly made by two or more entities or individuals, or made by an entity or individual in execution of a commission given to it or him by another entity or individual, the right to apply for a patent belongs, unless otherwise agreed upon, to the entity or individual that made, or to the entities or individuals that jointly made, the invention-creation. After the application is approved, the entity or individual that applied for it shall be the patentee. *Id.*

❾ *See 2009 Chinese Patent Act*, arts. 10, 46, 47.

all joint patent owners. ❶

This requirement is also reiterated in other legislations and regulations, such as article 4 of *Measures for Recording Mortgages on Patents*, ❷ which states that mortgaging a jointly-owned patent shall obtain the consent from all patent co-owners unless there is a prior agreement otherwise. ❸*Guidelines for Patent Examination*, ❹ section 6. 7. 2. 2 of chapter 1, part 1, states that:

[w] here the right of the applicant (or patentee) has been transferred because of assignment or gift, and a request for a change in the bibliographic data is submitted, the contract on the assignment or gift shall be submitted. If such a contract is concluded by any entity, the official seal of the entity or the seal specially used for concluding contracts shall be affixed. If the contract is concluded by any individual, it shall be signed or sealed by the person himself. Where there are two or more applicants (or patentees), a document certifying that all the right owners have agreed on the assignment or gift shall be submitted. ❺

In the event that a patentee requests to abandon his right in a patent after grant of the patent right, the *Guidelines for Patent Examination*, section 2. 3 of chapter 9, part 5 (Patentee Abandons Patent Right)❻ requires that the patentee "submit a declaration of abandonment of patent right with certifying materials of agreement of the abandonment of the patent right signed or sealed by all the patentees attached, or only submit a declaration of abandonment of patent right signed or sealed by all the patentees". ❼

With respect to the patent invalidation proceeding, the courts normally were careful in balancing all patent co-owner's interests due to the drastic outcome that may result from the proceeding, i. e., invalidity of the patent. In Yang Fu v. Patent Reexamination Board of SIPO, ❽ which was an appeal from a prior invalidation proceeding in the Patent Reexamination Board of SIPO, Yang Fu, a patent co-owner, argued that the Patent Reexamination Board failed to serve on him the Oral

❶ *See 2009 Chinese Patent Act*, arts. 15.

❷ *Measures for Recording Mortgages on Patents* (effective Oct. 1, 2010).

❸ *Id.*

❹ St. Intell. Prop. Off. of the P. R. C., *Guidelines for Patent Examination* 2010 [hereinafter SIPO *Guidelines*].

❺ *Id.* at Part I ch. 1 § 6. 7. 2. 2.

❻ *Id.* at Par. 5 ch. 8 § 2. 3.

❼ *Id.*

❽ *See* Final Written Administrative Judgment No. 542 (2007), by Beijing High People's Ct. Court.

Hearing Notification, resulting in his absence in the Patent Invalidation Oral Hearing, therefore, the proceeding was flawed. ❶In holding for the Reexamination Board, the court found that Yang Fu should have received the Oral Hearing Notification, which was sent by the Patent Reexamination Board, and he had actual knowledge that the Oral Hearing would be held at a specific time on a specific date based on the evidence of the Oral Hearing Notification of Invalidation Announcement Request issued by Patent Reexamination Board, the Recusal Request letter signed by Yang Fu and the other patent co-owner, and two reply letters signed by Yang Fu and the other patent co-owner in response to the Oral Hearing Notification of Invalidation Announcement Request issued by Patent Reexamination Board. ❷Thus, the court determined that Yang Fu had voluntarily abandoned his right to attend the Oral Hearing because he should have known and had actual knowledge of the Hearing date and time. ❸

Some scholars believe that the patent co-owners' right to control the patented invention should not include the right to invalidate one or more claims in the Invalidation Proceeding because validity of a patent is rather an issue of the public interest, which cannot be controlled by any patent owners. ❹Indeed, the nature of a patent is a contract between a patentee and the public, such that validity of the patent is not only the interest of patent owners but that of the public as well. ❺ Further, any person or entity may initiate an invalidation proceeding before the Patent Reexamination Board of the

---

❶ *See* Final Written Administrative Judgment No. 542 (2007), by Beijing High People's Ct. Court.

❷ *Id.*

❸ *Id.*

❹ *See* XINTIAN YIN. Introduction to the Patent Law of China [M]. Beijing: Intellectual Property Publishing House, 2011.
Does the patentee have the right to invalidate his own or a joint owned patent? As a matter of fact, the patent right is effective or can be deemed as a kind of right only when the patent is valid. The aim for invalidation is to question whether the patent should be granted, but not the effectiveness of said patent right. Once the patent is announced invalidity, said patent right is deemed nonexistent from the beginning. Although the *Chinese Patent Act* (2009) states that 'where, starting from the date of the announcement of the grant of the patent right by the patent administration department under the State Council, any entity or individual considers that the grant of the said patent right is not in conformity with the relevant provisions of this Law, it or he may request the Patent Reexamination Board to declare the patent right invalid', and the patentee himself is not ruled out from invalidation appeal, however, it is weird that the patentee invalidates his own or a joint owned patent. *Id.*

❺ MATTHEW GOLDBERG. The Viability of Stimulating Technology-Oriented Entrepreneurial Activity in China, Taiwan, Japan, and South Korea: How Regulations and Culture Encourage the Creation, Development, and Exploitation of Intellectual Property [J]. Int'l L & Mgmt. Rev., 2005 (1): 1, 6 (2005).

SIPO under the Chinese law. ❶In that case, why should a patent co-owner be excluded from doing so?

C. The Right to Make and Use the Patented Invention

A patent co-owner has the right to make and use the patented invention on his own, i. e., a patent co – owner may unilaterally make and use the patented invention without the consent from any other joint owners. ❷The Supreme Court of China stated in 2001 that a patent co-owner could make and use the patented invention individually if there was otherwise no conflicting agreement among patent co-owners, and that the patent co-owner who practiced the invention could keep the profit. ❸Article 15 of the *Patent Act* (2009), for that matter, is consistent with the historical judicial practice in China. ❹

D. The Right to License the Patented Invention

As mentioned above, the license rights of patent co-owners in China are expressly stated in Article 15 of the *Patent Act* (2009) to the extent that a joint patent owner only can make and use the patented invention on his own or grant a non-exclusive license to a third party absent any agreement, provided that he shares the profit generated from the license with other patent co-owners. ❺

In comparison, the U. S. law grants patent co-owners much broader rights to the extent that each of the patent co-owners will have an undivided interest in the whole patent absent any agreement, regardless the contributions made by each owner, and each of the patent co-owners "may make, use, offer to sell, or sell the patented invention" without consent of and without accounting to the other co-owners. ❻In other words, a patent co-owner in the U. S. may assign, or grant non-exclusive or exclusive license to a third party without permission or consent from any other patent co-owner. ❼

At first glance, this seems to be unfair to a patent co – owner whose contributions are significantly larger than other co-owners. However, the policy underly-

---

❶ *2009 Chinese Patent Act*, arts. 45–46.

❷ *Id.*, art. 15.

❸ See *Minutes of Issues on Examining Technical Contract Disputes In the Working Conference of Judging Intellectual Property By Nation Wide Courts*, The Supreme Court 2001.

❹ *2009 Chinese Patent Act*, art. 15.

❺ *Id.*

❻ 35 U. S. C. § § 261, 262 (2006).

❼ See Wis. Alumni Research Found. v. Xenon Pharm. Inc., 591 F. 3d 876, 882 (7th Cir. 2010).

ing such equal-interest property rule was explained by the U. S. court in the case Ethicon Inc. v. U. S. Surgical, ❶ where the court stated that joint inventorship (ownership) is a voluntary relationship and, therefore, any inequity resulting from the application of the equal-interest property rule must either be accepted by the inventors (owners) voluntarily, or be dealt with by express agreement among the parties claiming an ownership interest. ❷In balancing between the inequality and practicality, the U. S. legislature has chosen the easy way to deal with the issue, leaving the problems resulting from such co-ownership to the parties to resolve. ❸

A fundamental difference between Chinese and U. S. property law is that the Chinese does not allow unilateral licensing, exclusive or non-exclusive, the property interests by a joint owner of the property to a third party without consent from any other joint owners, while the U. S. property law does allow. ❹A rationale for the "consent" requirement in Chinese property law is that because jointly owned property is created jointly by the joint owners, it must be jointly controlled and transferred to maintain the integrity of the jointly owned property. ❺However, this appears to be more of a theoretical concern rather than a practical one. In reality, it is unlikely that any reasonable person would acquire a piece of property (or a patent for that matter) without an assurance that he would have the entire title, right and interest in such property. Thus, the concern that the integrity of the property would be destroyed absent the "consent" requirement seems unnecessary when an individual owner intends to transfer a jointly owned property.

Because the "consent" requirement of Chinese property law has become an impediment to the commercialization of technology and innovation, the *Chinese Patent Act* was amended to deviate from the General Principles of *Chinese Property Law* to the extent that the "consent" is not required in the situation where a non-exclusive license is granted as discussed above. ❻

---

❶ Ethicon, Inc. v. U. S. Surgical Corp. , 135 F. 3d 1456 (Fed. Cir. 1998).

❷ *Id*. at 1460, 1467-1468.

❸ Willingham v. Star CutterCo. , 555 F. 2d 1340, 1344 (6th Cir. 1977).

❹ *See* 35 U. S. C § 262; *c. f. 2009 Chinese Patent Act*, art. 15. (stating that *Chinese Property Law* does not allow unilateral licensing the property interests by a join owner of the property to a third party without the consent of other joint owners, while U. S. property law does).

❺ *See* CHENG YONGSHUN. Chinese Patent Litigation [M]. Beijing: Intellectual Property Publishing House, 2005: 70.

❻ *See* YAHONG LI. Pushing for Greater Protection: The Trend Towards Greater Protection of Intellectual Property in the Chinese Software Industry and the Implications for Rule of Law in China [J]. U. Pa. J. Int'l Econ. L. , 2002 (23): 637, 658.

While a non-exclusive license may be permitted without consent of the other owners, the law further requires accounting to the other owners of the profit generated by licensing. ❶ The reason for this profit sharing requirement may be out of a fairness consideration for other patent co-owners. ❷However, the Statute does not mention how the profit from the license should be shared among the patent co-owners. ❸Should it be shared equally or proportional to each individual's contribution? What happens when the contribution of each of the co-owners cannot be measured? Nevertheless, if the purpose of granting a non-exclusive license without consent is to facilitate commercialization of the patented invention, a requirement of accounting seems to operate in the opposite direction. ❹

Moreover, the Chinese legislature seems to feel uncomfortable with the idea that the patent co-owners may be treated unequally by their own choice. ❺Had the Chinese legislature taken one step further to consider the potential complication resulting from such accounting requirement, they would have appreciated the simplicity of the U. S. equal-interest property approach. ❻Indeed, the patent co-owners may be in a better position to weight and balance their own interests in the patented invention than any authorities. ❼

E. The Right to Sue

Prior to the third Amendment of the *Chinese Patent Act*, the issue whether commencement of a patent infringement suit requires all patent co-owners to participate

---

❶ *2009 Chinese Patent Act*, art. 15.

❷ *See* ELIZABETH CHIEN-HALE. Intellectual Property Aspects of Doing Business in China, in Doing Business in China: Resolving the Challenges in Today's Environment [G] //PLI Corporate Law and Practice Course Handbook Series, 2007: 109, 127, 140-141, (*available at* WL, 1626 PLI/Corp 109) .

❸ *2009 Chinese Patent Act*, art. 15.

❹ *C. f.* H. H. HENRY. Assignability of Licensee's Rights Under Patent Licensing Contract [M]. A. L. R. 2d 606 § 9 : 66

❺ *See 2009 Chinese Patent Act*, art. 15 (providing the owners the right to divide interests however they may choose).

❻ *See* 35 U. S. C. § 116; Israel Bio-Engineering Project v. Amgen Inc., 475 F. 3d 1256, 1263 (Fed. Cir. 2007).

❼ *See* Monsanto Co. v. Kamp, 269 F. Supp. 818, 824 (D. C. Cir. 1967).

was unsettled. ❶Yet, the third Amendment is still silent on this issue, leaving the discretion to the Chinese courts. ❷

In the current practice, the Chinese courts routinely allow cases to go forward in the absence of one or more patent co-owners. Any patent co-owner may bring an infringement suit against an alleged infringer unilaterally without consent of the other co-owners. The courts may name absent patent co-owners as joint plaintiffs or require absent patent co-owners to waive their litigation rights. In general, the courts are unwilling to prevent patent co-owners from enforcing their rights only because a co-owner of the patent refuses to join the suit.

The Chinese courts also took the position that a jointly owned patent as a whole requires the co-owners to act as a whole. ❸ This position is consistent with Section 56 of *The Supreme Court of China's Judicial Interpretation on Civil Litigation*, which sets forth procedural measures for property disputes. ❹A majority of the courts believe that a patent co-owner is a necessary party and must be joined with the plaintiff—other patent co-owners in a patent infringement suit. ❺For example, in Mao Shilun v. Chongqing Beipei Yongci Power Plant, ❻ the court allowed the case to go forward absent one of the patent co-owners Deng Xiandeng, on the basis that Deng had waived his right to sue, so that his necessary party status had been removed. ❼As such, he

---

❶ FENG. *supra* note 292, at 46; RACHEL T. WU. Awaking the Sleeping Dragon: The Evolving Chinese Patent Law and Its Implication for Pharmaceutical Patents [J]. Fordham Int'l L. J., 2011 (34): 549, 571; WILLIAM L. WARREN, LEI FANG. The Third Amendment to the Chinese Patent Law [EB/OL]. Sutherland (Mar. 9, 2009), http://www.sutherland.com/files/News/ddae6f2a - 7502 - 4740 - b58b - 060ced14e4bb/Presentation/NewsAttachment/2dbe51c9 - bb0a - 48bc - bfd9 - 8f6d7e663b25/TheThirdAmendment.pdf.

❷ *See 2009 Chinese Patent Act*, art. 15.

❸ EU - CHINA IPR2, Patent Protection in China, Roadmap for Intellectual Property Protection in China, 14 (2010) [EB/OL]. http://www.ipr2.org/storage/IPR2 _ Patent _ Roadmap-EN-update _ Feb _ 2010691.pdf.; JOHN RICHARDS. The Patent Law of the People's Republic of China [EB/OL]. Ladas & Parry (Nov. 5, 2009) [EB/OL]. http://www.ladas.com/Patents/PatentPractice/ChinaPatentLaw/index.html.

❹ *See* ISSUES APPLICABLE TO CIVIL PROCEDURE LAW OF P. R. C., art. 56, 31 Sup. People's Ct. Gaz. 70 (Sup. People's Ct. 1992) (China) (holding that if the jointly owned property right is violated by a third party, and not all of the co-owners sue that third party, the other co-owners shall be listed as the co-litigators).

❺ GARY MOORE. Joint Ventures and Strategic Alliances: Ownership of Developed Intellectual Property—Issues and Approaches [EB/OL]. Cooley China (Apr. 4, 2008), http://www.cooley.com/58741.

❻ *See* The Written Civil Judgment No. 81 (2005), by Chongqing No. 1 Intermediate People's Court.

❼ *Id.*

was not required to join the plaintiff. ❶

Based on the "joint ownership" theory, most Chinese courts, after the commencement of the action by a joint patent owner, follow the procedure that was set forth in Article 119 of *Civil Procedure Law of the People's Republic of China*, which states that "if a party who must participate in a joint lawsuit fails to participate in the proceedings, the courts shall notify the party to participate,"❷ and section 57 of the *Supreme Court's Judicial Interpretation on Civil Litigation*, which reads:

[w] hen the courts add a co-litigator as the party, the other parties should be notified. If the party who should be added as a plaintiff expresses unambiguously the party's intent to abandon its substantive right, the courts may not add such party as the plaintiff; if the party who does not want to join the litigation does not wish to abandon its substantive right, the courts shall still add the party as a co-plaintiff, and its absence in litigation shall not have any effect on any rulings in the case. ❸

These procedures are followed in order to notify the absent patent co-owners to join the plaintiff. ❹ If the absent patent co-owners refuse to join, the courts would require the absentees to sign a waiver stating that they had given up all their rights in the infringement suit at issue. ❺Once the courts received such written waiver, they would determine whether the plaintiff had established his standing as an independent plaintiff to allow the case to go forward. . ❻If the plaintiff was proven to be an independent plaintiff, the case would proceed. ❼In Luoyag Liming Machinery Co. v. Han Qihua,❽ the defendant moved to dismiss the complaint by raising the doubt on authenticity of the written waiver submitted by plaintiffs, who were two of the three patent co-owners. ❾ The court initiated, sua sponte, an investigation to determine whether the absent third patent co-owner indeed waived his rights to sue. ❿Based on the results of the investigation, the court held that the plaintiffs had standing to sue because the absent third patent co-owner had unambiguously waived his rights. ⓫

---

❶ *See* The Written Civil Judgment No. 81 (2005), by Chongqing No. 1 Intermediate People's Court.

❷ *See Civil Procedure Law of P. R. C.*, art. 119.

❸ *See Issues Applicable to Civil Procedure Law of P. R. C.*, art. 58, *supra* note 423.

❹ *Id*; *see Civil Procedure Law of P. R. C.*, art. 119.

❺ *See Issues Applicable to Civil Procedure Law of P. R. C.*, art. 58, *supra* note 423.

❻ *Id.*

❼ *Id.*

❽ *See* Final Written Civil Judgment No. 00078 (2008), by Hebei Higher People's Court (2008).

❾ *Id.*

❿ *Id.*

⓫ *Id.*

Even if a plaintiff-patent co-owner failed to obtain a written waiver from the absent joint patent owners, the courts normally still allowed plaintiff to litigate, relying on section 58 of the *Supreme Court's Judicial Interpretation on Civil Litigation.* ❶In Bei Rugen v. Shangyu Northern Elec. Mfg. Co. , plaintiff Bei Rugen jointly owned the patent right with another inventor Wang Qinghua to a Utility Model patent on a certain semiconductor device. ❷However, inventor Wang Qinghua did not join Bei Rugen in the suit. Nor could Bei Rugen provide any document showing that Wang Qinghua had waived the right to sue or given Bei Rugen a power of attorney to represent him in the case. ❸ The court mailed a notice to Wang Qinghua according to the address printed on the issued patent. The notice was returned because Wang Qinghua had moved and the new address was unknown. ❹Despite the fact that the absent patent co-owner Wang Qinghua could not be found, the court nevertheless allowed the plaintiff-joint patent owner Bei Rugen to sue. ❺In deciding the case, the court stated that protection of this patent was warranted because the patent had not expired and been challenged, and all requisite fees had been paid. ❻

Once an absent patent co-owner waived his litigation rights, all duties and obligations associated with the suit were allocated to plaintiff-patent co-owner. ❼In Liang Xiangrong v. Artificial Leather Factory of Yulin Town of City of Yulin, plaintiff Liang Xiangrong acquired the ownership of the patent on certain rubber composition by an agreement entered into with inventor Liu Guangjin. ❽The court held that plaintiff-patent co-owner Liang Xiangrong should bear all responsibilities and costs of the

---

❶ When the court adds a co-owner as a party, other parties should be notified. *See Issues Applicable to Civil Procedure Law of P. R. C.* , art. 58, *supra* note 423. If the party who should be added as the plaintiff declares clearly to abandon his substantive right, the court may not add him as a plaintiff; if a co-owner does not want to attend the litigation but will not abandon his substantive right, the court will still add him as a co-plaintiff, and his absence in litigation will not take any effect on judging the case. *Id.*

❷ Ruigen Bei v. Shangyu North Elec. Mfg. Co. , *see* No. 82 [Patent infringement litigation case], ((2007) Written Civil Judgment by Hangzhou Intermediate People's Ct. 2007).

❸ *Id.*

❹ *Id.*

❺ *Id.*

❻ *Id.*

❼ *Id.*

❽ Xiangrong Liang v. Yuli Leatheroid Factory, *see* No. 191 [Patent infringement litigation case] 191 (1997) (Written Civil Judgment by the Higher People's Ct. Court of Guangxi Zhuang Nationality Autonomous Region People's Court 2007) (noting that the agreement was entered into by Liang, Liu and another person Yang who acquired the ownership to a separate patent, which was not the issue in this case.)

suit, because the other two patent co-owners had waived their respective litigation rights. ❶

Notwithstanding, the Chinese courts typically required the patent co-owners, including those who did not join the suit to share in any recovery. ❷ Although this is a prevailing practice in China, some courts have expressed disagreement with this practice. ❸

This practice drastically differs from that in the U. S. , where a patent co-owner typically must be joined voluntarily by all other patent co-owners as a procedural requirement in U. S. law. ❹ Moreover, a patent co-owner cannot compel other co-owners to join in an infringement suit; neither can a co-owner make another co-owner a party-defendant.❺ There are three public policy reasons for the U. S. rule. ❻

First, there is a public interest in ensuring that patent owners have an opportunity to protect their substantive rights; second, there is a public interest in protecting defendants from being exposed to multiple suits, simultaneously or sequentially for the same patent; and third, there is a public interest in protecting the interest of co-owners in being able to license their patents to a third party without harassing other co-owners. ❼

These different approaches taken by Chinese and U. S. courts may reflect the differences of the two countries in terms of their respective public policies and culture. ❽The U. S. courts focus more on the balance of rights and interests among all litigants as well as that of the public by requiring all patent co-owners to participate in the suit, while the Chinese courts focus more on protection of property by allowing

---

❶ Xiangrong Liang v. Yuli Leatheroid Factory, see No. 191 [Patent infringement litigation case] 191 (1997) (Written Civil Judgment by the Higher People's Ct. Court of Guangxi Zhuang Nationality Autonomous Region People's Court 2007) (noting that the agreement was entered into by Liang, Liu and another person Yang who acquired the ownership to a separate patent, which was not the issue in this case.)

❷ See CUI GUOBIN. supra note 337, at 44, n. 13.

❸ Id. at 44 n. 9.

❹ Ethicon Inc. , v. U. S. Surgical Corp. , 135 F. 3d 1456, 1468 (Fed. Cir. 1998) ([A] s a matter of substantive law, all co-owners must ordinarily consent to join as plaintiffs in an infringement suit).

❺ Cilco, Inc. v. Precision-Cosmet, Inc. , 624 F. Supp. 49, 5152 (D. Minn. 1985).

❻ DALE L. CARLSON, JAMES R. BARNEY, The Division of Rights Among Joint Investors: Public Policy Concerns After Ethicon v. U. S. Surgical [J] J. L. & Tech. , 1999 (39): 251, 260.

❼ Id.

❽ See generally CHUN-HSIEN CHEN. Explaining Different Enforcement Rates of Intellectual Property Protection in the United States, China Taiwan, and the People's Republic of China [J]. Tul. J. Tech. & Intell. Prop. , 2007 (10): 211, 215-224 (discussing the effect of cultural differences on Intellectual Property Policyin the United States).

a property owner to act alone when its property is facing imminent harm. ❶

4. Conclusion

The *Chinese Patent Act* has been evolving in parallel to China's economic and technological development. ❷Although the concept of joint patent ownership under the Chinese Patent Act (2009) was derived from the General Principle of *Chinese Civil Law* and *Chinese Property Law*, it differs from conventional property joint ownership primarily because patents are considered a type of property that differs from other forms of property under Chinese law. ❸

Article 15 of the *Chinese Patent Act* (2009) defines the rights of patent co-owners. ❹Generally, a patent co-owner cannot act unilaterally with respect to the patented invention except for making and using the patented invention on his own or granting a non-exclusive license to a third party without consent from all patent co-owners. ❺ However, any patent co-owners may bring an action in the courts to enforce their patent rights without consent from all patent co-owners. ❻

The exception in Article 15 of the *Chinese Patent Act* (2009), permitting a patent co-owner to grant a non-exclusive license to a third party without consent of the other joint owners, reflects the legislative intent to promote innovation and technology transfer, although the accounting requirement in this provision seems to be inconsistent with such intent.

Unlike the patent law in the United States, which has been well established, the legislative history of Chinese patent law is relatively short, and many provisions of the *Chinese Patent Act* are still in their infancy and have yet to stand the test of time. ❼More issues will surface when the rules of law are applied in practice. It will be interesting to see how Chinese patent law continues to evolve in the future.

---

❶ *See* CHENG YONGSHUN. Chinese Patent Litigation [M] Beijing: Intellectual Property Publishing House, 2005: 172.

❷ *See* KONG QINGJIANG. The Political Economy of the Intellectual Property Regime - Building in China: Evidence from the Evolution of the Chinese Patent Regime [J]. Pac. McGeorge Global Bus. & Dev. L. J., 2008 (21): 111, 112

❸ *See* FENG. *supra* note 292, at 40-41.

❹ *Chinese Patent Act*, at art. 15.

❺ FENG, *supra* note 292, at 42.

❻ *Id.*

❼ *See*, *e. g.*, *2009 Chinese Patent Act*, art. 15.

Design Patent Prosecution and Enforcement: Latest Issues and Developments [*]

By: Qinghong Xu & Yan Huang

Design patents are a valuable, yet often overlooked, form of intellectual property protection that can play an important role in a company's business strategy. Often, design patents are utilized in industries where the aesthetic qualities of a product can enhance the brand and create customer loyalty. Apple's sophisticated and aggressive design patenting strategy covering iPhones and iPads is one such example.

In this article, we provide the latest issues and developments in the area of Chinese design patent prosecution and enforcement, and offer our insight into this area along with practical tips.

1. Insight into Design Patent Prosecution

For a design patent application, Chinese Patent Office will grant a patent right after a preliminary examination where no search concerning prior designs or conflicting applications will be conducted. However, some issues may come up when prosecuting an application for design.

A. Brief Explanation

According to the *Patent Law*[1] Article 59. 2, a brief explanation is required in a Chinese design patent. The law also provides that, the protection scope of the patent right for design shall be determined by the product design as shown in the drawings or photographs, while the brief explanation may be used to interpret the shown design. Id. Moreover, Rule 28 of the *Implementing Regulations*[2] specifies that a brief explanation shall indicate, among others, the essential feature of the design.

---

* First published at China IP Fous 2012, Managing Intellectual Property, United Kingdom, 2012.

[1] The *Patent Law* refers to the third amendment to the *Chinese Patent Law*, effective October 1, 2009.

[2] The *Implementing Regulations* refer to the *Implementing Regulations of the Patent Law*, effective February 1, 2010.

Indeed, a general principle of "overall observation and comprehensive judgment" has been laid out in both the *Examination Guidelines*❶ and the *Judicial Interpretations*❷ in the event of comparing the patented design with a prior design or an accused infringing product. However, it is unclear how the courts would use the brief explanation, particularly the described essential feature, to determine the patentability or infringement, while the *Judicial Interpretations* do specify the importance of the "distinctive design feature" (distinctive from the prior designs) of a patented design. See Article 11 of the *Judicial Interpretations*. Currently, most practitioners have drafted the brief explanation to broadly define the design to be patented.

B. Similar Designs

The *Patent Law* in Article 31. 2 provides, in part, that two or more similar designs for the same product or two or more similar designs incorporated in products belonging to the same class and sold or used in sets (individually and collectively "similar designs") may be filed as one application, which is intended to address the issue of an application's similar designs being precluded from patent protection.

Similar designs, by definition, refer to those "normally through overall observation, if the other designs and the main design have same or similar design features, and if the difference between them lies in slight changes in some fine details, usual design of this category of the products, the repeated and continuous arrangement of a design unit or mere change of color element". See the *Examination Guidelines*, Part I. Chapter 3. §9. 1. 2.

Specifically, the *Examination Guidelines* arbitrarily limit that no more than 10 similar designs in one application can be claimed. Worse yet, if an applicant tries to capture the embodiments beyond 10 designs in another application, one or both of the applications could be rejected for double patenting. ❸ Thus, it is suggested to carefully choose representatives of concept and claim similar designs that are patentably indistinct in order to effectively provide broader protection scopes.

---

❶ The *Examination Guidelines* refer to the *Guidelines for Patent Examination 2010*, effective February 1, 2010.

❷ The *Judicial Interpretations* refer to the *Interpretations of the Supreme People's Court Concerning Certain Issues on the Application of Law for the Trials of Cases on Disputes over Patent Infringement*, effective January 1, 2010.

❸ A type of multiple embodiment claiming used in the US with liberal dotted line practice is not allowed in China.

It should be noted that once an invalidation is asserted on a prior design basis, each of the claimed similar designs will be judged on its own merit and only the invalidated embodiment will fall.

C. Reference View

A design patent applicant often chooses to present reference views such as reference views of state in use in an application, which, according to the *Examination Guidelines*, are usually used to facilitate an understanding of "purpose of use, method of use, or place of use." See the *Examination Guidelines*, Part I. Chapter 3. § 4. 2. Simply based upon the function of the reference views, generally, it might be understood that the protection scope for a patented design should exclude those reference views. However, neither the *Patent Law* (Article 59. 2) nor the *Implementing Regulations* (Rule 27. 2) explicitly exclude the reference views from patent protection scopes.

Moreover, recent court decisions indicated that "the reference views of state in use", is excluded from patent protection scopes when determining the extent of protection scope, at least in some circumstances for example the case of "sofa bed (puzzle) ", ❶ which touched off a heated controversy.

In this "sofa bed (puzzle) " case, Beijing Intermediate People's Court upheld the Patent Reexamination Board's decision of invalidity of a design patent (2007, Beijing First Intermediate People's Court Administrative Case No. 97). Specifically, the court held that reference views of state in use, for a product classification purpose, should not be taken into account for the patent scope determination, and therefore, is excluded from the comparison to a prior design. The court reasoned that, instead of the reference views of state in use, the patentee has an option, but failed, to choose "views of state in use", which is used to define the protection scope and thus can be included in the comparison to the prior design, to protect variable states of a product and establish advantageous aspects that differ from the prior design.

At appeal, Beijing High People's Court affirmed the Intermediate People's Court judgment (2008, Beijing High People's Court Administrative Case No. 10),

---

❶ In an examination decision on a request for invalidation of a design patent "sofa bed (puzzle) " made by the Patent Reexamination Board, the Patent Reexamination Board considered that the protection scope of a product incorporating design with variations is determined by views with the title of front view, back view, left view, right view, top view and/or bottom view but not by reference views of state in use, and thusly declared the patented design invalid in whole (Examination Decision No. 8896) .

but further opined that the provisions concerning "reference views of state in use" in the *Examination Guidelines* do include the functions of determining the protection scope of a patented design and illustrating the protected object, and therefore do not violate the Patent Law and the Implementing Regulations.

Nevertheless, strictly speaking, since none of the *Patent Law*, the *Implementing Regulations* and the *Examination Guidelines* provide a clear definition for "reference views", its legal status needs to be clarified further when "reference views" is interpreted to include the functions of determining the protection scope of the patented design and illustrating the protected object.

Thus, it is suggested to carefully choose and use "reference views" in a design patent, in view of the Chinese patent practice.

D. View of State of Variation

Moreover, views of state of variation are also used for some products, which have different states when on sale and in use. The *Examination Guidelines*, in Part IV. Chapter 5. § 5.2.5.2, provide that every view of a comparative design may be used when it is compared with a patented design, while for a patented design, its state of use should be taken only to compare with a comparative design and a determination should be from various states of use taking comprehensive consideration into account. In contrast to the section 3 above (reference views of state in use), here the using-state views will be taken as the sole source for determining the patentability, while the only difference is the former being titled as "reference views". ❶ In this respect, the choice of titles of views may have an impact to the right-affirmation and enforcement of the Chinese design patents.

It is recommended to submit "views of state of variation" or "views of state in use" when the design shown in the views for illustrating variable states is the product per se shown in hexahedral views and space diagram (three-dimensional view), such that the variable states of the product are claimed to protect.

2. Insight into Design Patent Invalidation

As a design patent is granted without substantive examination, its validity will

---

❶ In the above "sofa bed" case, the Intermediate People's Court further considered that while "reference views of state in use" may include other shape, pattern or color outside the protection scope of patented design, "views of state in use" shall not include any design aspects outside the protection scope of patented design. Accordingly, the court concluded that if both have the same function, it would create confusion in the preliminary examination.

be challenged via an invalidation proceeding. The grounds for challenging include lack of novelty or inventiveness, and in conflict with a prior right. See the *Patent Law*, Article 23.

A. Ordinary Consumer

In deciding the novelty or inventiveness of a patented design against a prior design, the *Examination Guidelines* request that the comparison and judgment shall be made according to the knowledge and cognitive capability of an ordinary consumer. See the *Examination Guidelines* Part IV. Chapter 5. § 4. In the absence of a clear definition for the ordinary consumer, recently Supreme People's Court cases shed some lights on what capability such a hypothetical person should have—almost reaching the level of an ordinary designer.

In Honda v. the Patent Reexamination Board case (2010, Supreme People's Court Administrative Case No. 3) and Zhejiang Jinfei Machinery Group Co. Ltd v. Zhejiang Wanfeng Motorcycle Wheel Co., Ltd (2010, Supreme People's Court Administrative Case No. 5), the Supreme People's Court found that an ordinary consumer, in addition to looking at the design from overall appearance, is capable of knowing about the common means of design, the current design trend, the material and function limitations, as well as relevant technology and existing designs, and therefore, is able to look at individual portions of the design. Specifically, the Court considered the knowledge in the art, i. e. , what the state of art in the field of the product offers, in other words, what has been left for an innovative design given the limitations of product functionality, technology development, and existing designs (freedom of design). Further, according to the Supreme People's Court cases, an ordinary consumer would understand the design room (freedom of design) for one particular product, and accordingly make a determination regarding the similarity between designs.

B. Comprehensive Judgment

In the Honda case, supra, the Supreme People's Court confirmed the general principle of "overall observation and comprehensive judgment", and further considered the knowledge of the design room (freedom of design) understood by an ordinary consumer. The Court reasoned that when cars in certain categories adopt designs which have or appear a common configuration as a whole, this will have limited impact on the overall visual effect. Instead, distinctions in sectional design features such as the design of headlights, lateral view, and back view do bring a notable visual effect on the design of the car as a whole. Relying on this reasoning, it finally ruled that the existence of differences in the design of features such as head-lamps and side door windows have led an ordinary consumer to distinguish the paten-ted design from prior art. As a result, the challenged design patent remains valid.

Frankly speaking, the above opinion will with no doubt influence the determi-nation of future similar cases. However, as a question of facts, the outcome of com-parison will depend on the evidence presented in each case.

C. Inventiveness

Under the *Patent Law*, design patents are subject to inventiveness requirement under Article 23. A combined design does not meet the requirement if the "combina-tion, including mosaic and replacement, produces a design by merely aggregating two or more designs or design features, or replacing the design feature of one design with another design feature". See the *Examination Guidelines* Part IV. Chapter 5. § 6. 2. 3. While some details are provided with respect to what teachings and motivations are needed for this lack-of-inventiveness design, unique visual effect would be an effective showing of inventiveness.

3. Insight into Design Patent Enforcement

To infringe, an accused design must be identical or substantially identical to the patented design. The *Judicial Interpretations* specify that the comparison shall be made from "an ordinary consumer. Further, when determining whether a design is substantially identical, the ordinary consumer must make a comprehensive judgment in view of the overall visual effect of the design. based on the design feature (s) of each design". Nevertheless, the *Judicial Interpretations* are silent on what should be considered when making a "comprehensive judgment" of the overall visual effect.

A. Comprehensive Judgement and Distinctive Feature

As described above with respect to the Honda case, supra, the Supreme People's Court confirmed the general principle of "overall observation and compre-hensive judgment", which is also applicable to infringement cases. Moreover, the *Judicial Interpretations* introduce the "distinctive design feature" (distinctive from the prior designs) of a patented design which is different from the "key part of the design" in practice for years. See Article 11 of the *Judicial Interpretations*. Without any case under the distinctive design feature test, it seems to us that the Supreme

People's Court would like to limit the judges' discretion on key part 40 of the design test, ❶ where a judge would have a broad discretion interpreting the key part (s).

B. Infringement Activity

Under the *Patent Law*, the infringement of a design patent includes making, offering for sale, selling or importing a product incorporating the patented design for production or business purpose, while using the product will not constitute as infringement.

4. Conclusion

The third amendment to the *Patent Law* (effective October 1, 2009) has brought considerable changes in the standards of granting design patents, and as such, many new issues regarding design patent prosecution and enforcement are constantly emerging. We, as experienced patent attorneys, stand ready to update our clients on the developments and progresses, so we can help them to implement business strategies and achieve success in China.

---

❶ For example, in an earlier case, *Fiat Auto Spa v. Great Wall Motor Co. Ltd.* (2007), the court paid more attention to the front and rear parts of the vehicle where, according to the court, were the key parts usually most concerned by general consumers, and because of the differences in these parts, no infringement was found.

Exceptions to the Unity Principle

—Brief Discussion on Similar Designs and Designs of Products in Set

By: Xiangyun Jin & Yahui Dong

The principle of unity, which means that one patent application should only be limited to one invention–creation, is generally introduced and accepted in patent systems of all countries. However, this principle is not absolute at all. In regards to a patent application for design, the *Chinese Patent Law*❶ provides in Article 31.2 that an application for a patent for design shall be limited to one design. Two or more similar designs for the same product or two or more designs which are incorporated in products belonging to the same class and sold or used in sets may be filed as one application. The law, with respect to design patent application, sets forth both the unity principle as well as the exceptions, i. e. the similar designs and the designs of product in set can be filed in one design patent application.

This short article discusses the similarities and differences between the similar designs and the designs of product in set, as well as the strategies for filing these designs.

1. Two or More Similar Designs for the Same Product

As an exception to the principle of unity of the patent application for design, the similar design is newly–added in the third amendment of the *Patent Law*. In the old (pre – amended) *Patent Law*, the exception to the principle of unity only includes designs of product in set, and the old (pre–amended) *Implementing Regulations of the Patent Law*❷ has provided in Rule 13.1 that for any identical

---

❶ The *Patent Law* refers to the *Patent Law of the People's Republic of China* after 3rd amendment thereof, comes into effect from October 1, 2009.

❷ The *Implementing Regulations of the Patent Law* refers to the *Implementing Regulations of the Patent Law of the People's Republic of China* before 3rd amendment thereof, comes into effect from July 1, 2001.

invention-creation, only one patent right shall be granted.

However, in the practice, when a designer puts forward a new design to a product, a main design scheme and a plurality of designs similar to the main design scheme are often formed, and the designer generally wants patent protections both to the main design (basic design) and to the similar designs as well. Before the amendment of the *Patent Law*, if multiple similar designs of the same product were sought to be protected in one patent application for design, the application would be rejected for being not in conformity with the Article 31. 2 of the old *Chinese Patent Law*❶ for lack of unity; on the other hand, if the multiple patent applications for design are submitted respectively, they may be considered as "the same" invention – creation and thus would be rejected for being not in conformity with Rule 13. 1 of the old *Implement Regulations of the Chinese Patent Law* for double patenting. Accordingly, the patent application system of similar designs is added to the *Patent Law* for eliminating the afore-mentioned dilemma for the applicant.

When an application for two or more similar designs of the same product is filed, one design shall be designated as the main design in the brief explanation and the others are similar designs. The term "similar" means that through overall observation, if the other designs and the main design have same or similar design features, and if the difference between them lies in slight changes in some fine details, usual design of this category of the products, the repeated and continuous arrangement of a design unit or mere change of color element, they are considered as similar designs.❷

Illustrated below are the examples of two or more similar designs of the same product that are allowed to be filed in one application.

Example 1:

---

❶ The odd *Patent Law* refers to the *Patent Law of the People's Republic of China* before 3rd amendment thereof, came into effect from July 1, 2001.

❷ Taken form Section § 9. 1. 2 in chapter 3, part I of the *Guidelines for Patent Examination 2010* constituted by the State Intellectual Property Office (SIPO) of the People's Republic of China.

Front View of Design 1   Space Diagram of Design 1

Front View of Design 2   Space Diagram
of Design 2

Example 2：

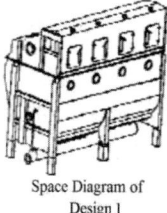
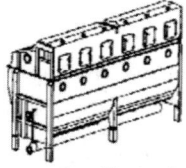

Space Diagram of
Design 1

Space Diagram of
Design 2

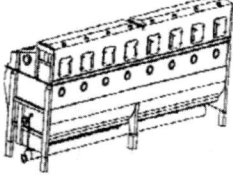

Space Diagram of Design 3

Example 3：

Front View of Design 1   Front View of Design 2

Front View of Design 3   Front View of Design 4

Example 4:

Front View of Design 1   Front View of Design 2   Front View of Design 3

Moreover, it should be noted that, when an application for two or more similar designs of the same product is filed, these designs shall involve the same product, and the name, type and use shall be identical; no more than 10 similar designs in one application may be claimed, as required by the *Implementing Regulations of the Patent Law*,❶ Rule § 35. 1.

The reason why "no more than 10 similar designs in one application may be claimed" lies in the fact: while providing conveniences to the applicant, it may also be taken care that an overlarge burden to both the patent examination and the protection of the patent right should be avoided due to an overly large number of design schemes in the application.

However, since the practical execution of the *Implementing Regulations of the Patent Law* from February 1, 2010, there is a large dispute on the provision in the industry of intellectual property, and it is generally believed that the provision "a maximum of **10** designs included in a patent application for design" cannot meet the current demand.

Practically, we think it is quite possible to amend this rule in the subsequent a-mendments of the *Implementing Regulations of the Patent Law*.

2. Two or More Designs for Products Belonging to the Same Class and Sold or Used in Sets

The *Implementing Regulations of the Patent Law* provides in Rule § 35. 2 that the two or more designs belonging to the same class and sold or used in sets as referred to in Article 31. 2 of the Patent Law mean that, each product incorporating the design belongs to the same class in the classification of products and is customari-

---

❶ The *Implementing Regulations of the Patent Law* refers to the *Implementing Regulations of the Patent Law of the People's Republic of China* after 3rd amendment thereof, came into effect from February 1, 2010.

ly sold or used at the same time, and the designs incorporated in each product have the same concept of design. The "classification" mentioned here refers to the *International Classification for Industrial Design*.

As for "the products being sold or used at the same time", it refers to the products that are customarily sold or used at the same time, for example, a multiple coffee set consisting of coffee cup, coffee pot, milk pot and sugar pot.

As for "the same concept of design", it refers to the unity of the style of design of each product, that means the design of the shape, pattern or their combination, or the combination of the color with shape or pattern of each product is unified.

3. The Patent Right as well as Protection of the Similar Designs and the Designs of Product in Set

When two or more similar designs for the same product and two or more designs of products in sets are granted a patent right, all the designs... in one patent are independent to each other. A declaration of invalidity of one of the designs does not necessarily result in the inevitable invalidity of the other designs.

When declaring patent right (s) of similar designs invalid, a certain similar design **cannot** be declared invalid only on the ground that it is similar to the main design.

Nevertheless, the assignment of the patent right shall occur at the same time. As regards to similar designs, they belong to one patent right and must be transferred altogether; in the case that the main design is declared invalid, all the other similar valid designs must be transferred again at the same time.

4. Application Strategies

The requirement of unity is a formal condition rather than a substantive condition for the grant of patent rights. In regards to the patent application for the similar designs and the designs of product in set, prior to the grant of patent, such applications may be rejected by the SIPO for being not in conformity with Article 31. 2 of the *Chinese Patent Law*. However, after the grant of patent, a patent right for design cannot be declared invalid for lack of unity, even the patent right for design is considered of being not in conformity with the provisions of the Article.

In view of this, for the applicant, in the case that the same product has the same or similar feature (s), as many similar designs as possible (but no more than 10) may be filed in one patent application for design. Even though some of these de-

signs may be rejected for being dissimilar with others by the examiner in the preliminary examination, the rejection could be overcome by filing divisional application
(s).

If more than 10 (e. g. , 15) similar designs are made for the same product,
when filing a patent application for similar designs, we suggest the applicant divide
the 15 similar designs into two patent applications for similar designs, or reduce the
number of designs from 15 to 10, in view of the provisions that no more than 10 similar designs in one application may be claimed. The following two schemes are illustrated with the diagram below (the numbers in the diagram represent the designs,
the adjacent designs are assumed most similar to one another).

Scheme 1: these 15 designs are divided into two patent applications for similar
designs to be filed, one application includes designs 1–7 and the other includes designs 8–15; for one application, design 4 is regarded as the "main design", and
for the other application, design 12 is the "main design";

Scheme 1: Two similar patent applications for design

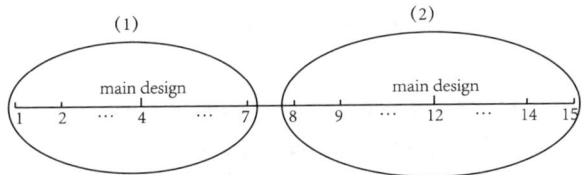

Scheme 2: One similar patent applications for design

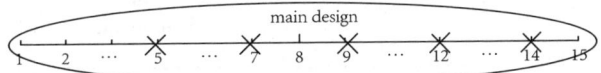

Scheme 2: delete 5 designs with high similarities (here, the "high
similarities" means the variations of the design features are small) and maintain only
10 designs.

In the case of adoption of scheme 1, as the 15 designs have the same or similar
design feature (s), when both patent applications for similar designs are granted
patent rights, the patent right for a certain design (e. g. **design 7**) in the
application (designs 1 ~ 7) or another design (e. g. **design 8**) in the other
application (designs 8 ~ 15) may be declared invalid for double patenting because
design 7 and design 8 are substantively identical and thus they belong to the same invention–creation, that is, the patent right for design 7 or 8 is declared invalid.
However, even the patent right for design 7 is declared invalid, the patent rights for
designs 1 ~ 6 is not necessarily inevitably invalid, so that a maximum protection

scope is able to be attained.

It should be noted that, one patent application for design should not include both the two or more similar designs and the two or more designs of product in sets. If an application includes a product set consisting of coffee cup, coffee pot, milk pot and sugar pot, and the coffee cup, coffee pot, milk pot and sugar pot each have 10 similar designs, it should be filed as similar designs. Otherwise, if the application is filed separately as 10 design applications of product sets consisting of coffee cup, coffee pot, milk pot and sugar pot, it is more likely that only one patent right could be acquired under the consideration that the designs of these 10 product sets belong to "identical invention-creation".

5. Conclusion

The application system for the similar designs and the designs of product in set is favorable to the applicant, the protection of the patent right, etc. If such system is used flexibly in a patent application for design to determine the strategy of application, the applicant can obtain the maximum and most stable protection scope with a relatively small expense.

At the end, the differences between the similar designs and the designs of product in set are summarized in Table 1 for easy reference.

Table 1

	Requirement for the product	Principle for determination	Illustration
Similar designs	The same product	Having the same or similar feature (s) of the design	Such as examples 1 to 4
Designs of product in set	products under the same class in the classification	Customarily sold or used at the same time; Having the same design concept	A coffee set consisting of coffee cup, coffee pot, milk pot and sugar pot

Inventiveness and Non-obviousness: Insights into Prosecution Practice in China and the United States

By: Yuyue Zhang

The inventiveness and non-obviousness reflect a same patentability requirement present in patent laws, according to which an invention should be sufficiently inventive, i. e. , non-obvious, to be patentable. Although the basic legal principle is roughly the same, the assessment of the inventiveness and non-obviousness varies from one country to another. The expression "inventiveness" is used in *Chinese Patent Law* under Art. 22 (3), while the expression "non-obviousness" is used in the *United States Patent Act* under 35 U. S. C. § 103. For the sake of simplicity, we use the expression "non-obviousness" for our discussions below.

As the United States and China are two major jurisdictions most entities would seek patent protection, this short article considers the ultimate condition of patentability—the requirement that the invention should be non-obvious in the United States and China, and focuses on their differences on the assessment of non-obviousness,❶ in order to help patent applicants have more precise prediction and more appropriate strategy for their inventions filed in the two countries.

1. Difference in application of laws with administrative rules during patent application examination

Non-obviousness, codified in 35 U. S. C. § 103 and similarly in Art. 22 (3) of *Chinese Patent Law*, is one of the requirements that an invention must meet to qualify for patentability. However, the statutory language in the patent laws is very generic for this requirement. 35 U. S. C. § 103 provides "a patent may not be obtained ... if the subject matter as a whole would have been obvious", while Art. 22 (3) of *Chinese Patent Law* requires that "an invention... has prominent substantive features and represents a notable feature. "

In examining whether an invention has met this non-obvious patentability re-

---

❶ This article addresses the obviousness issues for Chinese invention patents, not Chinese utility models.

quirement, the administrative agency (i. e. , the patent office in each country) applies the generic statutory language with specified administrative rules.

The *Manual of Patent Examining Procedure* (the MPEP) is applied by the United States Patent and Trademark Office ("USPTO"), but it doesn't belong to any legally binding law and thus needs to be adjusted in view of binding precedents of Courts. On the other hand, the *Guidelines for Patent Examination* (the GPE) is applied by the Chinese State Intellectual Property Office (SIPO), and has a legal validity not changing with decisions of Courts. This difference could be perceived from the amendment to " 2141 the examination guideline for determining obviousness" made by USPTO in response to the decision rendered by the Supreme Court in KSR Int'l Co. v. Teleflex Inc. (KSR), 550 U. S. 398, 82 USPQ 2d 1385 (2007).

The difference in responding to court decisions is originated from the disparity in legal systems, where the United States has a common law system contrasted with a civil law system in China. Given the difference, during a patent application examination, an applicant may have the following considerations:

(1) when pending claims of the patent application are rejected for being obvious, the applicant need to follow the examination criteria set forth in the GPE in China, while he may cite case laws in the United States, not necessarily the MPEP, to rebut the rejection, and

(2) when an obviousness issue is considered by a court (for example, appealed from the examination), a Chinese court may considers the rules stated in the GPE, while an American court will follow relevant precedent, and if there is no such precedent, it will create a precedent.

2. Difference in analytical roadmap for non-obviousness

Generally, determining non-obviousness involves a fact finding to an objective fact. However, it is a human person who makes the fact finding in view of his own experience level, recognition level, and is unavoidably being interfered with by objective limits and his subjectivity. For precluding the interference, SIPO and USPTO require the decision maker to step backward in time at the filing date of a patent application, and put himself into the shoes or enter into the mind of a hypothetical person having ordinary skills in the art to which the claimed invention pertains.

Practically, in China, the GPE requires the examination of non-obviousness by considering (1) whether the invention has prominent substantive features and

(2) whether the invention represents a notable progress. With respect to the former, SIPO applies a 3—step analytical method in order to decide whether an invention involves non—obviousness, i. e. , (i) identifying the closest prior art, (ii) determining distinguishing technical feature (s) and the technical problem actually solved; and (iii) examining whether or not the claimed invention would be obvious for one skilled person in the art. With respect to the latter, SIPO looks into whether or not the claimed invention brings any advantageous technical effect.

Indeed, the 3—step analytical method need to discern a subjective technical problem recorded in the original application documents and an objective technical problem. The objective technical problem, often different from the subjective technical problem, is formulated upon the determined distinguishing technical feature (s) between the claimed invention and the closest prior art, and varies in view of a prior art reference identified as the closest.

Pursuant to this 3—step analytical method, SIPO examiners readily use the claim in consideration as a blueprint where the technical problem which the claimed invention addresses and solves is treated as a known problem. Accordingly, the examiners would consider less of a motivation in combining several prior art references and/or common sense, and reject the claim for being obvious. Finally, obviously unimproved features are easily searched out, for example, in a prior art reference which is pertinent to the present application. Such a rationale will produce a strict non—obviousness standard.

Comparable to the non—obviousness requirement in China, 35 U. S. C. § 103 also requires an invention to be non—obvious. From the discussion above, the Chinese analysis employs a "problem and solution approach", where SIPO asks whether the technical solution that an invention provides to the objective technical problem being addressed would have been obvious to the person skilled in the art, rather than asking whether an invention is obvious in the American system.

Thus, in the United States, the method for conducting an obviousness analysis is a relatively straightforward analytical roadmap based on complex factual determinations. There isn't the dilemma of the subjective and object technical problems. In considering a combination of previously known elements, a teaching—suggestion—motivation test (the "TSM test")❶ has been used. With this test, only when the cited prior art references are relevant to each other and commonly point at the

❶ See e. g. , *Winner Int'l Royalty Corp. v. Wang*, 202 F. 3d. 1340, 1348 (Fed. Cir. , 2000).

claimed invention, i. e. all of them are relevant to the claimed invention, would those references be considered in determining whether one skilled in the art would be able to have conceived the claimed invention.

Consequently, such a rationale makes the American bar for non-obviousness lower than the Chinese one. However, the TSM test has been the subject of much criticism. The U. S. Supreme Court addressed this issue in KSR, supra, and held that the test analyzed the issue "in a narrow, rigid manner inconsistent with § 103 and our precedents". Accordingly, the Supreme Court decision in KSR raises the bar a bit, resulting in the following examination protocol in USPTO: If an obviousness decision may be made using the TSM test, then such a rejection should be made; If an obviousness decision cannot be made using the TSM test, then it is necessary to consider the ordinary skill and common sense in the art.

3. Difference in factors involved in a non-obviousness analysis

The general factual considerations in Chinese and the United States are roughly the same, it is like four Graham factors set forth by the Supreme Court in Graham v. John Deere Co. , 383 U. S. 1, 148 USPQ 459 (1966) as below:

(1) level of ordinary skill;

(2) scope and content of the prior art;

(3) differences between the claimed invention and the prior art; and

(4) secondary considerations.

Regarding factor (1), in China, a definition for a hypothetical person with ordinary skill in the art is given from the person's knowledge range (one knowledge range, which is common technical knowledge in the pertinent art) and capability's types (three kinds of capabilities, which consist of capability of applying routine experiment in the pertinent art, capability of accessing all the technologies existing before the filling date or the priority date in the pertinent art, and capability of accessing common technical knowledge and relevant prior art and applying routine experiment in the relevant art capability of being inspired by the technical problem), while in the United States, USPTO determines the level of ordinary skill by a fact inquiry with consideration of some or all of the following types of evidence (often in the form of expert witness testimony):

• Education level of the inventor;

• Education level of a typical worker (e. g. , whether the straw man would have a high school degree, college undergraduate degree, or graduate degree such as a master's or Ph. D. ;

- Type of problems encountered in the field;
- How quickly new innovation occurs in the field;
- Sophistication of the field (e. g. , is the invention a fishing lure or a method of cloning a gene?).

In this way, the level of ordinary skill in the art would vary with, e. g. , different technical field and problem to be solved. In litigation challenging a patent's validity for being obvious in the United States, the patentee usually will attempt to establish a level of ordinary skill as low as possible, such that the pending claimed invention would have been considered non-obvious by the largest possible number of persons while the challenger of validity typically will seek to raise that level.

4. Special analysis for non-obviousness in the United States

A. Teaching away

The Supreme Court in KSR, supra, stated that " [t] he Court relied upon the corollary principle that when the prior art teaches away from combining certain known elements, discovery of a successful means of combining them is more likely to be non-obvious". The 2020 USPTO KSR Guidelines also indicate that three "familiar lines of argument still apply" for traversing an obviousness rejection, including: (i) teaching away; (ii) lack of a reasonable expectation of success; and (iii) unexpected results. Thus, prosecuting a patent application before USPTO, a powerful argument to an obviousness rejection is that the reference "teaches away" from the claimed subject matter, i. e. , some language in the reference is inconsistent with the claimed subject matter, and would discourage or dissuade one skilled in the pertinent art from doing what the inventor actually and successfully did.

The GPE in China doesn't expressly state this analysis. But in practice, to consider whether the disclosures of several prior references, sometimes this analysis is used.

B. Other rebuttal evidence to traverse the ground of obviousness

The Supreme Court in KSR noted that the analysis supporting a rejection under 35 U. S. C. **103** should be made explicit. Accordingly, MPEP § 2141 exemplifies a few rationales that may support a rejection of obviousness:

(1) Combining prior art elements according to known methods to yield predictable results;

(2) Simple substitution of one known element for another to obtain predictable results;

(3) Use of a known technique to improve similar devices (methods, or products) in the same way;

(4) Applying a known technique to a known device (method, or product) ready for improvement to yield predictable results;

(5) "Obvious to try" – choosing from a finite number of identified and predictable solutions with a reasonable expectation of success;

(6) Known work in one field of endeavor may prompt variations of it for use in either the same field or a different one based on design incentives or other market forces if the variations are predictable to one of ordinary skill in the art;

(7) Some teaching, suggestion or motivation in the prior art that would have led one of ordinary skill to modify the prior art reference or combine prior art reference teachings to arrive at the claimed invention.

Thus, to rebut these rationales, the Applicant may submit rebuttal evidence including evidence of "secondary considerations", such as "commercial success, long felt but unsolved needs, [and] failure of others" (Graham v. John Deere Co. , 383 U. S. at 17, 148 USPQ at 467), and evidence of unexpected results. The evidence may be submitted to USPTO by way of affidavit or declaration under 37 CFR § 1. 132.

Similarly, in China although those rationales are not expressly stated, an examination opinion likely states that one with ordinary skill in the pertinent art would be able to obtain the claimed invention by "logical analysis, inference", "routine selection" and/or "limited number of experimentation". Also in China additional experimental data can be submitted to rebut a rejection for obviousness.

5. The destiny for the roughly same invention in the United States and China

It is clear that by common analysis rationale of non-obviousness, the standard in China is higher than that in the United States. The same invention may be likely patented in the United States while not in China. However, due to the different development levels in domestic economy, science and industry, the same invention may be patented in China while not in the United States, e. g. an invention in the computer science field may be patented in the United States because of the high level of ordinary skill in the United States. Furthermore, plus the difference of legal framework and language, the features and scopes of claims of the same invention adapted in the United States and China may be different, enlarged differences will exist in the non-obviousness analysis in the two countries.

Chinese Law and Practice on Determining Proximity of the Goods or Services

By: Di (Deland) Wu & Qinghong Xu

The determination of proximity of the goods or services and similarity of the marks, recited in many provisions, is the core of *Trademark Law of the People's Republic of China*❶ (*Chinese Trademark Law*) and an important factor for the establishment and enforcement of trademark rights. Under Article 8❷ of *Chinese Trademark Law*, the fundamental function of trademark is source–identifying, i. e. , distinguishing the goods of one's own from those of others. When the similarity of the marks is tested, one must consider whether the designated goods or services are similar.

In this article, we discuss the latest developments in China with respect to the judgment of similar goods or services.

1. Applicable Rules on Judgment of Similar Goods or Services

Applicable rules include the *Criteria for Trademark Examination* which was promulgated by the State Administration for Industry & Commerce of China (SAIC) in December 2005 and *Interpretation of the Supreme People's Court Concerning the Application of Laws in the Trial of Cases of Civil Disputes Arising from Trademarks* (the *Judicial Interpretation*) which was issued by the Supreme People's Court on October 12, 2002.

The *Criteria for Trademark Examination* prescribes that:

"Similar goods" means goods that are identical or similar in function, usage, raw material, that belong to the same or similar industry, that are sold through the same or similar sales channel (s), sale sites, and are aimed at the same or similar

---

❶ *Trademark Law of the People's Republic of China* refers to the second amendment to the *Chinese Trademark Law*, effective October 27, 2001.

❷ Article 8 of *Chinese Trademark Law* specifies: "An application for trademark registration may be filed for any visible mark including word, design, letter, number, 3D (three–dimension) mark or color combination, or the combination of the elements above mentioned, that can distinguish the commodities of the natural person, legal person or other organization from those of others.

group of consumers.

"Similar services" means services that are identical or similar to each other in purpose, content, way of serving and targeted consumers.

"Goods and services are similar" means that the goods and services are associated with each other and thus are likely to cause confusion.

Article 11 of the *Judicial Interpretation* prescribes that:

"Similar services" means services that are identical to each other in purpose, content, way of serving and target consumers; or the relative public tends to think the services are associated with each other and thus are likely to cause confusion.

"Goods and services are similar" means that the goods and services are associated with each other and thus are likely to cause confusion.

While the above rules are similar, the trademark administrative authority considers the proximity of the goods or services per se (in consideration of function, usage, production sectors, etc.) and the court emphasizes the likelihood of consumer confusion. Despite the difference, some commentators have suggested that the practice is consistent and the rules are just specified from different angles. ❶

2. The Function of Classification of Similar Goods or Services

Based on *International Classification of Goods and Services* (*Nice Classification*, 10th Ed), the *Classification of Similar Goods or Services* (the *Classification*) has been promulgated by SAIC and took effect on January 1, 2012.

The *Criteria for Trademark Examination* prescribes that:

China Trademark Office (hereinafter referred to as "CTO") and China Trademark Review and Adjudication Board (hereinafter referred to as "TRAB") shall use *Classification of Similar Goods or Services* as a reference. With regard to cases of trademark refusal review, opposition, opposition review, dispute, revocation or revocation review, when judging whether the goods or services are similar, the CTO and the TRAB shall make decisions on specific cases based on this criteria.

Article 12 of the *Judicial Interpretation* prescribes that:

When judging whether the goods or services are similar, the court shall make its judgment based on the average knowledge of the public pertaining to the goods or service. The *International Classification System of Goods and Services* and *Classification of Similar Goods or Services* can be used as references.

---

❶ Research on Administrative Adjudication of Trademark Rights [M]. Beijing: Intellectual Property Publishing House, 2008: 89.

Accordingly, both trademark administrative authority and the court regard the Classification as a reference not a legal basis.

However, to maintain the consistency of trademark registration, the trademark administrative authority applies the *Classification* literally and rigidly with few exceptions. In some cases, the TRAB held that, without much rationale, the *Classification* is perceived as black letter law. In contrast, a judge of the Beijing First Intermediate People's Court considered the *Classification* is procedural rather than substantive, and was of opinion that the judgment of similar goods based on the claims of the parties would be helpful in perfecting the Classification. ❶

3. Recent Cases

(1) Hunan Changkang Shiye Limited v. the TRAB and Changsha Jiajia Food Group Limited❷

The opposed trademark (applicant: Hunan Changkang Shiye Limited):

class/group/goods: 29/08/ Sesame oil

The cited trademarks (applicant: Jiajia Food Group Ltd.):

(cited trademark Ⅰ)　　　(cited trademark Ⅱ)　　　(cited trademark Ⅲ)

Note: according to the Classification, the designated goods "Sesame oil" in Class 29 of the opposed trademark are not similar to the designated goods "Soya sauce; etc. " in Class 30 of the cited trademarks.

In the adjudication No. 34098 issued on December 7, 2009, the TRAB reasoned that the designated goods "Sesame oil" in Class 29 of the opposed trademark can be differentiated from the designated goods "Soya sauce; etc. " in Class 30 of cited trademarks in terms of raw materials, production and sales channels, and held

❶　Research on Administrative Adjudication of Trademark Rights [M]. Beijing: Intellectual Property Publishing House, 2008: 94.

❷　Intellectual Property Trial Case Guide of the Supreme People's Court (Fourth Series) [M]. Beijing: China Legal Publishing House, 2012: 225.

that the goods are not similar, therefore there is no likelihood of consumer confusion. Accordingly, the opposed trademark should be approved for registration.

Jiajia Food Group Ltd. (Jiajia) appealed to Beijing First Intermediate People's court, who considered "Sesame oil" and "Soya sauce; etc." as similar goods as they are cooking spices and similar in sales channels and consumers. Assessing the likelihood of confusion to the public, the court first looked into the trademark reputation, where in this case, Jiajia produced a large amout of evidence showing the cited trademarks enjoyed certain reputation prior to the application date of the opposed trademark. The court further considered the similarity of the marks and decided that the opposed trademark was similar to the three citations. Accordingly, the adjudication No. 34098 was revoked, which decision was affirmed by Beijing Higher People's court.

In an appeal to the Supreme People's Court, the Court affirmed the lower courts' decisions on August 31, 2011, and further elaborated a few factors in determining whether confusion between related goods is likely, including the proximity of the goods, the reputation of the cited trademarks, and the similarity of the marks. The Court viewed that "sesame oil" and "Soya sauce; etc." are similar enough as cooking spices with similar packaging and that given the reputation of the cited trademarks, consumers would assume that they were offered by the same or affiliated source.

(2) Hangzhou Zhuomuniao Limited v. the TRAB and Qihao (Group) Limited❶

The disputed trademark (applicant: Hangzhou Zhuomuniao Limited):

 Class/group/goods: 25/01/ Shoes; Boots

The cited trademarks (applicant: Qihao (Group) Limited):

---

❶ Intellectual Property Trial Case Guide of the Supreme People's Court (Fourth Series), China Legal Publishing House, 2012, Page 232.

（引证商标一）

cited trademark I

（引证商标二）

cited trademark II

Note: according to the *Classification*, the designated goods "Shoes; Boots" in Class 25 of the disputed trademark are not similar to the designated goods "Clothing; etc." in Class 25 and the designated goods "bag; etc" in Class 18 of the cited trademarks.

Providing a similar reasoning to the case above, the TRAB decided that the goods are not similar based on the *Classification*, therefore the disputed trademark should be maintained for registration. The decision was first affirmed by Beijing First Intermediate People's court, and was then reversed by Beijing Higher People's court. The appellate court held that although the designated goods of the disputed trademark and cited trademarks are not fallen into the similar subclass according to the *Classification*, they belong to wearing goods , and if both are used in commerce, they would have confused consumers.

Upholding the appellate court's ruling, the Supreme People's Court has emphasized that the *Classification* shall not be applied mechanically, and that to answer the question of likelihood of consumer confusion, a few relevant factors, in combination of specific facts, have to be considered. Here, the Court opined that while "Shoes; Boots" and "clothing; bags; etc" differ in raw materials and usage, the modern marketing methods have unified those products in the same manufacturers, retailers or distribution networks, and thus the same consumers would confuse the origin of the disputed trademark and cited trademarks with an assumption of common source affiliation.

4. Conclusion

Thus, while judging whether goods or services are similar, the court pays more attention to whether consumers would confuse the origin of goods, taking the other factors into consideration, e. g. , the trademark reputation, the trademark originality, the trademark similarity, the goods relevancy and the bad faith.

The Supreme People's Court holds that once the related public tends to assume the goods or services were offered by the same or affiliated parties, the goods or services shall constitute similar. In addition, as similar goods or services should be determined based on a specific facts pattern, the conclusion should be drawn on a case-by-case basis. ❶

In addition, we, as experienced trademark attorneys, have found that the trademark administrative authority is mechanic and rigid in applying the Classification while the court is more liberal. It is advisable for the applicant to produce more use of evidence in trademark cases, which might become the basis for the authority not to strictly adhere to the Classification on specific cases.

---

❶ Intellectual Property Trial Case Guide of the Supreme People's Court (Fourth Series) [M]. Beijing: China Legal Publishing House, 2012: 239–240.

Eye on Amendments That Go beyond Original Disclosure

Similar to the law in most other jurisdictions, Article 33 of *Chinese Patent Law* prohibits amendments go beyond the scope of the original disclosure of the application❶ as filed. In recent years, Article 33 is always a hot topic in Chinese prosecution and litigation practice, and even has been labeled as a "Chinese-Style" provision by many foreign attorneys. While the ground of going beyond the scope of the original disclosure has constantly been asserted by a patent examiner or an invalidation requester, a question arises as to "why the content of the amendment is supported by the original application documents, but goes beyond the scope of the original application documents".

To answer this question, this article looks into Chinese prosecution and litigation practice about Article 33, with case studies and practical tips, in comparison with the practice about the support requirement under Article 26. 4 of *Chinese Patent Law*.

1. Guidelines For Examination

With respect to Article 33, *Guidelines for Examination* (the *Guidelines*) provide that an applicant may amend his or her application for a patent, but the amendment to the application for a patent for invention or utility model may not go beyond the scope of disclosure described in the initial description and claims based on a direct and unambiguous determination.

With respect to Article 26. 4, the *Guidelines* specify that the technical solution for which protection is sought in each of the claims shall be a solution that a person skilled in the art can reach directly or by generalization from the contents sufficiently disclosed in the description, and shall not go beyond the scope of the contents disclosed in the description based on the knowledge in the relevant prior art.

---

❶ The application refers to an invention or utility model patent or application, not a design.

2. Comparison between Article 33 and Article 26. 4

A. Legislative Intent

The commonness of legislative original idea for both Article 33 and Article 26. 4 is to balance the interests of the patentees and those of the public. The difference is as follows: Article 33 should reflect the first-filing-principle, preventing from obtaining unfair right through amendments; however, Article 26. 4 focuses on preventing from obtaining unfair right through over generalization.

B. Applicable Timing and Object

While Article 33 is directed to amended claims or description after filing, Article 26. 4 is directed to the original claims or the amended claims. During patent prosecution, once the claims are amended, the examination with Article 33 shall first proceed before that of Article 26. 4.

C. Considered Contents

The examination with Article 33 is based on the contents described in the original description and claims. However, the examination with Article 26. 4 is based on the disclosure of the original description, meanwhile, equivalents or obvious variants reasonably predicted are allowed to be added in the observations for responding to an office action.

3. Practice before the State Intellectual Property Office (SIPO)

A. Logical Criterion in Examination

In SIPO, for Article 26. 4, the scope of disclosure includes: contents literally described, contents determined directly and unambiguously, and equivalents or obvious variants reasonably predicted. For Article 33, the scope of described contents includes: contents literally described, and contents determined directly and unambiguously.

Taking a simple example, if only "Au, Ag or Cu" as conductor is described in the original description and generalization expression "metal" is described in the original claims, the scope of disclosure deemed by the examiner includes "Au, Ag or Cu" and other metal known as conductor in the art. However, if the generalization expression "metal" is introduced through amendments, not in the original claims, the scope of described contents deemed by the examiner includes only "Au, Ag or Cu", not allowing introducing other metals through the specific generalization expression "metal" based on the common knowledge in the art.

B. Misunderstandings to Be Avoided

1st Misunderstanding: The amended technical solution supported by the original description shall not cause the defect "going beyond the scope".

As the above-mentioned example, due to different logical criterion for "supporting" and "going beyond the scope", one claim with the same protection scope may have different fate, allowed or rejected, depending on whether the claim is original or amended.

2nd Misunderstanding: "amendments shall not go beyond the scope..." for one claim means that "not expanding the protection scope of a claim", so further limitation to claim would not cause the defect "going beyond the scope".

The true meaning of "not going beyond the scope" for one claim is: no new technical content is added, which is not just a problem of enlarging or narrowing protection scope. therefore one proposes that the expression "going beyond the scope..." is not exact itself, and needs to be modified to avoid the misunderstanding from public. Maybe, the expression "no amendments shall introduce new matter into the disclosure of the invention" in US patent law is more intelligible. Herein, it is expected to improve the corresponding expression in Chinese Patent Law.

3rd Misunderstanding: Adding the technical feature described in the original description would not cause the defect "going beyond the scope".

"Amendments shall not go beyond the scope..." for one claim means that the amended technical solution as a whole should be described in the original documents. Even if a single technical feature is described, but its combination with other technical features is not described, such amendments through such combination would still cause the defect "going beyond the scope".

4th Misunderstanding: Intermediate generalization within the protection scope of claims would not cause the defect "going beyond the scope".

In practice, amendments through generalization tend to have great possibility of "going beyond the scope", but this is not absolute. It still depends on the relationship among those technical features reflected in the original description.

For example, the original claim, which reads that "a Y, including A, B and C", is amended as a new claim, which reads that "a Y, including A, B, C and D", according to one embodiment of Y including A, B, C, D and E. If the relationship between D and E is close and codependent, such amended claim tends to be deemed as "going beyond the scope"; if not, such amended claim tends to be deemed as "not going beyond the scope".

4. Our Successful Reexamination Cases

Case 1: focusing on amendments based on drawings (ZL200580008197.2; Reexamination Decision No. 33336)

The present examination criterion for whether amendments based on drawings "go beyond the scope" or not is that, the person skilled in the art can not directly and unambiguously determine the quantitative information such as dimension or parameter from drawings, but can determine the qualitative information of components shown in the drawings, such as relative position and relative dimension relationship, when comprehending the whole of the description and drawings. Thereby, the technical features such as dimensions by measuring in the drawings are not allowed to be added into the application documents. In fact, even the qualitative information from the drawings is objected to by some "strict" examiner during the substantive examination, which increases the difficulty of responding to office action. The applicant struggles for patent rights through reexamination proceedings, for example, the reexamination case for ZL200580008197.2 below.

The original description reads that: a bi-negative pressure turbine comprises a plurality of impact tooth-plate. Each impact tooth-plate 20 includes a mounting portion 210 and a working portion 220 connected with the mounting portion. FIGs. 1 and 2 are front view and side view of the impact tooth-plate 20.

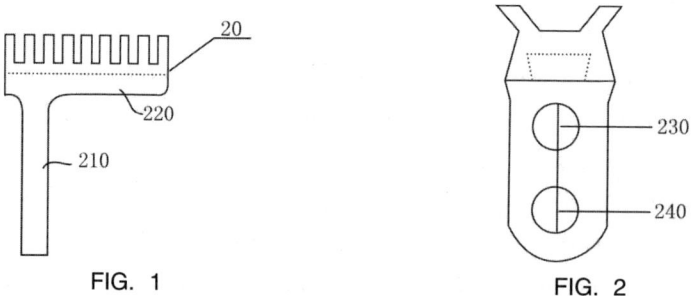

FIG. 1   FIG. 2

During the substantive examination, for emphasizing the advantages that such materials (e.g. Chinese medicinal materials) can be effectively crushed by the impact and shearing actions of the impact tooth-plate structure, in order to overcome a rejection for lack of the inventiveness, the following technical features obtained only from the drawings are added into the independent claim: "pairs of impact tooth-plates are formed at top of the working portion, wherein the impact teeth in each pair are inclined in such a manner that the distance between tops of the teeth in each pair is more far than that between roots of the teeth, and an acute angle is formed between the inclining direction of each tooth and a plane of teeth roots in each pair".

The viewpoints in the Rejection Decision:

(1) The added technical features cover many arrangements of tooth not shown in the FIG. 2. However, FIG. 2 just shows one arrangement of tooth having specific length, shape, dimensions.

(2) Although the drawings are part of the original disclosure, a drawing showing a new inclining manner of the teeth different from FIG. 2 can be obviously drafted according to the literal expression of the added technical features since the meaning of literal expression is more extensive than that shown in the specific drawing.

The Patent Reexamination Board withdrew the Rejection Decision based on the following reasons:

(1) The added technical features can be directly and unambiguously determined from the description and FIG. 2;

(2) Disapproving of the examiner's reasoning for the amendments going beyond the scope— the literal expression of the added technical features cover a new inclining manner of the teeth different from FIG. 2.

This case suggests that we should not deem a drawing as just one specific concept, but deem literal expression as generalized concept.

Case 2: focusing on amendments to correct an obvious error (CN200710138307.8, Reexamination Decision No. 45140)

The original description reads that: a voice coil motor positioning device comprises a fixed part 10, a movable part 12 and a connecting part 14, wherein, the movable part 12, movably arranged on the fixed part 10, comprises a lens component 120 and a winding component 122. The fixed part 10 comprises a first magnet assembly 102 including a first magnet 1022. An electrical field generated by the winding component 122 takes a mutual action with the magnetic field generated by the first magnet assembly 1022, thereby causing an electric-magnetic force for actuating the movable part 12. The first magnet 1022 is fixed to the lens assembly 120 and slidably disposed inside the winding component 122 with a clearance.

The applicant amended "The first magnet 1022 is fixed to the lens assembly 120" into "The first magnet 1022 is fixed to the fixed part 10".

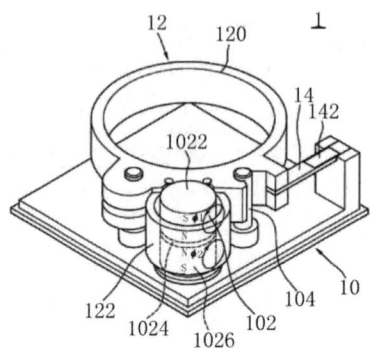

图 1

The examiner rejected such amendments for "going beyond the scope" based on the following reasons: The self-contradictory expression about connection relation between the first magnet 1022 and the lens assembly 120 in the original description only indicates that the first magnet 1022 is not fixed to the lens assembly 120. What can be directly and unambiguously determined from the scope of contents described in the original description is that "the first magnet 1022 is part of the fixed part 10", not "the first magnet 1022 is fixed to the fixed part 10".

The Reexamination Board concluded that the original description has clearly indicated that the first magnet 1022 is a part of the fixed part, the lens assembly 120 is a part of the movable part 12, and thereby "the first magnet 1022 is fixed to the lens assembly 120" is an obvious error and "the first magnet 1022 is fixed to the fixed part 10" can be exclusively determined from the original description, which conforms to the provision of Article 33.

By comparison between the examiner's reasoning and the Reexamination Board's conclusion, it can be found that, during the examination proceedings, the examiner tends to envision several possible amendments to the contradictory contents. If no ample reasons can convince the examiner that the amendments are exclusive, the amendments tend to be deemed as "going beyond the scope". However, the Reexamination Board will give an impersonal and direct technical judgment from the whole description not just in an exclusive thought.

5. Difference in Practice between Prosecution and Administrative Litigation

A. "Strict Criteria" in the Examination Department of SIPO

Due to the strict quality control procedure within SIPO, examiners mechanically apply the *Logical Criterion in Examination* in looking for express disclosure to support an amendment for compliance with Article 33, while overlooking what one skilled in the art would have recognized from the entire specification with respect to the contents disclosed expressly, implicitly or inherently.

B. "Fair Criteria" before the Patent Reexamination Board

The Patent Reexamination Board would further consider both the whole description and contribution to the prior art, and when appropriate, provides a suggestion as to amendments not "going beyond the scope" . For the application having the prospect of inventiveness and being rejected only under Article 33, the Reexamination Board may follow fair criteria to Article 33 by addressing what one skilled in the art would have recognized from the entire specification.

C. "Guiding Opinion" of the People's Court in Litigation

For the cases appealed from the Reexamination Board, the People's Court will not limit itself to the *Guidelines*, but address this issue in a variety of ways, according to the legislative intent of Article 33, with a strong presumption of validity of issued patents. However, the judicial opinions, though guiding, are not binding in SIPO.

For example, in patent administrative proceedings for invalidation of ZL00131800. 4 about "ink cartridge", the Beijing First Intermediate People's Court upheld the Patent Reexamination Board's decision to strike down the patent validity on the ground that amending "semiconductor storage device" into "storage device" goes beyond the scope of contents described in the original description and claims. However, the Beijing Higher People's Court overturned the lower court's decision considering the estoppel doctrine as the patentee has, if fact, construed "storage device" as "semiconductor storage device" in substantive examination and invalidation proceedings. Affirming with a different reasoning, the Supreme People's Court set forth a new standard for determining compliance with Article 33, by construing the as-filed-original disclosure to include literal and graphical contents together with some obvious content envisioned by the ordinary technicians in this art.

Another example is patent administrative trial for invalidation of ZL03150996. 7 about "Composition of Amlodipine and Irbesartan". In the invalidation proceedings, the recited ratio of Amlodipine to Irbesartan 1：10~50 was amended as 1：30, according to the described embodiment of 1mg/kg Amlodipine and 30mg/kg Irbesartan. The Patent Reexamination Board insisted that while this embodiment describes a fixed dosage, it can not be determined that other dosages satisfying the ratio of 1：30 can produce the same technical effects. The Supreme People's Court opined that the description of 1mg/kg and 30mg/kg supported the amendment to recite a 1：30 ratio, therefore the requirement under Article 33 was met. As to whether the fixed dosage species would have satisfied the ratio genus, according to the court, it shall be examined for compliance with Article 26.4, not Article 33.

6. Suggestion on Strategy of Patent Prosecution

(1) When drafting application documents, it would be beneficial to describe the technical solutions or features with different layers of scope such as intermediate-level generalization or higher-level generalization in the original description and claims.

(2) When drafting the application documents, structural features shown in the drawings should be literally provided in the description in detail, and improvement described in the description should be included in the original claims.

(3) When making amendments for responding to an office action, it is suggested to firstly point out the literal basis in the original description or claims. In a case where there is no literal basis, it is necessary to provide ample reasoning for the contents directly and unambiguously determined from the original description or claims. If the applicant has no option but to combine the common knowledge to deduce the amendments, it is suggested to provide the appropriate evidence and get ready for patent administrative proceedings.

(4) When making amendments for responding to an office action, if the intermediate generalization is desirable for a protection scope, it is suggested to use literal support in the description as much as possible.

(5) For important cases, on one hand, additional procedure such as reexamination or administrative proceedings should be fully employed to fight for patent rights of a valuable invention. On the other hand, it may be worthwhile to consider filing a divisional application for a patent right claiming a moderate protection.

As great attention has been drawn from applicants, patent attorneys from different countries or regions, SIPO and other judicial authorities, we are expecting that the law and practice of Article 33 will become imcreasingly reasonable.

Discussions on "A Defect Point" Included In a Claim under Chinese Patent Practice

By: Xiaoying Wu

The strength and predictability of the Chinese patent system is critical for a life-sciences company who seeks to boost its business in China. There are, however, several considerations a patent practitioner should be aware when advising a company whether to file and how to prepare a patent application for filing in China. One of these considerations is addressed in this article, i. e. , when the workability of an invention within claim scopes is reasonably doubted (e. g. , the existence of a defect point is disclosed), whether the "failure" of the invention can be accepted and if so, to what extent. Without a definite answer to the questions, we provide below recent cases, together with our thoughts and practical suggestions.

1. What is "A Defect Point"?

"A defect point" refers to a non-workable data point (i. e. , example) disclosed in a patent application which is unable to solve technical problems and achieve technical effects of a claimed invention. A claim will cover such a defect point when the scope of the claim is summarized to include such a non-workable example.

We will discuss hereinafter whether a defect point covered in a claim would influence allowance of the claim during prosecution procedure, and influence stability of an allowed claim based on two recent cases.

2. Legal Justification

The requirement that the applicant/patentee adequately disclose his invention to obtain the right to exclude others from making, using, selling, offering for sale, or importing the claimed invention is mandated by the *Chinese Patent Law*, Article 26, fourth paragraph (Art. 26. 4), which provides: " [t] he claims shall **be supported** by the description and shall define the extent of the patent protection sought for in a clear and concise manner. " (emphasis added.)

The emphasized term is one of the requirements from Art. 26.4, which requires both the written support for the claim language and enabling support for the claim scope. Although the law is silent with respect to a defect point, the *Guideline for Patent Examination* (the *Guideline*) specifies that if one skilled in the art would reasonably doubt that a claim includes a species within the claim scope unable to solve technical problems and achieve technical effects of the claimed invention, then the claim would be considered not supported. See Part II, Chapter 2, § 3.2.1.

3. Two Cases

Case I

A granted patent (patent No. 93109045.8), entitled "Stereoselective Glycosylation Process" and owned by Eli Lilly and Company (Eli Lilly), was challenged for validity before the Patent Reexamination Board (the Board) in 2006. Claim 1 of this patent relates to a process for preparing difluoronucleoside with concentrated β-anomer, wherein steps of the process and reactive conditions such as raw materials and temperatures of reactions are recited. This patent aims to provide a process for preparing difluoronucleoside with concentrated β-anomers and the technical problem to be solved is to produce the said product. In the description, there are 104 examples among which 11 examples failed to obtain the product of difluoronucleoside with concentrated β-anomers. However, the reactive conditions of the 11 examples making contributions to prior arts fall into the scope of claim 1. That is to say, claim 1 covers 11 defect points. The key issue in dispute was whether claim 1 meets the requirement of Art. 26.4.

The Board answered no (i.e., all the claims invalid) on the grounds that: Claim 1 comprises reactive conditions under which it is uncertain whether concentrated β-anomers would be produced. One skilled in the art would need a large amount of experiments or undue experiments to identify the technical solutions which solve the technical problem from claim 1. Thus, claim 1 is inconformity with the provisions of Art. 26.4.

Eli Lilly appealed to Beijing First Intermediate People's Court, arguing that the "undue experiments" cited by the Board, is not stipulated in the *Patent Law*, nor in the *Guideline*, and is not a correct criteria to evaluate the support issue. Eli Lilly further articulated that the presence of non-workable embodiments would not render claims non-supported as one skilled in the art would be able to determine the workability of the claims based upon the entire teaching in the specification with significant numbers of workable embodiments.

Beijing First Intermediate People's Court ((2007) No. 922) withdrew the Board's decision and concluded that the criteria to judge whether a claim is supported by the description depends on whether technical solutions claimed in this claim can be reached directly or generalized from the contents sufficiently disclosed in the description, and shall not go beyond the scope of the contents disclosed in the description, while the application of "undue experiments" was improper. On appeal, Beijing High People's Court overturned the lower court's ruling ((2008) No. 451), reasoning that where generalization of a claim includes contents speculated by the applicant and the effect thereof is difficult to determine or evaluate beforehand, the generalization shall be regarded as going beyond the scope of the contents disclosed in the description, or in other words, if the generalization of a claim is such that the person skilled in the art can reasonably doubt that one or more specific terms or options included in the generic terms or parallel options cannot solve the technical problem aimed to be solved by the invention or utility model and achieve the same technical effects, then it shall be taken that the claim is not supported by the description.

Rejecting the patentee's request for rehearing, the Supreme People's Court opined that a technical solution to be pursued in a claim should be that one skilled in the art can reach directly or generalize from the contents sufficiently disclosed in the description, and shall not go beyond the scope of the contents disclosed in the description. If the generalization of a claim is such that the person skilled in the art can reasonably doubt that one or more specific terms or options included in the generic terms or parallel options cannot solve the technical problem aimed to be solved by the invention or utility model and achieve the same technical effects, then it shall be taken that the claim is not supported by the description. In the description of the present invention, there are 11 examples cannot obtain difluoronucleoside with concentrated β-anomer. Furthermore, according to the description, there are a lot of factors to affect the stereoselective process, and the factors generalized in the claimed process of claim 1 are overly broad. One skilled in the art reasonably assumes that claim 1 includes many other technical solutions which cannot solve the technical problem in addition to the 11 non-workable examples. Meanwhile, it is not easy for one skilled in the art to obtain the technical solutions which can solve the technical problem according to routine experiments under a proper reactive condition selected from such many various reactive conditions recited in claim 1. Instead, it needs a large amount of experiments or undue experiments to determine the scope of claim 1. Thus, claim 1 cannot be supported by the description which is in conformity with the provision of Art. 26.4.

Case II

This case relates to an application with application number 2004800064116 having title "variants of α-amylase family" and was finally rejected for lack of support on February 12, 2010 in the substantive examination procedure. The rejection was maintained by the Board on March 16, 2012. The Board concluded that claim 1 cannot be supported by the description for the reason that one skilled in the art would not be able to predict reasonably all the enzyme variants included in claim 1 can solve the technical problem and achieve the technical effects in view that the description includes a non-workable example. In this application, claim 1 relates to an enzyme variant of a reference enzyme, wherein the amino acid mutation of the variant is A230V or one or more mutations in addition to the mutation of A230V compared with the reference enzyme, and said enzyme variant has a higher hydrolase activity. Although most of the examples in the description showed a higher hydrolase activity, the variant in example 4 with two mutations including A230V showed reduction of the hydrolase activity comparing the wild enzyme. Based on this, the Board reasoned that one skilled in the art would reasonably doubt any enzyme variants with mutations A230V and one or more mutations may increase the hydrolase activity or decrease the hydrolase activity of the wild enzyme, therefore he would not be able to reasonably predict all the enzyme variants with mutations A230V in combination other mutations would solve the technical problem and achieve the technical effects. Accordingly, the Board maintained the lack-of-support rejection for claim 1 under Art. 26.4.

4. Attitudes to "A Defect Point" of the Chinese Patent Office, Board and Court

It can be seen from the two cases above, whether in a prosecution procedure or in a procedure after grant, the Chinese Patent Office, Board and Court hold the same position that a claim covering a defect point cannot be supported by the description, despite that it seems a defect point is not a direct reason for such a conclusion. In the decision of the Board or opinion of the Supreme People's Court, it is quoted therein that "if the generalization of a claim is such that the person skilled in the art can reasonably doubt that one or more specific terms or options included in the generic terms or parallel options cannot solve the technical problem aimed to be solved by the invention or utility model and achieve the same technical effects, then it shall be taken that the claim is not supported by the description."

5. Discussions and Suggestions

The above cases raise the question: if the defect points have not been disclosed in the application documents, or the defect points have been excluded from the claims, would case II obtain a patent right and case I not be invalidated? Although none of the Patent Office, Board and Court regard defect points included in the claims as a direct reason for lack of support rejection, it appears that the defect points provide evidences for one skilled in the art to reasonabe doubt that one or more specific terms or options included in the generic terms or parallel options cannot solve the technical problem aimed to be solved by the invention or utility model and achieve the same technical effects. That is to say, the description of defect points causes the reasonable doubt.

Actually, in the prosecution procedure, it is impossible for examiners to validate experimental results described in an application. Without validation by experiments, how can "reason able doubt" be obtained? It is most convincing to provide evidences. In the case that an application discloses a non-workable example, the non-workable example provides the evidence to lead one skilled in the art to reasonabe doubt. Provided that the two cases have not disclosed the non-workable examples, how can one skilled in the art raise reasonabe doubt?

From this view, it is advantageous to the patentee or applicant not to disclose the defect points in the application documents, which, however, would be inequitable in some jurisdictions. Under such a situation, it is more important and feasible to consider how to disclose honestly the non-workable data and simultaneously to pursue a reasonable scope of protection.

Turning to case I, the defect points were pointed out in the invalidation procedure after grant, where the patentee is confined greatly to amend claims i. e., choosing from deleting a claim or technical solution and incorporating claims to reduce the scope of the protection. It is always unallowable to amend claim 1 by disclaiming the defect points in this procedure. It is likely to result in invalid claims due to no allowable amendments being reached. In view of this, it is critical to design a strategy for drafting an application document to leave some space for amending in the future. Not only should proper scopes of claims be considered, but also drafted at various levels in independent and dependent claims when drafting a set of claims. In other words, applicant may pursue a broad scope in an independent claim, and arrange different intermediate scopes in dependent claims. In such a way, a claim set contains not only a broad scope including a non-workable technical solution, but also a narrow scope excluding the non-workable technical solution to meet various countries or regions requirements. Thus, the applicant may have a chance to obtain a broad scope and can stably protect the crucial technical solution. Even though China, has a strict regulation on amending claims, such a claim set can avoid being in a passive position leaving no choice for case I in the invalidation procedure.

Patent Protection: Defenses—Options and Strategies[*]

By: Yan Hong & Qinghong Xu

In China, infringement allegations may put your products or services in jeopardy, and the very fact that a lawsuit has been brought may cause your customers to switch to other products, to seek costly indemnity from your company, and often, both. Lung Tin International Intellectual Property Agent Ltd. (Lung Tin) works with a variety of clients in patent litigation.

At Lung Tin, we understand the costs to defend alone can be large without even considering the downside risk of a finding of infringement. However, an effective, "business-first" defense can create opportunities which could turn these negatives into positive business opportunities. Thus, our very first questions in defending an infringement lawsuit are about your business and goals. Then, with your business and goals in mind, we will help you to design defense options and strategies in an effort to turn patent infringement claims into a positive opportunity or even re-position your company in the market.

In this short article, we will lay out some common strategies of defenses used in Chinese patent litigation. Determining and recommending the right strategy for you and your particular situation are our strengths.

1. Defenses Specified in *Chinese Patent Law*

A. Act not be patent infringement

According to provisions of *Chinese Patent Law*, the duration of the patent right commences from the filing date of a patent application while the patent right shall become effective as of the publication date. [1] This means the exploitation of a patent from the filing date to the publication date will not constitute patent infringement. If an alleged infringing act took place in this period, the defendant can make a defense

---

First published at China IP Focus 2011, Managing Intellectual Propety, United Kingdom, 2011.

[1] *See* Articles 39, 40 and 42 of *Patent Law of the People's Republic of China*.

of non-infringement. It should be noted that *Chinese Patent Law* also provides a pre-grant protection which allows a patent owner to obtain reasonable royalty damages for infringing activities that occurred after the publication date and before the issued date. ❶

B. Acts not be deemed as patent infringement

Article 69 of *Chinese Patent Law* stipulates five acts that shall not be deemed to be patent infringement. The five acts relate to the defenses of patent right exhaustion, prior use, temporary transit, scientific experimental use, and Bolar exception.❷

(i) patent right exhaustion

So far, there is no case law to the point concerning the patent right exhaustion doctrine. According to Chinese legislative interpretation, the right exhaustion is to a worldwide extent, Since China permits "parallel importation" of a patented product legally obtained outside of China. As for whether a patent owner is permitted to set forth reasonable restrictions on use imposed on its downstream customers, Chinese patent practice commonly holds an opinion of "first sale exhaustion,❸❹" such that the first unrestricted sale of a patented item effectively exhausts the patent owner's control over that item.

(ii) prior use

The prior use doctrine has been gradually accepted by Chinese patent practice and codified into *Chinese Patent Law* in 2008, which specifies that "[i] n a patent infringement dispute, if the accused infringer has evidence to prove that the technology or design exploited is an existing technology or design, the exploitation shall not constitute a patent right infringement. " See id. Article 62.

The following factors will be taken into consideration when the prior-use right is claimed: (a) the prior manufactured product/used method, or the product/method that has made necessary preparations for the manufacture or use, shall be identical to the patented technology; (b) the phrase "made necessary preparations for the manufacture or use" means (b1) main technical drawings or process documents necessary for implementing an invention have been completed, or (b2) main equipment or raw materials necessary for implementing an invention has been manufactured or pur-

---

❶ *See* Article 13 of *Patent Law of the People's Republic of China*.

❷ *See* Article 69 of *Patent Law of the People's Republic of China*.

❸ *See* YIN XINTIAN. Patent Protection [M]. Beijing: Intellectual Property Press, 2005: 92.

❹ Also *see* XIAO HAI. Summary of Seminar on Theory and Practice of Patent Infringement Defense [J]. China Patent & Trademarks, 2010 (1).

chased; (c) the original scope includes the scale of production which has existed and the scale of production which can be attained by using or according to an existing production equipment before the patent application date; (d) the prior-use right can not be assigned or licensed to any other party, but the product can be sold together with the company which has the right;❶ (e) the prior-use right includes the right to sell the product manufactured based on the prior-use right; and (f) the prior-use technology shall be self-developed or legally obtained. ❷

(iii) temporary transit

Defense of temporary transit will not be explained in details because it is seldom used in Chinese patent infringement litigation.

(iv) scientific experimental use

Although the scientific experimental use doctrine allows the use of a patented invention for purposes of scientific inquiry, the Chinese courts have applied this doctrine in a very strict manner. When the doctrine is claimed, the court will examine: (a) whether the accused infringer used the patented technology for gaining profits; (b) whether there is potential patent infringement when the patented technology is used for scientific experiments; (c) whether the plaintiff has suffered damages because of the utilization for scientific experiments; (d) when and how the patented technology is used. ❸ But some scholars have argued that in order to encourage research and development, the doctrine should not be examined too strictly, and when it is considered by the courts, the profitability shall not be a factor. ❹

(v) Bolar exception

Bolar exception was newly added to *Chinese Patent Law* in 2008, and its scope has not been interpreted in any cases. In the Seminar on Theory and Practice of Patent Infringement Defense held by Beijing No. 1 Intermediate People's Court on November 30, 2009, a research group of the same court raised an issue regarding the timing for filing a regulatory review of a generic drug application. The research group explained that regulatory examination and approval of pharmaceuticals usually take 2 to 3 years for final approval in China, if an application for regulatory review were

---

❶ *See* Article 15 of *Interpretation of the Supreme People's Court on Several Issues Concerning the Application of Law in the Trial of Patent Infringement Dispute Cases*; also *see* WANG Xiaozhong v. Zhonggao Company, (2002) GMZ No. 3.

❷ *See* No. 3 civil tribunal of Beijing High People's Court, Study On Intellectual Property Litigation [M]. Beijing: Intellectual Property Press, 2003: 44.

❸ *See supra* note 7 at 45.

❹ *See supra* note 5 at 97.

filed when a patent for a pharmaceutical would remain valid for 10 to 15 years, the applicant should not be exempted from liability. ❶ However, the Chinese regulatory authority has not enacted any rules to respond the Bolar exception.

2. Defenses in Practice

Except for the above defenses in law, there are some commonly used defenses in Chinese patent practice.

A. Right defenses

A valid patent legally obtained is the only basis for patent infringement litigation. So if possible, it would be quite advantageous for the defendant in patent infringement litigation to raise the issues regarding whether the patent in dispute is valid or whether the complaint i. e. , the patentee abuses its right.

(ⅰ) patent validity

In China, instead of arguing a defense in civil courts, it is preferable to instead argue that the patent to be enforced is invalid, however, before the Patent Reexamination Board (the PRB), particularly for a utility model or design patent which is not subjected to the substantial examination. Except for counter – attacking the plaintiff before the PRB, this defense will affect the legal proceedings and gain more time for the defendant. According to *Several Provisions of the Supreme People's Court on Issues Concerning the Application of Law in the Trial of Patent Disputes* which have quasi–legal force on lower courts in their trials of patent–related cases, if the defense of invalidity is raised before the PRB, the infringement court will stay the infringement proceeding unless the defense is obviously unreasonable when a utility model or design patent is involved;❷ or will stay the infringement proceeding unless the defense is quite reasonable when an invention patent is involved. ❸

(ⅱ) right abuse

In China, there is no law or authoritative case which prescribes whether right abuse is a legal defense in patent infringement litigation. Nevertheless, according to

---

❶ *See supra* note 5 at 99.

❷ *See* Article 9 of *Several Provisions of the Supreme People's Court on Issues Concerning the Application of Law in the Trial of Patent Disputes.*

❸ *See id.* at Article 11 In any case accepted by the people's court concerning a dispute over the patent for an invention or a dispute over a utility model or design patent in which the patent has been upheld following an examination carried out by the Patent Reexamination Board, where the defendant, during the presentation of its defense, makes a request that the patent be declared invalid, the people's court may nevertheless continue hearing the case.

an opinion of the authoritative experts, ❶ the acts of threatening a competitor by way of improper patent litigation belong to patent right abuse, where the acts may include initiating a patent infringement litigation based on a patent which the patentee knew to be unpatentable, initiating a patent infringement litigation based on a patent which the patentee knew would be certainly declared invalid by the PRB, initiating several patent litigations based on one patent infringement act, initiating a patent infringement litigation not upon knowing the infringement but after the infringement had grown. Therefore, if there is evidence that can prove that the intent of the patentee who took a patent infringement suit is improper, the defendant may defend himself by arguing that the patentee constitutes right abuse pursuant to principles of *Chinese Civil Law* or *Anti—Unfair Competition Law*.

B. Prior art

The prior art defense is commonly used in Chinese patent practice. Currently, Chinese courts hold an opinion on this defense as follows: (a) the prior art defense can be used in the cases for both literal infringement and infringement under the doctrine of equivalents; (b) the prior art used for the defense can be prior publicly used or known technology, or any published prior art owned by others; (c) the prior art used for the defense can be a technical solution or a combination of a technical solution and the common knowledge in the field, but not a combination of technical solutions; and (d) the prior art used for the defense can be a technology published or publicly used. There is a controversy regarding whether a conflicting patent application can be the prior art used for the defense, ❷ for example, Article 40 of *Provisions Of The Supreme People's Court On Several Questions In The Trial Of Patent Disputes* specify that prior art includes conflicting applications while some judges consider prior art to not include conflicting applications pursuant to current Chinese Patent Law. ❸

C. For non—production or business purposes

Under Article 11 of *Chinese Patent Law*, the phrase "production and business purposes" is a necessary element of patent infringement. Accordingly, in patent infringement litigation, a defendant may argue a defense based upon non—production

---

❶❷ *See* CHENG YONGSHUN. Chinese Patent Litigation [M]. Beijing: Intellectual Property Press, 2005: 226-227; also *see* CHENG YONGSHUN. Experts' Reasoning On Important Questions Of Intellectual Property [M]. Beijing: law press, 2010: 143-146.

❸ *See supra* note 5 at 98.

and business purposes. However, in practice this is seldom accepted by the court. In the Seminar on Theory and Practice of Patent Infringement Defense held by the Beijing No. 1 Intermediate People's Court on November 30, 2009, a research group of the same court recommended interpreting the phrase "for non-production and business purposes" as "used privately and not for profit-making purposes."

D. Other commonly used claims

In response to allegations of infringement, an accused infringing party, in addition to the defenses described above, will generally assert one of more of the following in court: (a) it was not practicing the patented invention either literally or under the doctrine of equivalents; (b) it was not performing any infringing act in China; (c) the patent has expired; and (d) it has obtained a license under the patent.

In patent litigation practice, there are some procedural items that can be used to help the defendant to drive the litigation go on as its willing, such as failure to meet statute of limitation, disqualification of a plaintiff and improper venue. These procedural items may take important effect to the patent litigation if used skillfully.